FREEDOM, STATE SECURITY
AND
THE RULE OF LAW

AUSTRALIA AND NEW ZEALAND
The Law Book Company Ltd.
Sydney : Melbourne : Perth

CANADA AND U.S.A.
The Carswell Company Ltd.
Agincourt, Ontario

INDIA
N. M. Tripathi Private Ltd.
Bombay
and
Eastern Law House Private Ltd.
Calcutta and Delhi
M.P.P. House
Bangalore

ISRAEL
Steimatzky's Agency Ltd.
Jerusalem : Tel Aviv : Haifa

MALAYSIA : SINGAPORE : BRUNEI
Malayan Law Journal (Pte.) Ltd.
Singapore and Kuala Lumpur

UNITED KINGDOM
Sweet & Maxwell Ltd.
London

Freedom, State Security and The Rule of Law

—*Dilemmas of the Apartheid Society*—

Anthony S Mathews

BA LLB PhD (Natal)

James Scott Wylie Professor of Law
University of Natal, Pietermaritzburg

LONDON

Sweet & Maxwell

1988

KRL 28

First published 1986
Published in 1988 by
Sweet & Maxwell Ltd. of
11 New Fetter Lane, London.

SET, PRINTED AND BOUND IN THE REPUBLIC OF SOUTH AFRICA
BY THE RUSTICA PRESS (PTY) LTD, WYNBERG, CAPE

ISBN 0 421 39640 7

To my wife Mary and my daughter Sarah.

Table of Contents

Introduction

The black people of South Africa for the most part encounter the security system as a brutal and repressive institution designed to frustrate the attainment of their legitimate social and political aspirations. The ruling whites perceive that same system to be their country's salvation from evil forces bent upon the destruction and take-over of the society in its present form. These immediate perceptions are being overshadowed, slowly but steadily, by the realisation that the 'law and order' machine has generated, and is now setting at large, forces that could engulf and destroy the personal security and aspirations of the members of all groups within the society whether black or white, ruling or dominated, majority or minority. The security system, in brief, has been transformed into an institution destined to serve the interests of *none* of the social segments of our society, and probably to undermine them all.

To those accustomed to taking a longer view, these dark consequences are a predictable outcome of the systematic demolition of the rule of law by security-law measures enacted during the past four decades. In effect, these measures enthroned a system of state lawlessness which has been countered by growing anti-state lawlessness, and been responsible for a great deal of anarchic violence as well. Most South Africans now living have neither experience nor understanding of the rule of law which the security establishment has undermined with methodical deliberation in the pursuit of its objectives. As a first task this study therefore seeks to explain the institution of 'government under law' that has been so disastrously destroyed in South Africa. Various approaches to the rule of law are presented in Part I and the most persuasive and sensible of them defended and adopted to serve as a principle of criticism and reform. This is followed in Part II by an exposition, made as readable as possible, of the legislation that has substituted executive dictatorship for legally limited and controlled administration. The story that unfolds there is of the displacement of constitutionalism by ministerial fiat as the principal mode of government in South Africa.

Part III is evaluative and begins by applying the requirements of the rule of law to internal security enactments. This is done in a comparative setting, with Israel (excluding the occupied territories) and Northern Ireland being the chief and contrasting examples. The effect of the comparison is to throw into relief the grossness of South African deviations from the rule of law and to question the asserted law-and-order function of the security system in South Africa. In the ensuing political analysis, the primary function of that system emerges and may be described, in fairly neutral language, as a sophisticated institution of political control. A security system so conceived and applied cannot be other than a disaster in terms of moral and political legitimacy. This lack of legitimacy is the chief reason for the system's manifest failure to guarantee the peace and stability that it was ostensibly enacted to bring about. Finally, and probably most controversially, an attempt is made in Part III to devise an alternative security system that will accommodate the requirements of the rule of law, the reality of social conflict, and the demands made upon the machinery of law and order by programmes of change. As a defence against potential critics, the reformed security system offered in Part III is presented only as the best that can be hoped for in the circumstances of our society.

The research that has culminated in this book was made possible by grants from the University of Natal, the Ernest Oppenheimer Memorial Trust, the Attorneys Notaries & Conveyancers Fidelity Guarantee Fund and the Human Sciences Research Council. Their helpful contributions are gratefully acknowledged. Discussions with colleagues in a variety of fields and countries have enriched this study immeasurably. I thank them for their invaluable contribution to my work. Two tributes cannot be made anonymously without injustice. These are to Ms Tamar Gaulan of the Department of Justice in Jerusalem who was an ever ready and efficient source of information about security law and practice in Israel; and to Val Rencken who rolled the manuscript off her word processor with unsurpassed speed and perfection.

November 1986   A S MATHEWS

Bibliography

A

Ackermann M F — *Die Reg Insake Openbare Orde en Staatsveiligheid*
Butterworths, Durban 1984

Adam Heribert — *Modernizing Racial Domination*
Univ of California Press 1971

Addison G N — *Censorship of the Press in South Africa During the Angolan War*
(unpublished thesis submitted to Rhodes University in 1980)

Aristotle — *The Nichomachean Ethics* (trans Browne)
Bell & Son Ltd, London 1914

Aristotle — *The Politics* (trans Jowett)
Oxford 1885

B

Barry Donald D (ed) et al — *Contemporary Soviet Law: Essays in Honour of John N Hazard*
Martinus Nijhoff, The Hague 1974

Barry Donald D (ed) et al — *Soviet Law After Stalin*
Sijthoff-Noordhoff, Netherlands 1979

Baxter L G — *Administrative Law*
Juta & Co Ltd, Cape Town 1984

Bell A N & Mackie R D A (eds) — *Detention and Security Legislation in South Africa*
University of Natal, Durban 1985

Bonner David — *Emergency Powers in Peacetime*
Sweet & Maxwell, London 1985

Boulle L J — *South Africa and the Consociational Option: A Constitutional Analysis*
Juta & Co Ltd, Cape Town 1984

Boyle Kevin, Hadden Tom & Hillyard Paddy — *Law and State: The Case of Northern Ireland*
Martin Robertson, London 1975

Boyle Kevin, Hadden Tom & Hillyard Paddy — *Ten Years On in Northern Ireland*
The Cobden Trust 1980

Breytenbach Breyten — *The True Confessions of an Albino Terrorist*
Taurus, Cape Town 1984

Burchell E M & Hunt P M A — *South African Criminal Law and Procedure*
2 ed Juta & Co Ltd, Cape Town 1983

C

Clutterbuck Richard — *Living with Terrorism*
Faber & Faber,
London 1975

Cosgrove Richard A — *The Rule of Law: Albert Venn Dicey, Victorian Jurist*
Univ of North Carolina Press 1980

Crick Bernard — *In Defence of Politics*
Penguin 1964

D

Dahrendorf Ralf — *Law and Order*
Stevens, London 1985

Dahrendorf Ralf — *Society and Democracy in Germany*
Doubleday, New York 1967

De Kock Alan — *Industrial Laws of South Africa*
Juta & Co Ltd, Cape Town 1982

Dicey A V — *Introduction to the Study of the Law of Constitution* 10 ed
Macmillan 1961

Dugard John — *Human Rights and the South African Legal Order*
Princeton Univ Press 1978

Dugard John   *South African Criminal Law and Procedure* vol IV
                               Juta & Co Ltd, Cape Town 1977
Dyson Kenneth H F   *The State Tradition in Western Europe*
                               Martin Robinson, Oxford 1980

F

Fine Bob   *Democracy and the Rule of Law*
                               Pluto Press, London 1984
Finnis John   *Natural Law and Natural Rights*
                               Oxford 1980
Forsyth Christopher   *In Danger for Their Talents*
                               Juta & Co Ltd, Cape Town 1985
Forsyth Christopher &   *Human Rights: The Cape Town Conference*
  Schiller J E (eds)   Juta & Co Ltd, Cape Town 1979
Foster Don & Sandler   *A Study of Detention and Torture in South Africa. Preliminary Report*
  Diane   Inst of Criminology, Univ of Cape Town 1985
Friedmann W   *Law in a Changing Society*
                               Univ of California Press 1959
Fuller Lon L   *Morality of the Law* revised ed
                               Yale Univ Press 1969
Fuller Lon L   *The Morality of Law*
                               Yale Univ Press 1964

G

Glanville Williams   *Criminal Law* 2 ed
                               Stevens, London 1961
Glanville Williams   *Salmond on Jurisprudence* 11 ed
                               Sweet & Maxwell, London 1957
Goren Dina   *Secrecy and the Right to Know*
                               Turtledove Publishing, Israel 1979
Grundy Kenneth W   *The Militarization of South African Politics*
                               Taurus & Co Ltd, London 1986
Guest A G (ed)   *Oxford Essays in Jurisprudence*
                               Oxford 1961

H

Hall Jerome   *General Principles of Criminal Law* 2 ed
                               The Bobbs-Merrill Co Inc, Indianapolis 1947
Halsbury   *The Laws of England* 4 ed vol 11
Hamson C J   *Executive Discretion and Judicial Control*
                               Stevens, London 1954
Hanf Theo et al   *South Africa: The Prospects of Peaceful Change*
                               Rex Collings, London 1981
Harris J W   *Legal Philosophies*
                               Butterworths, London 1980
Haysom Nicholas   *Mabangalala: The Rise of Right-Wing Vigilantes in South Africa*
                               Centre for Applied Legal Studies, Johannesburg 1986
Hewitt Patricia   *The Abuse of Power: Civil Liberties in the United Kingdom*
                               Martin Robertson, Oxford 1982
Horowitz Donald   *Ethnic Groups in Conflict*
                               Univ of California Press 1985
Huntingdon Samuel P   *Political Order in Changing Societies*
                               Yale Univ Press, New Haven 1968

J

Jennings I   *The Law and the Constitution*
                               Univ of London Press 1959

K

Kahn E (ed)   *Fiat Justitia: Essays in Memory of Oliver Schreiner*
                               Juta & Co Ltd, Cape Town 1983
Kronman Anthony T   *Max Weber*
                               Edward Arnold, London 1983

L

Lacqueur Walter   *A Dictionary of Politics*
                           The Free Press, New York 1974
Lansdown & Campbell   *South African Criminal Law and Procedure* vol 5
                           Juta & Co Ltd, Cape Town 1982
Locke John   *Treatise of Government*

M

MacCormick N   *Legal Reasoning and Legal Theory*
                           Oxford 1978
Mathews A S   *Law, Order and Liberty in South Africa*
                           Juta & Co, Cape Town 1971
Mathews A S   *The Darker Reaches of Government*
                           Juta & Co Ltd, Cape Town 1978
McIllwain C H   *Constitutionalism: Ancient and Modern*
                           Cornell Univ Press, revised ed 1947
McQuoid-Mason D J   *The Law of Privacy in South Africa*
                           Juta & Co Ltd, Cape Town 1978
Milton J R L   *South African Criminal Law and Procedure* 2 ed
                           Juta & Co Ltd, Cape Town 1982

N

Neethling J   *Persoonlikheidsreg* 2 ed
                           Butterworths, Durban 1985
Neumann Franz   *The Democratic and the Authoritarian State*
                           The Free Press, New York 1966
Nonet P & Selznick P   *Law and Society in Transition*
                           Harper & Row, New York 1978

P

Plato   *The Laws* (trans Taylor)
                           Dent & Sons Ltd, London 1934

R

Rawls John   *A Theory of Justice* Oxford 1972
Rees Mervyn & Day Chris   *Muldergate*
                           Macmillan, Johannesburg 1980
Rossiter Clinton L   *Constitutional Dictatorship: Crisis Government in the Modern Demo-
                           cracies*
                           Princeton Univ Press 1948
Rudolph Harold   *Security, Terrorism and Torture: Detainees' Rights in South Africa and
                           Israel—a Comparative Study*
                           Juta & Co Ltd, Cape Town 1984

S

Schreiner O D   *The Contribution of English Law to South African Law: and the Rule
                           of Law in South Africa*
                           Stevens 1967
Scruton Roger   *A Dictionary of Political Thought*
                           Macmillan, London 1982
Seervai H M   *Constitutional Law of India* 3 ed
                           Sweet & Maxwell, London 1983
Sergent Lyman Tower   *Contemporary Political Ideologies*
                           The Dorsey Press, Illinois 1981
Sharpe R J   *The Law of Habeas Corpus*
                           Oxford 1976
Shklar Judith N   *Legalism*
                           Harvard Univ Press 1964
Silver Louise   *A Guide to Political Censorship in South Africa*
                           Univ of the Witwatersrand, Johannesburg 1984
Snyman C R   *Criminal Law*
                           Butterworths, Pretoria 1984

Strakosch Henry E   *State Absolutism and the Rule of Law*
                             Sydney Univ Press 1967
Strauss S A, Strydom M J   *Die Suid-Afrikaanse Persreg* 3 ed
  & Van der Walt J C   Van Schaik, Pretoria 1976
Stuart K W   *The Newspaperman's Guide to the Law* 3 ed
                             Butterworths 1982
Stuart K W   *The Newspaperman's Guide to the Law* 4 ed
                             Butterworths, Durban 1986
Summers Robert S   *Lon L Fuller*
                             Edward Arnold, London 1984
Supperstone M   *Brownlie's Law of Public Order and National Security* 2 ed
                             Butterworths 1981

T
Thompson E P   *Whigs and Hunters*
                             Penguin 1977

U
Unger Roberto M   *Law in Modern Society*
                             The Free Press, New York 1976

V
Van Niekerk S J et al   *Privilegies in Die Bewysreg*
                             Butterworths, Durban 1984
Van Rooyen J C W   *Publikasiebeheer in Suid-Afrika*
                             Juta & Co Ltd, Cape Town 1978
Van Vuuren D J et al   *Change in South Africa*
  (eds)   Butterworths, Pretoria 1983
Van Zyl Slabbert Frederik   *The Last White Parliament*
                             Jonathan Ball, Johannesburg 1985
Vanderbilt Arthur T   *The Doctrine of the Separation of Powers and its Present Day*
                             Significance
                             Univ of Nebraska Press, Lincoln 1963

W
Wade H W R   *Administrative Law* 5 ed
                             Oxford 1982
Wiggins J R   *Freedom or Secrecy*
                             Oxford 1964
Wilczynski J   *An Encyclopaedic Dictionary of Marxism, Socialism and Communism*
                             Macmillan, London 1981
Wilkinson Paul   *Terrorism and the Liberal State*
                             Macmillan, London 1977

Z
Zola Emile   *Germinal*
                             Penguin 1958

Reports of Commissions, Committees of Inquiry and Conferences

The Rule of Law in a Free Society: Report of the Proceedings of the International Congress of Jurists Delhi 1959 (Delhi Report)

African Conference on the Rule of Law: Report of the Proceedings of the International Congress of Jurists Lagos, Nigeria 1961 (Lagos Report)

Executive Action and the Rule of Law: Report of the Proceedings of the International Congress of Jurists Rio 1962 (Rio Report).

Report of the Commission of Enquiry into Matters Relating to the Security of the State RP 102/1971 (Potgieter Report).

Report of the Commission to Consider Legal Procedures to Deal with Terrorist Activities in Northern Ireland Cmnd 5185, 1972 (Diplock Report).

Report of the Committee to Consider, in the Context of Civil Liberties and Human Rights. Measures to Deal with Terrorism in Northern Ireland Cmnd 5847, 1975 (Gardiner Report).

Report of the Commission of Enquiry into Alleged Irregularities in the Former Department of Information RP 113/1978 (Erasmus Report).

Review of the Operation of the Prevention of Terrorism (Temporary Provisions) Act 1974 and 1976 Cmnd 7324, 1978 (Shackleton Report).

Report of the Committee of Inquiry into Police Interrogation Procedures in Northern Ireland Cmnd 7497, 1979 (Bennett Report).

Report of the Commission of Inquiry into Reporting of Security Matters Regarding the South African Defence Force and the South African Police Force RP 52/1980 (Steyn Report).

Review of the Public Order Act 1936 and Related Legislation Cmnd 7891, 1980.

Die Verslag van die Kommissie van Ondersoek Na Veiligheidswetgewing RP 90/1981 (Rabie Report).

Freedom and Security Under Law Second Report of the Commission of Enquiry concerning certain Activities of the Royal Canadian Mounted Police, Canadian Government Publishing Centre, Ottawa 1981 (McDonald Report).

Review of the Operation of the Prevention of Terrorism (Temporary Provisions) Act 1976 Cmnd 8803, 1983 (Jellicoe Report).

Report on the Medical care of Prisoners and Detainees by an ad-hoc Committee of the Medical Association of South Africa, published as a supplement to the *South African Medical Journal* of 21 May 1983.

Review of the Operation of the Northern Ireland (Emergency Provisions) Act 1978 Cmnd 9222, 1984 (Baker Report).

Report of the Commission Appointed to Inquire Into the Incident which Occurred on 21st March 1985 at Uitenhage RP 74/1985 (Kannemeyer Report).

Table of Cases

Page

Table of Statutes

xxiii

PART I

The Rule of Law

Introduction

There is an intimate and permanent relationship between freedom and the rule of law. The rule of law does not constitute the whole of freedom but it certainly is a basic part of it.[1] Those who wish to understand what freedom means and who seek to secure it for society must also understand the rule of law. There is an equally important link between social justice and the rule of law[2] in the sense again that justice, while being a much broader idea, incorporates the rule of law as a fundamental part of its meaning. It follows that men and women working to advance either freedom or justice need to have a clear idea about the rule of law[3] and there, as Hamlet put it, lies 'the rub'.

The immediate cause of the rub is that even the experts cannot agree on a single theory of the rule of law. It is no surprise that politicians, who by general reputation if not by definition are not experts, hold widely different and often irreconcilable views on the meaning of the concept. Their grasp of the rule of law is frequently superficial and their attitude to it partisan. Most politicians view the rule of law as synonymous with their policies and its violation as a description of their opponents' actions. The result is that the rule of law is both confused and politicised by this group. While this is hardly surprising in the case of politicians, it is disappointing that 'experts' do not seem to have done much better. Their treatment of the subject may be less superficial but confusion and even politicisation, have certainly not been avoided. A learned judge once declared that a complaint that the rule of law has been infringed is a political and not a legal complaint;[4] and this remark encouraged the Rabie Commission, in the course of its investigation into South Africa's internal security

---

[1] Norman S Marsh has said that '(t)he Rule of Law is not identical with a free society although it is an important instrument of such a society': See 'The Rule of Law as a Supra-National Concept' in *Oxford Essays in Jurisprudence* ed A G Guest (Oxford, 1961) 223. John Rawls in *A Theory of Justice* (Oxford, 1972) 235 says: 'Now the rule of law is obviously clearly related to liberty.'

[2] John Rawls loc cit.

[3] In relating freedom (and also justice) to the rule of law, I have not overlooked the current in modern legal and political thought that represents true freedom as a product of 'spontaneously produced internal customs of each communal group' and which emphasizes the ' "living" or "inner" law of associations in contrast to the made rules of the state'. (Roberto M Unger *Law in Modern Society* (The Free Press, NY, 1976) 203.) I am sceptical of the 'freedom (or rights) without rules' thesis and remain convinced that what E P Thompson described as 'the negative restrictions of bourgeois legalism', in the *restricted* form that they are supported below, are essential to both individual and group freedom. It is only in its most expansive form (for example the Hayek proposition that the rule of law implies 'that government *in all its actions* is bound by rules fixed and announced beforehand') that the rule of law can be represented, as Unger represents it, as an instrument for the denial of freedom and equality rather than a means for achieving such ultimate human goals.

[4] O D Schreiner *The Contribution of English Law to South African Law: and the Rule of Law in South Africa* (Stevens, 1967) 100.

legislation, to discard the rule of law as a helpful guide in framing a new security policy.[5] Because some theorists of the rule of law, notably the International Commission of Jurists, have overcharged the doctrine with political values,[6] there is some excuse for this attitude; yet it remains surprising that many judges have not been perceptive enough to avoid the fallacy of discounting the rule of law as pure politics. It is bad enough that politicians have debased the rule of law; lawyers, one would have thought, have a greater degree of understanding and wisdom at their command.

There is only one sure way of avoiding the confusion and polemical disputes that surround and threaten to submerge the doctrine of the rule of law and that is to build on juridical bedrock. While no theory that is of any significance can be entirely purged of moral or political values, these must be subordinated to principles that are essentially legal if the theory is to command universal, or at least general, support. The essence of the approach to the rule of law adopted in this work is that juridical principles constitute the core of the doctrine and that these principles, which are central to the very notion of a legal order, must be assigned a dominating place in any acceptable description of that doctrine.

The argument that the rule of law is a juridical rather than a political concept should not be overstated. A doctrine concerned with the relationship between the government and the citizen and with the legal control of the government in the interests of freedom and justice cannot be without political import. The very choice between a system in which the government is subject to law and one in which it is not rests upon a political value judgment. As Judith N Shklar has said, the adherents of legalism frequently 'fail to recognize that they too have made a choice among political values'.[7] The essential point is that once the choice has been made in favour of a rule-of-law system, the cluster of principles, institutions and techniques that come into play are of a juridical rather than a political nature. If that were not so, if the rule of law were not concerned with fundamental principles of legal ordering, then the title of the doctrine would be a misnomer. The theory adopted in the ensuing pages seeks to give that title validity by unremitting attention to juridical core principles and the avoidance of propositions of pure politics.

Before explaining and defining the preferred theory of the rule of law, certain misconceived or inadequate approaches to the doctrine will have to be eliminated in a ground-clearing operation. All writings on the rule of law may be grouped under one of four theoretical categories, each corresponding to a broad approach to the meaning of the expression. These four categories are the following:

1. Law enforcement theories;
2. Theories of the rule of law as procedural justice;
3. The rule of law as justice in the material or substantive sense;
4. Theories of the rule of law as the protection of the citizen's basic rights through definite rules administered by independent tribunals.

[5] *Die Verslag van die Kommissie van Ondersoek Na Veiligheidswetgewing* RP 90/1981 paras 5.16 and 5.17. Referred to below as the 'Rabie Report'.
[6] Particularly in *African Conference on the Rule of Law: A Report of the Proceedings of the International Congress of Jurists* (Lagos, Nigeria, 1961). Referred to below as the 'Lagos Report'.
[7] Judith N Shklar *Legalism* (Harvard Univ Press, 1964) 8.

The first three approaches, while clearly embodying important elements or insights, will be rejected as unsatisfactory in this ground-clearing analysis. Theories falling into the fourth category will then be expounded and adopted as acceptable in the sense that they impose meaningful limitations on the power of governments over citizens and simultaneously hold fast to principles that are fundamentally juridical in character.

CHAPTER 1

The Law Enforcement Approach

The law enforcement theory is both basic and uncomplicated. Adherence to the rule of law means that the government[1] is required to act in accordance with valid law. The notion is best illustrated by an anecdote. Many years ago a minister of the ruling National Party government was being questioned at a political meeting about a restriction imposed on the liberty of an individual by arbitrary government action. The interlocutor asked him whether the government had acted in accordance with the rule of law in this instance. 'Of course we did' replied the minister, 'Parliament authorised the infringement of liberty'. The minister's proposition is the simple one that because the government's action was authorised by a valid law, it may be described as conforming to the rule of law.[2]

This first theory has rightly been described as a theory of rule *by* law, not of rule *under* law. Paradoxically, the law enforcement approach to the doctrine makes a point that is both important and inadequate. The inadequacy of the theory becomes obvious when we consider that it follows logically from it that a government can always conform to the rule of law by ensuring that there is prior legislative authority for its actions. Hitler covered most, if not all, of his official actions during the Third Reich by an enabling act passed on 23 March 1933 and entitled 'Law for the Relief of the People and the Reich'.[3] The Act conferred full legislative authority on his national-socialist cabinet and even gave it power to deviate from the constitution itself. It is therefore clear that the law enforcement theory legitimises the rule of most authoritarian and totalitarian governments as being in accordance with the rule of law because their actions are covered by law. Such a theory is not just inadequate, it is also dangerous. An apologist of the Nazi Party wrote in 1934 of *der deutsche Rechtsstaat Adolf Hitlers*[4]—of the German rule of law state of Adolf Hitler. When Hitler's rule is made to carry the imprimatur of the rule of law, we are clearly confronted by a dangerously distorted view of the doctrine.

[1] The rule of law is a doctrine of public law and concerns primarily the relationship between the government and the subjects of the state. Nevertheless, its prescriptions are binding on private citizens as well and it is a consequence of this theory that private as well as official action should be authorised by law.

[2] Norman S Marsh in 'The Rule of Law as a Supra-National Concept' (supra) 248, has expressed this proposition in more legalistic language: 'The Rule of Law in its most direct and literal application means that all action taken by the authorities of the State, as much as by individuals, must be based on and traceable back to an ultimate source of legal authority.'

[3] Arthur T Vanderbilt *The Doctrine of the Separation of Powers and its Present Day Significance* (Univ of Nebraska Press, Lincoln, 1963) 17.

[4] Kenneth H F Dyson *The State Tradition in Western Europe* (Martin Robinson, Oxford, 1980) 108.

   The inadequacy and danger of the first type of theory should not blind us to the fact that it expresses an important element of the rule of law. It is a requirement of all theories that government rule shall not be lawless. In early times, when the 'King's writ' did not extend to the borders of every society and feudal societies, to take a particular example, were gravely troubled by unruly barons, the transition to a society marked by 'public order maintained by the force of politically organized society'[5] was an important event. Today we take it for granted that society is governed in accordance with the prescriptions of law. For this reason a modern writer has described the first theory as being 'as unassailable as it is empty'.[6] The problem with the law enforcement theory is not that it is wrong, but that it limits the rule of law to a proposition that ought to be a starting-point. A theory of the rule of law that is meaningful must denote much more than simple law enforcement.

   Thomas Hobbes declared that life in a society without order would be 'solitary, poor, nasty, brutish and short'. Steve Biko lived in a society in which public order is maintained by law and yet his life, at its end, is well described by Hobbes' five adjectives. We need not seek far for the reasons. Only in a country where the rule of law means more than formal, legal validity will subjects enjoy real protection from official tyranny and abuse. A theory which has nothing to say about the form in which laws are expressed and the procedures by which they are administered cannot offer such protection. A theory that is totally silent on the content of the laws—which is reconcilable with anything that the legislature is prepared to authorise—is equally unhelpful. The weakness of law enforcement theories is that they prescribe nothing about the form, content and administration of a society's laws.

---

[5] W Burnett Harvey 'The Challenge of the Rule of Law' (1961) 59 *Mich L Rev* 603.
[6] W Friedmann *Law in a Changing Society* (Univ of California Press, 1959) 489. The proposition is, perhaps, not quite as empty as Friedmann declares since, according to one writer, it means that the citizen is entitled to rely on 'the law as it is expressed' even if the expressed meaning departs from the legislature's intention at the time of enactment; see T R S Allan 'Legislative Supremacy and the Rule of Law: Democracy and Constitutionalism', (1985) 44 *Cambridge LJ* 111, 117. Even in this extended form, the law enforcement theory is no more than a starting-point.

CHAPTER 2

The Procedural Justice Approach

Procedural justice theories are more advanced than theories of the first type in one major respect—they prescribe important requirements concerning the form and manner of administration of the laws. They do share with law enforcement theories the avoidance of any prescriptions about the content of laws and therefore leave the legislature free to command or forbid anything it pleases. However, the legislature is constrained by the requirement of the procedural justice approach that its laws be formulated in a certain manner and administered according to definite procedures. These requirements of form and administration are frequently expressed as 'the principle of legality' and the movement from law enforcement to procedural justice may be described as a transition from dry legalism to legality. A number of phrases have been used to express the essence of the procedural justice approach and it is captured also by terms such as 'due process', the *rechtsstaatsprinzip*, 'justice according to law' and 'justice as regularity', all of which mean broadly the same thing. In the discussion that follows, procedural justice and legality will be adopted as the preferred expressions and used synonymously.

The central idea, or ideas, in procedural justice or legality, though of ancient origin and complex in development, may be described in fairly simple terms. Legality demands that laws be so formulated that they will constitute a clear guide to human conduct and be evenly administered in practice under the control of independent courts or tribunals. This abstract idea will be more comprehensible if made clear by a concrete example, particularly an example of a law which violates the legality principle. Article 70 of the Russian penal code reads as follows:

> 'Agitation or propaganda carried on for the purpose of subverting or weakening Soviet authority or for the purpose of committing individual especially dangerous offences against the State, or circulating for those purposes slanderous fabrications which defame the Soviet State or social system, or circulating, preparing or keeping, for the same purpose, literature of such content is to be punished by deprivation of liberty. . . .'[1]

This is the provision under which many Russian dissidents have been convicted and sent to detention camps in Siberia. It manifestly does not meet the first requirement of legality that the laws should provide a clear guide to conduct. The law in question is phrased in vague and sweeping language: for example, there is no way of telling in advance what will constitute 'agitation' that will have the effect of 'subverting or weakening Soviet authority'. The conduct made punishable is too loosely

---

[1] Article 70 of the RSFSR Criminal Code.

described to enable the citizen to determine what the law commands or forbids.[2]

Where a law is framed vaguely, as in the case of art 70 of the Russian penal code, the courts could restrict the scope of the statute by a process of legal interpretation and thereby give it a meaning that is reasonably clear and definite. Since a narrowing interpretation will limit the use of the statute and consequently the powers of the authorities seeking to enforce it, only courts in a position of independence will be able to render vague language more precise by legal interpretation. The judiciary in the Soviet Union is neither in principle nor in practice an independent organ of government in the political or security sphere of its operations. In a careful study of the Soviet legal system, the continued political subjection of the courts to the Party was found to be a principle of the administration of justice even in the post-Stalin era. The author quotes a statement from a study by the Academy of Science's Law Institute to the effect that the Russian court 'does not stand and cannot stand outside of politics . . . beyond the guidance of the Party'.[3] The practice of Soviet courts in the post-Stalin period shows a movement towards legality, but this is not true in political cases where 'the rule of law gives way to unbridled arbitrariness'.[4] It is still the practice for the verdict and sentence in political trials to be determined in advance by the K.G.B. and the Party[5] and there is no record of anyone ever being adjudged innocent in a political trial.[6] Consequently, it is clear that all requirements of legality are violated in the administration of art 70. The law is vague and imprecise, as we have already observed; and its administration is not characterized by fair and even-handed administration under the control of independent courts. An expert on Soviet law has justly declared that art 70 might well be replaced by a rule saying: 'Any citizen who expresses ideas which the government or Party finds sufficiently objectionable, shall be punished by. . . .'[7] We may conclude that serious deviations from the principle of legality put the subject at the mercy of uncontrolled and indiscriminate government power.

The fundamental notion that underlies legality is that of government *under* law whereas, in law enforcement theories, it is government *by* or *through* law. Government under law, like so many other enduring ideas, originated with Plato and Aristotle. The Athenian in Plato's book *The Laws* praises the advantages of government under law in almost extravagant language:

[2] As one commentator on art 70 has observed, the provision is remarkable for a complete confusion of the objective (actus reus) and subjective (mens rea) elements of the crime: See F J M Feldbrugge 'Law and Political Dissent in the Soviet Union' in *Contemporary Soviet Law: Essays in Honor of John N Hazard* ed Donald D Barry et al (Martinus Nijhoff, The Hague, 1974) 60.
[3] Quoted by Robert Sharlet 'The Communist Party and the Administration of Justice in the USSR' in *Soviet Law After Stalin* ed Donald D Barry et al (Sijthoff-Noordhoff, Netherlands, 1979) Part III 325.
[4] Christopher Osakwe 'Due Process of Law and Civil Rights Cases in the Soviet Union' in *Soviet Law After Stalin* (supra) Part I 179.
[5] Robert Sharlet loc cit 367.
[6] Christopher Osakwe loc cit 213.
[7] F J M Feldbrugge loc cit 63.

'Where the law is overruled or obsolete, I see destruction hanging over the community; where it is sovereign over the authorities and they its humble servants, I discern the presence of salvation and every blessing Heaven sends on a society.'[8]

In Aristotle's writings we find some of the basic elements of legality, particularly in his discussion of the need for generality, certainty and impartiality in the laws of a society.[9] The idea of the supremacy of the law was again vigorously reasserted in Western medieval Europe of which it has been said that 'law therefore stood necessarily and indisputably above public authority. . .'.[10] However, there was no continuation of the Aristotelean analysis in the Middle Ages, and the principle of legality was asserted in the simple form of the subjection of political authority to law until the 19th century. In that century it was recognised that legality is a complex notion with a number of separate though related elements and writers began to make this explicit. The process started with the political writer John Locke who contrasted rule by 'extemporary, arbitrary decrees' with government by 'promulgated standing laws, and known authorized judges'.[11] It was continued by Dicey and more explicitly by the 19th-century jurist Salmond who elucidated the principle of legality in the form of 'justice according to law' which meant government under rules of law that are 'definite, certain, known and permanent'.[12] Early in the 20th century Roscoe Pound elaborated on justice according to law which he described as 'administration according to standards, more or less fixed, which individuals may ascertain in advance of controversy and by which all are reasonably assured of receiving like treatment'.[13] These writings were the forerunners of more sophisticated modern analyses of the principle of legality.

In modern analysis, the central principles are retained but their implications are worked out at a much higher and more detailed theoretical level. Jerome Hall, who wrote about legality in the context of criminal law, defined the concept in the following words:

'The principle of legality signifies that only after a thorough enquiry directed by rational procedure and aided by the long experience crystallized in precise rules of criminal law can defensible judgments be reached regarding the dangerousness of anyone.'[14]

[8] *The Laws of Plato* (trans Taylor: Dent and Sons Ltd, London, 1934) 99–100. Aristotle made the same point in different language: 'He who bids the law rule, may be deemed to bid God and Reason alone rule, but he who bids man rule adds an element of the beast; for desire is a wild beast, and passion perverts the minds of rulers even when they are the best of men. The law is reason unaffected by desire.' See *The Politics of Aristotle* (trans Jowett, Oxford 1885) I, 102.

[9] *The Politics of Aristotle*, (supra) 98–9; *The Nichomachean Ethics of Aristotle* (trans Browne, Bell and Son Ltd, London 1914) Book V, ch X para 4.

[10] Henry E Strakosch *State Absolutism and the Rule of Law* (Sydney Univ Press, 1967) 41. Medieval constitutionalism is well documented by C H McIlwain in *Constitutionalism: Ancient and Modern* (Cornell Univ Press, revised ed, 1947).

[11] John Locke *Treatise of Government* II XI 136.

[12] *Salmond on Jurisprudence* 11 ed by Glanville Williams (Sweet and Maxwell, London, 1957) 43–53.

[13] Roscoe Pound 'Justice According to Law' (1913) 13 *Colum L Rev* 696 and 14 (1914) *Colum L Rev* 103.

[14] Jerome Hall *General Principles of Criminal Law* 2 ed (The Bobbs-Merrill Co Inc Indianapolis 1947) 51.

However, this definition is part of an extended and intricate analysis of such questions as the principle's implied prohibition on the extension of penal statutes to similar or analogous conduct under the dangerous rule of 'legal analogy'[15] and of the relation between legality and the rule against retroactive penal statutes. Lon L Fuller's analysis culminates in eight 'imperatives' of legal government which may be briefly described as (1) the requirement of general rules; (2) the promulgation of such rules; (3) the prohibition on retroactive laws; (4) the requirement that the rules be clear; (5) the avoidance of contradiction in the rules; (6) the avoidance of rules demanding the impossible; (7) the constancy or durability of rules, and (8) conformity between the rules and their application in practice.[16] In a more recent exposition, Joseph Raz expresses the procedural justice approach in the form of eight principles which overlap with Fuller's 'imperatives' but incorporate more detailed requirements concerning the administration of rules by the courts.[17] The ensuing attempt to provide the reader with an up-to-date version of the principle of legality that recognises its complexity but preserves simplicity of expression as far as possible, will draw heavily on the analysis by Joseph Raz.[18]

The eight principles that form the substance of Professor Raz's exposition are divided by him into two clusters of related principles, the first three forming the first cluster and the last five the second. Each of the two clusters will be discussed separately, and then related to each other.

First Principle

Laws should be general, prospective, open and clear

If laws are not prospective, they cannot serve as a guide to human conduct and retroactive penal laws are irreconcilable with the legality principle.[19] The requirement that laws be 'open' restates Lon L Fuller's proposition that the laws should be promulgated and accessible to the citizens.[20] The requirement that the laws should be clear involves both the avoidance of ambiguity and a positive demand for precision in drafting. The demand that the laws be precise is closely connected with the requirement of generality. If laws are not expressed in the form of specific rules designed to achieve 'the maximum possible certainty'[21] their application is likely to be indiscriminate rather than general. This perception is well expressed by Franz Neumann who remarked that 'general laws *which have no specific reference* are nothing but a mask under

---

[15] Where the courts do not interpret penal statutes with reasonable strictness and use them to punish conduct that contains some elements in common with the prohibited conduct, the result is to 'widen the net of punishability' and make the law uncertain in its application.

[16] Lon L Fuller *The Morality of Law* (Yale Univ Press, 1964) 39, 46–94.

[17] Joseph Raz 'The Rule of Law and Its Virtue' (1977) 93 *Law Quarterly Rev* 195.

[18] Professor Raz's approach will be modified in this presentation, partly by the incorporation of the principle that the laws should be general as a first principle of legality. His eight principles will be reformulated and linked to the writings of others where relevant.

[19] See, for example, Jerome Hall, op cit 58 and Lon L Fuller op cit 51.

[20] Op cit 49.

[21] The quotation comes from Jerome Hall, op cit 47 where he declares that: 'The principle of legality can do no more than implement the attainment of the maximum possible certainty resulting from the operation of specific rules in a social milieu.'

which individual measures are hidden'.[22] Vague laws, in other words, lead to arbitrary and uneven application; generality is lost when the laws are imprecise.

Second Principle

Laws should be relatively stable

As Fuller has expressed it, this requirement is one prescribing 'the constancy of law through time'.[23] While it is recognised that the law must change and adapt, where alterations are excessively frequent the citizens will be unable to adjust their conduct to the law's prescriptions. The important notion expressed by the second principle is the notion of the relative durability of laws.

Third Principle

Open, stable, clear and general rules should govern subordinate legislation and particular orders having legal effect

It is common for statutes to delegate to officials or official bodies the power to make rules designed to give effect to the statutory programme. In addition, statutes frequently authorise persons or bodies to issue orders that will be legally binding. The third principle requires that such subordinate legislation or orders be contained within a framework of rules that comply with the first and second principles. In Professor Goodhart's words, the delegation of legal authority to any officer should be in the form of 'specific provisions controlling his actions';[24] or, as another commentator has said, legal authority to exercise a discretion must be so formulated that it is possible to pass judgment on the question whether, in an individual case, the discretion has been exercised 'within the meaning of the law'.[25] To sum up, the law must subject delegations of authority to legislate or to make legal orders to the control of specific criteria.

These principles making up the first cluster are all intended to further the objective of making the law a clear and effective guide to human conduct. We turn now to the second cluster of principles.

Fourth Principle

There must be an independent judiciary charged with the application of the law to cases brought before it

This recalls Dicey's famous proposition that no one shall be punished except for a breach of law established before the ordinary courts of the land.[26] Dicey's reference to the ordinary courts need not be retained today so long as the adjudicating tribunals enjoy an independent status. Whether the tribunals be the regular courts or specialist bodies with an

---

[22] Franz Neumann *The Democratic and the Authoritarian State* (The Free Press, New York, 1966) 29.
[23] Lon L Fuller op cit 79.
[24] A L Goodhart 'The Rule of Law and Absolute Sovereignty' (1958) 106 *Penn L Rev* 943, 956.
[25] Hans Klecatsky 'Reflections on the Rule of Law and in particular on the Principle of the Legality of Administrative Action' in (1962–3) 4 *Journal of the International Commission of Jurists* 209.
[26] A V Dicey *Introduction to the Study of the Law of Constitution* (Macmillan, 1961) 10 ed 188.

independent status, the point remains, as Lon L Fuller has said, that 'all are agreed that the courts are essential to the rule of law'.[27]

Fifth Principle

The Principles of Natural Justice should be observed

Tribunals adjudicating on citizens' rights are required to adhere to the basic rules of a fair hearing. As an irreducible minimum this means that the judge must be free from bias or direct interest in the case, and that the affected party has a right to be heard. In recent times, because of the rigidity of the law surrounding the principles of natural justice, the courts have evolved a more flexible notion in the form of the duty to act fairly.[28] Both concepts express the same idea — that of a fair and reasonable hearing. In a criminal trial, the elements of a fair hearing are much more technical and complex. A fair hearing before a criminal court is usually said to involve such requirements as a clearly formulated charge, the presumption of innocence, the privilege against self-incrimination, the right to counsel, and so on.[29] Procedural justice in criminal law is a subject on its own and it will be sufficient to record here that the central notion of the fifth principle is that the subject is entitled to 'a meaningful day in court'.

Sixth Principle

Review powers should be vested in the courts to guarantee the implementation of the above principles

The actions of officials or official bodies should be reviewable by the courts or other independent tribunals to ensure that they act according to the standards prescribed by the law and in accordance with fair-hearing requirements. This principle reformulates in different language the requirement of judicial control of executive actions to which almost all theories of the rule of law attach central significance.[30] Joseph Raz extends court review to the legislature itself to ensure that the foregoing principles are honoured in statutory law; but while being desirable, review of the enactments of the legislative branch is not generally regarded as an essential attribute of legality.

Seventh Principle

The courts should be easily accessible to subjects of the state

The courts, someone once sardonically remarked, like the Ritz Hotel, are open to rich and poor alike. This principle demands that it should

[27] Lon L Fuller 'Forms and Limits of Adjudication' (1978) 92 *Harv L Rev* 353, 372.

[28] See, for example, L G Baxter 'Fairness and Natural Justice in English and South African Law' (1979) 96 *SALJ* 607.

[29] The Geneva Conventions for the Protection of War Victims provide what may be regarded as an irreducible minimum in their specification of procedures for the trial of prisoners of war. Articles 99–108 prohibit punishment under retroactive laws, provide for a hearing with the assistance of counsel, the specification of charges, a speedy trial, the right to call witnesses and a right of appeal: See Conventions for the Protection of War Victims, Geneva, 12 August 1949 (HMSO, London 1971).

[30] See, for example, the reports of the congresses on the Rule of Law held by the International Commission of Jurists at Delhi (*The Rule of Law in a Free Society*, 1959) and Lagos (*African Congress on the Rule of Law*, 1962). (Referred to below as the *Delhi* and *Lagos Reports.*) Control of the executive is regarded by A L Goodhart loc cit 962 as being of prime importance. Hans Klecatsky loc cit, passim is of the same opinion.

genuinely be within the power of all, including the weak and the poor, to set the law in motion. In modern times, this invariably implies an effective system of legal aid.

Eighth Principle

The discretion of the crime-preventing agencies must not be allowed to pervert the law

The authorities have a discretion whether to investigate crime and whether to prosecute following investigation. If this discretion is not kept within bounds by the adoption of reasonable standards for its exercise, generality and even-handed administration will be lost and legality undermined.

The second cluster of principles (five to eight) are designed to ensure that the rules constituting a clear guide to official action (established by the first three) will not be distorted in their application and that legal remedies will be available for their enforcement. All eight principles may be epitomised in the following proposition: Legality means government according to general, preannounced and clear rules which are faithfully administered by independent and accessible courts according to fair-trial procedures.

The notion of legality is without any doubt whatever an important, rich and fruitful concept which no satisfactory theory of the rule of law can dispense with.[31] Therefore, the vital question is not whether legality is meaningful but whether a theory of the rule of law that is limited to legality is meaningful enough. Exponents of the procedural justice or legality approach consciously avoid any linkage with substantive rights. Raz specifically disclaims any relationship between his theory and 'spheres of activity free from governmental interference' and adds that the theory is compatible with 'gross violations of human rights'.[32] A L Goodhart has also denied that the rule of law has a specific point of reference and emphatically rejects its association with 'basic rights'.[33] Quotations such as these, which insist on the purity of the legal principle, simultaneously underline the inadequacy of a theory of the rule of law that eschews substantive values or goals. The problem is that legality, while purporting to be a limitation on governmental power in the interests of the citizen, may become an effective instrument of authoritarian control:

> 'The uniformity, regularity and stability which characterize law recommend legality to autocratic states no less than to democracies.'[34]

A theory which is useful to an authoritarian state and which may even serve to legitimise its rule, does not go far enough.

Exponents of the rule of law as legality recognise this dilemma and have attempted to credit the procedural justice approach with substantive moral significance. Raz, for example, argues that it presupposes that men are 'rational autonomous creatures' and that it enlarges their freedom in the sense of 'an effective ability to choose between as many options as possible'.[35] John Finnis has said that legality is premised upon the rights

---

[31] It is also, more arguably, central to all legal ordering. However, Lon L Fuller's view that it constitutes an internal morality of the law is much disputed.
[32] Loc cit 204.   [33] Loc cit 945.
[34] Jerome Hall op cit 68.
[35] Joseph Raz loc cit 204–5.

of humans to 'respectful consideration' and to the dignity of being 'responsible agents'.[36] These assertions fail to recognise the fact that particular laws, and even whole legal systems, may conform to all the requirements of legality and yet reduce human autonomy and eliminate individual choice. This is true, for example, of many of the laws which have formed the corner-stones of apartheid such as influx control restrictions and the pass laws. As demonstrated elsewhere, these laws were expressed in the form of general, pre-announced and clear rules which fall under the control of the ordinary courts;[37] yet they unquestionably restricted the choices of people subject to them and scarcely dealt with them as subjects entitled to respectful consideration. The conclusion must be that legality alone, as significant as it may be to the doctrine of the rule of law, does not go far enough. An adequate theory of the rule of law will have to join legality to substantive rights, though the precise nature and extent of this marriage between procedural and material justice is one of the most controversial problems in writings on the rule of law. The material justice approach falls under the third category of rule of law theories and, unlike the first two, incorporates prescriptions concerning the *content* of laws in addition to directions about their form and administration.

[36] John Finnis *Natural Law and Natural Rights* (Oxford, 1980) 272–3.
[37] A S Mathews 'The Rule of Law—A Reassessment' in *Fiat Justitia: Essays in Memory of Oliver Schreiner* ed E Kahn (Juta & Co, Cape Town, 1983) 294, 298 et seq.

CHAPTER 3

The Material Justice Approach

The first two approaches to the rule of law, the law enforcement and procedural justice approaches, are silent on the content of the laws of a society; they avoid all reference to the social and political goals or values towards which legal enactments are, or may be, directed. The substantive or material justice approach seeks to correct the omission by making the rule of law almost synonymous with the achievement of full social and political justice. Such theories transform the rule of law into an instrument for the attainment of the perfect social order; some of them scarcely distinguish between the two.

The chief exponent of the material justice approach is the International Commission of Jurists. At its first congress on the rule of law held at Athens the Commission adhered, with some variations, to the traditional doctrine associated with the name of A V Dicey. It did associate the rule of law with substantive rights but limited these to basic personal and spiritual freedoms and political rights.[1] However, at the Delhi conference held in 1959, the restraint of the Athens declaration was abandoned and the Commission announced that the rule of law stands for the values of a free society in which the 'supreme value of human personality' is accorded the fullest respect.[2] Respect for the value of human personality embraces man's economic and social needs in addition to his spiritual and political freedom.[3] The final step was taken at the Lagos conference in 1961 at which the following grand statement was adopted:

'The Rule of Law is a dynamic concept which should be employed to safeguard and advance the will of the people and the political rights of the individual and to establish social, economic, educational and cultural conditions under which the individual may achieve his dignity and realize his legitimate aspirations in all countries, whether dependent or independent.'[4]

In this declaration the doctrine of rule of law and the Universal Declaration of Human Rights are fused into one, and a supporter of the doctrine thereby becomes committed to mankind's aspiration for complete social justice.[5]

[1] The Act of Athens of 18 June 1955, in which the findings of the congress are summarised, identifies the rule of law with freedom of speech, press, worship, assembly and association and with the right to free elections. Freedom of the person is not specifically mentioned but must have been intended by implication in the reference to the rights of individuals.

[2] Delhi Report 194–6.

[3] Ibid.

[4] Lagos Report, 11.

[5] The identification of the rule of law with human rights in the broad sense had been previously made at a Chicago Colloquium on the rule of law: See (1959) IX Annales de la Faculte de Droit d'Istanbul 14. The culmination of this view is the Lagos Report published in 1961.

The reasons for the International Commission's transformation of the rule of law into the reign of justice are documented in its Delhi report. The traditional Diceyan approach, being a product of developed countries of Western Europe, emphasised rights that expressed spiritual and intellectual values. To the third world countries that were strongly represented at Delhi, such rights fell into the category of luxuries that meant little to the peoples of societies in which basic material needs had yet to be satisfied. Freedom of expression, for example, has a relatively low appeal to a subject whose stomach is empty, who has no secure roof over his or her head and who is uneducated. It seemed logical and reasonable to the Delhi Conference that economic and social rights, so neglected in traditional teaching about the rule of law, should be accorded a primary place and that the rule of law should be expanded to accommodate such essential needs of the human race.

The identification of the rule of law with justice in the broadest sense is characteristic also of the so-called material *rechtsstaat* theories. The procedural *rechtsstaat* doctrines which correspond broadly to the legality principle discussed earlier, became discredited in some quarters for two main reasons. First, they were powerless against the fascist and totalitarian movements in Europe on account of their failure to incorporate and defend the traditional human values of Western culture. Second, they took no account of the evolution of political systems in Western Europe towards welfare state programmes and thereby lost touch with current social developments. The material *rechtsstaat* doctrine is therefore one which avowedly seeks to accommodate and advance all the values of the modern liberal/socialist welfare state.[6] In essence the material *rechtsstaat* does not differ from the dynamic theory of the International Commission of Jurists. Both approaches seek to identify the rule of law with the attainment of individual and social justice in the fullest sense.

It is scarcely imaginable that anyone will disagree with the proposition of these broad theories that 'good should triumph'[7] and that all of us, including lawyers, should seek to establish a fully just social order. It is equally unthinkable that anyone will dispute the desperate need to provide all humans with the basic material necessities for a decent life in society. However, such beliefs are not inconsistent with the view that the doctrine of the rule of law should not be transmogrified into an all-embracing political and social philosophy. The validity of the expression 'rule of law' is seriously in question when related to the search for the components of the good life or the quest for the meaning and realisation of justice in the broad sense. It would be strange if Plato had given his book *The Republic* the title of *The Rule of Law*; and the latter expression would be a singularly inapt title for John Rawls' great work on justice. This is not to say that the rule of law may not constitute one of the elements of a just social order.

[6] See, for example, Eikema Hommes 'De Materiele Rechtsstaatsidee', 1978 *TSAR* 42. A more moderate and defensible view of the material *rechtsstaat* is that it represents the attempt to extend elements of legality, especially procedural fairness, into the whole area of state administration: See A S Mathews 'The Rule of Law—A Reassessment' (supra) 306–7.

[7] Joseph Raz loc cit 195–6.

There are sound reasons for repudiating the material justice theories of the rule of law. The intellectual output of the world's greatest thinkers has brought no unanimity on the nature of the just society or on the meaning of the good life. Such questions are as far from settled now as they were at the dawn of civilisation and we may confidently predict that they will never be fashioned into an established truth. If the rule of law is thrown into this seething sea of contention, it will be deprived of all claims to objectivity and relatively settled meaning and, as a consequence, will lose the chance of a broad transcultural recognition. In short, it will become a hapless victim to the fierce moral and ideological conflicts of our times.

The more fundamental reason for rejecting the material justice approach is that it envisages a totally unrealistic role for law and the courts in society. There are two aspects to this lack of realism. First, the social tasks devised for the courts by the material justice theory—the provision of jobs, education, housing and the like—are well beyond the resources and powers of the judicial branch of government. Second, the judiciary is an institution which operates in terms of 'formal claims of right and wrong' and its adjudication of such claims must be in terms of settled rules with a reasonably clear meaning. The judicial role is essentially one involving the application of pre-established standards or rules to problems that are brought before it. Many of the social programmes implicit in the material justice theory, such as the creation of an economy that can provide jobs and a good education for all, cannot possibly be expressed in the form of clear and definite rules that are administerable by ordinary courts or similar tribunals. These social tasks are not susceptible, or only partially susceptible, to the rule-making process. Exactly why adjudication around formal rules is unworkable in many areas of government has been illustrated in a seminal study by Lon L Fuller on the limits of the adjudicative process. The social tasks that lie outside the scope of adjudication in terms of formal claims of right and wrong are described by Fuller as polycentric tasks. A polycentric task is one which by reason of the multiplicity of the parties involved, the fluid or rapidly changing context in which it is located or the complex and wide-ranging repercussions of decisions within the field, cannot be resolved by proofs and arguments revolving around established rules of right or wrong. This abstract description of polycentric tasks will be made clearer if illustrated by one of Fuller's own examples:

'As a second illustration suppose in a socialist regime it were decided to have all wages and prices set by courts which would proceed after the usual forms of adjudication. It is, I assume, obvious that there is a task that could not successfully be undertaken by the adjudicative method. The point that comes first to mind is that courts move too slowly to keep up with a rapidly changing economic scene. The more fundamental point is that the forms of adjudication cannot encompass and take into account the complex repercussions that may result from any change in prices or wages. A rise in the price of aluminium may affect in varying degrees the demand for, and therefore the proper price of, thirty kinds of steel, twenty kinds of plastics, and infinitude of wood, other metals etc. Each of the separate effects may have its own complex repercussions in the economy'.[8]

---

[8] Lon L Fuller 'Forms and Limits of Adjudication' (1978) 92 *Harv L Rev* 353, 394.

Clearly, for such a task, the formulation and application of clear, general and durable rules is neither realistic nor even conceivable. Polcycentric characteristics are also evident in matters such as foreign policy, fiscal decisions (for example, devaluation and the determination of interest rates) and economic policy. The decision to adopt a programme of industrial decentralization is one of economic policy and can hardly be guided or regulated by clear rules administered by courts. As Lon Fuller would have said, this is an area of human endeavour which cannot 'endure' a delimiting in terms of rights and wrongs and which is therefore not susceptible to adjudicative determination.[9] The same appears to be true where decision-making concerns issues in which complex technical matters and public policy questions are intertwined, as has occurred in the United States over the allocation of broadcasting licences.[10] Our conclusion must be that the principle of legality cannot be given 'across the board' application in public administration.

The argument that legality is inappropriate for the achievement of many social tasks does not carry the corollary that law is totally excluded from the process of their solution. In such cases the law will inevitably lay down ground rules for the exercise of public authority. These rules will necessarily fall far short of the prescription of general, clear and durable standards required by the principle of the legality. However, elements of legality may be applicable or desirable, such as the duty to afford a fair hearing. If the material *rechtsstaat* means that the requirements of fair hearing should be extended as fully and as far as possible into the administrative process, it is quite acceptable so long as this mission is not confused with the rule of law. The rule of law demands much more than a fair hearing. The more basic and anterior demand is that there be clear, general rules which govern disputes in judicial hearings. The central principle, as a writer on the rule of law has remarked, is that the law is the ultimate reference, not the judges.[11] Confining the rule of law to a fair hearing is equivalent to advocating a lawless judicial power.

We may conclude that the material *rechtsstaat*, in the sense of a complete programme for social justice, is refutable because it envisages social tasks that would submerge the principle of legality; and without legality the expression 'rule of law' loses its validity. If the material *rechtsstaat* means the extension of the right to a fair hearing over the whole area of administrative law, it stands only for an element of the rule of law. In neither form does the material *rechtsstaat* offer a satisfactory account of the doctrine of the rule of law.

---

[9] Robert S Summers *Lon L Fuller* (Edward Arnold, London 1984) 91.
[10] In *National Broadcasting Co v United States* 319 US 190 (1943) 87 L Ed 1344, 1362 & 1367, the United States Supreme Court validated a delegation by Congress of authority to make regulations even though the exercise of subordinate rule-making authority was not confined by precise standards. The court held that power was to be exercised according to the touchstone of 'public interest' and that this was a criterion 'as concrete as the complicated factors for judgment in such a field . . . permit'. This seems to be a clear acknowledgement that fixed rules or criteria would be unworkable in the complex task of the allocation of broadcasting licences.
[11] Luke K Cooperrider 'The Rule of Law and the Judicial Process' (1961) 59 *Mich L Rev* 501, 503.

CHAPTER 4

The Protection of Basic Rights Approach

The first two approaches to the rule of law, the law enforcement and procedural justice theories, were indifferent to the content of laws and were pronounced inadequate partly for that reason. The third approach, the material justice approach, is guilty of over-correction since it seeks to fill the doctrine of the rule of law, in cornucopian fashion, with every imaginable form of social good. The well-intended zeal of theorists in that tradition is certainly misguided since it relegates to a peripheral role that principle of legality which alone establishes the right or title of any theory to the description 'rule of law'. Between the extremes of excessive social benevolence on the one hand, and total indifference to the ends or goals of legal ordering on the other, there must be an approach which keeps the search for material justice firmly anchored to the core principle of legality. What is required is a theory that will respect legality by restricting its operation to areas of social concern in which it is both relevant and workable. This is precisely the great strength of Dicey's theory and the reason that, despite the strictures of eminent constitutional lawyers like Jennings, it is one that has 'conquered something for everybody, as an achievement of mankind'.[1] While Dicey did not coin the phrase 'rule of law'[2] he popularised it in the first full-blown exposition of the doctrine published in the later 19th century. His approach, with some modernising changes, ends our search for the most compelling theory of the rule of law.

Dicey left his reader in no doubt that his theory went beyond the form and manner of administration of the laws. His concern with material or substantive goals is evident in his categorical statement that for him the concept meant 'the security given under the English Constitution to the rights of individuals'.[3] An examination of Dicey's text shows that he was primarily concerned with freedom of the person, freedom of expression, freedom of movement and the right to hold meetings. In expounding his theory, therefore, he was putting forward the principle of the legal protection of civil liberties. In contemporary terminology 'civil liberties'[4] are broader than Dicey's description and refer to the guarantee through law of the freedoms of person, conscience, speech, information, movement, meeting and association. Nevertheless, the material or substantive content of Dicey's theory, considered either in its original or revised

[1] G Treves 'The Rule of Law in Italy' (1959) IX *Annales de la Faculte de Droit d'Istanbul* 113, 118.

[2] Richard A Cosgrove in *The Rule of Law: Albert Venn Dicey, Victorian Jurist* (Univ of North Carolina Press, 1980) 67 and 87n70, says that the expression 'rule of law' was first used by W E Hearn in 1876.

[3] A V Dicey, op cit 184.

[4] The expression 'civil liberties' is used here in a narrow sense as excluding social and political rights.

modern form, is strictly limited to individual liberty. Those who follow
Dicey do *not* associate the rule of law, as in material justice theories, with
economic, social and political justice. In short, Dicey's theory has a
substantive content but it is limited to basic civil rights.

Dicey's text reveals a concurrent concern with the form and administration of the laws. This concern is reflected in the three principles which
constitute his definition of the rule of law:

First Principle

No man is punishable or can be lawfully made to suffer in body or goods
except for a distinct breach of the law established in the ordinary legal
manner before the ordinary courts of the land;

Second Principle

No man is above the law but every man, whatever be his rank or
condition, is subject to the ordinary law of the realm and answerable to
the jurisdiction of the ordinary tribunals;

Third Principle

The general principles of the constitution (as for example the right to
personal liberty, or the right to public meeting) are the result of judicial
decisions determining the rights of private persons in particular cases
brought before the courts.[5]

Closer examination reveals that these principles are simply an
unsophisticated statement of the principle of legality. The first principle,
through the use of the phrase 'distinct breach of the law', establishes the
notion of pre-announced and clear rules. It also insists on the jurisdiction
of independent courts applying fair-trial procedures ('established in the
ordinary legal manner'). The second insists that these rules should be
equally, and therefore *generally*, applied by those impartial courts.[6] The
third declares that freedom through the law will be more effective if it is
part of the ordinary law of the land enforced by the ordinary courts. The
basic elements of legality—pre-announced, clear and general rules
administered by independent tribunals applying fair procedures—are all
contained within Dicey's three propositions.

The preceding analysis has shown that Dicey's theory incorporates the
legality principle but also transcends it by advocating the protection of the
civil rights of the citizen. However, though his exposition reveals a
commitment to justice in the substantive or material sense, legality retains
a central and dominant place. He makes legality serve only a defined and
limited aspect of justice, not the whole of it as in the case of the
International Commission of Jurists. The proposition that civil liberties
constitute the prime sphere for the operation of legality or formal justice
has stood the test of time and has recently found reaffirmation in the

[5] The three principles have been slightly reworded and shortened here. They are
extensively discussed by Dicey in *Introduction to the Study of the Law of the Constitution*, (supra)
188–203.

[6] Despite some incautious language, Dicey was not here advocating the broad equality
between ruler and ruled which Jennings caricatures in his treatment of Dicey: See I Jennings,
The Law and the Constitution (Univ of London Press, 1959) 5 ed 312. What Dicey is saying is that
the basic freedoms are protected against all in society, including those in high office.

writings of John Rawls. Rawls' exposition of social justice centres on two great principles, the first of which is that 'each person is to have an equal right to the most extensive basic liberty compatible with a similar liberty for others'.[7] What Rawls means by basic liberties is made explicit in the following passage:

> 'The basic liberties of citizens are, roughly speaking, political liberty (the right to vote and to be eligible for public office) together with freedom of speech and assembly; liberty of conscience and freedom of thought; freedom of the person along with the right to hold (personal) property, and freedom from arbitrary arrest and seizure as defined by the concept of the rule of law.'[8]

According to Rawls there is a necessary association between liberty in this sense and formal justice or, as he prefers to call it, justice as regularity. This association falls away in the discussion of the second great principle of Rawls' work on justice, a principle that is concerned with economic and social justice. Rawls does not discuss legality or 'justice as regularity' in the context of his search for a just economic and social system.

The substantive rights which Rawls associates with formal justice are broader than Dicey's in one major respect: his concept of liberty guaranteed by general rules includes the right to vote and to be eligible for public office (political liberty). We have seen that the International Commission of Jurists, in its first more moderate pronouncement on the rule of law at the Athens Congress, also included political liberty as a rule-of-law concern. The question that now arises in sharp form is whether the Diceyan model should be widened by including political rights among those protected by the legality principle. Though the right to vote and hold public office certainly could be formulated in clear and precise rules,[9] on balance it seems undesirable to incorporate them into the doctrine of the rule of law. The reason for excluding political freedom from the ambit of the rule of law is institutional, as Ralf Dahrendorff shows incidentally in his illuminating analysis of the 'elements' of citizenship in modern society.[10] He divides citizenship into three parts—

(a)   The 'civil element' in which is included primarily the rights necessary for individual freedom, such as liberty of 'the person, speech, thought and faith'. The institutions most directly associated with civil rights are the courts of justice.

(b)   The 'political element' which means 'the right to participate in the exercise of political power, as a member of a body vested with political authority or as an elector of the members of such a body'. In this case, the corresponding institutions are parliament and the councils of local government.

(c)   The 'social element' covering the whole range from 'the right to a modicum of economic welfare and security to the right to share to the full in the social heritage and the life of a civilized being . . .'.

The institutions connected with this element are the educational system and the social services.

---

[7] John Rawls loc cit 60 and 302.   [8] Ibid 61.
[9] Considering the varying and technical nature of voting systems and the complexity of their administration, political rights are probably less amenable to clear, general rules than civil rights.
[10] Ralf Dahrendorff *Society and Democracy in Germany* (Doubleday, New York, 1967) 70.

Though these divisions neither are, nor were intended to be, entirely separate and watertight, they do demarcate the primary spheres of interest of each of the major institutions of government. And since, as Lon Fuller has said, 'all are agreed that courts are essential to the "rule of law" ',[11] it would seem sensible to exclude the protection of the non-civil elements of citizenship (the political and social elements) from the scope of the rule of law. The courts are by nature ill-equipped to be effective guarantors of political and social rights and their involvement in these spheres of 'citizenship' is at best marginal. Even in the United States, where the courts have a broader function than in most societies, the judiciary for decades declined petitions to reapportion constituencies in which there was gross inequality between rural and urban voters on the ground that voting was a legislative matter. When finally in *Baker v Carr*[12] the court invalidated a reapportionment scheme on account of conflict with the equal protection clause, its role remained a peripheral one. No court would undertake the positive task of reapportioning constituency boundaries or of imposing specific reapportionment solutions on the legislature since these are political enterprises with all the characteristics of a polycentric undertaking. Equally inappropriate for judicial determination is the matter of the basic framework for political rights in society. Voting systems, for example, are best selected and formulated by parliaments or constituent assemblies with courts cast in the subordinate role of supervising the technical administration of the electoral scheme. We may conclude that certain elements of political liberty do not lend themselves to enactment in the form of clear and general rules[13] and that they are therefore not fully susceptible to rule-of-law enforcement. Moreover, as the weakest branch of government, the judiciary cannot be expected to have a decisive influence on the form and substance of the political element of citizenship.

Civil liberties, on the other hand, traditionally fall within the scope of judicial protection. In societies where the rule of law holds, the judiciary has been primarily responsible for guaranteeing personal freedom. The habeas corpus writ, and the Roman-Dutch equivalent, the interdictum de libero homine exhibendum, are essentially court-evolved remedies to protect citizens against official invasions of their right to personal freedom.[14] Courts have frequently protected liberty of the person by giving criminal statutes a narrow and restricted reading, thereby restricting the possibility of their use to suppress unpopular ideas or punish the people who hold them. In the United States, where the 'Smith Act'[15] declared the advocacy of the overthrow of government by force or violence to be a punishable crime, the court restricted the scope of the provision by requiring proof of the advocacy of illegal *action*;[16] mere theoretical talk about revolution or resistance to established authority was

---

[11] Lon L Fuller 'Forms and Limits of Adjudication' (supra) 372.
[12] 369 US 186 (1962) 7 L Ed 2nd 663.
[13] Some elements are obviously susceptible to expression in the form of exact rules, for example, eligibility to vote and to hold public office.
[14] See, for example *Halsbury's Laws of England* 4 ed, vol 11 1457 and R J Sharpe *The Law of Habeas Corpus* (Oxford 1976).
[15] 18 USCA para 2385.
[16] *Yates v United States* 354 US 298 (1957).

accordingly placed beyond the reach of the criminal law. In *Brandenberg v Ohio*[17] the court gave a restricted interpretation to a state criminal syndicalism law which punished advocacy of the 'duty, necessity or propriety of crime, sabotage, violence or unlawful methods of terrorism as a means of accomplishing industrial or political reform'. It declared that the prohibited advocacy was not criminal unless it was directed towards 'inciting or producing imminent lawless action' and, by so doing, once again limited the scope of official interference with basic rights. Though the American Supreme Court invoked the First Amendment in these two cases, the judicial narrowing of criminal statutes is both possible and proper without a constitutional mandate. In *Ndabeni v Minister of Law and Order*[18] a South African court limited the scope of the crime of furthering the objects of an unlawful organisation by requiring proof that the accused had advocated objects that were distinctive of the banned organisation. The judiciary can further the principle of legality in relation to other basic rights as well. For example, in *Sa'ar et al v Minister of Interior and Police*[19] the Supreme Court in Israel struck a blow for the right of assembly when it set aside a prohibition on a procession in the absence of the apprehension of a 'real danger' of disturbances based on 'specific facts'. There is no need to multiply these instances to make the point that the judiciary is exercising a manageable rule-of-law task in protecting basic liberties by demanding adherence to clear standards or norms. This task, moreover, is an entirely proper one for the courts to undertake since it involves the application of the legality principle—a principle that is implicit of the very notion of a legal order—to an area of human conflict where it has a proven relevance.

SUMMARY AND CONCLUSIONS

In the course of surveying the four major theories of the rule of law, two became automatic candidates for elimination: the law enforcement approach because it stood for very little and the material justice approach for the opposite reason that it embraced everything. Between the niggardliness of the one and the munificence of the other, we discovered two more persuasive approaches. The procedural justice theory is of cardinal importance, not as a complete theory but rather as the kernel or core principle of the doctrine of the rule of law. Standing alone it lacks a frame of reference since it has no identifiable social context and is potentially applicable to each and every task of government.[20] Its compatibility with tyranny, even if it is a tyranny of rules, means that it is not necessarily a restraint on governmental power but potentially an instrument of it. These weaknesses of the procedural justice doctrine make the fourth and final approach—Dicey's theory—the most compelling of all. Dicey allied procedural justice with substantive goals in such a way that the core principle is retained, rather than being submerged as in

---

[17] 395 US 444 (1969) 23 L Ed 2d 430.
[18] 1984 (3) SA 500 (D).
[19] (1980) (II) 34 PD 169. The judgment is reviewed in (1981) 16 *Israel L Rev* 116.
[20] The rule of law, a principle of constitutional law, relates more to the power relations between government and citizen than to the social justice expectations of the ruled. As T R S Allan has said, it is concerned 'with the position of the individual in political society': (1985) 44 *Cambridge LJ* 111, 134.

material justice doctrines. Of equal importance is the fact that the material values incorporated into his doctrine, when enforced by the courts, will constitute a substantial check on political power. That surely is the true and historical function of the rule of law.

Having elevated Dicey's doctrine to the status of the chosen theory, we can reformulate its main propositions in modern form:

First Proposition

Government according to the rule of law means that with a view to the preservation of the basic rights enumerated in the second proposition below, the relevant laws[21] shall take the form of pre-announced, general, durable and reasonably precise rules administered by regular courts or similar independent tribunals according to fair procedures;

Second Proposition

The basic freedoms of person,[22] conscience, speech, information, movement, meeting and association shall be equally guaranteed by the law to all citizens of the society;

Third Proposition

Any limitations on the civil rights or freedoms enumerated in the second proposition shall be in the form of rules conforming to the requirements of legality expressed in the first proposition. Furthermore, restrictions on the basic freedoms shall be limited in scope and, except in times of genuine crisis or emergency,[23] shall not encroach upon the essential content of such freedoms.[24]

The basic rights sought to be realised and protected through adherence to legality in this redefinition of the rule of law will not impose an undesirable rigidity upon the social institutions or values of the society. This is because the fundamental freedoms have a dual character, being simultaneously substantive rights to be realised for their own sake and instrumental rights through which social objectives can be expressed and achieved. Citizens who enjoy the freedom of person, speech, association and so on, are able to defend or attack the status quo and to advocate and work towards alternative social and economic policies. The protection of basic rights through general, durable and clear rules facilitates constant reassessment of current policies and the re-evaluation of social purposes, needs and consequences. Where legality is given a wider scope of application, it degenerates into a legalism in which the 'focus on rules tends to narrow the range of legally relevant facts, thereby detaching legal thought from social reality'.[25] This tendency of legality to retard and

---

[21] That is, those touching upon the basic rights.

[22] Freedom of the person is essentially the right of physical integrity. It means that everyone's personal liberty shall be respected and that no one shall suffer physical constraint (such as arrest or imprisonment) except for a violation of laws conforming to the first proposition both in their form and administration.

[23] The rule of law and emergency government is discussed in chapter 11 below.

[24] Article 19(2) of the Basic Law for the Federal Republic of Germany declares: 'In no case may the essential content of a basic right be encroached upon.'

[25] P Nonet and P Selznick *Law and Society in Transition* (Harper & Row, New York, 1978) 64.

obstruct reform when given too much emphasis in the economic and social life of a nation, was clearly perceived by Max Weber who recognised, in the words of one of his commentators, that '[a] legal order that seeks to promote individual freedom by guaranteeing a maximum degree of calculability will therefore inevitably work to the advantage of those who possess economic power and to the disadvantage of those who do not—will in other words, sharpen and stabilize existing disparities in the material well-being of different individuals and classes in society'.[26] The material justice theories, by seeking to broaden the application of fixed rules, carry the danger of social policies being frozen through law. One of the great virtues of the basic rights approach to the rule of law is that it advocates the legal protection of those substantive rights that would facilitate rather than freeze social development. And in so doing, it avoids Roberto Unger's strictures that the rule-of-law state is an instance of a failed attempt to legitimise the domination that flows from the identification of the state with one or other faction or group in society.[27] The protection of the basic civil rights of citizens involves no commitment to any group or faction in society, or to a set of values or goals that would favour any such group or faction. The basic rights theory is also not susceptible to Marxist critiques of the rule of law. These critiques make the valid point that the law, especially the law governing economic relations, frequently disguises private interests behind outwardly objective legal forms and that legal relations thereby tend to misrepresent social reality.[28] In a recent discussion of Marxism and the rule of law, a writer has expressed the problem in the following way:

'Far from an autonomous, egalitarian sphere, the legal realm for classical Marxism was rooted in the social relations of production whose oppressiveness it not only did not counteract, relieve or even escape, but indeed which it ratified, mystified and enforced.'[29]

The quotation makes it clear that what enlightened Marxists are critical of is the *role* of law in society, not the *rule* of law. We may concede that, in the economic sphere of human relations, the pretensions of the law to be a neutral arbitrator between rival claimants[30] have frequently been false; but this concession does not in any way weaken or diminish the basic rights theory of the rule of law.[31] Far from being grounded in 'the social relations of production', the basic rights approach makes possible the continual reassessment of social and economic policies by guaranteeing equally to all citizens the liberty to participate in the public debate. The rule of law in this restricted sense, and not the *role* of law in general, is what E P Thompson has referred to as an 'unqualified human good'.[32]

---

[26] Anthony T Kronman *Max Weber* (Edward Arnold, London, 1983) 94.

[27] Roberto M Unger *Law In Modern Society* (supra) 181.

[28] See for example Bob Fine *Democracy and the Rule of Law* (Pluto Press, London, 1984) 139, 156–7.

[29] M Mandel, 'The Rule of Law and the Legalisation of Politics in Canada' (1985) 13 *Int J of the Sociology of Law* 273, 274.

[30] Bob Fine, op cit 157.

[31] The Marxist critique is more relevant to material justice theories of the rule of law.

[32] E P Thompson *Whigs and Hunters* (Penguin, 1977) 266. The author's actual words at this place are worth citing: 'But the rule of law itself, the imposing of effective restrictions upon power and the defence of the citizen from power's all intrusive claims, seems to me to be an unqualified human good.'

A more recent Marxist re-evaluation of the rule of law, although still retaining the utopian belief in the disappearance of law in developed communist states, does recognise the interim need to forge an alliance 'with liberalism in defence of çivil liberties'.[33] In such revisionist approaches to the rule of law[34] we may discern the final virtue of the basic rights approach—its capacity to bridge the ideological divide between conservatives, liberals and radicals. It is the only theory that holds any promise of something approaching universal acceptance.

[33] Bob Fine op cit 188.
[34] These writings are revisionist because they do not join in the more general rejection of the rule of law as an obstacle to the despotism of the Party in communist societies.

CHAPTER 5

Procedural Aspects

Up to this point the rule of law has been discussed and developed as a concept or idea with only incidental reference to the institutions and procedures through which the idea is realised in practice. The International Commission of Jurists, in its deliberations at Delhi, made a useful distinction between the 'substantive content' of the rule of law (the ideal which it expresses) and the 'procedural machinery' with which the ideal is associated.[1] The procedural machinery, in the words of the Commission's report, consists of legal institutions, procedures and traditions which have been proved necessary to 'give practical reality' to the ideal.[2] Though the earlier discussion of the concept itself has demonstrated that a complete separation of the idea and its institutional form is impossible, we shall now focus more specifically on the procedural aspects of the doctrine. We do so because rights are rather pointless without remedies[3] and because there is a sense in which procedures outweigh principles. Speaking of the protection of personal freedom through the habeas corpus writ Dicey said: 'The Habeas Corpus Acts declare no principle and define no rights, but they are for practical purposes worth a hundred constitutional articles guaranteeing individual liberty.'[4] The existence of effective legal machinery to make rights work in practice is of paramount importance.

The procedural aspects of the rule of law are most conveniently considered in relation to the main institutions of government: the legislature, the executive and the judiciary.[5]

The Legislature

The approach to the rule of law adopted in this work[6] requires that the legislature, either by external constraint or self-imposed restraint, shall observe two main principles in its enactment of laws. First, the principle of legality must be observed in legislation touching on civil liberties; and, second, any statutory limitations on civil liberties must be such that the basic essence of each right is preserved. These injunctions imposed upon the legislature by the rule of law carry the corollary that what the legislature is prohibited from doing itself may not be performed by any other person or body under its authority. The delegation of rule-making authority or of the power to make orders must therefore subject the

---

[1] *Delhi Report*, 191.
[2] Ibid.
[3] As the Romans said: ubi ius ibi remedium.
[4] Op cit 199.
[5] This follows roughly the method adopted at the Delhi Conference where the procedural aspect was discussed in relation to the legislature, the executive, the criminal process, the judiciary and the legal profession.
[6] As outlined in ch 4 above.

recipient of that authority or power to the same restraints as the delegating body is obliged to observe. At its conference held at Lagos in 1961, the International Commission of Jurists expressed the principle admirably in the statement that 'legislation should as far as possible be delegated only in respect of matters of an economic and social character and the exercise of such powers should not infringe upon fundamental human rights'.[7] An example of a delegation of legislative authority which ignores this principle is to be found in a provision of the Black Administration Act[8] which grants to the State President power to legislate, without any limitation as to subject-matter, for designated black areas of the Republic. He may exercise this power by proclamation and any such proclamation, even if it takes away basic rights, will have full legislative force unless and until Parliament disapproves by resolution.[9] An unfettered power to 'ban' both persons and organisations (that is, to impose orders having legal effect) was granted to executive officials by the Internal Security Act of 1950.[10] The banning power conferred by these provisions undermined the principle of legality and authorised the almost complete abrogation of the personal liberty, and the freedom of expression, movement and association of banned persons. Similar powers have been conferred by the new Internal Security Act[11] and although such powers are now subject to certain safeguards,[12] they still violate legality and authorise executive abrogation of liberty. In these two instances, Parliament has delegated legislative authority and the power to issue binding legal orders in obvious violation of the rule of law.

Because of the tendency of some legislatures to derogate from legality and basic rights in the manner just indicated, it is sometimes suggested that the rule of law should incorporate the principle of constitutionally entrenched procedural and substantive basic rights. The constitutions of both the United States of America and the Federal Republic of West Germany provide two excellent examples of the effective entrenchment of such rights. In these countries the rule of law has been incorporated into the constitution and the legislature is generally powerless to undermine it. Nevertheless, the rule of law applies in many countries which do not have entrenched bills of rights and it would be wrong to regard such a constitutional scheme as a constituent element of the doctrine. The late Professor Beinart perceptively observed that in America there is little discussion of the rule of law because its advocates need only appeal to the constitution;[13] in Britain and South Africa, on the other hand, where the constitution is unhelpful, the rule of law enjoys great prominence in legal and political writing. In societies where legislatures are legally sovereign, the rule of law enjoys a more precarious existence, but a sensible parliament will observe the twin principles of legality and basic rights and achieve by self-restraint what is elsewhere required by fundamental law.

[7] *Lagos Report* 15. I would substitute the expression 'fundamental civil rights' for 'fundamental human rights' in this quotation.
[8] Act 38 of 1927, s 25.
[9] Ibid.
[10] Act 44 of 1950, ss 2, 9 & 10.
[11] Act 74 of 1982, ss 4, 18, 19, 20 & 21.
[12] Analysed in Part II below.
[13] B Beinart 'The Rule of Law' 1962 *Acta Juridica* 99, 135.

The Executive

It is widely, almost universally, agreed that the subjection of the executive branch of government to legal control is central to the realisation in practice of the rule of law. An Austrian judge has said that the 'demand that the executive be subject to the laws was the main postulate of the Rule of Law state'.[14] The growth of executive and bureaucratic power in this century underlines the continuing relevance of this concern. What precisely do we mean by the legal control of the executive? The theory of the rule of law adopted in this work simplifies the problem of executive control considerably. In contrast, the expansive material justice theories have to confront, and provide adequate solutions to, the vast and complex problem of the legal control of executive discretion in all areas of governing, including the economic, cultural and social. The solutions offered must perforce be of a general and even questionable nature, as in the proposals adopted at Rio after a full conference devoted to executive action and the rule of law. Among the conclusions reached at Rio is that an 'inviolable right of access to the courts' shall lie 'whenever the rights, interests or status of any person are infringed or threatened by executive action'.[15] This statement either claims too much for the rule of law by suggesting that legal remedies are (or should be) available for every prejudicial executive action; or it avoids the question of precisely when an actionable invasion of rights, interests or status takes place and thereby becomes an admirable but rather unhelpful aspiration.

In contrast, the basic rights approach implies more limited and specific requirements for the legal control of the executive. The restraints on legislative competence discussed earlier ensure (1) that the executive will not have the power to abrogate or substantially erode basic civil rights and (2) that any power conferred on executive officials to modify such rights in practice will respect the principle of legality by being both narrow and precisely defined. Where, for example, the executive (or one of its officers) is given the power to regulate meetings and processions, the consequent restriction upon freedom of movement and assembly should be in accordance with clear standards or norms, such as an objectively established threat to peace and order, and supervised by independent courts. The power of the Minister of Law and Order, granted to him by the Internal Security Act of 1982,[16] to abrogate the right of assembly throughout the Republic, is a classic example of the complete violation of rule-of-law requirements in relation to the executive. The Minister may abolish the right of assembly and, in doing so, is controlled neither by clear legal standards nor by the courts.[17] A less serious but still unacceptable deviation from the rule of law is to be found in the British Public Order Act of 1936[18] which authorises public authorities to ban processions along highways if serious public disorder is apprehended.

[14] Hans Klecatsky, loc cit 209.
[15] *Executive Action and the Rule of Law—A Report of the Proceedings of the International Congress of Jurists* (Rio 1962) 27 (Referred to below as the *Rio Report*).
[16] Act 74 of 1982, s 46(3).
[17] For details, see ch 8 below.
[18] 1 Edw 8 and 1 Geo 6 c6.

Though the Act does specify a clear standard or criterion, the test of whether it is met appears to be subjective and the British courts lack the power to review a decision on the merits. A government appointed commission which investigated the Act in 1980 declared that court review on the merits would be 'a new departure'.[19] It follows that while the Act does specify precise standards, they need not be objectively established by the authority in question and are legally unenforceable against it. The recently published Public Order Bill, which is intended to replace the Public Order Act of 1936,[20] makes the power to impose conditions on processions or assemblies, or to ban processions, subject to the reasonable apprehension that serious disorder, damage to property or disruption of community life is likely to occur. It follows that controls over processions and assemblies may be challenged before the courts for non-compliance with the specified criteria.

The preceding examples, relating to only one of the basic civil rights (freedom of assembly), have been given to illustrate the general proposition that the rule of law, when applied to the executive arm of government, means primarily that where discretion is granted to executive officials to limit the enjoyment of any civil right, that discretion will be exercised according to clearly defined statutory criteria upon the presence or absence of which the courts, in a given case, have jurisdiction to pronounce. Where the power of an executive official to interfere with the enjoyment of basic rights is controlled neither by prescribed standards or criteria, nor by the courts, that official acts arbitrarily and in violation of the rule of law.

The formal subordination of the executive to legal control must be complemented by appropriate remedies which citizens can invoke before the courts. Where, for example, a person is subjected to illegal arrest or other physical constraint, a remedy in the nature of habeas corpus is essential to give practical meaning to his personal freedom. The habeas corpus writ entitles such a person (or anyone with an interest in his welfare) to challenge the legality of his incarceration by an expeditious[21] and non-technical procedure, and to be set free if the authorities cannot justify their action. South African detention laws which incorporate the formula that 'no court of law shall have jurisdiction to pronounce' on any action taken under their provisions,[22] in effect remove the remedy of habeas corpus. The rule of law and habeas corpus have always been rightly regarded as inseparable.

Apart from habeas corpus there is a range of remedies which should be available if the executive is to be truly subject to law in respect of basic rights. Officials who violate the legal rights of the individual should be amenable to criminal prosecution and, in appropriate cases, to a civil action for damages.[23] In addition, the state should be liable for the

---

[19] 'Review of the Public Order Act 1936 and Related Legislation' (Cmnd 7891 1980) 16–17.
[20] Printed on order of the House of Commons on 5 December 1985.
[21] It was inexcusable for the lower court in Ganyile v Minister of Justice 1962 (1) SA 647 (E) to reserve judgment for the lengthy period of almost two months in a habeas corpus application.
[22] As, for example, in s 29(6) of the Internal Security Act 74 of 1982.
[23] See B Beinart loc cit 123–8.

misdeeds of its servants. Procedures to interdict the government or its officials from acting unlawfully in respect of basic rights, to compel them to carry out their legal duties (a mandamus) or for a declaratory order establishing a citizen's rights, constitute the basic apparatus of the legal control of executive government[24] and should be available to the subjects in a rule-of-law state.

It is widely agreed that the executive may require broader powers during times of emergency and that these will often include the authority to suspend basic rights and to act in violation of legality. However, since emergency rule (or crisis government, as it is sometimes called) is a subject of its own, and involves special and distinct dangers to the rule of law, the entire problem will be discussed separately below.[25]

The Judiciary

The rule of law and an independent judiciary vested with power to adjudicate over basic rights, are so closely related to each other as to be like opposite sides of the same coin. Though it is conceivable that both legality and the protection of basic rights could be realised by vesting jurisdiction in independent tribunals other than the ordinary courts, there are cogent reasons for Dicey's insistence on the control of 'the ordinary courts of the land'. Professor Beinart has offered eight reasons for the belief that control by the regular courts is preferable, and these include professional habit and training, the reasoned and open style of court adjudication, a system of appeals to correct errors, the recognised fairness and impartiality of judges and judicial preference for moral authority over personal ambition for power.[26] While courts do not necessarily have these virtues, and sometimes even fail to grasp the requirements of the rule of law itself, they are more likely to possess them than other tribunals. Judicial deviations from rule-of-law standards are not unknown but seem to be exceptional. A startling example of judicial inadvertence to legality in Britain is to be found in *McEldowney v Forde*[27] in which the House of Lords, against two cogent and reputation-salvaging minority judgments, held that a ministerial order banning 'Republican Clubs' or 'any like organisation howsoever described' was not too vague to be enforced. The following salutary observations come from an Irish commentator on this finding:

> 'Since the political cliques learned how to control Parliament in the nineteenth century the citizen's only protection against tyranny has been those marvellous be-gowned, be-wigged and fearless freedom fighters on the Bench. When they start to capitulate, even moderate men may start looking to the streets.'[28]

[24] For a comparative survey of such remedies (now somewhat dated) see the *Delhi Report* 229–34.
[25] See ch 11 below.
[26] B Beinart 'The Rule of Law' (supra) 113–15.
[27] (1969) 2 All ER 1039 (HL). Lord Diplock, in his dissenting judgment, expressed the legality rule in relation to delegation of power in the following words: 'A regulation whose meaning is so vague that it cannot be ascertained with reasonable certainty cannot fall within the words of delegation' (at 1074). This gives proper effect to the requirements of legality.
[28] H G Calvert 'The "Republican Clubs" Case' (1970) 21 *Northern Ireland Legal Quarterly* 91, 193.

South African courts, no doubt, have qualified more regularly for such strictures on account of judicial neglect of basic rights, due process and legality. Obvious examples are *Rossouw v Sachs*[29] (detainee held not entitled to reading matter and writing materials even though legislation silent on question); *Minister van Justisie v Alexander*[30] (banned person seeking to set aside his banning order not even entitled to a 'discovery order' listing by description the papers on which the minister allegedly relied in imposing the order); and the more recent case of *S v Meer*[31] in which the requirements of legality were ignored by a unanimous court (prohibition on attending social gatherings, defined as any gathering at which those present 'also have social intercourse with one another', upheld even though there is manifestly no clear guide as to what constitutes criminal conduct). Lamentable though these departures from the rule of law may be, they are not so gross as to make the judiciary an inappropriate instrument for achieving basic rights and due process in South Africa. They call instead for renewed commitment in all branches of the profession to the values associated with the rule of law and for an educational effort designed to reinforce the propriety of judicial concern with strivings towards legality and due process. There are judgments in which the validity and appropriateness of that concern is recognised. The most important among these are *Hurley v Minister of Law and Order*[32] and *S v Ramgobin*[33] which have done wonders to revive the flagging faith in the judiciary. These judgments illustrate that the judiciary at its best is the most hopeful institution to nurture and expand the idea of the *rechtsstaat* in South Africa.

Of course, there is little point in proclaiming the virtues of an independent judiciary unless it actually possesses jurisdiction over disputes concerning basic rights. The South African habit of excluding the courts from these traditional judicial concerns has already been mentioned as a violation of the rule of law. A more insidious practice is to retain court jurisdiction but to limit the powers of the judges in such a way that their control becomes ineffectual. An example of this will be found in a provision of the Criminal Procedure Act[34] which authorises 180-day detention after application to the court by the attorney-general but makes no provision for representations to the court by the detainee. This law requires the court to act contrary to the basic rule audi alteram partem (hear the other side) and offers the illusion rather than the substance of court protection. Banning orders imposed under the Internal Security Act of 1950 could theoretically be challenged if the victim was able to show that the minister had acted mala fide or for improper considerations. The near-impossibility of proving such official misconduct is poignantly illustrated by *Kloppenberg v Minister of Justice*[35] in which the

---

[29] 1964 (2) SA 551 (A).   [30] 1975 (4) SA 530 (A).
[31] 1981 (4) SA 604 (A). See also A S Mathews 'A *Meer* Débâcle—The Law and Social Gatherings' (1982) 99 *SALJ* 1.
[32] 1985 (4) SA 709 (D). Since confirmed on appeal in *Minister of Law and Order v Hurley*, 1986 (3) SA 568 (A).
[33] 1985 (3) SA 587 (N).
[34] Section 185 of the Criminal Procedure Act 51 of 1977. The 'court' consists of a judge in chambers. A similar example is to be found in s 50 of the Internal Security Act 74 of 1982.
[35] 1964 (4) SA 31 (N).

minister declared that he had valid reasons for banning the applicant but could not disclose them for fear of injuring public policy. The court upheld both the refusal to give reasons and the banning order. Though the *Kloppenberg* ruling on record is no longer valid in the light of *Nkondo & Gumede v Minister of Law and Order*,[35a] the burden of proving that a minister has acted in bad faith remains forbidding. Where the court can only interfere upon proof of bad faith or improper purpose, and where it cannot examine all the evidence because the executive has the final say on what evidence may be excluded for reasons of state security,[36] its power to render justice is gravely impaired and court control becomes a cynical charade. A further dangerous consequence of compelling the courts to operate under reduced standards of due process is that the judiciary loses its credibility because 'the better the quality of participation by affected parties, the more legitimate the process and its outcome in that case'.[37] Banning under the Internal Security Act of 1982[38] is an improvement, in the procedural sense, on the 1950 statute since it provides for review of the minister's decision by a review board. However, the review board is not required to give the banned person a hearing if the chairman concludes that this is not in the public interest;[39] and the only form of recourse to the judges is the obligation of the minister to lay the papers before the Chief Justice where he (the minister) imposes a more stringent banning than the board recommends.[40] The Chief Justice, or some other judge designated by him, does not conduct a hearing but merely reviews the decision as presented in the papers submitted to him. He may set aside a banning order only if satisfied that the minister has exceeded his powers, acted in bad faith or taken legally irrelevant considerations into account.[41] Courts of law are precluded from pronouncing on the findings of the Chief Justice or designated judge of appeal.[42] Clearly these procedures constitute a highly attenuated form of court control and do not meet the basic requirements of procedural justice.[43] The rule-of-law requirement that the citizen is entitled to have his basic rights judged by the regular courts is still far from being met by the recently enacted Internal Security Act.[44] Examples such as these demonstrate that when court control is not totally excluded it is frequently whittled down to the point of extinction. This reduction of jurisdiction over basic rights is a serious rule-of-law violation.

The courts are almost invariably in control of the administration of criminal justice. Criminal prosecution is potentially harmful to basic rights, especially the right to personal freedom.[45] It is therefore a

---

[35a] 1986 (2) SA 756 (A).
[36] Section 66(1) of the Internal Security Act 74 of 1982 makes the minister the final arbiter on this question.
[37] Roberts S Summers *Lon L Fuller*, (supra), 104.
[38] Sections 18, 19, 20 and 21 of Act 74 of 1982.
[39] Section 38(4).
[40] Section 41(1).
[41] Section 41(2).
[42] Section 42(4).
[43] These procedures are more fully evaluated in ch 8 below.
[44] Other examples of this failure will be discussed in Part II below.
[45] All except trivial crimes contain a threat to the personal liberty of the accused and it is primarily in relation to the criminal law that Pound's remark about the relation between hard-and-fast rules and liberty has special validity.

requirement of the rule of law that legality should apply fully in the area of criminal law. That means, in the first place, that crimes should be narrowly and precisely defined—nullem crimen sine lege. It follows, as Glanville Williams has said, that there must be certainty in the definition of criminal laws, that they must not be retrospective and that they must be accessible and intelligible.[46] These requirements are violated by over-broad common-law crimes like sedition and by many statutory political crimes.[47] In the second place, legality in the area of the criminal law means that the courts must operate under fair-trial procedures. The meaning of a fair trial is worthy of a full and separate work and we can only note in passing such basic rights as the presumption of innocence, specification of charges, speedy trial, fair rules of evidence, open court proceedings, legal defence and appeal.[48] The complete abrogation of these rights is uncommon but the courts in South Africa have been severely hampered in the task of administering criminal justice according to the rule of law by provisions reversing the onus of proof, authorising the detention and interrogation of witnesses in solitary confinement, and the like. The maintenance of essential procedural rights in criminal law is a vital component of the rule of law, as well as being the barometer of civilisation in society.

The Procedural Aspects Summarised

All theories of the rule of law, except the law enforcement approach, recognise the absolute centrality of procedural justice. This is obviously true of the basic rights theory which imposes upon parliament the duty to observe the principle of legality in enactments touching on the fundamental liberties of the subject, and upon the executive the obligation to act within the meaning of the law articulated by the legislature. The executive will therefore be controlled by preannounced and clear standards administered by courts whose procedures conform to the requirements of fair hearing. The basic rights doctrine of the rule of law underlines the old truth that the ultimate guarantee of liberty is to be found in meticulous adherence to due process.

[46] Glanville Williams *Criminal Law* 2 ed (Stevens, London, 1961) 601–4. See also Jerome Hall op cit 36.
[47] Many of these will be discussed in Part II below.
[48] See, for example, *Delhi Report* (supra), 8–11, 247–78.

The Security System

Introduction

The purpose of this part is to introduce the reader to the corpus of internal security legislation in South Africa. The presentation is largely descriptive and analytical, critical judgments about the laws being reserved, in the main, to Part III. However, the horrendous nature of much of the material examined has meant that critical comments have forced their way to the surface from time to time and overwhelmed the writer's pre-ordained judgmental reserve. These aberrations from the intended style of Part II seem excusable in relation to a body of laws that could well be introduced to the reader with Dante's ominous words: 'All hope abandon, ye who enter here.'

All the main security enactments are examined in this part but the coverage is by no means exhaustive.[1] The aim is to acquaint the reader with the principal features of the security system, not to overwhelm him with massive detail. As far as the technical nature of much of the material permits, the style of presentation is designed to make the material accessible to the non-specialist reader.

---

[1] For example, the Control of Access to Public Premises and Vehicles Act 53 of 1985 has been omitted, as have laws relating to explosives and firearms. Common-law security crimes such as treason, public violence and the like are fully dealt with in many general works on criminal law and therefore not included in this part.

CHAPTER 6

Security Crimes

Acting on the assumption[1] that the established common-law crimes for the protection of the state (treason, sedition, public violence and the like) are woefully inadequate for the task of securing order in contemporary circumstances, the legislature has crammed the criminal statute book with special security crimes which range across the spectrum of social activity with a generous but unbenign sweep. Though collectively they may seem to criminalise almost everything, our first assignment will be to determine the scope of each separate crime and to specify, in so far as one can be exact about inexact language, the kind of conduct or activity at which it is directed. This analysis will make use of the basic elements into which criminal lawyers have divided crimes, namely, the conduct made punishable by the statute and the criminal intent required for guilt. These elements are known in technical language as the actus reus (criminal deed) and the mens rea (guilty mind). When the dissection process has been applied to each crime they will be reconsidered[1a] with a view to an evaluation of the legal, political and moral implications of the entire corpus of security offences.

1. TERRORISM

Introduction

Some Western nations, of which Great Britain is a good example, have enacted legislation to deal with terrorism without creating a special crime of terrorism. Since the acts committed by terrorists usually fall within the ambit of a number of common-law crimes such as murder, attempted murder, malicious damage to property and the like, legislation in Great Britain has focused on such matters as the outlawing of terrorist organisations, the deportation of suspected terrorists, the prohibition of support for terrorist groups and short-term arrest for the interrogation of suspects, and the trial of security-law offenders without juries and in accordance with modified procedures.[2] South Africa has not followed this tradition of legislative restraint and the government decided to enact the independent crime of terrorism in 1967.[3] With a lack of discrimination that would shame a magpie, the draftsman of this notorious law sought to criminalise a broad range of ill-defined activities, many of which were not terroristic in any meaningful sense; and the courts, with only limited success, attempted to confine the statutory monster to acts that bore some resemblance to the phenomenon denoted by the word

---

[1] Which will be critically examined in Part III of this work. [1a] In ch 12.

[2] See the Prevention of Terrorism (Temporary Provisions) Act 1984 and the Northern Ireland (Emergency Provisions) Act 1978.

[3] The Terrorism Act 83 of 1967.

terrorism.[4] The Terrorism Act of 1967 was repealed by the Internal
Security Act of 1982[5] and this later Act introduced a new crime of
terrorism[6] of a somewhat less forbidding nature than its predecessor. We
turn now to the current crime of terrorism.

Basic Elements of Terrorism

The Criminal Conduct

In simple and non-technical language, the conduct made punishable by
the offence of terrorism is the commission of an act of violence.[7] This is an
improvement on the old crime which criminalised 'any act'[8] committed
with a specified intent. 'Violence', for the purposes of the new crime of
terrorism, is defined as *including* 'the inflicting of bodily harm upon or
killing of, or the endangering of the safety of, any person, or the damaging,
destruction or endangering of property'.[9] This definition presents us with
our first problem. What are the unincluded forms of violence to which the
definition alludes? The court is apparently given a discretion to punish
forms of violence other than those directed at persons or property, though
it is hard to imagine what they would be.[10] A second problem, perhaps
more easily disposed of, turns on the meaning of the word 'property' in the
definition of violence. Property here seems to connote tangible things[11] so
that a boycott of goods which diminishes goodwill or the value of shares
should not qualify as an act of violence. Yet another problem relates to the
degree of violence required. On its face the language of the statutory
definition covers trivial assaults and minor damage to property. This
suggests that terrorism may be committed, if the relevant intent is present,
by a person who pushes another or kicks open the door of a house. Since
the statute does not expressly exclude trivial forms of harm the only
possible solutions are either the application of the principle that the law
does not concern itself with trivialities (de minimis lex non curat) or a
resort to the intention of Parliament which could scarcely have intended
to confer the status of terrorist on a political brawler. Finally, there is the
question of what an *act* of violence means. The statute helps in part by
declaring that undergoing training and possession of substances and
things are deemed to be 'acts'.[12] Whether speech or writing can constitute
an act is rendered moot by a provision, shortly to be discussed, which
makes incitements and encouragements to acts of violence punishable as
terrorism.

---

[4] For a brief analysis of the main judgments, see A S Mathews, 'The Terrors of
Terrorism' (1974) 91 *SALJ* 381.
   [5] Act 74 of 1982.
   [6] Section 54(1).
   [7] Section 54(1)(i).
   [8] That is, an act of any and every kind.
   [9] Section 1(xxiii).
   [10] Possibly a protest march at which persons 'psych' themselves up by brandishing
weapons or firing guns harmlessly into the air. This example raises the question whether
undirected 'violence' should be regarded as a form of punishable terrorism. However, it
would be undesirable for the courts to punish what the legislature has not specifically
prohibited.
   [11] As does the word 'goed' in the Afrikaans definition.
   [12] Section 54(7).

The determination of what constitutes prohibited conduct for purposes of the crime of terrorism ceases to be a simple and non-technical question when we find that the relevant section extends the offence to threats or attempts to commit acts of violence,[13] to the performance of acts 'aimed at causing, bringing about, promoting or contributing towards' an act or threat of violence,[14] to a conspiracy to bring about an act or threat of violence or an act aimed at causing such act or threat,[15] and to various forms of encouragement or incitement to any such acts or threats.[16] A person who uses language which will encourage another to commit an act which is aimed at producing a threat of violence is punishable as a terrorist if he has the requisite criminal intent even though his conduct is at least two removes from a manifestly terroristic act. Criminalising conduct at several removes from a violent deed can raise tricky problems of causation, as in the determination of whether an act performed by the accused was 'aimed at . . . contributing towards' a threat of violence. If at a political meeting, a member of the audience opines that the speaker richly deserves to be cuffed about the ears and this spurs on another member to jump on to the stage with raised fists, is the first member guilty of terrorism (assuming that he has the necessary intent) in that he has 'advised' another to perform an act which 'is aimed at . . . bringing about . . . a threat of violence'? A fanciful example, no doubt; but the fact that it is potentially within the proscribed conduct tells us much about the scope and obscurity of the crime of terrorism.

We may conclude that the conduct rendered criminal by the definition of terrorism, while covering such obvious terroristic acts as machine-gunning people or bombing property, also incorporates a rather ill-defined range of less obnoxious activities. What is significant about these other activities is not that they embrace the fanciful examples of statutory terrorism just alluded to, but, more ominously, that political protestors could fall within their reach. Whether, and in what circumstances, they do is best considered after analysis of the criminal intent requirement of terrorism.

The Criminal Intent

The conduct described in the preceding section is punishable only if it is accompanied by a prescribed intent. While the intent requirement may be easy to describe in relation to many crimes (for example, murder requires an intention to kill) this is not so in the case of terrorism since the Act specifies four different kinds of intent,[17] the presence of *any one* of which will render the conduct criminal. The four forms of intent are:

(a) intent to overthrow or endanger state authority in the Republic. What seems to be required here is an intent to render the established institutions for the government of the state completely or substantially unworkable;

---

[13] Section 54(1)(i).
[14] Section 54(1)(ii). This subsection further includes consenting to, or taking steps to perform, such an act.
[15] Section 54(1)(iii).
[16] Section 54(1)(iv).
[17] Section 54(1)(a), (b), (c) & (d).

(b) intent to promote or bring about any constitutional, political, industrial, social or economic aim or change in the Republic. This is exceedingly broad since it appears to refer not just to a change in the general direction of policy but also (on account of the words 'any' and 'aim') to a limited and specific goal, such as the amendment of a section of the constitution or higher wages for a group of workers;

(c) intent to induce the Government of the Republic to do or refrain from doing any act or to adopt or abandon a particular standpoint. Here is another example of overbreadth, made worse by the fact that 'Government' includes a provincial administration or even a local or similar authority.[18]

(d) intent to put in fear or demoralise the general public, a particular population group or the inhabitants of a particular area in the Republic or to induce any of these to do or abstain from doing any act.

The breadth of the intent requirement becomes apparent if one asks a simple question: 'Is there any activity in the public domain which will not be characterised by at least one of these forms of intent?' The answer seems to be negative because any public activity that is not entirely purposeless will be directed at altering official standpoints or actions or bringing about some kind of change. Bearing in mind that we are dealing with terrorism, the intent requirement should have been limited to the overthrow or endangering of state authority or the intimidation (putting into fear) of the government, the public or a section of it.

A number of provisions in the Act[19] facilitate proof by the prosecution of the prescribed intent. If the act alleged to have been committed by the accused in the charge resulted, or was likely to have resulted, in the achievement of the 'objects' (sic) specified in the intent provision (for example caused or was likely to have caused the endangering of state authority or some form of political, social, et cetera change) then the accused is presumed, unless he proves the contrary, to have committed the act in question with the intent of achieving that objective.[20] Where the act with which the accused is charged is the possession of certain specified dangerous weapons[21] (or ammunition or component parts thereof) or of any 'grenade, mine, bomb or explosive' and it is proved that he unlawfully had any of these in his possession, it is presumed unless the accused proves the contrary, that he possessed them with intent to achieve the objectives specified in the intent section by the commission of a prohibited act of terrorism.[22] This evidential provision means that an accused proved to be in unlawful possession of even a single round of ammunition for one of the specified weapons, must disprove both the intent and the criminal conduct requirements of the crime of terrorism or be adjudged guilty. Where the act with which the accused is charged is the unlawful

[18] Section 54(8).
[19] The Internal Security Act 74 of 1982. This measure will be referred to in the text as 'the Act'.
[20] Section 69(5). The accused will have to discharge this onus on a balance of probabilities, not by proof beyond a reasonable doubt as under the Terrorism Act of 1967.
[21] Such as automatic and semi-automatic rifles, machine-guns and machine pistols, rocket launchers, recoilless guns or mortars.
[22] Section 69(6)*(a)*.

possession of firearms or ammunition other than those specified in the provision just mentioned,[23] and it is proved that he unlawfully had in his possession any such other firearm or ammunition, or more than one such firearm, and the court concludes that the nature, surrounding circumstances or quantity of the firearms or ammunition possessed justify the inference that they were possessed with prohibited intent, the accused is again required, on pain of being found guilty, to disprove both elements of the crime of terrorism.[24] Finally, where membership of, or association with, an organisation is relevant to a charge of terrorism, the court is required to take into account the *fact* that certain unlawful organisations specified in Schedule 4 to the Act, have as their object the achievement by means of violence or threats the objective of overthrowing or endangering State authority.[25] This statutory deeming of criminal intent on the part of specified organisations may virtually 'cook the goose' for the accused.

A number of procedural provisions of the Act in relation to terrorism must be mentioned. Prosecutions require the written authority of the attorney-general.[26] Provision is made for the secrecy of trials to such an extent that even applications for a terrorism trial to be held behind closed doors must be held in camera.[27] Separate offenders may be prosecuted together for the crime of terrorism.[28] Trials of persons charged with terrorism do not have to be held by courts having jurisdiction over the place where the alleged offence was committed but may be held where the accused 'happens to be' or where the Minister of Justice directs.[29] Each of these provisions carries the possibility of prejudice to the accused.

The Scope of the Crime of Terrorism

While the security situation in South Africa may lend force to the argument that the country needs a special crime of terrorism, there is no justification for making a capital[30] crime as broad as the new definition of the offence. If a local authority announces an increase in rents for low-paid workers, and some of them storm its offices and break a few windows to dissuade it from acting, they fall within the definition of the crime since they have committed violent acts in order to dissuade the authority from 'doing any act' or to persuade it to 'abandon a particular standpoint'. Such acts are already punishable at law but making them a capital crime is sheer extravagance. If the much-battered Crossroads squatters decide to resist the police on their next eviction raid, they too seem guilty since they will have advised acts which may lead to violence with the intent of altering the government policies concerning squatters. The conclusion is inescapable that the protest politics of the disenfranchised in South Africa will fall within the definition of terrorism even if only a limited degree of

[23] These may be described as less dangerous firearms and will include ordinary handguns, shotguns, et cetera.

[24] Section 69(6)(b).

[25] Section 69(7)(a). The State President may add new organisations to those specified in Schedule 4: s 69(7)(b).

[26] Section 64.

[27] Section 65.

[28] Section 67.

[29] Section 68(1) & (2).

[30] The penalty is that prescribed for treason: s 54(1).

violence is involved. This is a chilling thought, especially when we take
into account the power of the police to detain indefinitely for interrogation
any person suspected of being guilty of terrorism or having information
about it.[31]

2. SUBVERSION

Introduction

Subversion is nominally a new security crime created by the Internal
Security Act of 1982.[32] In fact it has a spiritual parentage in the old crimes
of terrorism[33] and of sabotage[34] from which the bastard crime of
subversion has been fashioned. Unfortunately, modifications to the
offspring will make comparisons with its predecessors generally unfruitful.
In the discussion of the basic elements of subversion below, the order of
treatment will be reversed and the criminal intent requirement discussed
first, it being the same as that prescribed for the new crime of terrorism.
What distinguishes these two crimes is that the criminal conduct specified
for subversion is different, being both more complex and more obscure.

Basic Elements of Subversion

The Criminal Intent

The criminal intent required for subversion (as for terrorism) is, in
summary, an intent to overthrow or endanger State authority, to bring
about specified forms of change, to induce the government to act or refrain
from acting or to change a standpoint, or to put in fear or demoralise the
general public or parts of it.[35] If the relevant criminal conduct is
accompanied by any one of these forms of intent, the accused will be guilty
of subversion.

The Criminal Conduct

No less than eleven forms of conduct are listed by the Act[36] any one of
which, if accompanied by the intent just described, will constitute
subversion. Each of the eleven categories of criminal conduct contains
subcategories and, when these are taken into account, the number of
criminal acts which can constitute the crime probably runs to several
hundred. It is therefore extremely difficult to describe the range of
conduct made punishable by the crime and almost impossible to know
what activities are likely to land one in the dock on a charge of subversion.
In the ensuing account, a selection of the forms of punishable conduct will
be made and paraphrasing will be resorted to quite extensively. There is
no other way to make reasonable order out of the statutory chaos.

[31] Section 29. M F Ackermann in *Die Reg Insake Openbare Orde en Staatsveiligheid*
(Butterworths, Durban, 1984) 24 says that the legislature could not have intended to punish
as terrorism 'aangeleenthede van 'n relatief beusselagtige aard'; but it is doubtful that the
examples given in this paragraph would be regarded as trivial.
[32] Section 54(2) of Act 74 of 1982.
[33] Section 2 of the Terrorism Act 83 of 1967.
[34] Section 21 of the General Law Amendment Act 76 of 1962.
[35] Section 54(1)*(a)*, *(b)*, *(c)* & *(d)*, discussed in detail under terrorism above.
[36] Section 54(2). The first eight of those listed constitute substantive forms of conduct and
the remaining three cover, in a broad fashion, attempts, conspiracies and encouragements to
perform the substantive acts.

The crime of subversion prohibits any person (with the intent described above) from causing or promoting general dislocation or disorder at any place in the Republic,[37] from crippling, prejudicing or interrupting any industry or undertaking or the production, distribution or supply of commodities or foodstuffs, from interrupting, impeding or endangering, the manufacture, storage, generation, distribution or supply of various products or services,[38] from endangering, damaging, destroying, rendering useless or putting out of action any installation for the supply of any such service[39] or any prohibited place or any public building,[40] from preventing or hampering or deterring any person from assisting in the maintenance of law and order, from impeding or endangering the free movement of traffic (land, air or sea), from causing encouraging or fomenting feelings of hostility between population groups or parts thereof or from destroying, polluting or contaminating any water supply intended for public use.[41] In addition, a person who performs any act, or attempts, consents or takes steps to perform any act which results in or could have resulted in, or promotes or could have promoted, any one of the multifarious activities just listed, is guilty of subversion, as he would also be if he conspired to bring about either such act or the resultant activity, or aided in their commission, or encouraged or advised them in various ways.[42] It follows from this last category that a statement advising conduct that is likely to cause an act which will result in an obstruction to the free movement of traffic (for example) constitutes a form of conduct prohibited by the crime of subversion. This takes criminal conduct almost to the point of its genesis in the mind of the doer and has the obvious effect of extending the range of the inchoate crimes, such as attempt and incitement, to cover all preliminary acts.

From this brief résumé of the activities proscribed by the crime of subversion, we can see that comprehensiveness is not one of the measure's failings; in fact, it conjures up the vision of a draftsman with a manic desire to criminalise every form of public human activity that can be envisaged by a fevered imagination. The extent to which that desire has been given force of law will be discussed after brief examination of some procedural matters.

Procedural and Evidential Provisions

As in the case of terrorism, proof that the act alleged against the accused in the charge resulted in, or was likely to have resulted in, the achievement of any of the objectives described in the criminal intent provision (for example, in any kind of political or social change) casts

[37] As in the case of terrorism, if the offence was committed outside the Republic, only citizens, residents and persons who have entered the country illegally may be tried for offence.
[38] Examples are water, fuel, energy, light, medical, educational, police, ambulance, radio and television services or products. The full list (in s 54(2)(c)) is followed by the words 'or any other public service'.
[39] That is, any of the services selectively described in the preceding footnote.
[40] 'Prohibited place' means one as defined in s 1 of the Protection of Information Act 84 of 1982. A 'public building' is one occupied either wholly or partly by the State or a provincial or local government: s 54(8).
[41] Section 54(2)(a)−(h).
[42] Section 54(2)(i)−(k).

upon the accused the burden of demonstrating that he did not have such an intent.[43] Where the objects of an organisation are relevant to the charge, the court must take account of the fact that organisations specified in Schedule 4 to the Act are statutorily deemed to have the objective of overthrowing or endangering state authority.[44]

Prosecutions for the offence of subversion require the written consent of the attorney-general.[45] The same provisions for in camera hearings, joint prosecutions, and trials at places where the accused happens to be (or where the Minister of Justice directs) as were shown to be applicable to terrorism are equally applicable to subversion.[46]

Scope of the Crime of Subversion

There is a temptation to describe the scope of this crime by some single word such as 'total' or 'cosmic', and leave it at that. Unfortunately, this will not do; the crime may be excessively broad, but it presumably has some boundaries or outer limits. The task of specifying what these limits are is awesome, for several reasons. First, though many of the activities listed as forms of criminal conduct by the section will be per se unlawful, unlawfulness is not specified as a requirement and is probably not an essential element of the crime. It seems that a person who has local government permission to organise a protest march through a town or city may be guilty of subversion if the march 'impedes . . . the free movement of any traffic on land'[47] even though the march and consequent disruption were not per se unlawful. (The criminal intent requirement will be easily satisfied in such a case as the protest march will necessarily have as an objective the achievement of some 'political . . . social or economic aim or change'.[48]) Second, the activities covered by the prohibition may vary enormously in scale or degree; for example, interrupting the 'supply or distribution of commodities or foodstuffs'[49] may range between knocking a delivery man off his bicycle and sabotaging a goods train. Is every kind of activity between these extremes included; or is there some limiting principle? Third, the language of the section gives rise to difficult problems of causation. It is no simple matter to decide in what circumstances a statement will be punishable because it constituted advice or encouragement to the performance of 'any act . . . which could have resulted in'[50] 'general dislocation'[51] or 'feelings of hostility between different population groups'.[52] Fourth, many of the concepts employed by the draftsman are obscure or vague. What, for example, does it mean to 'interrupt' or 'impede' postal or telecommunication services?[53] For these

---

[43] Section 69(5).
[44] Section 69(7)(a). The State President may add to the specified organisations by acting in terms of s 69(7)(b).
[45] Section 64.
[46] Sections 67 & 68(1) & (2).
[47] Section 54(2)(f). A lawful act, if accompanied by the necessary intent, may constitute treason: R v Wentzel 1940 WLD 269, 275.
[48] Section 54(1)(b).
[49] Section 54(2)(b).
[50] Section 54(2)(i) & (k).
[51] Section 54(2)(a).
[52] Section 54(2)(g).
[53] Section 54(2)(c).

and, no doubt, many other reasons, the crime of subversion has a daunting opaqueness.

However vague the contours of the crime may be, there is no doubt that much of the protest politics of opposition groups falls within its ambit. Without the necessity of proving any act of violence against an accused person, that person may be guilty of subversion, and liable to a sentence of up to twenty years,[54] if he has made a speech which causes 'general dislocation or disorder at any place'[55] or which promotes feelings of hostility between population groups or parts thereof.[56] As we have already observed, meetings, processions or marches that impede traffic also put the organisers and participants in danger of conviction. A politically motivated strike which interrupts the production, supply or distribution of foodstuffs is prima facie a form of criminal subversion. There are other kinds of conduct which the provision proscribes with more legitimacy such as acts of sabotage (crippling an industry) but these are punishable, in any event, either as terrorism or as sabotage.

There appear to be at least three ways in which a court, if so minded, could restrict the rampant quality of the statutory definition of subversion. It could, in the first place, exclude all but the most serious forms of forbidden acts from the scope of the prohibited conduct. For example, only a substantial or serious interruption of the supply of commodities or prejudice to an industry should be held to fall within the statutory prohibition. In the second place, the courts are likely to take a strict view of the mens rea (or guilty mind) requirement of the crime. A person accused of subversion should be set free unless his intention encompassed both the act which he performed *and* the consequences which, according to the statute, invest that act with criminal significance. Where the causative link between the act and the consequences is weak, there should be clear proof that the accused's intent extended both to the act and to its consequences. It follows from this suggestion for limiting the ambit of the crime that negligence is insufficient to satisfy the requirement of mens rea. Thirdly, the acts specified in the definition of subversion are in the nature of positive acts of commission, and omissions (for example a work stay-away) appear to fall outside the scope of the crime.

3. SABOTAGE

Introduction

The process of repealing and rearranging the old crimes of terrorism and sabotage has spawned sabotage in a new form, as well as the security offence of subversion just discussed. In the earlier form of sabotage,[57] seven specified forms of conduct were listed as constituting the proscribed criminal conduct (these being similar but not identical to those proscribed by the new crime of subversion) and the accused was guilty unless he or she demonstrated that the conduct proved by the prosecution was not committed with the intent of achieving any one of ten prescribed

---

[54] Section 54(2)(i); or twenty-five years if the act resulted in violence which the accused should have foreseen: s 54(2)(ii).
[55] Section 54(2)(a).
[56] Section 54(2)(g).
[57] Section 21 of the General Law Amendment Act 76 of 1962.

objectives.[58] The earlier form of sabotage is the model on which
subversion has been based (that is, linking several prescribed forms of
conduct with specified kinds of intent), while the older offence of terrorism
is the model for the new crime of sabotage in that sabotage now consists of
the commission of 'any act' (that is, unspecified conduct) committed in
conjunction with one of a number of listed objectives. The objectives (the
intent requirement of sabotage) correspond broadly, but not exactly, with
the forms of criminal conduct specified for subversion. The nutshell
difference, then, between subversion and sabotage as they now exist, is
that what are prescribed as the prohibited forms of criminal conduct for
subversion, become the intent requirements for sabotage, which consists
of the performance of unspecified conduct ('any act') which is coupled
with one or more of those intent requirements.

Elements of Sabotage

The Criminal Conduct

The basic conduct made punishable by the offence of sabotage is the
commission of an act.[59] Also criminalised is an attempt to commit an act,
a conspiracy to bring about its commission, the giving of aid in its
commission, and various forms of incitement or encouragement towards
the commission thereof.[60] However, whatever form the prosecution takes,
there must be some *act* which the accused is alleged to have performed,
attempted, advised, et cetera. That little word appears to cover the whole
spectrum of deliberate human activity. One limitation on its scope is
discernible: it will not embrace the undergoing of training or the
possession of things or substances since the legislature specifically
incorporated these into the meaning of 'act' in relation to terrorism, but
has not done so in relation to sabotage. Other than this there appear to be
no limits to the scope of the provision. The act does not have to be per se
unlawful; at least, there are no indications to that effect. Verbal or written
statements can clearly constitute acts. Even human excretory functions
are apparently covered and to put it crudely, a person who pees into
public water with the intent of polluting, or contaminating it[61] is a
criminal saboteur. Even the act of human copulation, if performed by
persons uninhibited enough to do it in a street, could qualify as sabotage
in that it has impeded the free movement of traffic on land. Our legislature
has raised fornication to a new level of excitement and significance. But
enough of this levity. Let us consider with what intent the act must be
coupled (to continue the metaphor) if it is to be punishable as sabotage.

The Criminal Intent

If the act proved against the accused was carried out with intent to
achieve any one of six specified objectives, he or she will be guilty of
sabotage and liable to a maximum of twenty years' imprisonment. The
objectives listed by the Act[62] are, in summary, endangering the safety,

---

[58] For an account of the old offence, see A S Mathews, *Law, Order and Liberty in South Africa*
(Juta & Co, Cape Town, 1971) 164.
[59] Section 54(3). The Act describes the criminal conduct as 'any act'.   [60] Ibid.
[61] See the discussion of the intent provision below.
[62] Section 54(3).

health or interests of the public at any place;[63] destroying, polluting or contaminating any water supply intended for public use; interrupting, impeding or endangering at any place, the manufacture, storage, generation, distribution, rendering or supply of various products or services;[64] endangering, destroying, damaging, et cetera any installation for the supply of any of the services just specified, or any prohibited place[65] or public building;[66] crippling, prejudicing or interrupting at any place any industry or undertaking, or the production, distribution or supply of commodities or foodstuffs, and impeding or endangering the free flow of traffic (air, sea or land) at any place. There is little need to elaborate on the vast range of activities covered by the specified objectives.

Procedural and Evidential Provisions

While the presumptions which may be invoked to prove intent on a charge of terrorism and subversion are not applicable to a prosecution for sabotage, the same provisions for joint trials of separate offenders and for the trial to take place where the accused 'happens to be', or the Minister of Justice directs, are applicable to sabotage.[67] Prosecutions require the written consent of the attorney-general[68] and applications for in camera hearings must be heard behind closed doors.[69]

Scope of the Crime of Sabotage

Some indication of the omniverous quality of sabotage was given in the section dealing with the prohibited criminal conduct. One or two examples, more related to political realities, will suffice to underline the overbreadth of the offence. A person who organises a school boycott will have committed an act which 'interrupts . . . educational services'[70] and will therefore be chargeable for sabotage. An unlawful strike[71] will usually 'interrupt . . . the production, supply or distribution of commodities or foodstuffs'[72] and therefore fall under the broad mantle of the offence of sabotage. These two simple examples provide chilling evidence of the potential impact of security crimes on protest politics and industrial action in South Africa.

[63] If the offence was committed outside the Republic, only South African citizens, residents or persons who have entered the Republic illegally may be prosecuted for it: s 54(5).
[64] Examples are fuel, petroleum products, energy, light and water, educational, police, fire-fighting, ambulance, postal and telecommunication services, radio and television services and 'any other public service'.
[65] As defined in s 1 of the Protection of Information Act 84 of 1982.
[66] 'Public building' means any building which is entirely or partly occupied by the State or a provincial or local government authority: s 54(8).
[67] Sections 67 and 68.
[68] Section 64.
[69] Section 65.
[70] Section 54(3)(c). M F Ackermann op cit 34 suggests that the interests protected by the crime of sabotage are the safety, health and interests of the public; but even this suggestion for narrowing the crime leaves it unacceptably wide and does not exclude the examples given in the text.
[71] Presumably, there cannot be a conviction if the strike is legal in terms of labour legislation.
[72] Section 54(3)(e).

Offences Related to Terrorism, Subversion and Sabotage

Any person who harbours or conceals or directly or indirectly assists another person, or who fails to report his or her presence to the police, when he has reason to suspect that that other person intends to commit or has committed the offence of terrorism, subversion or sabotage, is guilty of a crime and liable to the same punishment as is provided for the crime which the other person committed or intended to commit.[73] Similarly, a person who is aware of the presence at any place of another person who is suspected of intending to commit or of having committed any such offence and who harbours or assists such person, or fails to report his presence, is liable to the same punishment.[74] Thus if I harbour, assist or fail to report the presence of, a terrorist or a potential terrorist or a person suspected of terrorism, I am punishable as if I were a terrorist myself; and the same applies to subversion and sabotage. A judge of the Appellate Division, in relation to the similarly worded crime of the now-repealed Terrorism Act of 1967, suggested that the crime is committed even if the person suspected of being a terrorist (and, under the present Act, of having committed subversion or sabotage) is in fact not a terrorist (or subversive or saboteur).[75] Even if this astonishing interpretation was applicable to the earlier provision, the precise wording of the present crime is different and should preclude punishment of persons who helped, or failed to report the presence of, a person who was not a terrorist (or subversive or saboteur) but who was (or should have been) suspected of being one.

If this crime was confined to harbouring, assisting or not reporting a terrorist or saboteur in the true sense (for example someone who had shot people or bombed buildings, or was planning to do so) it would be more acceptable. Giving refuge or assistance to such persons are acts which most states would wish to punish; and even the failure to report terrorism can legitimately be criminalised in a society with a civilised legal and social system.[76] But when these crimes are defined so as to encompass virtually the whole range of protest politics such as marches, school boycotts and industrial action, the crime of harbouring, assisting or failing to report takes on a grotesque character. I am potentially liable to a long prison sentence if I admit a boycotter or striker to my house and fail to report his presence to the police. I must also report, on pain of suffering the same penalty, any person who declares that he is going to boycott educational institutions or organise a strike. It goes without saying that such a crime gives the police enormous power over people whose actions are innocuous or, perhaps, even humane. The existence of this power is made worse by the fact that the crime is committed also by persons who negligently fail to suspect that the person assisted (or not reported) is a terrorist, subversive or saboteur; it is not confined to *intentional* assistance to such persons.

---

[73] Section 54(4).
[74] Ibid.
[75] *S v Imene* 1979 (2) SA 710 (A) 712. This interpretation is surprisingly supported, in relation to the present crime, by M F Ackermann, op cit 37n67.
[76] The 'Jellicoe Report' on the prevention of terrorism in Britain concluded that it was proper to punish persons for failing to report an offence as reprehensible as terrorism: *Review of the Operation of the Prevention of Terrorism (Temporary Provisions) Act 1976* (Cmnd 8803, Feb 1983) paras 214–33.

4. Furthering the Objects of Communism

Of the security crimes considered so far, this is the first explicitly ideological offence in the sense that it authorises the criminal punishment of persons who give support to a defined set of political beliefs. It had a forerunner in the Internal Security Act of 1950[77] which penalised the advocacy of communist doctrine or belief in the generally understood sense but which, in addition, made it criminal to advocate certain schemes for change in South Africa by means that included disorder or the commission of crimes, whether or not such schemes were in furtherance of communist ideology.[78] The new version of the crime avoids the identification of change involving disorder or the commission of crimes with communism[79] but makes itself vulnerable to serious criticism of a different kind by a definition of communism which ranges well beyond the accepted tenets of that ideology. The legislature has again followed the old practice of giving with the one hand and taking with the other.

The Basic Elements of the Crime

The Criminal Conduct

Two forms of conduct fall within the scope of the crime. The first subjects to criminal punishment any person who 'advocates, advises, defends or encourages the achievement in the Republic of any of the objects of communism'.[80] The second penalises a person who 'performs any other act of whatever nature calculated to further the achievement' of any such object in the Republic.[81] In a nutshell, the crime is committed by a person who either advocates an 'object' of communism directly or who does so indirectly by performing an act which is likely to further such an object.

The attitude adopted by the courts on four issues of interpretation will determine the scope of the crime. These issues are the meaning of advocacy, the nature of the acts that are calculated to further the objects of communism, the meaning of an 'object' of communism and, finally, the definition of communism itself. Turning to the first issue, we have seen that advocating, advising, encouraging or defending the achievement of an object of communism is prohibited by the Act. Do these words imply that the accused must have proposed the achievement of an object of communism *as a plan of action* or will it be sufficient if he intellectually identifies with the attainment of such an object? This distinction is based on that drawn by the American Supreme Court between 'the language of incitement' and abstract discussion, in its interpretation of the 'Smith Act' prohibition on advocacy of the overthrow of government by force, violence or the assassination of the officers of government. Faced with similar language[82] to that with which we are concerned, the highest court in the

[77] Section 11(a) & (b) of Act 44 of 1950.
[78] On the interpretation of the crime of furthering the objects of communism under the 1950 Act, see A S Mathews *Law, Order and Liberty in South Africa* (supra) 96 et seq.
[79] The advocacy of such change may still be punishable under the crimes already considered (terrorism, subversion or sabotage) or under crimes still to be considered.
[80] Section 55.   [81] Ibid.
[82] The 'Smith Act' makes a person guilty of a crime if he or she '. . . advocates, abets, advises or teaches the duty, necessity, desirability or propriety of overthrowing or destroying the government . . .': see 18 US CA 2385.

United States decided that while advocacy of action was caught up by the statutory words and was therefore punishable, theoretical or academic talk was not.[83] Though it is true that the court was influenced in its judgment by the prescriptions of the First Amendment in relation to free speech, the same conclusion could be reached on the South African law by statutory interpretation. It is doubtful that the legislature intended to prohibit classroom discussions in which, to take only one example, a lecturer or student expressed the view that social justice would be better achieved in South Africa by nationalisation of the major assets of production. Whereas such discussion should be regarded as legally innocent, encouraging people to *work towards* such an objective[84] might constitute a contravention of the statutory prohibition on the advocacy, encouragement, et cetera of certain ideological goals. In short, the provision should not be interpreted in a way that will put certain ideas out of circulation but only in a way that will prohibit the practical implementation of the disfavoured ideology. It is not to be lightly assumed that Parliament intended the censorship of mere ideas when they are unrelated to a programme of action or of 'achievement', to use the key word in the prohibition. In *R v Adams*[85] the court decided that advocacy implied communication of the prohibited material to an audience; but the effective curtailment of the crime requires that, to be criminal, the advocacy must be directed, in addition, to a plan of action.

A person who has performed 'any act of whatever nature calculated to further the achievement' of any of the objects of communism is also punishable in terms of those words of the provision which we have described above as the indirect advocacy of communism. The effect of this prohibition depends largely on whether 'calculated' means likely or whether it means 'intended'. In its interpretation of the earlier crime of furthering the objects of communism, the court held[86] that 'calculated' does not refer to an intention to achieve an object of communism but makes punishable any act that, in the objective sense, is likely to have that result. This interpretation introduces difficult problems of causation, such as whether the giving of any kind of aid and comfort to a person known to be an active communist constitutes a criminal act. Does it place a bar upon humanitarian assistance to Marxists? The best way to prevent that kind of result would be to interpret 'calculated' to mean 'intended'; failing that the requirement of causation could be made strict so as to qualify for punishment only those acts that have a direct or substantial bearing on the achievement of the object in question.

The resolution of the next issue, the meaning of an 'object' of communism, is more problematic than any of the others. What did the draftsman mean to import by the notion of an 'object' of communism? He could have meant only those ideas which are central to the ideology of communism such as one-party proletarian government and the public ownership of all property excluding personal effects. While this is the

[83] See, for example, *Dennis v United States* 341 US 494 (1951) and *Yates v United States* 354 US 298 (1957).
[84] Which we shall assume to be a prohibited object of communism for the moment.
[85] 1959 (1) SA 646 (SCC) 674.
[86] As we shall see in the discussion of criminal intent below.

narrowest and most sensible of possible interpretations of the law, it is by no means free from difficulty. The problem of what ideas are central to the ideology of communism is not capable of easy resolution and is likely to be disputed both within the ranks of the faithful as well as by those outside it. Thus, in relation to Marxism, the most influential of theories of communism, it has been said that 'there are currents, strains, heresies and rival interpretations in the theoretical sphere which make it additionally difficult to pin down any particular doctrine as giving the essence of Marxism'.[87] Theoretical descriptions of communism and Marxism tend to emphasize three main features: (1) a classless society in which private property is abolished and the means of production and exchange are owned in common; (2) proletarian government through the instrumentality of the Communist Party (the emphasis here is on the identity of interest between the proletariat and the Party); (3) mono-party government characterised by the supremacy of the state over the individual and authoritarian control of politics and the economy.[88] However, at least at the theoretical level, these features are not universal, partly because there is a strong contemporary school of Marxist theorists who argue that a non-authoritarian communism is the 'only correct line of development from Marx'.[89] The communist parties in France and Italy, moreover, have modified theory to incorporate multi-party government[90] and to give some scope, admittedly limited, to private enterprise.

It is by no means clear that the legislature in prohibiting the furtherance of the 'objects' of communism, was concerned exclusively with theory and that the *practice* of communist movements is irrelevant to the determination of what objectives are proscribed by the Act. Scruton refers to Marxist revolutionary movements which 'tend to see the world in terms of a class struggle and attempt to align themselves with the oppressed in that struggle' and which 'nourish themselves . . . upon a variety of left, socialist and equalitarian doctrines'.[91] It appears likely that the courts will regard participation in the class struggle with revolutionary aims as an 'object' prohibited by the Act for, as we shall see below, the definition of communism does take account of communist practice as well as theory.

The conclusion towards which this discussion leads is that the expression 'objects of communism' should be limited to those theoretical features and practical goals of the ideology which constitute its distinctive nature. The corollary to this proposition is that objectives which communism shares with all or several other political movements are not part of the core concept of the ideology and their pursuit should not be punishable under the Act.

The final issue of interpretation concerns the meaning of communism. The statutory definition[92] declares that any one of three kinds of doctrine,

---

[87] Roger Scruton *A Dictionary of Political Thought* (Macmillan, London, 1982) 290.
[88] Roger Scruton op cit 81, 291; Walter Lacqueur, *A Dictionary of Politics* (The Free Press, New York, 1974) 108; J Wilczynski *An Encyclopedic Dictionary of Marxism, Socialism and Communism* (Macmillan, London, 1981) 91–2.
[89] See for example Lyman Tower Sergent *Contemporary Political Ideologies* (The Dorsey Press, Illinois, 1981) 79–80.
[90] Lyman Tower Sergent op cit 112. There is disagreement on whether the belief in elections and multi-party government will survive success at the polls by a communist party.
[91] Op cit 291.   [92] Section 1(iv).

ideology or scheme will constitute communism for purposes of the Act. The first is one which is 'based on, has developed from or is related to' the tenets of the major Marxist theorists[93] and which 'aims at the establishment of any form of socialism or collective ownership'. This language is disturbingly wide and, at first blush, it seems that a doctrine of democratic socialism will fall under it since such a doctrine appears to be 'related to' Marxist tenets and to aim at the establishment of a 'form of socialism'. Whether Scandinavian socialism or West German social democracy fall under the definition is a serious problem which Parliament ought to have avoided by more judicious use of language. However much the words of the definition may dictate such conclusions, the courts would make the law, and more importantly themselves, very foolish by ruling that the ideologies of a large number of the countries of Western Europe are forms of prohibited communism. Democratic Marxism can probably not be saved but non-Marxist democratic socialism may reasonably be put beyond the reach of the criminal law.[94]

The second doctrine, ideology or scheme which falls under the definition of communism is one which by means of class or group polarisation seeks to place one group or class in power and to establish a one-party despotic system of government.[95] This language more closely reflects the essential or core features of communism alluded to earlier and is for that reason much more acceptable as a form of communism.

The third and final kind of doctrine, ideology or scheme which constitutes communism under the Act is one which seeks to bring about change[96] in the Republic under the direction or guidance of, or with the co-operation of, a foreign government or foreign international institution or organisation which has as a purpose,[97] whether declared or not, the achievement within the Republic of any social or economic system characterised by the features of the first kind of doctrine, ideology or scheme discussed above (ie by the tenets of Marxism) or of a government characterised by the features of the second of such doctrines, ideologies or schemes (ie one arising from the polarisation of class or group conflict and taking the form of despotic, one-party control).[98] In brief, the third kind of doctrine, ideology or scheme which constitutes communism under the Act is one which aims at change in collaboration with foreign governments or organisations which aim to achieve either of the first two in the Republic. The third form of communism will therefore be narrow or broad, and offensive or less offensive to democratic politics, according to whether the first two (and particularly the first) are restrictively or loosely interpreted. If democratic socialism falls under the first kind, then collaboration with any foreign body which advocates such an ideology in order to achieve change in South Africa will be punishable as communism. Nobody could

---

[93] Those specifically mentioned are Marx, Engels, Lenin and Mao Tse-Tung; but any other recognised theorist in, or exponent of, these tenets is included.
[94] This conclusion will follow if the courts hold that an ideology, to be based on, or related to, the tenets of Marxism, must be *substantially* based on or related to those tenets.
[95] See s 1(iv)(b) for the detailed wording.
[96] The definition refers to 'any political, economic, industrial or social change within the Republic'.
[97] Or as one of its purposes.
[98] Section 1(iv)(c).

then collaborate with a socialist trade union abroad to achieve any kind of change (for example improved worker protection) in the Republic. As already indicated, such absurdities may be avoided by assigning a narrow meaning to the first form of communism.

The Criminal Intent

There is little doubt that a person charged with the direct advocacy of an object of communism is not guilty unless the state proves that he intended to bring about the object that forms the basis of the charge. However, as we have seen, the Act also criminalises the performance of 'any other act of whatever nature calculated to further the achievement'[99] of an object of communism; and 'calculated' in the similarly worded old provision, was held to mean 'likely'.[100] This finding is said to carry the corollary that the state need not prove a subjective intention on the part of the accused to further an object of communism by the performance of the act charged.[101] The mens rea requirement will be satisfied if the state proves that the accused intentionally committed the act charged and that this act was reasonably likely to have furthered an object of communism. This line of reasoning now appears to be discredited, and rightly so. In several judgments concerned with the use of similar statutory language, the courts have held that the accused's guilty mind must extend not just to the act charged but also to the prohibited consequences thereof.[102] Some of these judgments, while requiring proof that the act alleged to have the prohibited consequence was intentionally committed, hold that negligence or culpa is sufficient to satisfy the guilty-mind requirement in relation to the consequence.[103] It follows that a person who intentionally commits an act that is likely to further an object of communism is guilty even if he did not intend the consequence, so long as he was negligent in foreseeing that the consequence would flow from his act. There seems to be no reason, however, why the courts should not require proof of intention (dolus) both as to the act and the consequences. The word 'calculated' is commonly used to denote a positive deliberative activity and even though it appears at first sight to qualify the word 'act' in the statutory formulation of the crime, the language is open to the construction that the consequence must have been 'calculated' in the mind of the accused.[104]

Scope of the Crime

If the crime of furthering the objects of communism is interpreted broadly so as to include virtually any socialist doctrine or ideology, it is

---

[99] Section 55.

[100] *S v Nokwe* 1962 (3) SA 71 (T).

[101] *S v Nokwe* (supra) 74. See also *S v Byleveld* 1964 (1) SA 269 (T).

[102] See, for example, *S v Mdingi* 1979 (1) SA 309 (A) 316, *S v Dalindyebo* 1980 (3) SA 1049 (TkSC) 1052 and *S v Ntshiwa* 1985 (3) SA 495 (T) 504.

[103] *S v Dalindyebo* (supra). See also Burchell & Hunt *South African Criminal Law and Procedure* 2 ed (Juta & Co Ltd, Cape Town, 1983) vol 1 218.

[104] The language of the section in question is quite capable of bearing the construction 'calculated by the accused' to further the objects of communism. Though the Appellate Division appears to have thought differently in *S v Arenstein* 1967 (3) SA 366 (A) 381 this aspect of the judgment appears to be obiter. M F Ackermann op cit 46 accepts that the reading 'calculated by the accused' is a permissible interpretation of the section.

clearly a measure that violates democratic principles of government and is likely to be destructive of them in practice. If interpreted narrowly, it is less vulnerable to the charge that it is undemocratic but the question of the efficacy of criminalising an ideology remains to be answered. The presence of this crime on the statute book since 1950 has certainly not diminished support for Marxist doctrine in South Africa and it may be suggested that remedial activity in the social and economic sphere, rather than the criminal law, is more likely to counter the apparently growing attractiveness of communism in South Africa.

5. FURTHERING THE AIMS OF AN UNLAWFUL ORGANISATION

While this section on security crimes is concerned chiefly with substantive security crimes and not those flowing from breaches of restrictions imposed under the Act,[105] it will be helpful to mention briefly at this point the crime of furthering the aims of an unlawful organisation since it is analogous to the offence of furthering the objects of communism. As indicated elsewhere,[106] the Act confers a virtually unrestricted power on the Minister of Law and Order to declare organisations unlawful.[107] He can also declare, apparently without any possibility of 'interference' from the judiciary, that any organisation is in fact the same as one already declared unlawful and it will follow from such a declaration that, in any criminal proceedings, an act or omission proved in relation to the first mentioned organisation is deemed to be proved in relation to the unlawful organisation.[108] Moreover, officers, office-bearers and members of the first organisation (i e the one declared to be the same as one that is unlawful) are deemed to be officers, office-bearers and members of the unlawful organisation. As indicated below, the criminal consequences of a declaration of unlawfulness or a declaration of equivalence are of a drastic nature.

Once an organisation is declared unlawful it becomes a criminal offence to become, continue to be, or to perform any act as, an office-bearer, officer or member of the organisation, to carry, be in possession of or display anything indicating that the person in question was at any time and in any way associated with the organisation, to contribute or solicit anything for the direct or indirect benefit of the organisation; to take part in any activity of the unlawful organisation or to carry on in its direct or indirect interest any activity in which it was or *could have been engaged* at the date of the declaration of unlawfulness, or to advocate in various ways the achievement of any of the objects of the unlawful organisation or of objects *similar to the objects of such organisation* (or to perform any act calculated to have that effect).[109] For each of these prohibited activities a penalty of imprisonment up to ten years is provided,[110] the severity of which is illustrated by a judgment on the earlier equivalent section[111] in which the court held that a person who becomes a member, puts on a membership

---

[105] The Internal Security Act 74 of 1982 (referred to below as 'the Act').
[106] See ch 7 below.
[107] Section 4(1).
[108] Section 4(2).
[109] Section 13(1)(a).
[110] Section 56(1)(a) read with 56(1)(i).
[111] Section 3(1)(a) of the Internal Security Act 44 of 1950.

badge and then solicits a small donation would theoretically expose himself to a possible total sentence of thirty years.[112] The italicised words above provide a clear indication of the potential breadth of the restriction, especially the prohibition on the advocacy of any object which is similar to an object of the unlawful organisation.[113]

Prohibitions of this kind would carry more conviction if restricted to the activities of proven terrorist organisations. In fact, the prohibitions are applicable to any organisation declared unlawful[114] by the minister and to any body which he deems to be equivalent to an unlawful organisation. The banning of the Christian Institute in October 1977 (along with seventeen other groups) is one clear example of an organisation being declared unlawful for what may legitimately be described as protest politics. Moreover, organisations such as the African National Congress had many laudable objectives at the time when it was banned though it had by then, in desperation, abandoned its non-violent strategy. It is nevertheless an offence to further any of the objects of these two organisations, whether admirable or reprehensible, lawful or unlawful; or to further any object in which they could have engaged or which are similar to those in which they did engage.

Fortunately, the ambit of the crime of promoting the objects of a banned organisation has been subjected to a narrowing interpretation in the significant judgment of Didcott J in *Ndabeni v Minister of Law and Order*.[115] In a judgment remarkable for politically realistic and clear-minded analysis, the court declared that guilt depended on proof that the accused had furthered objects that were distinctive of the banned organisation. On the facts before it, it declined to hold that the simple advocacy of the philosophy of black consciousness amounted to the advocacy of an object that was distinctive of the banned organisation SASO (South African Students' Organisation). The importance of *Ndabeni* is that general political or social objectives or programmes, which are not peculiarly or specially identified with a banned organisation, are not put under quarantine simply because that organisation happened to espouse or adopt them. Of course, it remains an offence to continue to carry on, in the interests of the banned organisation, any activity in which it was (or could be) involved.[116] We may conclude that though the prohibition remains wide, much of its sting has been removed by the judgment in *Ndabeni* and the subsequent approval of it by the Transvaal court in *S v Ntshiwa*.[117]

[112] *S v Xoswa* 1964 (2) SA 459 (C). More recently, in *S v Mgijima* 1982 (1) SA 886 (E) the court held that where different acts are part and parcel of one intention and one course of conduct, the different counts should be taken as one for purposes of sentence. However, it remains clear that separate convictions for each act are possible.

[113] The prohibition on advocating similar objects was added after *S v Nokwe* (supra) in which the court held that the accused was not punishable if he tried to achieve similar objects independently of the unlawful organisation.

[114] The definition of unlawful organisation in s 1(xxii) makes it clear that all organisations which were unlawful under previous legislation at the date of the coming into operation of the Act, remain unlawful.

[115] 1984 (3) SA 500 (D).

[116] Section 13(1)(a)(i) & (iv). Didcott J made the further important point that some objectives of a banned organisation may be so 'mundane or innocuous' that the legislature could not have contemplated outlawing them: *Ndabeni v Minister of Law and Order* (supra) 508.

[117] 1985 (3) SA 495 (T) 506.

6. CRIMES OF PROTEST

Introduction

The web of restrictive and discriminatory laws which constitute the legalised aspect of apartheid bear down heavily on South Africans who are not classified as whites and most heavily upon the African (indigenous) segment of the non-white peoples of the country. Black South Africans[118] initially sought to free themselves from legalised discrimination by lawful protest and negotiation but these methods were unsuccessful and apartheid was progressively intensified and extended through legislation after the National Party came into power in 1948. On 26 June 1952 black organisations launched a campaign of non-violent defiance aimed at securing the repeal of discriminatory legislation and by the end of that year more than eight thousand persons had been arrested for participation in the organised contravention of the laws of apartheid, more particularly pass laws, curfew regulations and regulations for the segregation of public facilities.[119] The government responded by enacting a law which introduced fierce penalties for crimes that were committed by way of protest and similar penalties for encouraging protest crimes or organising or assisting in campaigns to break laws by way of protest. This law, known as the Criminal Law Amendment Act of 1953,[120] broke the defiance campaign and has effectively eliminated non-violent disobedience as a strategy for the disenfranchised in South Africa. The provisions of the Criminal Law Amendment Act of 1953 have now been incorporated into the Internal Security Act of 1982[121] with only minor amendments.

Basic Features of Crimes of Protest

This branch of security crimes consists of three main provisions. The first provides increased penalties for offences which are committed by way of protest; the second criminalises encouragement to the commission of offences by way of protest; and the third penalises certain forms of assistance to those involved in protest crimes. Each will require separate treatment.

(a) Increased penalties

This provision[122] of the Act does not introduce a new substantive crime but provides that a person convicted of any offence 'which is proved to have been committed by way of protest against any law or in support of any campaign against any law or in support of any campaign for the repeal or modification of any law or for the variation or limitation of the application or administration of any law' shall be liable to a fine of not exceeding three thousand rands or imprisonment not exceeding three

---

[118] The term black is used in the text to denote all the 'non-white' groups—African, Coloured and Asian.

[119] For details of the campaign the reader may consult *A Survey of Race Relations in South Africa* (1951–2) 11 et seq and (1952–3) 27 et seq.

[120] No 8 of 1953. For a detailed discussion of this law and its interpretation by the courts, see A S Mathews *Law, Order and Liberty in South Africa* (supra) 184 et seq.

[121] Act 74 of 1982. As before, this law is referred to in the text as 'the Act'.

[122] Section 58.

years, or both the fine and imprisonment.[123] However trivial the penalty provided for the crime actually committed, once the motive of protest or alteration of the law is proved, the accused becomes liable to the heavier penalties just indicated. The effect is to convert a vast array of minor and technical offences into major crimes if the accused had the requisite political motive. A presumption in the Act[124] facilitates proof by the prosecution of this motive. If it is established that the offence was committed in the company of two or more persons who have been or are being charged with similar offences committed at the same place and approximately the same time, then it is presumed, unless the accused proves the contrary, that the motive was to protest against, or seek the alteration of, a law or laws.

It is clear that the increased penalties are not applicable if the offence committed by the accused was done in the course of, or incidentally to, a protest without the specified motive. For this reason, the accused in *S v Peake*,[125] having defaced property in the process of carrying out a protest, was held not liable to the additional penalties. But where the accused commits the offence in the company of several others, he will be presumed, as in *S v Pungula*,[126] to have the necessary motive unless he proves otherwise. In *Pungula's* case the operation of the presumption made the accused subject to the higher penalties.

(b) Inciting Protest Crimes

It is a substantive crime under the Act[127] to encourage[128] any other person or persons in general to commit any offence by way of protest against any law or in support of a campaign against any law or a campaign for the repeal or modification of any law, or for the variation or limitation of its application. It is also an offence to use any language or to do any act or thing 'calculated' to have that effect. A person found guilty of the crime is liable to a fine not exceeding five thousand rands or imprisonment not exceeding five years, or to both the fine and imprisonment.[129]

The reach of this crime is quite impressive. If a speaker says to an audience of blacks that they will never free themselves of their servitude if they do not ignore discriminatory laws, he will be guilty, and subject to the severe penalties indicated, for using language that was likely to encourage others to commit protest crimes or to embark on a campaign to change the law, if not for direct encouragement to do so. In *S v Nathie*[130] the court, while acquitting the accused because he was charged only with direct encouragement, expressed the view that a provocative political

---

[123] The penalty of ten lashes, which was one of the pleasant alternatives introduced by the 1953 Act, no longer applies. It should be noted that the increased penalty has been held applicable to any offence whatever, including the inchoate crime of incitement: *R v Sesidi* 1953 (4) SA 634 (GW).

[124] Section 69(8).

[125] 1962 (3) SA 572 (C).

[126] 1960 (2) SA 760 (N).

[127] Section 59.

[128] The relevant words are 'in any manner whatsoever advises, encourages, incites, commands, aids or procures . . .'.

[129] Section 59.

[130] 1964 (3) SA 588 (A).

speech in which the speaker referred with approval to the actions of others who had defied an apartheid law, was a contravention of the similarly worded predecessor of the provision under discussion.[131] What the offence does, therefore, is to eliminate civil disobedience as a political option and even to render criminal, in certain circumstances, the favourable mention of civil disobedience as a strategy.

Where direct encouragement is the basis of the prosecution, the accused will not be guilty unless he intended to encourage another or others to commit a protest crime or to embark on a campaign for changing laws by means of the commission of crimes. On the other hand, if the charge against the accused is that he used language 'calculated' to have that result, he may be found guilty on the basis that he negligently failed to appreciate the impact of his words. This is because 'calculated' in this context is almost invariably given the meaning of 'likely to result in' and is not interpreted so as to require proof of a subjective intent to encourage protest crimes. However, as already mentioned,[132] the word 'calculated' can equally be construed to mean 'intended'; and it should be so interpreted in the present context as well. Unless the courts accept this alternative reading, the law will function as a severe restriction on political speech, as the obiter dictum in *Nathie* portends.

Finally, two points of minor consolation may be mentioned. If the person incited is not capable of committing the offence in question because, for example, he was under sixteen years of age and therefore not required to carry a pass as in *R v Molorane*,[133] no offence will have been committed by the inciter. But where the accused has addressed an audience consisting of persons who could either then, or in the future, commit the crime in question, he may be found guilty without actual proof that the persons present were then capable of committing the offence.[134] The second point of consolation is that the presumption[135] of guilty intent that arises from commission of the crime in the company of two or more persons, probably does not apply to the offence under discussion because the words creating it refer to a prosecution in which the *offence charged* was committed by way of protest.[136] The crime we are presently discussing requires that the offence incited, not the offence charged, must be a protest offence.

(c) Assistance to protest offenders

The Act creates a further substantive crime which will be committed by any person who solicits or accepts, or offers or gives, money or goods[137] from or to any other person or group of persons for the purpose of assisting a campaign, conducted by means of unlawful acts or omissions, against any law (or its application or administration) or for the purpose of

---

[131] The accused is said to be guilty because of the use of language likely to cause others to break the law by way of protest, or to secure its alteration. (See the court's obiter dictum at p 597 of the judgment.)

[132] See n 104 above and the accompanying text.

[133] 1960 (4) SA 353 (C).

[134] *S v Peake* 1962 (4) SA 288 (C).

[135] In s 69(8).

[136] *R v Moilwayana* 1957 (4) SA 302 (T).

[137] The relevant wording of the section is 'money or other article'.

assisting any person to commit an offence by way of protest against any law or in support of a campaign for the repeal or modification of a law or the variation of its application, or for the purpose of unlawfully assisting a person who has committed any such offence.[138] The penalties for this crime are a fine of five thousand rands, imprisonment of up to five years, or both.[139] In addition to the penalty which it imposes, the court is required to declare forfeited to the state any money or goods in the possession or under the control of the accused which were given or received for any of the purposes mentioned above.[140]

The criminal conduct which falls under this prohibition is reasonably clear and consists of any kind of material assistance towards the protest crimes discussed above[141] whereas under the old provision the giving of legal aid to those involved in protest crimes was arguably a criminal offence.[142] Material assistance to those who have already committed protest offences is now punishable only if it is unlawful.[143] Giving aid will be unlawful if it is specifically for the purpose of furthering protest crimes or campaigns. The criminal intent required for guilt should be strictly interpreted in this case to mean an intention to further protest crimes or campaigns. The rationale of *S v Peake*[144] is equally applicable here and the fact that the accused gave money to a campaign in which unforeseen protest crimes were incidentally committed, should not render him liable. As the court implied in *R v Moshoe*[145] the accused must have contemplated the commission of offences in order to be guilty. Foresight is required and mere proof of negligence on the part of the accused is not enough.

Procedural Provisions

A civil disobedient recognises that there is a price to pay for breaking the law and is usually prepared to go to jail as part of his protest against laws that are discriminatory and unjust. In fact, campaigns are sometimes intended to make the laws in question unworkable by filling the jails with dissenters. The crimes now under discussion seek to raise the price of dissent by imposing a heavy fine and sentence of imprisonment for violation of what are in essence minor crimes. Since even such punishments may enhance the symbolic effect of the protest, the legislature has introduced a provision to enable the government to avoid filling the jails with prisoners of conscience but simultaneously to strike back savagely at the offender. This provision[146] authorises the court which sentences a protest offender to issue a warrant for the attachment of his property if any fine imposed is not paid within forty-eight hours. The movable property of the offender must first be attached and, if that is insufficient, immovable property may be sold in execution. The provision

---

[138] Section 60(1).
[139] Ibid.
[140] Section 69(2).
[141] That is, under paras *(a)* and *(b)* above.
[142] And the court so held in at least one case: see A S Mathews *Law, Order and Liberty in South Africa* (supra) 189; *S v Sobale* 1962 (1) SA 411 (E).
[143] Section 60(1)*(c)* refers to 'unlawfully assisting any person' whereas the old provision spoke only of 'assisting'.
[144] Supra.
[145] 1953 (4) SA 119 (T).
[146] Section 61.

therefore contemplates the possible impoverishment of the offender of conscience and of his immediate family. It is this procedural provision in particular which reduces the prospect of a successful programme of disobedience to discriminatory laws in South Africa.

Finally, the trial of protest offenders may take place where the accused 'happens to be',[147] may be held before an ordinary magistrate's court with jurisdiction to impose higher-than-usual penalties,[148] and may take the form of a joint trial for separate offenders who are charged with offences committed at the same place and approximately the same time.[149]

7. INTERNAL SECURITY ACT CRIMES—GENERAL

Apart from the major substantive crimes created by the Act,[150] there is a host of crimes, some with quite severe penalties, which flow from breaches of administrative orders issued under its terms. For example, persons who print, publish, or disseminate a prohibited publication, or possess without consent any publication of any unlawful organisation, are guilty of an offence and liable to heavy punishment.[151] Condign punishment also awaits a banned or listed person who fails to give notice of a change of address or, when called upon to do so by a policeman, fails to give his or her name or address or furnishes a false or incorrect name or address.[152] Various provisions of the Act make it criminal to break any of the conditions of a banning order and to reproduce or disseminate in various ways any speech or writing of a banned person.[153] We have already observed that furthering the objects of an organisation declared unlawful is a crime under the Act. It would be both tedious and unnecessary to examine each and every one of these ancillary[154] crimes; and, in any event, many of them are dealt with briefly in the chapters concerned with the administrative powers granted by the Act. However, at this point we simply record that a fine mesh of criminal regulation has been brought into being by the Act and that not even the smallest of fish is likely to slip through.

8. THE CRIME OF INTIMIDATION

Introduction

Certain provisions of the Riotous Assemblies Act of 1956[155] rendered criminal a variety of intimidatory, threatening or even disrespectful actions designed to compel persons to act or not to act in various ways or to subject them to threats or ridicule for having acted (or not acted) as they did.[156] In their original form these provisions were concerned with

---

[147] Section 67.
[148] Section 68(4). The penalties authorised are a fine of not exceeding R3 000 or imprisonment for not exceeding three years.
[149] Section 67.
[150] Act 74 of 1982.
[151] Imprisonment of up to ten years for the first-mentioned offence and three years for the second. Section 56(1)(b) & (c) read with s 56(1)(i) & (ii).
[152] Section 54(1)(d) & (e) read with s 56(1)(i).
[153] See, for example, s 56(1)(f), (i), (k), (l), (m) & (p).
[154] Ancillary, that is, to administrative orders issued under the Act.
[155] Sections 10–15 of Act 17 of 1956.
[156] For a detailed description of these provisions, see A S Mathews *Law Order and Liberty in South Africa* (supra) 191–5.

employer–employee relations and, particularly, with the aggressive use by labourers of any economic muscle which they might have possessed. The provisions were later given a universal application by elimination of the requirement that the intimidatory or similar conduct had to be 'in respect of employment'. In 1982 the Intimidation Act[157] repealed these provisions of the Riotous Assemblies Act and replaced them by a single crime with a brevity that belies its cosmic scope.

Elements of the Crime of Intimidation

Briefly stated, the offence of intimidation is committed by a person who without lawful reason assaults, injures or causes damage to any other person, or who threatens to do so, with the intention of compelling some particular person to do or not to do any act or to assume or abandon a particular standpoint.[158] The penalties provided are a fine not exceeding twenty-thousand rands or imprisonment not exceeding ten years, or both.

The Criminal Conduct

The accused, acting without lawful reason, must be proved to have assaulted, injured or caused damage to any other person or in any manner to have threatened to do so or to kill any other person.[159] As in the case of almost all security crimes examined so far, these words confront us with a spectrum of human activity ranging from relatively innocuous conduct at one end to serious behaviour at the other. An accused person who has badly beaten up another, or burned down his house, in order to compel that person to toe some political line, *is* guilty of reprehensible conduct. Such conduct already constitutes a crime at common law for which substantial punishment may be imposed by a court. However, while a serious threat to assault someone else is punishable at common law as a form of assault, threatening to burn down a house does not appear to be a non-statutory crime. There may therefore be some justification for criminalising such conduct where it is used to induce others to act or refrain from doing so, or to alter any standpoint. But, if we move to the other end of the spectrum, we will discover that the crime of intimidation covers some remarkably trivial or innocuous activities. If a speaker wishes to make a point at a meeting and I push him down into his chair to stop him from speaking, I appear to be guilty because I have assaulted him with a view to inducing him to 'abstain from doing' an act. More seriously, since the provision speaks of causing damage to any person (and is not limited to injury to tangible property) an unlawful[160] striker likewise appears to be guilty of intimidation since the strikers will have caused damage to the employer with a view to altering his standpoint on working conditions. Equally, any kind of physical threat to a reluctant striker appears to constitute criminal conduct.

---

[157] 72 of 1982.
[158] Section 1(1) of the Intimidation Act 72 of 1982.
[159] Ibid.
[160] Since the conditions under which a strike of workers in South Africa will be lawful are onerous and require adherence to elaborate and long-winded procedures, it is not surprising that most strikes are unlawful: see s 65 of the Labour Relations Act 28 of 1956. Where a strike is unlawful, the accused will presumably not have a 'lawful reason' for his threat or other prohibited action.

The accused is guilty only if he acted 'without lawful reason'.[161] This qualification is unlikely to limit the scope of the crime to any substantial degree since the forms of conduct prohibited are per se unlawful and will become lawful only where the accused is clothed with some kind of legal authority to act as he did or where, for example, he acted legally in self-defence.[162] As already observed, a strike that is unlawful under the Labour Relations Act, and even an incitement to such a strike,[163] could constitute intimidation since the accused could hardly have had lawful reason to act where the strike is legally prohibited. A strike by certain classes of workers, for example municipal workers, is automatically illegal.[164] The accused is required to establish the lawful reason unless a statement indicating its existence has been made before the close of the prosecution case by or on behalf of the accused.[165]

Where the basis of the charge against the accused is a threat to kill, injure or cause damage (and not the commission of the substantive acts of killing, injuring, et cetera) the threat, according to the wording of the Act, must have been directed against 'a particular person' or 'any other person'. This language precludes a finding of guilt where the accused has directed his threats generally, and not against a particular person or persons. The court, in *S v Mohapi*,[166] acquitted the accused where the threats were directed against the inhabitants of a particular area. In doing so, it observed that more general threats appeared to be covered in any event by the crime of terrorism. The finding in *Mohapi* is clearly correct.

The Criminal Intent

Little need be said about the criminal intent requirement of the Intimidation Act except that it is all-encompassing. The accused must have intended, when he performed the criminal conduct, to cause some particular person either to act or not to act, or to take up or abandon a particular standpoint. An intent requirement can hardly be more unfocused than that. However, the judgment in *R v Foster*,[167] which was concerned with similar Rhodesian legislation, adopted the partially limiting rule that the accused must have intended to alter a standpoint in the form of a clearly held belief or opinion.

Scope of the Crime of Intimidation

Though the origin of this crime is in the field of labour relations, and one of its principal functions in practice is to convert strikes into security offences,[168] its application is a great deal wider than that. In October

---

[161] Section 1(1).

[162] For example, a policeman dispersing a meeting by force in the exercise of statutory powers.

[163] Section 65 of the Labour Relations Act 28 of 1956.

[164] Section 65(1)*(c)* read with section 46(1) of the Labour Relations Act 28 of 1956. Workers engaged in the provision of 'essential services' (defined as the provision of light, power, water, sanitation, passenger transport or fire-fighting) are also prohibited from striking in any circumstances.

[165] Section 1(2) of Act 72 of 1982.

[166] 1984 (1) SA 270 (O).

[167] 1962 (1) SA 280 (SR) 285.

[168] A leading authority on industrial legislation takes the view that strikes are covered by the Act: Alan de Kock *Industrial Laws of South Africa* (Juta & Co Ltd, Cape Town, 1982) 652.

1983, at a meeting in the Pietermaritzburg City Hall addressed by the Prime Minister on the subject of the referendum on the constitution, members of the Black Sash stood peaceably in the hall holding a protest banner. They were manhandled by National Party supporters and physically ejected from the hall. Did the Prime Minister, who is reported to have smilingly watched those proceedings, recognise that he was witnessing the commission of the crime of intimidation by his followers? The manhandling of the protesting women constituted an assault which was clearly done with the intent that they should 'abstain from doing' the 'act' of displaying a banner.[169] No doubt, the commission of a crime was far from his mind since his government, when it enacted this law, had other people and other events in contemplation. History teaches the lesson that when new rulers take over some unexpected persons tend to become the victims of dragnet laws like the Intimidation Act. The legislature would have been wiser to restrict the crime of intimidation to serious harm (or threats thereof) and to limit the concept to actual or threatened damage to property.

9. INCITEMENT TO PUBLIC VIOLENCE

The new security law dispensation of 1982, consisting mainly of the Internal Security and Intimidation Acts already discussed, resulted in the repeal of almost all the provisions of the Riotous Assemblies Act of 1956.[170] Among the provisions left unrepealed is one[171] which broadens the common-law crime of incitement to public violence. It declares that a person who has acted in a manner, or spoken or published words, that are likely to cause his audience or members of the public to commit public violence, is guilty of incitement to the crime of public violence. This changes the requirements of the crime at common law by eliminating the necessity of proof by the state that the accused intended to incite public violence or that such violence would be an immediate consequence of his actions or words.[172] This slackening of the requirements of incitement to public violence should not be interpreted to permit punishment of a person who goes no further than to arouse feelings about legitimate grievances of disadvantaged groups in society.

10. ATTEMPT, CONSPIRACY OR INCITEMENT TO COMMIT OFFENCES

Another unrepealed provision[173] of the Riotous Assemblies Act of 1956 declares that an attempt to commit an offence against a statute or statutory regulation, or a conspiracy or incitement to commit such an offence or an offence at common law, shall be a crime and, in the absence of specific provision, shall be subject to the same penalties as are provided for the substantive crime itself. It follows that in respect of any security crime whatever, the accused may be charged also with attempting to commit the crime in question, or with incitement or conspiracy to do so.

---

[169] See the wording of s 1(1) of the Act.
[170] Act 17 of 1956. The repealed provisions have been re-enacted in slightly modified form.
[171] Section 17 of Act 17 of 1956.
[172] *R v Radu* 1953 (2) SA 245 (E); *R v Maxaulana* 1953 (2) SA 252 (E).
[173] Section 18 of Act 17 of 1956.

11. Promoting Racial Hostility

It has long been an offence under the Black Administration Act of 1927[174] to promote feelings of hostility between 'Blacks and Europeans' in South Africa. This offence remains on the statute book but has since been complemented by a provision of the Internal Security Act of 1982[175] which punishes the promotion of hostility 'between population groups or parts of population groups of the Republic'.[176] It makes it an offence to utter words or to perform any other act with the intention of causing, encouraging or fomenting such feelings. As in the case of the similar offence under the Black Administration Act,[177] it is clear that there must be a specific intent which can be drawn by the court as the only reasonable inference from the accused's words or conduct.[178] Even though the new provision speaks of parts of population groups as well as population groups as a whole (as opposed to Blacks and Europeans in the Black Administration Act or 'population groups' under the Second General Law Amendment Act of 1974), it is submitted that the crime is not committed where a restricted group is attacked, such as farmers or lawyers or businessmen, unless they are attacked as representatives of a racial group.[179] The phrase 'feelings of hostility', which is common to both provisions, was declared in *R v Bunting*[180] to refer to the creation of discord, enmity, estrangement, disaffection or unfriendliness between race groups.[181]

There is nothing inherently undesirable in criminalising incitement to racial hostility in plural societies. The exploitation of racial differences may cause tension and even violent conflict. In Britain, incitement to racial hatred is a crime which was stiffened in 1976[182] by removing the need to prove an actual intent to stir up racial hatred. The intent requirement had made it difficult to secure convictions for blatantly racialistic language.[183] However, in a mixed society where one group is

---

[174] Section 29(1) of Act 38 of 1927.

[175] Section 62 of Act 74 of 1982.

[176] The penalty is a fine of up to R2 000 or imprisonment of up to two years, or both. This section replaced a similar prohibition in s 1 of the Second General Amendment Act 94 of 1974.

[177] Which is analysed by A S Mathews in *Law, Order and Liberty in South Africa* (supra) 208–12.

[178] *R v Sutherland* 1950 (4) SA 66 (T); *R v Nkatlo* 1950 (1) SA 26 (C); *R v Bunting* 1929 EDL 320; *S v Kubhaka* 1974 (3) SA 443 (N); *S v Singh* 1975 (1) SA 330 (N).

[179] An example would be an accusation that white farmers are fascist oppressors. In *S v Mbiline* 1978 (3) SA 131 (E) the court required proof of incitement against population groups as a whole. Even though s 1 of Act 94 of 1974, with which it was dealing, did not contain the phrase 'parts of population groups' it is submitted that it is still a requirement that the group in question must be attacked *as such*. However, in view of the changed wording an intention to attack entire population groups is no longer a requirement.

[180] (Supra) at p 332.

[181] However, 'estrangement' and 'unfriendliness' appear to be weaker forms of 'hostility' which is what the statute is aimed at preventing. If the legislature had intended to include these weaker forms, it would surely not have limited itself to the word 'hostility'.

[182] See s 5A of the Public Order Act 1936. In the Public Order Bill published late in 1985, the crime of inciting racial hostility is extended further by criminalising the publication of written matter (or its possession with a view to publication) or the use of words or gestures in a public place which are intended to stir up, *or are likely to stir up*, racial hatred.

[183] See *Brownlie's Law of Public Order and National Security* (2 ed by M Supperstone, Butterworths, 1981) 15–19.

dominant, this type of law tends to be used almost exclusively against the disadvantaged groups or their supporters. Most or all of the reported cases in South Africa refer to promotion of hostility against the white group. In an unequal society, laws of this kind are likely to be used in a discriminatory way and this makes it desirable to retain the specific intent requirement. The courts have correctly insisted on proof of actual intention to incite hostility; had they not, many vigorous attacks on the white ruling party for its apartheid policy would have led to convictions under the law.

CHAPTER 7

Detention

Detention has become a prevalent and, among the ruling group at least, acceptable practice of government in South Africa. It has also been institutionalised by its incorporation into permanent law.[1] The word 'detention' has a euphemistic air about it and the nature of the act it signifies would be better captured by an expression such as 'incarcerated' or, even better, 'locked up'. The reality of political control in South Africa is more realistically conveyed by the statement that the government frequently locks up its citizens than by the softer statement that it detains them. This should be constantly kept in mind when 'detention', the more common and convenient word in legal and political discourse, is used in the analysis below.

Though detention is not confined in South Africa to state security operations,[2] our concern with the phenomenon here is in the national security context. Internal security law makes provision for six forms of detention which are classifiable into the categories of preventive detention and pre-trial detention. Preventive detention, which is sometimes referred to as internment, is designed to remove certain actors from the stage of public life because they are deemed to be a threat to its orderly conduct. Pre-trial detention has the different purpose of obtaining information by questioning or interrogation, or of securing the attendance of persons at court in the capacity of witness or accused. Though the two forms of detention are functionally distinct, in practice the dividing line may not be clear particularly where the criteria for a detention order are vague and there is an absence of external court control. A detaining authority that is accountable to no one may use a pre-trial detention provision for preventive purposes and vice versa. But because court jurisdiction is seldom totally annihilated, and such an improper purpose would be legally significant if proved, the distinction is worth preserving both for legal and expositional reasons. We deal first with preventive detention and later with pre-trial detention.

A. PREVENTIVE DETENTION

Present-day security law authorises three forms of preventive detention. The first is the potentially indefinite preventive detention which may be imposed by the Minister of Law and Order;[3] the second is short-term preventive detention which may be ordered by a police officer for forty-

---

[1] The Internal Security Act 74 of 1982. This law is referred to below as 'the Act'.

[2] Detention may be ordered in non-security cases under s 185 of the Criminal Procedure Act 51 of 1977 and s 13 of the Abuse of Dependence-producing Substances and Rehabilitation Centres Act 41 of 1971.

[3] Under s 28 of the Act.

eight hours and extended by magisterial warrant to a maximum of fourteen days;[4] and the third is a new 180-day detention provision[5] forced through Parliament in June 1986 with the aid of the President's Council after the Houses of Delegates and Representatives had declined to pass the measure without the incorporation of safeguards. The seldom used provision of the Code of Zulu Law, which authorises another type of preventive detention for black persons, will not be dealt with here.[6]

Indefinite Preventive Detention

The Minister of Law and Order has the power to issue a notice[7] for the detention of any person for such period as he may specify therein.[8] There is no outer limit to the period which he may fix for detention, nor is there a legal barrier to the indefinite re-issue of lapsed notices. In short, he may directly, or indirectly by renewals, detain a person for his or her lifetime.

This severe power is part of permanent law and may be used even in times of peace without any need for the declaration of an emergency. It may be exercised by the minister on any one of three grounds, namely, (a) that he has reason to apprehend that the person in question will commit the offence of terrorism, subversion or sabotage[9] or (b) that he is satisfied that the detainee will endanger the security of the state or the maintenance of law and order or (c) that he has reason to suspect that a person who has committed a specified offence[10] is likely to endanger state security or the maintenance of law and order.[11]

The breadth of the detention power is underlined by two features of the wording of the Act. First, an ill-defined and wide range of human activity is encompassed by the crimes of subversion and sabotage[12] and by the notion of a threat to state security or law and order. The mere apprehension that the detainee is likely to be involved in any act falling within that broad spectrum of activity justifies the decision to order a detention. Such an apprehension might easily be formed about almost any extra-parliamentary political activist and, indeed, about officials of government who make provocative speeches or take provocative actions, even although coverage of the latter was not intended by the promoters of the legislation. Secondly, the phrases 'if in his opinion', 'is satisfied', and 'has reason to suspect', all so-called subjective discretion clauses, have generally been held by the courts to confer an almost uncontrolled discretion to act upon the empowered authority, at least in the context of

---

[4] Under s 50.

[5] Section 50A introduced by s 1 of the Internal Security Amendment Act 66 of 1986.

[6] It is briefly discussed in *The Law of South Africa*, vol 21 para 368.

[7] Signed by him and directed to an officer in charge of a prison. A signed or certified copy of the notice must be delivered or tendered to the person named in it and is deemed to be a warrant for his arrest and detention: s 28(3)(a). A police officer who has received information of the issue of a notice may arrest the person concerned and keep him in custody for a period not exceeding seven days so that the notice may be served on him: s 28(4). A telegram from the minister to the effect that a notice has been issued has the same effect as a notice: s 28(5).

[8] Section 28(1) of the Act.

[9] As shown in Chapter 6 above these are very broad crimes created by s 54(1), (2) and (3) of the Act.

[10] A wide range of security or political offences is specified in Schedule 2 to the Act.

[11] Section 28(1).

[12] See the analysis of these crimes in Chapter 6 above.

national security. According to the judges, the question for determination by the courts in such cases is not whether there are grounds for the suspicion, opinion or apprehension, but whether the authority (the minister in respect of detention) in fact entertained the suspicion or apprehension or held the necessary opinion. In technical language, the exercise of power under a subjective discretion clause may be challenged, according to the traditional doctrine, only on the ground that the relevant authority did not apply its mind to the issue or, if it did, acted mala fide—in bad faith.[13] Since proof of either is a rather fanciful possibility, it is hardly surprising that there is no recorded case of a high official of state having been found to have acted mindlessly or dishonestly in exercising a security power.

In non-security cases, phrases like 'reason to believe' and 'is satisfied' have not been given the subjective interpretation which they have magically acquired in the sphere of internal security. 'Reason to believe', Jansen J declared in *London Estates (Pty) Ltd v Nair*,[14] 'is constituted by facts giving rise to such a belief'; and in *Brits Town Council v Pienaar NO*[15] the court held that an administrative official who had to be 'satisfied' was required to exercise his discretion as a reasonable man would in relation to the relevant facts. In both these cases, the court was prepared to judge the exercise of discretion by reference to objective facts and to regard it as improper where the facts could not support the finding. Common sense, apart from legal authority, appears to dictate the rule that a person cannot be of the opinion or satisfied that a certain state of affairs exists unless there are grounds upon which the opinion or satisfaction is based. Only in an 'Alice Through the Looking Glass' world would an irrational, manufactured or fictional judgment be graced with the description 'opinion', 'state of satisfaction', and the like. Until recently, courts that have understood this perfectly well in a non-security context appear to have taken leave of good sense once there is a legislative or ministerial incantation of the national security justification. The recent exceptions are the judgments in *Hurley v Minister of Law and Order*[16] and in *Minister of Law and Order v Hurley*;[17] and also in the Namibian case of *Katofa v Administrator-General for South West Africa*.[18] In *Hurley*, both at the provincial and appeal court level, the finding was explicitly restricted to the phrase 'has reason to believe' and both courts declared, obiter no doubt, that detention decisions under the provision that is our present concern (s 28 detention) are not reviewable on an objective basis. Only in *Katofa* has the court broken decisively with past thinking by declaring that the statutory requirement that the detaining authority must be 'satisfied'

[13] In *Sachs v Minister of Justice* 1934 AD 11, in which the subjective discretion clause read 'whenever the Minister is satisfied . . .', the court declared that 'no decision affirms the right of a court to interfere with the honest exercise of a duly conferred discretion' (at 37) and went on to say that if the minister was satisfied he could act even in the absence of the grounds upon which his satisfaction is supposed to be formed.

[14] 1957 (3) SA 591 (D). See also *Watson v Commissioner of Customs and Excise* 1960 (3) SA 212 (N) 216.

[15] 1949 (1) SA 1004 (T) 1030.

[16] 1985 (4) SA 709 (D).

[17] 1986 (3) SA 568 (A).

[18] 1985 (4) SA 211 (SWA). There is an excellent review of this judgment in (1986) 2 *South African Journal on Human Rights* 74.

that there are reasons for a detention does *not* preclude the court from investigating the grounds for the decision. *Katofa* was neither followed nor referred to in the Appellate Division judgment in *Hurley* and that court remains committed to a non-interventionist approach where the grant of authority to interfere with basic rights is prefaced by phrases like 'is satisfied', 'is of the opinion', et cetera.

Departures from good sense are not characteristic only of South African courts, and the most notorious British example is the House of Lords judgment in *Liversidge v Anderson*[19] in which it was held that the words 'if the Secretary of State has reasonable cause to believe' meant no more than his belief that reasonable cause existed. The court thereby precluded itself from enquiring into whether there was an objective basis for the Secretary's belief that Liversidge was of 'hostile origin or associations' and consequently liable to internment under wartime regulations. This finding has caused British lawyers much discomfort and the courts of that country soon began to manifest their disquiet, first in *Nakkuda Ali v Jayaratne*,[20] and later by the sideswipe in *Ridge v Baldwin*[21] that *Liversidge* was a 'very peculiar decision'. Disapproval was later followed by explicit rejection of the *Liversidge* ruling in *Inland Revenue Commissioner v Rossminster Ltd*[22] and implicit rejection in *Attorney-General of St Christopher v Reynolds*.[23] In *Rossminster* Lord Diplock said '. . . I think the time has come to acknowledge openly that the majority of this House in *Liversidge v Anderson* were expediently and, at that time, perhaps inexcusably wrong and the dissenting speech of Lord Atkin was right';[24] and in *Reynolds* the Privy Council refused to hold that a regulation which authorised detention 'if the Governor is satisfied upon reasonable grounds' meant 'if the Governor thinks that etc' or that the regulations 'could be properly construed as conferring dictatorial powers on the Governor'.[25] *Liversidge v Anderson* now lies discarded on the juristic scrapheap together with other unfortunate relics of the legal past.

The *Liversidge* ruling was concerned with the phrase 'has reasonable cause to believe' but its overturning is applicable also to similar formulas such as 'has reason to apprehend', 'is of the opinion', 'is satisfied' and the like. Though it may be possible to devise a formulation which will render an administrative decision entirely subjective, the standard expressions ('is satisfied', 'is of the opinion', etc) should not be held to preclude reference by the courts to the objective facts. As Lord Denning said in *Secretary of State for Education and Science v Tameside Metropolitan Borough Council*,[26] much depends upon the matter upon which the official has to be satisfied. If Parliament envisaged that the minister's judgment (his 'satisfaction' or 'opinion') would depend on a review of broad policy

[19] [1942] AC 206.
[20] [1951] AC 66, 76.
[21] [1964] AC 40, 73.
[22] [1980] AC 952.
[23] [1980] AC 637 (PC).
[24] At 1011.
[25] At 656.
[26] [1977] AC 1014, 1025. Lord Atkin did concede in *Liversidge*, unwisely it seems, that 'is satisfied' conferred unlimited discretion: *Liversidge v Anderson* (supra) 233. Lord Denning felt that this construction held only in times of war when speedy executive action was required.

issues, an objective evaluation of the grounds for the decision is usually precluded; but if the issue for decision is one of fact rather than policy, then even standard formulations such as 'is satisfied' should not preclude objective judicial assessment of the basis of the decision. The verbal formulation of the grant of power is not decisive; and the statutory language has to be interpreted in the context of the nature or type of judgment which the holder of delegated power is required to exercise.

In South Africa, the rejection of the *Liversidge* doctrine has not assumed the 'root and branch' dimensions that characterise its repudiation by British courts. The ghost of *Liversidge* has been laid to rest only in relation to detention statutes that employ the 'reason to believe' formula and the narrowness of the *Hurley* decision means that it will continue to haunt judicial corridors where the executive officer's discretion that is challenged depends upon his opinion or state of satisfaction. This is both unfortunate and indefensible. The various formulas employed by statutory draftsmen to confer administrative powers do not have a magical quality by which their meaning is inflexibly and self-evidently conveyed to the reader or interpreter. As a matter of language, it is impossible to maintain that phrases like 'has reason to believe' and 'is of the opinion' have a fixed meaning and that this meaning is necessarily different for the two phrases. Court judgments are themselves testimony to the fact no constant meaning can be assigned to such language since judges have given the same phrases a different interpretation depending on whether they are being considered within or without a national security context. Even within the national security context, different courts have assigned different meanings to the same phrases,[27] as the Namibian court has done in *Katofa* by refusing to follow the old established attitudes to 'is satisfied' clauses. The truth is that all the phrases with which we are presently concerned ('has reason to believe', 'is satisfied', 'is of the opinion', 'has reasonable cause to believe') are capable of being read either as a subjective grant of power or as a grant of power controlled by the objective facts, depending on the relevant context.[28] The only defensible approach for the court to take in choosing between these two readings, is to look at the language in the broader context of the statute in question. The most important feature of the context will be the type of decision that the executive official is required to take, and particularly whether it is essentially a decision of fact (that is, objective in nature) or essentially one of policy (which will be subjective rather than objective). On this approach, the minister's decision to order preventive detention (under s 28) is *not* a grant of subjective power which the courts are precluded from examining in relation to the underlying facts. When the minister orders a detention under s 28, the law requires him to be satisfied about two matters. First, he must be satisfied that the words or conduct of the person in question are such that the commission of specified offences or a threat to security or law and order may be apprehended; and, secondly, he must be satisfied that the apprehension of the said dangers justifies the detention of that person. The first matter, the assessment of the words or

---

[27] Usually at different times, as in the contemporary rejection of *Liversidge* by British courts.

[28] This is not to deny that some of the phrases have a more subjective 'ring' than others.

conduct of the detainee, is a sufficiently clear-cut issue for court review of the minister's finding, while the second appears to be one of policy to be decided according to the subjective discretion of the minister. On the first matter, the detainee should be permitted to challenge the minister's finding on an objective basis and a court should be willing to review his grounds for it. This does not mean that it becomes the decision-maker in the place of the minister but only that it is required to determine, in the words of Lord Denning, whether the finding is one that 'is, or can be, supported with good reasons or, at any rate, is a decision which a reasonable person might reasonably reach'.[29] On this approach there is no usurpation of the minister's power, only a long-stop check to ensure that it is rationally exercised and not misused. The court, it has been said, does not determine whether the minister's decision is *correct* but undertakes the more modest task of determining whether it is reasonable.[30]

Unfortunately for the detainee, the law as it stands at present enables the minister to detain on the basis of opinion rather than fact. As if this was not bad enough, court judgments failed until 1986 to give body and substance to clauses in the Act which require the minister to give reasons for restrictive actions taken by him. When the minister orders a detention under s 28, he is required to provide the detainee with reasons for the order, together with so much of the information on which he acted as in his opinion can be disclosed without prejudice to the public interest.[31] While duty to provide reasons is imperative and unqualified, the minister need only give background information if the public interest will not be prejudiced by its revelation. A conceptual confusion appears to be responsible for the judicial failure to enforce the unqualified statutory obligation to give reasons. There is a clear, notional distinction between the minister's *finding* (or decision) that the detainee is a threat to state security or the maintenance of order, the *reasons* for that finding and the *information* on which the decision is based. In *Kloppenberg v Minister of Justice*,[32] a decision relating to the similarly worded duty to give reasons for a banning order, the court confused the first two concepts by holding that the detainee had to be satisfied with a ministerial statement which expressed only the minister's *finding* that the detainee was a threat to security in words that were a mere repetition of the statutory ground for issuing a detention notice. The court also qualified what is imperative and absolute in the Act by declaring that if the minister cannot give reasons without disclosing information which he believes to be prejudicial to the public interest, he need not give reasons either. The decision in *Kloppenberg* represents the low-water mark of judicial support for due process and individual right.

After many years of ministerial non-compliance with the duty to give reasons for restrictive orders issued under the Act (or its predecessor), the

[29] *Secretary of State for Education and Science v Tameside Metropolitan Borough Council* (supra) 1025.

[30] Etienne Mureinik 'Liversidge in Decay' (1985) 102 *SALJ* 77, 80 and 88.

[31] Section 28(3)(b). The detention notice served upon the detainee must be accompanied by a statement from the minister setting out his reasons and the information which he feels able to disclose.

[32] 1964 (1) SA 813 (D); upheld on appeal: 1964 (4) SA 31 (N).

meaning of the statutory obligation imposed upon the minister when he orders a detention under s 28 came sharply before the Natal court in *Gumede v Minister of Law and Order*.[33] In that case, the detention notice was accompanied by the following statement by the minister:

> 'Statement by the Minister of Law and Order in terms of s 28(3)*(b)* of the Internal Security Act 74 of 1982
>
> *(a)* Reason for the detention of Archibald Jacob Gumede in accordance with a notice issued in terms of s 28(1) of the Internal Security Act, 1982: I am satisfied that the said Archibald Jacob Gumede engages in activities which endanger maintenance of law and order.
>
> *(b)* Information which induced me to issue the said notice:
> By acts and utterances the said Archibald Jacob Gumede did himself and in collaboration with other persons attempt to create a revolutionary climate in the Republic of South Africa thereby causing a situation endangering the maintenance of law and order.
> No other information can in my opinion be disclosed without detriment to the public interest.'

In paragraph *(a)* of the minister's statement his *finding* that the detainee endangered the maintenance of law and order is presented as if it were a *reason*. The ministerial confusion is compounded in paragraph *(b)* of the statement where what is essentially a *reason* (though a vague and generalised one) is described as *information*. Moreover, the misdescribed reason is entirely unhelpful in acquainting the detainee with the basis of the minister's case for acting against him. The nebulous phenomenon of a 'revolutionary climate', which the detainee was supposed to have created, is nowhere mentioned in the Act and is arguably something which the government itself has created over the years by its 'acts and utterances'. So compelling were the minister's reasons (described by him as information) that they might well have provided him with a justification for his own detention, or that of his more belligerent colleagues in the government.

Despite the fact that the minister's statement in *Gumede* was a vague conceptual mess, the Natal court came to his rescue rather than that of the detainee. The process by which the court arrived at its remarkable decision will not be analysed here since it has been decisively rejected on appeal in *Nkondo & Gumede v Minister of Law and Order*.[34] The judgment of the Appellate Division now makes it clear that it is not sufficient to inform the detainee of the statutory ground upon which the minister has acted and that the reasons given must be such as to afford the detainee a fair opportunity to make representations against his detention. The court has therefore given effect to the unqualified statutory duty on the minister to give reasons for detentions and to make his statement of reasons meaningful. The only issue that remains unclear is what degree of detail will be required from the minister in the specification of reasons. This in turn raises the question of the meaning of the concepts of *reasons* and *information*, and more specifically of the difference between them.

Information is the raw data which the minister receives to enable him to decide whether there are legal grounds for ordering the detention of a

[33] 1985 (2) SA 529 (N).
[34] 1986 (2) SA 756 (A).

person. The raw data will presumably consist of papers and documents and security force reports of the actions and utterances of the proposed victim of a detention order. It is this raw data which the minister may withhold, presumably on the ground that its revelation may uncover sensitive information about sources and methods of information-gathering. 'Reasons' appear to be an abstraction from, or intellectual re-working of, the raw data so as to provide a statement of its general import and its relation to the statutory grounds for imposing a detention order. It should not be beyond the wit of the minister to provide a fairly detailed résumé of the data without disclosing sources or sensitive information, or beyond the power of the court to order him to do so. In short, the courts can reasonably be expected to demand substantial detail from the minister so as to enable the detainee to refute his case by joining issue on specific allegations; and, with a little intelligence, the minister can respond to such a court demand without revealing sensitive information. The guiding principle must be that the detainee is entitled to a degree of specificity that will enable him or her to understand and answer the official case for detention.

Are the courts required to respond supinely to the standard ministerial assertions that no information whatever can be provided because to do so would prejudice the public interest? Though in the past a simple ministerial say-so has been accepted unquestioningly by the judges, such absolute deference is out of accord with modern views on the limits of judicial supervision of administrative action. Assuming that the minister does have the final authority to refuse information, he could be required by the judges to satisfy them that there are grounds which make it proper to do so. The American case of *Vaughn v Rosen*,[35] decided in the context of an executive claim that information is exempt from disclosure under the Freedom of Information Act, is a good example of the possibility and value of a little judicial assertiveness. The court refused to accept 'conclusory and generalised allegations of exemptions'—a perfect description of the style of ministerial statements in South Africa—and declared that the government was required to justify its assertion that information is not disclosable by relatively detailed analysis on affidavit. Demanding a persuasive justification from the minister for refusing to disgorge information is arguably within the competence of the court since this would not require disclosure of the information itself. There is good reason to believe that the courts could go even further and require in camera inspection of the information to satisfy themselves that the minister's refusal to reveal information is not designed to mask the absence of any real justification for detention. The existence of such a power was reaffirmed in *Van der Linde v Calitz*[36] and there is no reason to infer a statutory repeal of that power in a provision which authorises the minister to exclude information, not from the courts, but from the statement delivered to the detainee. The minister has been given the power to keep the courts in the dark by relying on the absolute state privilege provided for in another section of the Act;[37] but unless he takes

[35] 484 F 2nd 820 (DC. Cir. 1973).
[36] 1967 (2) SA 239 (A).
[37] Section 66.

that drastic step, a provision in the same Act which does not explicitly preclude court supervision should not be read as if it does.

A fair summary of the legal position of the s 28 detainee is that, like the curate's egg, it is good in parts and bad in others. The detainee is entitled to meaningful reasons for the detention order and the availability of these reasons may be of some assistance in proceedings to set the detention aside or in the review proceedings discussed below. In terms of due process, the detainee's situation would be even better if the court assumed a supervisory function over ministerial decisions to withhold information even if, in the last resort, the minister can effectively block access to the raw data on which he relied. The bad part of the detainee's legal position is that the courts have interpreted the language of s 28 as conferring a subjective power of decision-making on the minister. The onus will therefore be on the detainee to show that the ministerial judgment was improperly exercised. Notwithstanding the subjective reading that the judges have given the language which confers the detention power upon the minister, there is some reason to be hopeful about the possibility of judicial intervention in detention cases, especially now that meaningful reasons have to be provided by the minister. Local developments in the judicial control of administrative actions have provided some helpful material to a court inclined to make the power of the minister less dictatorial even on the assumption that the statutory language confers a subjective power of decision. Of that local material, the most useful is the refinement by the courts of intervention on the basis of the failure of an authority to apply his or her mind to the matter. As Corbett JA pointed out in *Goldberg v Minister of Prisons*[38] a failure to apply one's mind to something includes a failure to direct one's thoughts to relevant data or considerations or a reliance on irrelevant considerations. Court intervention is not limited to cases where a 'sinister motivation' can be established or where the authority acted with total mindlessness; it includes, in other words, instances of a malfunctioning mind. The significance of this development is that there is a modicum of judicial control even over so-called subjective jurisdictional facts and that the public authority is not free to err with impunity because of the subjective formulation of the statutory grant of authority. A commentator on detention laws in India has expressed this well in the following passage:

'The wording of section 3 clearly showed that it was the subjective satisfaction of the central and state Governments which had to be established, and an objective test in a court of law cannot be substituted for it. But the satisfaction of the Government must be based on some grounds, for there could be no satisfaction if there were no grounds for it.'[39]

'Is satisfied' clauses do not preclude all enquiry into the rationality of decisions taken by the empowered authority even when they are given a subjective reading.[40] There is no reason why the courts should not evaluate decisions against the facts and reasons put forward by the

[38] 1979 (1) SA 14 (A) 48.

[39] H M Seervai *Constitutional Law of India* 3 ed (Sweet & Maxwell, London 1983) vol 1 839.

[40] See L J Boulle 'Detainees and the Courts: New Beginnings' (1985) 1 *SA Journal on Human Rights* 251, 256.

detaining authority and declare them invalid if the opinion on which they were based is not of the kind envisaged by the Act.[40a]

The Act itself purports to provide safeguards against the abuse of the ministerial power to detain by giving the detainee some limited remedies. The first hardly qualifies as a remedy at all since it merely enables the detainee, within fourteen days after delivery of the detention notice, to make written representations to the minister.[41] Though the minister has power to withdraw a detention order at any time,[42] he is not bound in any way to act upon the detainee's representations. There is a second safeguard which on the surface has a more substantial look about it. The minister is required by the Act to submit every decision to detain to a board of review for investigation and consideration.[43] He must do this 'as soon as possible' after the expiration of the fourteen-day time limit[44] for the institution of proceedings to declare a detention notice invalid. The minister must submit to the review board (a) a copy of the detention notice; (b) a statement of the reasons for the decision and all the information on which it was based; (c) a copy of any representations or information submitted by the detainee; and (d) such additional report or information as the minister may deem necessary.[45] The board of review to which the minister refers the detention is directed to investigate and consider the detention and may hear oral evidence or receive representations from any person.[46] The detainee may apply in writing to give oral evidence to the board and his request must be acceded to unless the chairman is of the opinion that to do so would be contrary to the public interest.[47] Various procedural provisions relating to advisory committees appointed under the Act are applicable to boards of review.[48] Among these are provisions denying legal assistance to witnesses (including the detainee) at a hearing, restricting the persons entitled to be present at a hearing, preventing inspection of the record of the proceedings, prohibiting disclosure of the board's deliberations and recommendations, and excluding the jurisdiction of the ordinary courts in respect of the functions and recommendations of a board of review. In short, a board of review functions in secret, without the presence of legal representatives[49] and free of the control of the regular courts.

[40a] As the court did in *The Bishop of the Roman Catholic Church of the Diocese of Port Elizabeth v The Minister of Law and Order* (unreported judgment of the Eastern Cape Division delivered on 1 August 1986, Case No 1101/86).

[41] Section 28(9). For this purpose the detainee is entitled to the assistance of a legal representative who is not 'listed' (under s 16) or restricted under the Act and the 'no-access' clause of s 28(8) is specifically modified to permit access to the representative: s 28(8). The detainee may consult his legal representative out of the hearing of the authorities: *Mokoena v Commissioner of Prisons* 1985 (1) SA 368 (W).

[42] Section 28(10).

[43] Section 38(1).

[44] Section 42(1) requires a detainee to institute proceedings to declare a detention notice invalid within 14 days of the service of the notice upon him and s 42(2) declares that such proceedings must be concluded within 12 months, subject to the power of the court to extend this period if the delay is not the fault of the applicant. A court may not suspend or postpone the effect of a detention order pending such proceedings: s 42(2).

[45] Section 38(2).   [46] Section 38(3).

[47] Section 38(4).

[48] Section 39 declares applicable those contained in subsecs 8(2)–8(12) inclusive.

[49] The detainee is only entitled to the assistance of a legal representative in preparing written representations: s 28(8).

When a board of review has investigated a detention order referred to it by the minister, it is required to furnish him with a written report stating whether grounds exist for the amendment or withdrawal of the notice and setting out its recommendations.[50] The minister must notify the detainee of the findings and recommendations of the board[51] but he is not obliged to give effect to them.[52] However, if the effect of the minister's refusal to accept a recommendation is that stricter measures than those recommended by the board will remain in force, he must submit, within fourteen days of his refusal, all the papers to the Chief Justice of South Africa.[53] The Chief Justice (or some other judge of the Appellate Division designated by him) will therefore review all cases in which the minister has refused to accept a board recommendation for the alleviation or withdrawal of the detention order.[54]

If on consideration of all the documents by the Chief Justice, or the judge designated by him, it appears that the minister exceeded the powers conferred on him by the Act, acted in bad faith or based his decision on considerations other than those specified by the Act,[55] the detention order may be set aside.[56] Otherwise, the Chief Justice (or designated judge) must endorse the minister's statement of reasons for the detention to the effect that no grounds exist for setting it aside.[57] Courts of law are specifically precluded from pronouncing on the finding of the Chief Justice or designated judge.[58]

A detainee may have his case placed before a review board at intervals of not less than six months after being notified of the outcome of the original investigation by the board.[59] The rules and procedures that govern the initial review and referral of the matter to the Chief Justice apply mutatis mutandis to a second or subsequent review.[60] Preventive detention under the Act is therefore subject to periodical review but the question arises whether the review procedure constitutes an effective safeguard.

In assessing the review procedure, a number of shortcomings have to be taken into account. First, the initial review of a detention does not take place if a detainee challenges the validity of the order before the ordinary courts,[61] though the right to request periodical reviews thereafter is not affected. Secondly, the referral to the Chief Justice, who unlike the review committee has power to nullify the detention, takes place only if that committee disagrees with the minister's decision to detain.[62] Review of his decision by a member of the ordinary courts depends therefore on review

---

[50] Section 38(5) and (6).
[51] Section 38(7).
[52] Section 41(1).
[53] Section 41(1). The papers submitted will be all those presented to the review board, a copy of that board's report, and such further report as the minister deems necessary.
[54] Section 41(2).
[55] Specified, that is, by s 28(1).
[56] Section 41(2). Reasons for doing this must be given to the minister: s 41(5). The detainee need not be given reasons for a refusal to set aside a detention.
[57] Section 41(3).
[58] Section 41(4).
[59] Section 43.   [60] Ibid.
[61] Section 42(3).
[62] Or believes that the detention should be continued but its terms alleviated.

committees developing an independent and spirited attitude and thereby avoiding the tame acceptance of government security perceptions. The manner of appointment, if not the composition, of the review board seems to make such an attitude unlikely. It is appointed by the State President on the recommendation of the Minister of Justice.[63] One member, the chairman, must be a judge or former judge, or a person who has held office as a chief or regional magistrate, or a person entitled to be admitted to practice as an advocate who 'has been concerned in the application of law for a continuous period of not less than ten years' after his admission.[64] Of the other two members, one must hold a degree or diploma in law.[65] The period for which a member of the review board holds office is determined by the State President.[66] These conditions governing appointment, composition and tenure of office do not hold out much promise of a toughly independent board coming into being. The members appointed to review boards so far, to the extent that they are known, have no reputation for holding an independent set of security perceptions or beliefs. One must therefore conclude that regular and substantial disagreement with the Minister of Law and Order, the condition upon which an effective review of detention orders might be exercised, is unlikely to occur. In 1985 a total of fifty-four cases of detention came before the review board and it did not recommend withdrawal of the detention notice in any one of these cases. A release rate of nil per cent does not say much for the usefulness of the review procedure.[67] Thirdly, even if the matter does reach the Chief Justice on account of disagreement between the minister and the review board, the chances of nullification of the detention order seem remote. Though the Chief Justice sees both the reasons for the detention and the background information, he has no independent powers of investigation and no statutory authority to resolve conflicts by calling for evidence. Furthermore, the Chief Justice may set aside the detention order only if he is satisfied that the minister acted in bad faith (a remote possibility) or that he exceeded the powers conferred by the Act (powers so broad, if literally interpreted, that a feat of mental gymnastics would be required to go beyond them) or that he based his decision on considerations other than those specified by the Act (which the Chief Justice is unlikely to know if he cannot investigate the factual case of the minister).[68] While the last ground for setting aside the order does appear to authorise a finding on the rationality of the decision to detain judged by the available facts, even a boldly assertive Chief Justice, a rather improbable figure in contemporary South Africa, may be reduced to impotence by his inability to test the official facts. Of course, the Chief Justice would be in a better position to adjudicate on the rationality of the decision if the quality of bold

[63] Section 35(3).
[64] Ibid.   [65] Ibid.
[66] Section 36(1).
[67] These figures were reported to Parliament by the Minister of Law and Order: see *Natal Witness* 25 February 1986.
[68] These are the grounds specified by s 41(2). If the section in question (s 28(1)) is given the more objective reading suggested earlier in the text, then the minister may be said to have exceeded his powers whenever the decision to detain is not one that could reasonably be arrived at on the available facts.

assertiveness characterised the enquiry by the review board; but this seems to be an even remoter contingency. To summarise, the review procedure of the Act is so flawed that only aggressively resourceful and sceptical review authorities are likely to convert the flawed procedure into an effective safeguard. Unfortunately, such qualities are short-supply commodities in South Africa.

What is the detainee's position where the minister fails to submit the matter for review,[69] or is guilty of unreasonable delay in so doing? The same question arises in relation to any procedural failures in issuing the notice and accompanying statutory statement, or in delivering them to the detainee. The basic principle must be that a procedural failure will invalidate so drastic an action as the removal of personal freedom by detention order. In the first of the 'consular six' applications, Mr Justice Law set aside detention orders because the minister neither provided information nor declared that he could not do so without injury to the public interest.[70] The failure to provide the detainee with adequate reasons for his detention resulted in a declaration of invalidity in *Nkondo & Gumede v Minister of Law and Order*.[71] An equally strict attitude towards other procedural failures seems desirable as exemplified, for example, by the Israeli courts in their pronouncements on detention.[72] However, where the procedural failure occurs after the issue of an initially valid detention order, such as a failure to submit the matter for review, there is less certainty about the right to have the order set aside. In the Zimbabwean case of *Minister of Home Affairs v Dabengwa*[73] the court decided that such subsequent failures should be cured initially by a mandamus—an order on the authorities to comply, for example by carrying out the required review. This approach appears far too lenient, especially where the detaining authority is itself required to submit the matter for review and fails to do so.[74] In South Africa, the minister who issues a detention order is himself required to submit the matter to the review board 'as soon as possible';[75] and, if he refuses to accept the recommendation of the board, to submit the papers to the Chief Justice within fourteen days of his refusal.[76] If the minister does not refer the matter to the review board expeditiously or fails to meet the fourteen-day deadline for submission of the papers to the Chief Justice, a serious procedural failure affecting the liberty of the subject will have occurred, and the order should be set aside.

The conditions under which s 28 detainees are to be held are prescribed by the Act and by regulations promulgated under it. The Act restricts the right of access to the detainee, except where permission has been obtained from the minister or the commissioner, to the minister himself, the director of security legislation, judges, a chairman of a board of review or

---

[69] That is, to the review board in terms of s 38(2) or the Chief Justice under s 41(1).
[70] *Gumede v Minister of Law and Order* 1984 (4) SA 915 (N). An appeal against this judgment failed in *Nkondo & Gumede v Minister of Law and Order* (supra).
[71] Supra.
[72] (1978) 8 *Israel Yearbook on Human Rights* 296, 310, 313. The failure to specify a place of detention, for example, was held to be a fatal defect.
[73] 1984 (2) SA 345 (ZS).
[74] This was not the case in *Minister of Home Affairs v Dabengwa* (supra).
[75] Section 38(1).   [76] Section 41(1).

other persons acting by virtue of their office in the service of the state.[77]
This means that relatives, friends, doctors and lawyers (other than a
lawyer assisting the detainee in the preparation of his representations)[78]
do not have a right to visit the detainee and that to this extent there is
authority to imprison in isolation. The regulations[79] published by the
minister confer upon detainees the status of awaiting-trial prisoners and it
seems to follow that solitary confinement is not permitted except to the
extent that it is possible for such prisoners. The published regulations
make written communications between the detainee and other persons[80]
subject to official approval, provide for the separation of the detainee from
other prisoners and for medical examination and treatment. While these
regulations may not be invalidated by a court of law,[81] there is authority
that they confer enforceable rights upon the detainee[82] since enforcing
regulations is not the same as pronouncing on their validity. Their status
as awaiting-trial prisoners will give the detainees access to reading matter,
though *Goldberg v Minister of Prisons*[83] is not at all encouraging to a detainee
who wishes to challenge prison authority discretion as to access to reading
matter. If the authorities employ to the full their powers under the Act,
the regulations and the prison regulations, they could make the detainee's
prison life extremely unpleasant.

Short-term Preventive Detention

(a) Fourteen-day Detention

A police officer, of or above the rank of warrant officer may arrest, or
order the arrest of, any person without warrant and cause him to be
detained in a prison or police cell or lock-up for an initial period of forty-
eight hours and thereafter, under warrant from a magistrate, for a total
period of fourteen days, including the initial forty-eight hour period.[84]
The arrest and detention may be ordered by a police officer if he is of the
opinion *(a)* that the actions of the person in question are contributing to
the continuation of a state of public disturbance, disorder, riot or public
violence which exists at any place in the Republic and that the detention
will help to combat or terminate such a state of affairs or *(b)* that the
detention of such person will assist in the prevention or resumption of
such a state of affairs anywhere in the Republic.[85]

There is at least one jurisdictional fact which is a prerequisite to the
invocation of this detention power—a state of public disturbance,
disorder, riot or public violence which either exists at the time of the
detention, has recently existed or is about to erupt.[86] Assuming the
presence of that jurisdictional fact, the police officer may arrest and detain

[77] Section 28(8).   [78] Ibid.
[79] GN No R1685 (*GG* 8331 of 6 August 1982).
[80] Except the communications permitted by ss 28(9) and 38(4).
[81] Section 28(7).
[82] *Cassiem v Commanding Officer, Victor Verster Prison* 1982 (2) SA 547 (C).
[83] Supra.
[84] Section 50(1) and (2).
[85] Section 50(1).
[86] Where the state of affairs does not actually exist, and the police officer relies on a past
or imminent breakdown of peace and order, it is submitted that this should not be too remote
or fanciful and that, if it is, the detention will not be valid.

if he is 'of the opinion' that the detention will assist in combating or terminating the breakdown of peace and order or in the prevention or resumption of such a state of affairs. Though the wording is again in subjective terms, it is arguable that this serious invasion of a citizen's right to personal freedom at the instance of a low-ranking policeman must be based on a second jurisdictional fact, namely, some rational link between the detainee's conduct and the actual or apprehended state of disorder, riot and the like. There must be some ground, in other words, for associating the detainee with an actual, recent or imminent breakdown in order.

The procedure for extension of detention beyond the initial forty-eight hour period by a magistrate[87] is totally unsatisfactory from a due process point of view. An application for extension must be made on oath by a police officer and the magistrate who hears it must do so behind closed doors.[88] The Act makes no provision for the magistrate to hear the detainee or to receive representations from him, and it has been held that the audi alteram partem rule is impliedly excluded.[89] The court reasoned that short-term preventive detention was premised on the need for urgent and effective action to contain unrest and that the legislature did not contemplate a right to be heard since this would undermine the expeditiousness of the power which it intended to confer. But would it? The right to be heard does not mean the right to a trial-type hearing.[90] If the courts were to insist on a right to be heard by the magistrate but simultaneously declare that this right is satisfied by giving the detainee an opportunity to respond at an informally conducted hearing, it is hard to see how the effectiveness of the measure would be undermined.

The grounds upon which the magistrate may order an extension of detention beyond the initial forty-eight hour period are the same as those governing the initial detention.[91] According to *Groenewald v Minister van Justisie*,[92] the decision of a magistrate who is authorised to issue a warrant if of the opinion that certain conditions exist, is not reviewable on objective grounds. If the Appellate Division does not adopt the more enlightened approach to so-called subjective discretion clauses suggested earlier in this chapter, the magistrate's order will be absolute in all cases except those in which the detainee achieves the impossible and proves bad faith or excess of jurisdiction on the part of the magistrate. The effect of denying detainees a hearing and the right to seek a review on objective grounds is to make it possible for the police to lock persons up at will in times of trouble.

A short-term detainee may be released on the order of a magistrate at any time prior to the expiration of the fourteen-day period.[93] The Commissioner of Police is required to notify the minister of the name of

---

[87] 'Magistrate' includes an additional or assistant magistrate: s 50(2)*(d)*.
[88] Section 50(2)*(b)* and *(c)*.
[89] *N v Minister of Law and Order* 1986 (3) SA 921 (C).
[90] L G Baxter *Administrative Law* 542 et seq.
[91] Section 50(2)*(b)*.
[92] 1973 (3) SA 877 (A). See also *Gafoor v Commissioner of Police*, unreported judgment of the Eastern Cape Division delivered on 15 November 1985 (case No 1842/85).
[93] Section 50(5).

the detainee and the place of his detention but a failure to do so is excused where the detainee is released before this can reasonably be done.[94] Detainees are held in accordance with the provisions of the Prisons Act relating to awaiting-trial prisoners.[95]

(b) 180-day Detention

A police officer, of or above the rank of warrant officer, who is of the opinion that the arrest and detention of any person will help to combat, prevent or terminate various forms of unrest (public disturbance, disorder, riot or public violence) at any place in the Republic, may arrest such person without warrant and cause him or her to be detained in prison for a period not exceeding forty-eight hours.[96] A commissioned officer, of or above the rank of lieutenant-colonel, who is of the same opinion, may order the further detention of such person for a period not exceeding 180 days after arrest.[97] Both the initial arrest and detention, and the extension of the detention beyond forty-eight hours, may be ordered if the designated officers are 'of the opinion' that such action will further the purposes disclosed by the enabling section;[98] and this means, according to the prevailing judicial attitude towards administrative action which may be based on opinion, that the courts will not enquire into the existence of objective grounds for the arrest and detention. Though the court's attitude to 'of the opinion' clauses has been criticised and declared to be wrong in preceding discussion relating to detention, it was reaffirmed (though obiter) by the court in *Minister of Law and Order v Hurley*[99] and it follows that 180-day detention will rest upon official opinion of the detainee's conduct rather than upon the conduct itself.

It is clear that the officer who affects the initial arrest and detention need not afford the detainee a hearing. Though less clear, it is probably also true that the extension of detention may be done without a hearing. Since the commissioned officer who orders an extension must act within forty-eight hours after arrest, it is hardly practicable to impose the requirement of a hearing. This leaves the detainee without an effective right to procedural justice. The safeguards which the Act purports to grant him are illusory. The first enables him at any time to make representations to the minister and the minister is empowered, though not obliged, to order his release.[100] There is no provision for a statement of reasons for the detention and representations to the minister will therefore have to be in the nature of a futile protestation of innocence. The second 'safeguard' takes the form of referral of the detention to a review board if the detainee has not been released at the expiration of three months from the date of his arrest.[101] The review board is required to consider any written representations which the detainee may wish to submit but has a

[94] Section 50(4).
[95] Section 50(3).
[96] Section 50A(1).
[97] Section 50A(2).
[98] Section 50A(1) and (2).
[99] Supra.
[100] Section 50A(3). Section 50A(8) requires the Commissioner of Police to notify the minister of detentions unless the detainee is released before this can be done.
[101] Section 50A(9)(a).

discretion as to whether to grant the detainee a right to make oral representations.[102] After considering the matter the review board is required to report to the minister.[103] The review procedure is almost valueless for several reasons. Since the detainee has no right to reasons, he will have to argue his case in the dark and there is little point, it has been said, in disputing with a sphinx. The minister can ignore the findings and recommendations of the review board. The record of board reviews of s 28 detentions inspires no confidence since the procedure appears to have resulted in no releases whatever. In any event, review can be avoided by the simple expedient of ordering detentions for less than three months or by releasing the detainee prior to the expiration of three months and re-detaining afterwards.

180-day detainees will be held under conditions prescribed by the Minister of Justice by regulation.[104] The regulations will be ultra vires if they attempt to make the position of the detainee harsher than the principal Act envisages, for example by authorising interrogation in solitary confinement. This form of detention is clearly preventive and its nature cannot be transformed or altered by subordinate legislation.

The power to detain under the 180-day clause will be available only if so determined by the State President by proclamation in the *Gazette*.[105] The State President appears to have the authority to make 180-day detention operative for so long as he determines.[106] Proclamations are required to be tabled in Parliament.[107]

The 180-day detention provision was drafted so as to avoid the judgment in *Nkondo & Gumede v Minister of Law and Order*,[108] which requires the minister to provide meaningful reasons to s 28 detainees, and the judgment in *Minister of Law and Order v Hurley*,[109] which decided that the grounds for a s 29 detention (discussed below) could be examined by the courts. The specific objective of the new detention clause is to abolish any effective safeguards and controls over the exercise of the power to detain. The 180-day detention provision carries arbitrariness to its limits.

B. Pre-Trial Detention

Three forms of pre-trial detention are currently operative throughout South Africa: indefinite detention under s 29 of the Internal Security Act,[110] the detention of witnesses under s 31 of that Act, and the 'no bail' clause contained in s 30 of the same Act. There are in addition pre-trial detention provisions that have a more restricted operation in the geographical sense, for example 'ninety-day' detention for purposes of interrogation is permitted by proclamation issued by the State President for certain districts of Natal.[111] The analysis that follows will concentrate

---

[102] Section 50A(9)*(b)*.   [103] Section 50A(9)*(c)*.
[104] Section 50A(5). A failure to comply with such regulations is an offence: s 50A(7).
[105] Section 50A(10)*(a)*.
[106] Section 50A(10)*(b)*.   [107] Section 50A(10)*(c)*.
[108] Supra.   [109] Supra.
[110] 74 of 1982, referred to below as 'the Act'.
[111] Proclamations R103 (*GG* 3873 of 19 April 1973), R266 (*GG* 6188 of 20 October 1978) and R67 (*GG* 7525 of 3 April 1981). On the right of a detainee under these proclamations to access to a lawyer, see *Ngqulunga v Minister of Law and Order* 1983 (2) SA 696 (N). See also 'Public Safety' in *The Law of South Africa* vol 21 s 353.

on the nationally operative provisions and the local detention regulations will not be discussed. Pre-trial detention for non-security purposes[112] will also be omitted from the ensuing analysis.

As we have seen, the main function of preventive detention is to remove allegedly dangerous persons from society. The purpose of pre-trial detention is quite different since it is usually employed to obtain information or evidence (or both) from the detainee. This makes it a far more dangerous restriction of personal liberty especially where it is indefinite and there are few external controls. The most severe forms of pre-trial detention (such as indefinite detention under s 29) create a situation in which police officials have under their absolute power a defenceless detainee from whom they are usually determined to extract information. It is not surprising that this form of detention, since its inception in 1963,[113] has resulted in the deaths of at least fifty detainees, many in circumstances strongly suggestive of physical or mental maltreatment.[114] Indefinite detention for purposes of interrogation and without adequate safeguards is a legal invitation or incentive to the ill-treatment and abuse of detainees.

Indefinite Detention (s 29)

A commissioned officer of the police, of or above the rank of lieutenant-colonel, may order without warrant the arrest and detention for interrogation of any person who he has reason to believe *(a)* has committed (or intended or intends to commit) the offence of terrorism or subversion or the offence of harbouring, assisting or failing to report the presence of someone reasonably suspected of having committed terrorism or subversion or *(b)* is withholding from the South African Police any information relating to the commission or intended commission of any such offence.[115] A person so detained will be held according to directions issued by the Commissioner of Police[116] until such time as the commissioner orders a release when satisfied that he or she has satisfactorily replied to all questions or that no useful purpose will be served by further detention.[117] This means that the detainee may be held indefinitely subject only to certain internal procedural requirements.[118]

[112] For example s 185 of the Criminal Procedure Act 51 of 1977 and s 13 of the Abuse of Dependence-producing Substances and Rehabilitation Centres Act 41 of 1971.

[113] The forerunners of the present pre-trial detention laws were '90-day' detention under s 17 of the General Law Amendment Act 37 of 1963, '180-day' detention under s 12B of the Internal Security Act 44 of 1950, indefinite detention under s 6 of the Terrorism Act 83 of 1967 and '14-day' detention under s 22 of the General Law Amendment Act 62 of 1966.

[114] According to the research department of the South African Institute of Race Relations at least fifty persons have died in detention since the introduction of detention laws in 1963. The number could be as high as seventy but in the additional cases it is not absolutely clear that the victims had detainee as opposed to awaiting-trial status. The Detainees' Support Committee has calculated that 79 people have died in detention: *Sunday Tribune* 11 May 1986.

[115] Section 29(1).

[116] Subject to directions issued by the Minister of Law and Order.

[117] A detainee may be held even after the interrogation has concluded where the matter is referred to the attorney-general for a decision as to whether to prosecute. On referral to the attorney-general, the detainee may be held until the attorney-general makes known his decision not to prosecute, until the service of the indictment where he decides to prosecute or until the minister orders the detainee's release, whichever event occurs first: s 29(1).

[118] These will be discussed fully below where it will be shown that they do not constitute effective safeguards.

The basis of the decision to detain is a reasonable belief that the person in question has committed (or intends to commit) a specified offence or is withholding information about such an offence. The offences specified by the Act—terrorism, subversion or harbouring, assisting or failing to report a suspected terrorist or subversive—are serious in terms of the punishment provided[119] but wide-ranging and ill-defined in terms of scope.[120] The offence of subversion, for example, is broad enough to cover many forms of protest politics such as a protest march that interrupts the flow of traffic, to cite only one possible example. In short, there is a serious danger that a reasonable belief that a person has committed subversion, or has information about the commission of the offence, could easily be formed about many active opponents of the government. In technical language, the jurisdictional fact upon which the decision to detain must be based could be found, created or concocted without much difficulty in many cases.

The phrase 'reason to believe', which appeared also in s 6 of the Terrorism Act,[121] the statutory precursor to s 29 detention under present law, was assumed (without any direct authority on the point) to preclude an enquiry by the courts as to whether objective grounds existed for the belief that the detainee had committed the prescribed offences or was witholding information about them. The first indication that the courts might be responsive to a legal challenge to this assumption was given in Transkei. In *Sigaba v Minister of Defence and Police*[122] and *Honey v Minister of Police*[123] the court was prepared to investigate the grounds for detentions which were premised upon 'reason to believe' that they were justified by the facts, and in each case declared the detention orders to be invalid. These two cases were soon contradicted by two further Transkei judgments[124] which re-asserted the outmoded, stodgy and pro-executive approach of *Liversidge v Anderson*.[125] Then followed a curious decision of the Ciskei court, *Sebe v Government of Ciskei*,[126] in which the court accepted that it could investigate the basis of a detention on objective grounds, and that the onus was on the detaining authority to justify the detention order; but then inexplicably accepted the mere say-so of the detaining authority that grounds for detention existed. The decisive breakthrough came in *Hurley v Minister of Law and Order*[127] in which Leon J held that s 29 detentions were reviewable on an objective basis and set aside a detention for interrogation for which the minister had declined to give reasons. We have already seen that this judgment was affirmed by the Appellate Division in *Minister of Law and Order v Hurley*[128] in which Rabie CJ, on a

---

[119] Terrorism is a capital crime and subversion carries a maximum penalty of twenty years' imprisonment (or twenty-five years where there is an element of violence which the accused should have foreseen): s 54(1) and (2)

[120] See Chapter 6 where these crimes are analysed.

[121] 83 of 1967.

[122] 1980 (3) SA 535 (Tk).

[123] 1980 (3) SA 800 (Tk).

[124] *Mnyani v Minister of Justice* 1980 (4) SA 528 (Tk) and *Mbane v Minister of Police* 1982 (1) SA 223 (Tk). *Mbane* has been criticised and virtually demolished by Etienne Mureinik in 'Liversidge in Decay' (1985) 102 *SALJ* 77.

[125] [1942] AC 206.

[126] 1983 (4) SA 523 (Ck).

[127] 1985 (4) SA 709 (D).   [128] Supra.

narrow basis and without any express avowal to that effect, joined in the contemporary repudiation of the *Liversidge* line of thinking. The Appellate Division also resolved a point which Leon J had left open in the lower court by holding that the onus is on the detaining authority to justify a detention under s 29.[129] This decision on onus of proof is of great importance to s 29 detainees.

The consequences of the *Hurley* ruling may be summed up in a number of propositions. First, the court is empowered to investigate the factual basis of a s 29 detention to determine whether a reasonable man, in the case before it, could have believed that the detainee had committed, or intended to commit a prescribed offence, or had information about it. Secondly, if the objective facts do not warrant such a belief, the detention will be invalid however much the detaining authority may have believed it to be necessary. Thirdly, where there is evidence on which a reasonable man might have formed the required belief, the court will not substitute its own view for that of the detaining authority.[130] Fourthly, the burden of establishing a valid detention falls on the detaining authority and if it fails to provide an adequate justification or refuses to acquaint the court with the necessary information on the ground that it is privileged from disclosure,[131] the detention will be invalid for failure to establish the jurisdictional facts that are prerequisites to the exercise of the detention power.

Subject to what was said earlier about the breadth and vagueness of the crimes to which s 29 detention is related, the legal position of the detainee *as to the decision to detain* has been much improved by the *Hurley* decision. The law governing his right to release after an initially valid detention remains objectionable. Whereas the decision to detain is justiciable on objective grounds, the decision not to release a detainee is probably open to challenge only on proof of bad faith or improper purpose. The provision in question declares that the detainee shall be held until the Commissioner of Police orders his release 'when satisfied that the said person has satisfactorily replied to all questions at the interrogation or that no useful purpose will be served by his further interrogation . . .'.[132] Though it has already been suggested that the use of the phrase 'is satisfied' does not necessarily indicate that the decision-maker's state of mind need bear no relation to the objective facts, there is less authority for giving the expression 'is satisfied' an objective reading than there is for so

---

[129] This decision on onus is clearly correct on the basis that where the statutory formula for conferring discretionary power, on a true interpretation, requires grounds which are objectively present as a basis for a decision to detain, the detaining authority must prove their existence since they are a prerequisite to the valid exercise of the power conferred on that authority. The approach of the House of Lords to onus was the same in *Inland Revenue Commissioner v Rossminster* [1980] 1 All ER 80 (HL), a case which dealt with a search warrant. If our courts were to hold that a power to detain or restrict which may be premised on the detaining authority's 'belief' or 'satisfaction' requires the presence of objective facts which may reasonably support that belief or satisfaction, the onus would likewise be on the authority in question to justify its action by proving the necessary jurisdictional facts.

[130] According to Rabie CJ, this approach gives effect to the clause (s 29(6)) ousting the court's jurisdiction in s 29 cases.

[131] Under s 66 of the Act the minister has an absolute right to withhold information from a court on the ground that it is privileged.

[132] Section 29(1).

interpreting the phrase 'has reason to believe'. The more important point, however, is that the matter on which the commissioner has to be satisfied—whether the detainee has satisfactorily replied to all questions—is unlikely to be a clear-cut issue capable of relatively easy judicial resolution. Whether the detainee has replied satisfactorily to his interrogators is something that cannot easily be decided without a full knowledge of the general course of the interrogation and without personal observation of the detainee during that interrogation. In legal jargon, this is a matter on which the legislator must have intended the commissioner to be the final arbiter. That being so, the court is unlikely to interfere except on proof that the detainee is being held not for interrogation but for punishment or revenge, or some similar misuse of the detention provision. In addition, where it is evident that the interrogational purpose of the detention cannot be realised because, for example, the detainee is mentally disturbed, the court should order his release.[133]

Detainees who do not have the resources to challenge detention decisions before the ordinary courts will be forced to rely on a number of unhelpful provisions somewhat meretriciously dressed up as safeguards. The first provision prescribes that no person may be detained for a period exceeding thirty days from the date of arrest except under written authority for further detention granted by the Minister of Law and Order.[134] The minister shall not grant such authority unless he is satisfied, by a written application signed by the commissioner and setting out in full reasons why the detainee should not be released, that further detention is necessary for interrogation.[135] The audi alteram partem rule does not apply to an extension of detention authorised by the minister and an extension will be valid even if the detainee has not been given an opportunity to dispute it.[136] The requirements of a signed application by the commissioner and written authority by the minister are expressed in peremptory language and it follows that further detention will be illegal in the event of non-compliance; but since the entire procedure is internal to the Department of Law and Order, there is really no chance that a failure to comply will ever be revealed. The courts have been unhelpful in cases of dispute about compliance with technical requirements and in *Real Printing Co (Pty) Ltd v Minister of Justice*[137] they refused to order the minister to disclose documents to prove that an analogous procedural requirement prior to the banning of a newspaper had been complied with. Though the question is academic on account of the internal and secret nature of the procedure for extension of detention beyond thirty days, there appears to be no reason whatever to uphold a minister's claim of state privilege for his written authority (which will reveal nothing except that he has or has not given that authority) in the unlikely event of the matter ever reaching

---

[133] *Morarjee v Minister of Law and Order* 1986 (3) SA 823 (D) 839.
[134] Section 29(3)*(a)*.
[135] Section 29(3)*(b)*. The detainee may be held, pending the result of the application, as if the application had been granted: s 29(3)*(c)*. No time-limit for the processing of the application is provided.
[136] *Morarjee v Minister of Law and Order* (supra).
[137] 1965 (2) SA 782 (C).

a court of law.[138] We may conclude that a procedure which operates in the secret and sinister recesses of a police department, and which involves no external check of any kind, is no safeguard at all.

There are several further procedural requirements of an internal nature. The commissioned officer who orders the arrest and detention of any person is required 'as soon as possible after the arrest' to notify the Commissioner of Police thereof; and he in turn is required to notify the minister of the name of the detainee and the place of detention 'as soon as possible after having been so notified'.[139] These internal procedures are supplemented by the requirement of reference of the matter to a board of review if the detainee has not been released at the expiration of a period of six months from the date of his arrest.[140] The provision in question requires the Commissioner of Police, either in person or through a commissioned officer designated by him, to adduce reasons to the board as to why the detainee should not be released at the end of the initial six-month period of detention and thereafter to do so at intervals of 'not less than three months'.[141] The statutory duty to notify the commissioner and the minister of a detention, and the duty to place the matter before the review board at intervals, are all expressed in peremptory language. It follows that an unreasonable delay in complying with the notification procedures and, certainly, a failure to submit the matter for review, should result in the detention being illegal. Our courts might well take a leaf out of the Israeli book and treat a procedural failure, where it concerns as vital a matter as the personal liberty of the subject, as a fatal flaw.[142] In the Zimbabwean case of *Minister of Home Affairs v Dabengwa*[143] the court decided that a delay in reviewing a detention should be cured initially by an order to comply (a mandamus) and that it did not per se render the detention invalid. It distinguished between failures 'that go to the legality of the detention order itself and those that go to the obligations that must thereafter be discharged . . .'.[144] An example of the first is the failure to specify the place of detention as required by the statute, which the Supreme Court in Israel held fatal to the legality of the detention in *Al-Khouri v Chief of Staff*.[145] An example of an obligation that 'must thereafter be discharged' is the requirement of the submission of detention orders for review, and it is in respect of such failures that *Minister of Home Affairs v Dabengwa* decided that an order of illegality is inappropriate. The distinction between irregularities affecting the initial detention and those

---

[138] The minister's claim that the commissioner's signed application for extension of detention is privileged is more likely to be successful in any court proceedings.

[139] Section 29(2)(a).

[140] Ibid.

[141] Ibid. The phrase 'not less than three months' appears to be a mistake. The drafters must have intended 'not more than three months'. This mistake seems to deprive the detainee of the right to regular subsequent review of his detention but it should be treated as a mistake and read by the courts to require three-monthly reviews. Alternatively, it should be interpreted as requiring the commissioner to adduce reasons within a reasonable time after the end of each three-monthly period.

[142] See the cases reviewed in (1978) 8 *Israel Yearbook on Human Rights* 296, 310, 313.

[143] 1984 (2) SA 345 (ZS).

[144] At 356.

[145] 4 P.D. 34 A, 46. See the discussion of this case by Harold Rudolph in *Security, Terrorism and Torture* (Juta 1984) 76.

occurring thereafter is unsatisfactory and should be rejected. The
immediate consequence of the distinction is to treat subsequent procedural failures as less injurious to a detainee and to the protection of his or her
liberty even though there is no logical reason why this should be so. The
Israeli Supreme Court ignored the distinction in *Al-Karbutli v Minister of
Defence*[146] and declared a detention invalid because at the time it was
made a review committee had not been appointed even though the review
committee would be required to operate only after the detention came into
effect. The rule that any procedural failure that is serious and substantial,
even if it occurs after an initially valid detention, entitles the detainee to a
declaration of illegality, would be more in accordance with the much-
vaunted judicial concern for individual freedom. The failure of the
detaining authority to refer a case for review in accordance with a
peremptory statutory duty, is a serious and substantial failure and,
contrary to the finding in *Dabengwa*, our courts should be ready to grant
an order nullifying the detention in such a case.[147] Such a judicial
approach would ensure greater respect by the authorities for the
detainees' rights and would reflect a real and *effective* concern for personal
freedom.

The board of review to which s 29 detentions are referred after the
initial six months, is appointed by the State President on the recommendation of the Minister of Justice.[148] The power of the government in office
to determine the composition of the board is the first reason for concern
relating to the review procedure. A board of review will consist of three
members, one of whom (the chairman) is required to be legally
experienced;[149] of the remaining two members, one is required to hold a
degree or diploma in law.[150] Boards may take decisions by a majority (i e
of two members) but have powers of recommendation only[151] — a second
reason for concern about the review procedure. Moreover, there is no
provision for reference of the matter to the Chief Justice (as in the case of
preventive detention under s 28) where a board's recommendation differs
from that of the detaining authority. A third ground for concern is that the
members of a board of review do not enjoy real security of tenure and may
be replaced by the State President 'for good cause'.[152] Yet another
disturbing feature of the review procedure is that no time period is
specified by the Act within which the board must conclude its proceedings
and make a recommendation.

The procedures prescribed for a review board provide further cause for
disquiet. While the board is required to consider any representations

---

[146] 2 P.D. 5. The case is discussed by Harold Rudolph op cit 76.

[147] In *Minister of Home Affairs v Dabengwa* (supra) it was made clear that the detainee in
Zimbabwe had a right to see his legal representative whereas s 29 detainees in South Africa are
held incommunicado. This is a further reason for not insisting on mandamus proceedings since
the chances of any incommunicado detainee being able to initiate them are virtually nil.

[148] Sections 1(ii) and 35.

[149] The chairman must be a judge or a person who has held office as a judge or as a senior
magistrate or a person entitled to be admitted as an advocate who has been involved in the
application of law for a continuous period of not less than ten years: s 35(3).

[150] Section 35(3).

[151] Boards are directed to make a written report to the minister by s 29(2)*(c)*; nowhere is
the minister required to give effect to a review board's findings.

[152] Section 35(4).

which the detainee wishes to submit, it is not required to hear oral evidence from him.[153] Furthermore, no duty is imposed upon the detaining authority to provide the detainee with a statement setting out the grounds for his further detention[154] thereby jeopardising his ability to make effective representations to the board. Other rules of natural justice, such as the rule against bias, are apparently inapplicable.[155] A review board operates in secrecy and no person may attend its proceedings except the Director of Security Legislation, a person engaged in giving evidence, or a person in the service of the state whose presence is considered necessary by the chairman.[156] Legal representatives have no right to attend. Taking into account the procedures prescribed for boards, their composition and lack of power, they clearly do not constitute an effective safeguard.[157] The most one can say about this weak form of external review is that it is marginally better than nothing.

The combination of several provisions of the Act makes the position of a s 29 detainee one of complete powerlessness and vulnerability. The Act directs that the detainee shall be held in accordance with such directions as the commissioner, subject to directions from the minister, may issue from time to time.[158] There is an ouster clause which states that no court of law has jurisdiction to pronounce 'upon the validity of any action taken in terms of this section . . .'[159] and which is clearly designed to free the detaining authority from court control in respect of the conditions of detention. Finally, the isolation of the detainee is assured by a provision which limits access to the detainee to the minister, and to officials of the state acting in their professional capacity, unless consent for a visit is given by the minister or the commissioner.[160] This last provision authorises incommunicado interrogation of detainees.

Since *Rossouw v Sachs*[161] in which the court surprisingly denied a detainee[162] access to reading matter and writing materials and lamented the fact that the court had to pronounce on conditions of detention,[163] the jurisdiction of the court over the treatment of the detainee has been all but eradicated. Acting in accordance with his statutory power to issue directions governing s 29 detentions, the minister has promulgated a

---

[153] Section 29(2)(b).
[154] Formal directions issued by the minister under s 29(1) of the Act (GN 877 of 1982 (*GG* 8467 of 31 December 1982)) do require the commissioned officer, as soon as possible after the arrest of the detainee, to inform him of the reasons for detention. However, this requirement does not refer to the subsequent decision not to release a detainee and, in any event, reasons may be provided informally and be too bald to be helpful.
[155] On this point, see *Beukes v Administrator General SWA* 1980 (2) SA 624 (SWA).
[156] Section 8(8) which is made applicable by s 29(2)(d).
[157] The right of a detainee to make representations at any time to the minister (s 29(4)) and the power of the minister to order the release at any time of a detainee (s 29(5)) do not qualify as safeguards for obvious reasons.
[158] Section 29(1).
[159] Section 29(6).
[160] Section 29(7). As we shall see below, the detainee will be visited by the Inspector of Detainees and by a magistrate and district surgeon.
[161] 1964 (2) SA 551 (A).
[162] Under the now repealed ninety-day form of pre-trial detention.
[163] Ogilvie-Thompson JA (at 558A of his judgment) virtually invites the government to take over the determination of the conditions of detention, an invitation which it was not reluctant to accept.

statutory code for the treatment of detainees.[164] The issue of this code is a form of 'action taken in terms of this section' on the validity of which the court is specifically precluded from pronouncing.[165] To the extent that these directions do provide protection for the detainee (a minimal protection, as will be shown below) they are legally binding and, subject to practical difficulties, enforceable by the courts. In *Cassiem v Commanding Officer, Victor Verster Prison*[166] similar regulations issued in respect of s 28 detainees (those held under preventive detention) were treated as being enforceable and there appears to be no reason why directions issued by the minister in terms of a power conferred on him by s 29 of the Act should be regarded as having 'no legal effect'.[167] The real problem about enforcement is not that the directions lack legal force but that the detainee and the courts are denied access to each other and that enforcement is therefore a practical impossibility. One of the directions issued by the minister[168] declares that a detainee 'shall be afforded ample opportunity to sleep and to do physical exercise'. If a detainee, in accordance with a common practice of interrogators, was being denied sleep and exercise to soften him up, the court should have no difficulty about issuing an appropriate order on application by or on behalf of the detainee. The problem is that there will be no such application because the detainee is confined incommunicado with no right of access to a lawyer. After discharge from detention an action for damages is in principle available, but the problem of proof for a person held in isolation is virtually insurmountable. The practical effect of the detainee's isolation and his lack of access to the courts, is that the authorities have been appointed their own guardians—a situation in which we cannot anticipate much respect even for the minimal rights which the law affords the detainee. It is therefore no surprise that since the minister's directions for the 'protection' of detainees were issued in 1982, several detainees have died in detention.

The self-policed directions issued by the minister are in any event full of reservations and qualifications. Apart from the direction regarding sleep and exercise already mentioned, there is one other which is expressed in categorical language:

> 'A detainee shall at all times be treated in a humane manner with proper regard to the rules of decency and shall not in any way be assaulted or otherwise ill-treated or subjected to any form of torture or inhuman or degrading treatment.'[169]

However, one should avoid being too impressed by this direction and keep in mind that the government has been careful to ensure that the

---

[164] 'Directions regarding the Detention of Persons in Terms of Section 29(1) of the Internal Security Act, 1982' in GN 877 of 1982 (*GG* 8467 of 3 December 1982).

[165] Section 29(6).

[166] 1982 (2) SA 547 (C) 553.

[167] Harold Rudolph op cit 36, 39. It was wrongly stated in Bulletin No I of Lawyers for Human Rights (Feb 1983) 28 that the directions are not binding 'as they are not issued in terms of any enabling statute'. The Government Notice in question specifically states that the Internal Security Act of 1982 (s 29(1)) is the enabling statute. At p 38 of the same bulletin, legal effect to the regulations is denied because they are not 'regulations'. There seems to be no reason why the use of the word 'directions', which appears also in s 29(1), should deprive the minister's notice of legal effect.

[168] Paragraph 16.   [169] Paragraph 15.

courts do not administer it and that it adds little to the basic common-law rights of the detainee which are, in the words of *Rossouw v Sachs*,[170] to be 'released with his physical and mental health unimpaired'. Until the minister provides for external and independent supervision over the treatment of the detainee, the direction as to humane treatment will remain a paper guarantee. All the other directions which might contribute to the better treatment of detainees are qualified. The nearest relative of the detainee need not be informed of the detention if 'this will hinder any investigation or endanger the security of the State';[171] the provision of an exercise area and adequate washing and toilet facilities must be provided 'where practicable';[172] interrogators may not take firearms into the interrogation cells 'unless there are compelling security reasons for doing so'.[173] (Considering that a detainee has been shot in the head and killed by an interrogator, there should be an absolute prohibition on firearms in the interrogation cell.)[174]

The minister's directions are also significant for what they omit. There is no provision for observation by closed circuit television of interrogation sessions.[175] There are no detailed prohibitions on specific forms of ill-treatment such as stripping prisoners, forcing them to maintain unnatural postures, and so on.[176] Visits by private doctors are not generally allowed. In short, the directions do not go far enough as well as being heavily qualified and of a self-policing nature.

While the legislature has done its damndest to neutralise the role of the courts in relation to detention, there remains a small residuum of authority which the judiciary should not hesitate to exploit if it still wishes to be seen as a defender of individual freedom. Nothing in the Act authorises the physical or mental maltreatment of the detainee and the court retains its jurisdiction to respond to such illegal action on the part of the detaining or interrogating authorities. If information leaks out that the detainee is being ill-treated, the court has the power to grant a prohibitory interdict against the offenders.[177] Where the information is too thin, the court can authorise, as suggested in *Nxasana v Minister of Justice*,[178] the taking of evidence on commission by one of the persons who is legally authorised to visit the detainee.[179] Such an order should be granted on a mere apprehension of ill-treatment since the detainee's isolation precludes

[170] 1964 (2) SA 551 (A) 561.
[171] Paragraph 7.
[172] Paragraph 13.
[173] Paragraph 22.
[174] The report of the conviction of the interrogator on a charge of culpable homicide arising out of this incident appears in the *Sunday Tribune* of 26 February 1984.
[175] This is standard practice in Northern Ireland following the Bennett Report (Cmnd 7497, March 1979). The Baker Report (Cmnd 9222, April 1984) has since recommended that a sound-track be added.
[176] See Baker Report, (n 175) para 180.
[177] See, for example, *Essop v Commissioner of SA Police* 1972 (1) PH H5 (T) 4; 1972 *Annual Survey* 14. See also *Gosschalk v Rossouw* 1966 (2) SA 476 (C) and *Nestor v Minister of Police* 1984 (4) SA 230 (SWA).
[178] 1976 (3) SA 745 (D). The contrary judgment in *Cooper v Minister of Police* 1977 (2) SA 209 (T) is clearly wrong. *Nxasana* has been followed, and *Cooper* rejected, in *Ngxale v Minister of Justice of the Ciskei* 1981 (2) SA 554 (E) and *Mkhize v Minister of Law and Order* 1985 (4) SA 147 (N).
[179] For example, the magistrate or Inspector of Detainees.

the production of evidence to that effect. While the *Nxasana* judgment is admirable in authorising the taking of evidence on commission, it was a shade too strict in its demand that the court should be presented with a prima facie case of ill-treatment. In an unfortunate judgment, *Scherm-brucker v Klindt*,[180] the court, on an interpretation of the similarly worded '90-day' detention law, precluded itself from taking the only really effective action to determine the truth and to protect the detainee, by declaring that it could not require the authorities to produce a detainee in court to give direct evidence of the conditions of his detention and interrogation. A different finding on this issue of the production before court of s 29 detainees would bring our judiciary local and international recognition for serious and effective concern for the well-being of the most defenceless of security-law victims in South Africa.[181]

The power to isolate detainees is conferred by a provision of the Act which declares that no person other than the minister or a person acting by virtue of his office in the service of the state shall have access to the detainee except with the consent of the minister or Commissioner of Police.[182] The detainee's isolation will be broken only by visits from the Inspector of Detainees,[183] who is required to visit detainees 'as frequently as possible',[184] and by the stipulated visits of a magistrate and district surgeon who must each call at least once a fortnight.[185] Notable omissions from the list of those who may visit without special permission are legal representatives of the detainee, close members of the detainee's family and private doctors.[186] All these omissions are serious but none is more devastating to a detainee's common-law right to be unharmed either physically or mentally than the exclusion of all medical practitioners other than doctors in the service of the state. An ad hoc committee of the Medical Association of South Africa has drawn attention to the lack of clinical independence on the part of district surgeons and has made certain important recommendations for assuring their full medical independence and for the medical examination of the detainee by an independent medical practitioner either of his own choice or from a panel set up by the association.[187] For a long time the authorities appear to have treated these important recommendations as so much chaff in the wind. Recently, however, under pressure from the Medical Association, an agreement has been arrived at, but not yet implemented, in terms of which a detainee will be able to request the district surgeon to arrange for a 'second opinion' which will be provided by a member of a local panel set up by the association.[188] An obvious weakness of the scheme is the failure

---

[180] 1965 (4) SA 606 (A).

[181] The minority judgment in *Schermbrucker's* case is preferable and provides a good basis for a new ruling: see A S Mathews *Law, Order and Liberty in South Africa* 140.

[182] Section 29(7).   [183] Appointed in terms of s 44 of the Act.

[184] Section 45(1).   [185] Section 29(9).

[186] Paragraph 28 of the minister's directions makes provision for the services of a medical practitioner other than the district surgeon where the latter is not available for reasons of emergency.

[187] Report on the 'Medical Care of Prisoners and Detainees by an ad hoc Committee of the Medical Association of South Africa' adopted by the Federal Council of the Association on 10 May 1983 published as a supplement to the *South African Medical Journal* of 21 May 1983.

[188] Information supplied by Mr A Volschenk, legal adviser to the Medical Association of South Africa. At the time of going to press, it was announced that the panels had been set up and were ready to function.

to permit a close relative or friend of the detainee to arrange for a visit by a panel member (the detainee could easily be pressured not to ask for a private practitioner); moreover it is not clear whether the request must be acceded to and how expeditiously it will take place. Judgment will have to be reserved until the scheme comes into effect.

Though the courts have decided that the detainee's isolation cannot be broken by an order that he or she be produced in court,[189] there appears to be legal authority for a judge to visit a detainee in prison—of moving the mountain to Muhammad, as it were. In terms of prison regulations, judges have a right to visit a prison or any part of it and to interview any prisoner.[190] The definition of prisoner in the Prisons Act[191] is wide enough to encompass a detainee. Here, it seems, is a residual piece of court jurisdiction over detainees which can still be employed and which should be vigorously exercised, especially where the issue of the maltreatment of a detainee is before the court. A failure on the part of the judges to act will inevitably suggest that their general impotence to protect the victims of security laws is in part self-imposed and not entirely unwelcome.

The government's response to the local and international surge of shock and anger following the deaths in detention of Steve Biko and Neil Aggett remains shamefully inadequate. The compulsory visits to the detainee, at least once a fortnight, of a magistrate and a district surgeon have proved to be ineffective in the past. These persons are viewed by detainees as part of the state apparatus and this alone deprives their visits of much of its protective significance. The institution of an Inspector of Detainees,[192] who must visit as often as possible, was an improvement but his visits have also not prevented further deaths. There is evidence that detainees have 'not been available' on some occasions when a statutory visitor has called.[193] The central reason why these visits have proved to be inadequate is that the detainee remains at all times in the control of the security police who have the ability to make things much more unpleasant following complaints to any of the official visitors. This problem will remain so long as the detainee is isolated from all contact with people concerned for his or her safety and well-being (such as family, friends, private doctors and priests) and from the courts which have the necessary authority to order remedial action if the facts can be placed before them.

The detainee's isolation is increased by the construction of a legislative information barrier around the detention cell: no person other than the minister or a person acting by virtue of his office in the service of the state is entitled to any information relating to or obtained from a detainee.[194] This provision, while not making information about the detainee an official secret, entitles the authorities to refuse to give out any information

---

[189] *Schermbrucker v Klindt NO* (supra).

[190] See the chapter on Prisons in *Law of South Africa* vol 21 para 179 and *Goldberg v Minister of Prisons* 1979 (1) SA 14 (A) 28. See also D M Davis 'Judicial Protection of Detainees' (1986) 2 *South African Journal on Human Rights* 80.

[191] 8 of 1959, s 1.

[192] An Inspector of Detainees is directed to visit detainees 'as frequently as possible' (s 45(1)) and to make reports on his visits to the minister and, if in his opinion an offence has been committed in relation to the detainee during his detention, to the attorney-general (s 45(4) and (5)).

[193] Unpublished memorandum by the Detainees Parents' Support Committee.

[194] Section 29(7).

about them.[195] 'Disappearance in the night', that dread phenomenon of a police state, has been made a reality by this law. Fortunately, the information barrier does not prevent a court from taking evidence about the detainee's state of health on commission through one of the official visitors.[196] There were conflicting judgments as to whether the similarly worded provision of the Terrorism Act[197] prohibited a detainee who is charged with a crime from demanding[198] written statements made during his detention but the matter has been settled, adversely to the detainee, by the present Act which entitles him to demand such statements only if the prosecutor puts any part thereof to him at the trial.[199] The isolation of the detainee from his own statements is a revealing indication of the nature of security legislation in South Africa. The information barrier does not prevent the prosecution from using statements obtained in detention in the subsequent trial of the detainee.[200]

The use in a subsequent trial of statements obtained from a detainee, and the acceptance of evidence from detainees who have been through the interrogation-in-isolation routine, both raise issues of central importance to the criminal process. The framers of s 29 clearly intended to set up an oppressive regime for detainees which would enable the police to extract information from them. An essential part of this regime is the authorisation of lengthy detention coupled with sensory deprivation (attendant upon isolation in a single cell) and aggressive interrogation. Though aggressive interrogation does not *legally* include the use of mental or physical torture, given the absence of proper controls such practices are inevitable. Under these conditions, according to scientific evidence to be considered below, the subject of interrogation may become suggestible, confused and unreliable. This is so even where illegal methods of interrogation are not used. The basic elements in s 29 detention, therefore, are coercion and the consequential danger of a suggestible and unreliable informant. These are the very elements which modern and civilised systems of criminal procedure seek to exclude from the trial of alleged offenders so as to ensure that the trial becomes an effective instrument for the determination of truth. The central features of s 29 detention and the principles of fair trial are in direct opposition and it is this crucial conflict which has not been adequately appreciated and addressed by South African courts.

Lengthy and potentially indefinite incarceration in a solitary cell, with no access to family, friends, doctors and lawyers, is a traumatic experience for most persons. The trauma is heightened by the hostility of official interrogators whose uncontrolled access to, and power over, the detainee constitute an intimidating and ever-present sense of menace, even when that menace is not translated into verbal or physical aggression or into subtle or unsubtle forms of mental torture. The immense power of the interrogators, and total vulnerability of detainees, has been described in

---

[195] *Nxasana v Minister of Justice* (supra).
[196] On this point, see particularly *Mkhize v Minister of Law and Order* (supra).
[197] Section 6(6) of Act 83 of 1967.
[198] In terms of s 335 of the Criminal Procedure Act 51 of 1977.
[199] Section 29(8).
[200] *S v Mzo* 1984 (3) SA 954 (E). See also *S v Moumbaris* 1973 (3) SA 109 (T).

grim poetry by Breyten Breytenbach after his firsthand experience of the system. He says of the interrogators:

'There's nothing, there's nobody, no power anywhere in the world that has any say over them. They can keep you forever. They can put their heavy hands on you. They can break you down. They may even go red in the face and really let rip.'[201]

On the situation of the detainee he says: 'I can understand how the mouse is paralysed although still alive whilst being eaten by the snake— celebrating with open eyes its own death.'[202] The medical condition of a detainee held in such circumstances has been characterised by a leading expert, Dr Louis J West, as the D.D.D. syndrome, that is, the debility, dependency and dread syndrome.[203] The D.D.D. syndrome is a convenient shorthand expression for describing the physical and psychological impact of enforced isolation and interrogation on detainees which several decades of medical research has established with adequate clarity. That research reveals that persons held and interrogated under the conditions described may experience one or more of the following states or conditions: a feeling of extreme helplessness; intense fear for himself and close family; mental confusion (ranging from a mild to an extreme degree); disturbance of concentration and of the memory function; malleability in the hands of those who control his destiny during detention; suicidal tendencies and mental breakdown; and the experience of hallucinations and the development of delusions.[204] There is always the danger, especially where detention in isolation is prolonged, that the experience of the traumas just described will cause lasting psychological damage to the detainee. This was one of the findings of the ad hoc committee of the South African Medical Association in its investigation of the medical care of prisoners and detainees.[205] Because of the absence of effective safeguards and external controls over detention, there is a good chance that many people suffering such permanent damage will be innocent of criminal or subversive behaviour.

If a detainee makes an admission or confession after undergoing one or more of the experiences described above, or if his co-operation is the result of the fear of being subjected to such treatment, it is difficult to see how the admission or confession could be regarded as free and voluntary. The court recognised that this was so in a perceptive judgment given by

[201] Breyten Breytenbach *The True Confessions of an Albino Terrorist* (Taurus, Cape Town 1984) 19.
[202] Op cit 49. Elsewhere he speaks of a detainee being like 'the rabbit assisting open-eyed and without kicking at one's own eating' (39).
[203] This syndrome was explained in detail by Dr West in the evidence given by him in the unreported case of *S v Gwala* (July 1977—NPD). Both the credentials and the general tenor of the evidence of Dr West were accepted by the court.
[204] Much of the scientific literature establishing these consequences was reviewed by Mathews & Albino in 'The Permanence of the Temporary: An Examination of the 90 and 180 day Detention Laws' (1966) 83 *SALJ* 31. Dr West's evidence in the *Gwala* case (supra) incorporated the results of more recent scientific work: see J J Riekert 'The D.D.D. syndrome: Solitary confinement and a South African Security Law Trial' in A N Bell & R D A Mackie (eds) *Detention and Security Legislation in South Africa* (University of Natal, Durban 1985) 121. Recent scientific evidence is also referred to by D Fine 'Re-examining the Validity of Detainee Evidence: A Psycho-Legal Approach' (1984) 8 *SACC* 156.
[205] Ad hoc report of the Medical Association of South Africa (n 187) para 3.9.

Milne JP in *S v Ismail (1)*[206] at a time when indefinite detention was not possible. In that case Milne JP said:

> 'To contemplate being detained for 90 days in solitary confinement, without being able to see one's relatives or friends, is in its nature a grievous thing. And it is perhaps even more so if the person who contemplates his detention has a family dependent upon him.'[207]

Since that statement was made by the court, detention has become indefinite and detainees are aware of the treatment that was suffered by Biko and others, and of the numerous deaths in detention. There is every reason, therefore, to describe interrogation in isolation as an oppressive and frightening set-up,[208] or as a scheme to subjugate 'the individual to the will of his examiner',[209] with the obvious consequence that admissions or confessions by the detainee will be involuntary and inadmissible. Breyten Breytenbach, writing of his interrogation under indefinite detention in South Africa, has left us in no doubt about the strength of will of the examiner or interrogator. He says of his interrogators that they 'were and are fanatically committed to their view of reality, to the justness of their analysis of the situation, and finally to their way of life'. He adds that 'not only do they believe their cause to be just, but so convinced are they that the whole world is ranged against them, that any and all methods used in breaking and destroying those they figger as the enemy are justified'.[210] The circumstances will have to be truly exceptional to support a finding that an admission or confession made by a detainee interrogated in isolation was of a voluntary character. There is the technical difficulty that an apparently voluntary admission or confession which is reduced to writing by or in the presence of a magistrate is regarded as voluntary unless the contrary is established by the person who made it.[211] But the courts have demonstrated an admirable strictness in relation to the conditions under which the onus of proof will shift to the maker of the admission or confession, thereby requiring him to disprove voluntariness;[212] and even where the onus does shift, the courts can (and should) treat the burden of proof as discharged where the detainee shows that he was interrogated in isolation for a lengthy period or that he acted under the threat of such interrogation. Leaving aside, for the moment, technical questions about the burden of proof, it seems clear that the realities of detention in isolation in South Africa require the courts to reject detainee admissions and confessions as a general principle, and to allow exceptions to that principle only in cases in which the absence of coercion is manifestly clear.

Unfortunately, the approach of Milne JP in *S v Ismail (1)*[213] has been treated as an aberration by another court[214] and side-stepped by the

---

[206] 1965 (1) SA 446 (N).
[207] At 448–9.
[208] See *R v Prager* [1972] 1 All ER 1114 (CA) 1119 in which the principle that confessions obtained through oppressive questioning are inadmissible, was adopted.
[209] *Miranda v Arizona* 384 US 436 (1966) 16 L Ed 2nd 694.
[210] Breyten Breytenbach op cit 34.
[211] Sections 217(1)*(b)* and 219A(1)*(b)* of the Criminal Procedure Act 51 of 1977.
[212] See the judgment in *S v Mpetha (2)* 1982 (2) (SA) 406 (C) and the authorities reviewed therein.
[213] Supra.   [214] *S v Hlekani* 1964 (4) SA 429 (E).

Appellate Division in *S v Alexander (1)*.[215] More recently, in *S v Christie*[216] the Appellate Division decided that being held in detention under a fourteen-day detention law[217] did not in itself deprive a statement of the quality of voluntariness. It did so despite the fact that the detainee claimed that he believed that he was being held under indefinite detention and despite the power of the police to convert a fourteen-day detention to indefinite detention at any time. In fact, it seems certain that had Christie not co-operated by the time his short-term detention expired, he would have been held thereafter under the indefinite detention provision. In the result, Christie's conviction on several of the charges depended entirely on his statements made in detention. The Appellate Division appears to have passed up once again the opportunity to adopt a tough-minded stance (which would fully accord with the medical and psychological evidence) towards the acceptance of detainee admissions or confessions. The time is overdue for this court to accept the logic of the proposition that 'the principle that confessions are inadmissible unless made voluntarily, cannot meaningfully co-exist with a police power to detain and interrogate indefinitely and until all questions are answered "satisfactorily" '.[218]

The attitude of the Appellate Division to the credibility of evidence given in court by a detainee is equally indecisive and unresponsive to the clear import of the scientific evidence. When a detainee gives evidence in court there is no legal bar to its admission, as in the case of admissions and confessions that are not voluntary, but there is the serious question of whether a court should attach any credibility to such evidence. In the leading judgment on this question, *S v Hassim*,[219] the court did not adopt a resolutely sceptical attitude towards detainee evidence but merely put itself under the duty to exercise extra 'vigilance and scrutiny'. The court, moreover, seemed reasonably confident of its ability to determine the truth and reliability of the evidence by the usual methods of evaluation. Expert investigations into the mental effects of prolonged isolation suggest that the courts should be strongly sceptical both about the reliability or veracity of information or evidence obtained from a detainee and about their own ability to evaluate the information or evidence. As to reliability and veracity, the following conclusion of the committee of experts appointed by the Medical Association of South Africa, is worthy of note:

> 'Information gathered from a detainee under conditions outlined above[220] will often result in evidence lacking all reliability and therefore of limited use to the interrogators either for further investigation or legal proceedings. A statement could be made quite contrary to the individual's true belief or knowledge. The above methods of detention would render the detainee susceptible to suggestion with no limit to the potential distortion of the information obtained.'[221]

---

[215] 1962 (2) SA 796 (A) 814.
[216] 1982 (1) SA 464 (A). The judgment is strongly criticised by J van den Berg in 'Treason: Evaluating the Evidence of Political Detainees' (1985) 9 *SACC* 252.
[217] The now repealed s 22 of the General Law Amendment Act 62 of 1966.
[218] R C Williams in (1984) 101 *SALJ* 7, 8.
[219] 1973 (3) SA 443 (A).
[220] By the interrogation of detainees held in isolation.
[221] Report of the Ad Hoc Committee of the Medical Association of South Africa (n 187) para 3.8.

As this conclusion indicates, there is a *likelihood* that detainee evidence will be unreliable and untrue.[222] Furthermore, it is not self-evident that a court of law can determine, with a sufficient degree of certainty and conviction, that a particular piece of evidence, or a particular part of it, is reliable and truthful and therefore deserving of credibility. On the contrary, as Dr West said in his evidence given in the *Gwala* case:

'The nett judgment from a scientific point of view that would have to be applied to information forthcoming under these conditions would be that it was all tainted. You'd never know what part was true, what part was false and you couldn't really even rely on the witness if he was assured of the protection of the court from that moment on to ascertain at the time he was giving testimony whether it was true or not.'[223]

A court therefore deceives itself in believing that it can evaluate the evidence of a detainee subjected to prolonged isolation by the usual methods of assessment. The trauma experienced by detainees who are interrogated in isolation makes a reliance on the witness's demeanour, and on general impressions of him, extremely dangerous. The test of corroboration by other witnesses is obviously unacceptable where the others are detainees who have been subjected to the same treatment;[224] but even if they are not, the test of corroboration remains a dangerous guide since evidence tainted by interrogation in isolation is so questionable as to be incapable of supporting, or being supported by, other evidence that is credible. The court should not lean on a broken reed.

There is only one approach to detainee evidence that is consistent with the evidence of scientists and the requirements of a fair trial—to reject such evidence unless there are cogent and compelling reasons for believing that it is both truthful and reliable. This was the approach of the judge in *S v Hoffman*[225] in which the court declared itself unable to proceed with any confidence on the evidence of a detainee held under an indefinite detention provision.[226] In contrast, the acceptance, in another case, of evidence from a witness who had been detained for over five hundred days[227] is enough to boggle the mind and to destroy confidence in political justice in South Africa. It is not sufficient to sound dire warnings about

---

[222] Untruth and unreliability need not necessarily refer to the basic facts of a case since these may not be in dispute as between interrogator and detainee. The untruth or unreliability will most frequently refer to the complexion or framework of purpose which the interrogator seeks to put upon the agreed facts through extended interrogation. In the case of Breyten Breytenbach, the framework into which the admitted fact of his visit to South Africa, and the contacts which he made while in the country, was placed by the investigators, was totally different from the framework in which Breytenbach operated. In the end, the 'official' framework prevailed in court, and resulted in his severe punishment (imprisonment for nine years); but it now seems clear that the actual framework was quite different and that without the drastic process of interrogation, a different picture altogether would have been presented to the court.

[223] Cited by D Fine op cit 182.

[224] They will almost invariably have been questioned by the same interrogation team. In' *S v Hassim* (supra) the court did not react adversely to the principle of one detainee corroborating another. This suggests a real failure on the part of the court to understand the import of scientific evidence on the effects of isolation.

[225] Unreported judgment of the Cape Provincial Division in 1976. On this judgment, see the paper by C R Nicholson 'Admissibility and Reliability of Detainee Evidence' *Detention and Security Legislation in South Africa*, 105, 109.

[226] The now repealed s 6 of the Terrorism Act 83 of 1967.

[227] See D Fine op cit 162.

the danger of detainee evidence, as in *S v Mpetha (2)*[228] if the court then
proceeds to rely on it. What the courts should have done was to adopt a
basic rule that denies credibility to the evidence of detainees who have
been held for anything but very short periods of detention.[229] Their failure
to react decisively against detainee evidence has been a lost opportunity to
render full justice in security trials. As a former member of the attorney-
general's office in Natal has said, they (the courts) 'have not distinguished
themselves in coming to the assistance of ex-detainee witnesses who testify
under continued police pressure, or even to show themselves fully aware of
the difficulties faced by such witnesses and the pressures to which they
might have been subjected in detention'.[230] It is still not too late for the
judiciary to review its attitude; and it may be predicted that the institution
of indefinite detention for purposes of interrogation will not long survive a
bloody-minded decision from the court on the use of detainee statements
and evidence in political trials.

Detention of Witnesses (s 31)

The power to order the detention of a potential witness vests in the
attorney-general. If he is of the opinion that any person likely to give
material evidence for the state in any criminal proceedings relating to
certain specified offences may be tampered with or be intimidated, or that
such person may abscond, or whenever he deems it to be in the interests of
such person or the administration of justice, he may issue a warrant for
the arrest and detention of such person.[231] The specified offences are those
listed in a schedule to the Act[232] which in general covers sedition, carrying
on the activities of an unlawful organisation,[233] terrorism, subversion,
sabotage (and related offences),[234] furthering the aims of communism[235]
and treason. Any conspiracy, incitement or attempt to commit any of
these offences, except treason, is also covered. A person arrested by virtue
of a warrant issued by the attorney-general must be taken as soon as
possible to the place specified in the warrant and detained there, or at any
other place determined by the attorney-general from time to time, in
accordance with regulations made by the Minister of Justice. The
detainee will be held in detention for a period terminating on the day on
which the criminal proceedings in question are concluded[236] unless the
attorney-general orders that he be released earlier or unless no charge
sheet has been lodged or indictment served within a period of six months
from the date upon which the detainee was arrested. In the latter case, he
must be released on the day on which the period of six months expires.[237]
A person unfortunate enough to have evidence to give in a trial
concerning one or more of the specified offences may therefore be held in

---

[228] 1983 (1) SA 576 (C).
[229] The court may even have to reject the evidence of a short-term detainee when the
methods of interrogation have been severe enough to raise doubts about its credibility.
[230] J van den Berg op cit 260.   [231] Section 31(1).   [232] Schedule 3.
[233] Made an offence by s 13(1)*(a)*(iv) of the Act.
[234] As defined in s 54 of the Act.
[235] As defined in s 55 of the Act.
[236] Which, it is submitted, will not include the period during which an appeal is being
pursued.
[237] Section 31(3).

isolation and interrogated for the duration of the trial and, even where no trial materialises, for a maximum period of six months. Detention in South Africa is not reserved for persons thought to be subversive but may be applied to those who are thought to know about subversives, even though they themselves are entirely innocent. It is dangerous not just to speak or do 'evil', but to see or hear it as well.

The question arises whether the decision of the attorney-general to invoke this remarkable power of arrest and detention may be attacked in court on the basis that there are no grounds, in the objective sense, to justify that decision. A detainee might argue, for example, that he has no relevant evidence to give, or that the evidence which he can give does not relate to a specified offence. He might also argue, where this is the reason for detaining him, that he is not likely to abscond or be tampered with; or that these dangers can be prevented by other less drastic means. If he does so argue, does the court have the power to enquire into the basis of the attorney-general's decision? This question was answered adversely to a detainee held under the '180-day' detention law,[238] a similarly worded predecessor to the current provision. Marais J decided in *Singh v Attorney- General, Transvaal*[239] that the legislature intended the attorney- general to be the dominus of the entire proceedings, that *his opinion* that the prerequisites of the detaining power are satisfied in a particular case is the relevant criterion of a proper exercise of that power, and that the section does not therefore prescribe criteria which have to be objectively satisfied. What this means is that in order to become a victim of this detention power, you need not be an actual witness to an actual offence, but that you need only be *thought* to be a witness to an apprehended offence.

Even though the power to detain is premised on the attorney-general's 'opinion' that the detainee is a potential witness, and even though conventional legal wisdom holds that bad faith or improper purpose or considerations are the only invalidating grounds in such cases, *Singh's* case ought to be reversed. The more recent decisions in Britain, reviewed above in relation to other powers of detention,[240] turn on the question of whether the matter in respect of which the opinion has to be formed is susceptible to judicial evaluation. If an exercise of discretion relates to matters of broad policy which do not lend themselves to relatively clear-cut court evaluation, the decision-maker's judgment will not be evaluated by reference to objective facts. On the other hand, where the prerequisites for the exercise of power lend themselves to hard-and-fast determination, the court will examine the facts to ascertain whether they could reasonably form a basis for the decision arrived at. Into what category do the prerequisites for detention fall in the present case?

According to the wording of the provision authorising the detention of witnesses there are two matters on which the attorney-general must be satisfied: (1) that the detainee can give material evidence for the state in a

---

[238] Section 215*bis* of the now repealed Criminal Procedure Act 56 of 1955.
[239] 1967 (2) SA 1 (T). See also *Thuntsi v Attorney-General, Northern Cape* 1982 (4) SA 468 (NC).
[240] See particularly *Secretary of State for Education and Science v Tameside Metropolitan Borough Council* [1976] 3 All ER 665 (CA) 670–1.

trial involving a specified offence[241] and (2) that the detainee may abscond or be tampered with or intimidated or that it is in the interests of the detainee or the administration of justice that a detention should be ordered. The first matter is certainly not a question of broad policy; and whether the detainee has evidence to give which relates to a specified offence does seem to be capable of reasonably clear-cut determination. The question is essentially one of whether the material which the detainee can place before the court is relevant to a specified offence, that is, whether the evidence and the alleged offence are rationally linked. The second matter on which the attorney-general must be satisfied, though a blend of fact and policy, is not very different from bail decisions which are regularly given by the courts. In bail cases, courts do have to assess the danger that a person will abscond or interfere with state witnesses and this is not therefore something which has hitherto been regarded as non-justiciable. Even where the attorney-general acts on the ground that detention is required in the interests of the detainee (who is himself the best judge of that!) or of the administration of justice, the court seems capable of assessing his specific reasons for reaching such a conclusion. It follows that if a detainee challenges the detention on the basis that one or other of the requisite jurisdictional facts are not present, the court must investigate them and determine whether there was a reasonable basis for the attorney-general's decision.[242]

A witness detained under warrant issued by the attorney-general is also subject to a 'no-access' provision since the Act declares that except with the consent of the attorney-general (or a person to whom he has delegated the authority) and subject to such conditions as he may determine, no person other than one acting by virtue of his office in the service of the state, shall have access to the detainee.[243] While such a person may be held in isolation, and interrogated while so held by a person in the service of the state,[244] he must be visited in private not less than once a fortnight by a magistrate and a district surgeon.[245] Because the statutory purpose underlying the detention of witnesses is different from the intention ascribed to Parliament in the case of indefinite detention, the 'no-access' provision will be interpreted less rigidly. Thus in *S v Heyman*[246] the court, in relation to the similarly worded '180-day' law,[247] held that a detainee giving evidence in court when facing a charge of unlawful refusal to testify

---

[241] On a proper grammatical reading of s 31(1) this requirement is not conditional upon the attorney-general's opinion but rather independent of it. In *Singh's* case the court declined to hold that grammatically speaking only the second prerequisite (that the witness was likely to abscond et cetera) was a matter for his opinion.

[242] If the minister prevents the court from making an investigation into these questions by invoking state privilege under s 66, the court should find that the grounds for detention are not established. The ouster clause contained in s 31(7) does not preclude court action where the relevant jurisdictional facts are not present since, in their absence, the detainee cannot be said to 'be detained under subsection (1) . . .'.

[243] Section 31(4).

[244] It was held in *Gosschalk v Rossouw* 1966 (2) SA 476 (C) 489 that, subject to certain limitations, there is a common-law right to interrogate. The fact that such interrogations take place in isolation means that the considerations discussed under indefinite detention in relation to confessions, admissions and evidence are also applicable here.

[245] Section 31(5). An Inspector of Detainees is not required to make visits: s 45(1).

[246] 1966 (4) SA 598 (A).

[247] Section 215*bis* of the Criminal Procedure Act 56 of 1955.

was entitled to see a lawyer even though still technically a detainee. It
seems to follow clearly from the reasoning in *Heyman's* case that the
decision in *Schermbrucker v Klindt NO*,[248] that a detainee alleging
maltreatment could not be brought before a court to give evidence, will
not be applicable to detained witnesses since the statutory purpose of
preventing intimidation or abscondence could scarcely be frustrated by
such an appearance.[249] Nevertheless, because access to detained witnesses
and the conditions thereof are under the control of the attorney-general,
and the jurisdiction of the court excluded in respect of such consent or
conditions,[250] there are practical difficulties in the way of a detainee
bringing allegations of maltreatment to the attention of a court of law. If
despite these difficulties he succeeds, the court has power to order his
appearance to give evidence. It is astonishing that a person who is
detained simply because he is a potential witness does not have a right to
see a lawyer. Such access would help to prevent ill-treatment and would
not frustrate the purposes of detention.

The ouster clause just referred to also has the effect of precluding a
court of law from ordering the release of a detained witness or
pronouncing on the conditions under which he is held. As argued above
under indefinite detention, this will not preclude the court from taking
appropriate action in respect of illegal treatment such as the grant of an
interdict against the offending officials. The conditions governing a
detained witness are governed in part by regulations made by the
Minister of Justice. According to the regulations currently in force[251] the
detainee is entitled, subject to the provisions of the Act and to the
regulations made thereunder, to be treated as an awaiting-trial prisoner.
However, the regulations specifically provide that the right to communicate by letter with persons outside and the right to purchase stationery
and literature is subject to official approval. It follows that there is power
to make the detainee's isolation virtually absolute. Courts of law are
specifically prohibited from pronouncing upon the validity of the
regulations.[252]

A detained witness, for purposes of s 191 of the Criminal Procedure
Act,[253] is deemed to have attended the criminal proceedings in question as
a witness for the state for the whole of his period of detention.[254] The effect
of this is to entitle him to expenses as a witness.

The 'No Bail' Clause (s 30)

If a person has been arrested on a charge of having committed an
offence referred to in Schedule 3 of the Act,[255] the attorney-general may

[248] Supra.
[249] See A S Mathews *Law, Order and Liberty in South Africa* 144.
[250] Section 31(7).
[251] GN No R1281 (*GG* 5228 of 16 July 1976). These regulations remain in force by virtue
of s 73(2) of the Act.
[252] Section 31(7). This does not mean that the regulations cannot be enforced by the
courts: see *Cassiem v Commanding Officer, Victor Verster Prison* 1982 (2) SA 547 (C).
[253] Act 51 of 1977.   [254] Section 31(6).
[255] The offences listed in Schedule 3 have been described above in the discussion of the
detention of witnesses. In brief these offences are sedition, carrying on the activities of an
unlawful organisation, terrorism, subversion, sabotage, furthering the aims of communism,
and treason.

order that such person shall not be released on bail or warning[256] if he considers such an order necessary in the interests of the security of the state or the maintenance of law and order.[257] Once such an order has been made, no person shall be released on bail or warning notwithstanding the provisions of any other law.[258] The only exception to this is that the attorney-general may himself withdraw an order before its expiration.[259] The chief effect of this section is to withdraw from the courts their traditional power to order release of an accused person on bail or otherwise.[260]

When a person arrested for one of the specified offences applies to be released on bail or on warning, and the prosecutor informs the court or presiding officer that the matter has been referred to the attorney-general for an order prohibiting release on bail or warning, such person shall not be released on bail or warning pending the decision of the attorney-general; but if such order is not issued within fourteen days of the date on which the court or presiding officer has been so informed, the person in question may again apply for release on bail or warning and the court may then order release.[261] A telegraphic copy of an order by the attorney-general prohibiting release on bail or warning, is regarded as prima facie proof of the contents thereof.[262]

Though the provision in question removes the power of the court to order release of an accused on bail or warning, this is only so where the accused has been arrested on a charge of having committed an offence listed in Schedule 3. This is a precondition and the issue of an order by the attorney-general without it being satisfied would be illegal.[263] In *S v Ramgobin*[264] the court held that the mere naming of the offences with which the arrested person was to be charged is insufficient and that being charged with one or more of the specified offences means a *decision* by the appropriate authority to lay such a charge or charges against the accused. The court appeared to accept that the decision to charge could be reached by methods falling short of the actual service of an indictment but did not specify what these less formal methods might be. It is clear, however, that an order by an attorney-general prohibiting bail will not be valid unless preceded by at least two jurisdictional facts, namely, (1) the arrest of the accused on a Schedule 3 offence and (2) a clear decision to charge the accused with such an offence. These jurisdictional requirements are prerequisites to the 'issue' of an order denying bail. The case of *S v*

---

[256] Under the Criminal Procedure Act 51 of 1977.

[257] Section 30(1). A clause in similar form was introduced into the Internal Security Act 44 of 1950 (s 12A) in 1976. This clause, in turn, had predecessors which are discussed in A S Mathews *Law, Order and Liberty* 156–8.

[258] Section 30(2)(a).   [259] Section 30(3).

[260] This power has also been withdrawn in respect of certain non-security offences: see s 61 of the Criminal Procedure Act 51 of 1977 read with Part III of Schedule 2. In a judgment of 29 March 1984 (as yet unreported) the Witwatersrand Local Division held that the section did not apply to a person once convicted, since he cannot then be described as an 'arrested' person. It follows that the attorney-general may not refuse bail pending the hearing of an appeal.

[261] Section 30(2)(b).   [262] Section 30(4).

[263] Once the accused has been convicted, the attorney-general may not withhold bail pending the hearing of an appeal, since a convicted person is no longer an 'arrested' person in terms of s 30(1) (unreported judgment of the WLD of 29 March 1984).

[264] 1985 (3) SA 587 (N).

Baleka[265] demonstrates that 'issue' does not have a clear legal meaning and that an order denying bail which is served on the accused immediately after the indictments are handed over may be invalid as having been issued prior to the charge.[266] Much more important than this technical point are two further issues raised by *Baleka* and *Ramgobin*. The first is whether there is not a further jurisdictional fact, which must precede the attorney-general's order, that the accused should have been afforded the opportunity to make representations against the denial of bail. Only one judge in *Baleka* decided that affording a hearing (audi alteram partem) was a prerequisite to the validity of the attorney-general's order; but his reasons for demanding a hearing are more convincing than the majority's denial of this basic right. The second issue was alluded to in *Ramgobin* and it relates to the question of the power of the court to review the decision of the attorney-general to refuse bail. *Ramgobin* suggests, correctly it is submitted, that upon review of the attorney-general's order the court may investigate and pronounce upon the factual basis for the jurisdictional requirements of the arrest of the accused and the preferment of a charge for a scheduled offence. In his judgment Friedmann J expresses the opinion that the court may set aside the attorney-general's order 'where the "decision to charge" was made in relation to allegations of conduct which were not reasonably capable of constituting the offence with which the appellants were charged'.[267] While there is some authority, therefore, for an objective assessment by the courts of the facts alleged to constitute the basis of the jurisdictional prerequisites of an order denying bail, it is not clear that the courts will so assess the attorney-general's belief that the interests of justice or state security require the issue of his order. Such a function was assumed by the court in *S v Hartman*[268] but the wording of the relevant provision was different. Nevertheless, it is arguable that because the attorney-general does not occupy a policy-making office, and the discretion which he exercises is of a prosecutorial kind, the court should be prepared to hear argument that the interests of justice and security do not require, in the case before it, that the court be deprived of its normal authority to grant or refuse bail. There is a growing tendency to subject prosecutorial discretion to judicial review[269] and this extended jurisdiction seems appropriate where the attorney-general exercises a professional function. While the court probably cannot investigate the factual basis of his belief that justice or security require the issue of an order, it certainly could evaluate its rationality in relation to his stated reasons.

In conclusion, it seems shameful that the legislature has not responded to the condemnation of statutory interference with the court's traditional power to determine bail by the judges in *Ramgobin* and by the Judge President in the later case of *S v Ramgobin*.[270]

---

[265] 1986 (1) SA 361 (T).

[266] Two judges held that the service of the notice withdrawing bail was not premature but Preiss J found (and could be upheld by the Appellate Division) that the notices were issued as soon as they were handed to an officer for official implementation.

[267] *S v Ramgobin* (supra) 594.

[268] 1968 (1) SA 278 (T). On this case, see A S Mathews *Law, Order and Liberty in South Africa* 157 and (1968) 86 *SALJ* 234.

[269] Lawrence Baxter *Administrative Law* 333.   [270] 1985 (4) SA 130 (N).

CHAPTER 8

Banning

The words 'ban' and 'banning' are not official, legal terms but popular descriptions of arbitrary forms of administrative action. Such action may be taken in South Africa against organisations, publications, individuals and assemblies; that is to say, the government may ban an organisation, a publication, an individual or a meeting. The popular words 'ban', 'banning' and 'banning order' accord with general usage in public discussion, especially in the press; they will therefore be used below alongside similar expressions such as 'proscribe' (in respect of organisations and publications) and 'restrict' (in respect of individuals).[1] The word 'ban' and those derived from it are also preferable because less euphemistic than the official legal jargon.

Until quite recently the guiding principle of government action in the sphere of internal security has been 'if it moves, ban it'. In the eighties the banning of individuals has become less common and has virtually been replaced by the rule 'if it moves, detain it'. Only one organisation has been banned in the eighties,[2] though all those formerly banned remain unlawful. Publications and meetings continue to be banned at a steady rate. Despite the lower frequency of the banning of individuals and groups at the present time, the banning power remains a formidable instrument in the government security arsenal quite capable of full revival at any moment. It will therefore receive extensive treatment below.

I The Banning of Organisations

The power to proscribe an organisation is conferred on the Minister of Law and Order by the Internal Security Act of 1982.[3] It has existed as a permanent, peace-time power since 1950 when the Suppression of Communism Act[4] was introduced in that year. The power was supplemented by the Unlawful Organisations Act of 1960[5] mainly on account of a rare government squeamishness about using an Act ostensibly directed at communism to outlaw the organisations that became the principal vehicles of African nationalism.[6] By the time that the Internal Security Act was passed in 1982 some thirty-two organisa-

---

[1] The official terminology is too clumsy for general use: for example the law grants the power to declare an organisation to be an unlawful organisation, and to prohibit the printing, publication or dissemination of a publication.

[2] The Congress of South African Students was banned by GN No R 1977 (*GG* 9914 of 28 August 1985).

[3] Act 74 of 1982, s 4 (referred to below as 'the Act').

[4] Act 44 of 1950 which was subsequently re-named the Internal Security Act 44 of 1950.

[5] Act 34 of 1960.

[6] Both the African National Congress and the Pan-Africanist Congress were banned under the Unlawful Organisations Act.

tions had been banned, including the South African Communist Party, the African National Congress (ANC) and the Pan-Africanist Congress (PAC). In 1977, in a 'night of the long knives operation' eighteen organisations were eliminated by a stroke of the official pen. The victims of this operation were mainly black groups, including the South African Students Organisation (SASO). However, whites were also affected in the banning of the Christian Institute headed by Dr Beyers Naudé (who was also banned during that year). The Internal Security Act of 1982 has repealed the earlier legislation authorising banning but retains in force all the bannings of organisations that took place under that legislation.[7] There has been only one' banning under the 1982 Act but there are constant rumblings about the United Democratic Front and new proscription orders could be imminent.

Under present law the minister may declare any organisation unlawful if he 'is satisfied' that it engages in activities which endanger the security of the state or the maintenance of law and order, or that it propagates the principles or promotes the spread of communism, or that it engages in activities for the achievement of any of the objects of communism, or that it is controlled by an organisation which is committed to any of these objectives or that it carries on (or was established to carry on) the activities of an unlawful organisation.[8] The banning (declaration of unlawfulness) must be by notice in the *Gazette*[9] and will not be invalid because the organisation in question is dissolved before the notice takes effect.[10] The requirement that the minister must be 'satisfied' that the specified prerequisites for banning are present in a given case confronts us once again with a typical subjective discretion clause. This same formula appearing in the banning clauses of the earlier statute was held by the court to preclude judicial investigation into the objective existence of the grounds relied upon by the empowered official.[11] The minister's decision, apart from procedural failures, is susceptible to attack only on the basis that he acted mala fide, mindlessly or for improper considerations. The fact that no minister has ever been found to have so acted, and that the secrecy with which ministers can legally cloak their decisions means that they never will, illustrates that the alleged basis of attack is one of those carefully nurtured fictions of the law designed to suggest that the courts are still exercising a supervisory function over ministerial action. Theoretically the mala fides et cetera ground of review does exist; in practice it is almost worthless in the security field and it is time for the judiciary to transform it into a more effective instrument of control or to acknowledge the fictional character which it has been accorded.

'Is satisfied' and similar clauses were examined in the earlier chapter on

---

[7] Definition of 'unlawful organisations' in s 1(xxii).

[8] Section 4(1) which has been paraphrased in the text. Under s 6 the minister is empowered to order an 'authorised officer' (see definition in s 1(1)) to conduct a far-reaching investigation into an organisation that he suspects ought to be declared unlawful. The authorised officer has virtually unrestricted powers of entry, search, seizure and questioning under s 6(3). The minister, without any derogation from his banning powers, may warn any organisation to desist from specified activities (s 70).

[9] Such a notice may be withdrawn by the minister by like procedure: s 4(3).

[10] Section 4(5).

[11] *South African Defence and Aid Fund v Minister of Justice* 1967 (1) SA 31 (C).

detention[12] where it was argued that such clauses do not necessarily prohibit court examination of the relationship between the minister's decision and the objective facts. The arguments presented there are relevant in the present context since the matters on which the minister has to be satisfied when he bans an organisation, for example, the question whether the organisation has fostered the objectives of communism (which is defined in the Act) or whether it is carrying on the activities of a banned organisation, are susceptible to relatively clear-cut determination. The acceptance of those arguments will involve the court in unaccustomed activism in the sphere of security law. Unfortunately, the appeal court judgment in *Minister of Law and Order v Hurley*[13] is confined to the phrase 'has reason to believe' and does not signal a new judicial approach to differently worded subjective discretion clauses. It is a consequence of the narrow approach adopted by the court in *Hurley* that organisations may be banned not for what they do but for what the minister says they are doing.

Though the minister may proscribe an organisation without notice to it,[14] prior to banning he must have considered a factual report and recommendation on the organisation by an advisory committee appointed under the Act.[15] The advisory committee will consist of three members appointed by the State President on the recommendation of the Minister of Justice.[16] Two of its members are required to have certain legal qualifications.[17] The advisory committee is required by the Act to enquire into all matters relating to the organisation which are considered relevant to a decision as to whether it should be banned and to furnish the minister with a factual report and recommendation.[18] It must consider all facts and representations submitted to it in writing and, in its discretion, may hear oral evidence from any person.[19] The chairman, by written notice to the organisation or one of its office-bearers, is required to inform it of a right to submit written representations and to present oral evidence unless the committee decides that this is not in the public interest.[20] Under earlier legislation, the courts decided that the organisation in question did not have a right to be heard by the investigating committee.[21] The legal position concerning a hearing is somewhat better under present law in that a hearing will be accorded unless the committee decides that this will be contrary to the public interest. The circumstances will indeed have to be exceptional to bring a fair hearing into conflict with the public interest.

---

[12] Chapter 6.
[13] 1986 (3) SA 568 (A). The lower-court judgment (*Hurley v Minister of Law and Order* 1985 (4) SA 709 (D)) was also restricted in its application.
[14] Section 4(1).
[15] Section 7(1).
[16] Section 7(2).
[17] These are specified in s 7(2) and are the same as those for review committees discussed in chapter 6 on detention.
[18] Section 7(3). The decision of two members constitutes the decision of the committee: s 8(1). The procedure of an advisory committee is determined by the chairman (s 8(2)) and it has power to subpoena witnesses and administer the oath (s 8(4), (5) and (12)). The secretarial work is performed by public servants designated by the Minister of Justice (s 9).
[19] Section 7(4).
[20] Section 7(5).
[21] *South African Defence and Aid Fund v Minister of Justice* 1967 (1) SA 263 (A).

It is undesirable, moreover, that the exercise of so basic a right of civilised systems of jurisprudence should depend on the discretion of the investigating committee. The language of the provision which confers this discretion upon the committee is in subjective terms[22] and this suggests that an adverse decision on the right to be heard will be reviewable only on that mythical ground of mala fides or improper purpose. Because the advisory committee operates in secret[23] and its reasons for refusing a hearing are not therefore discoverable, this ground for challenging a decision will be even more mythical than usual. A further obstacle is that the Act prohibits the courts from pronouncing upon the functions or recommendations of an advisory committee;[24] but this should not disarm a court of law in the unlikely event of there being evidence of mala fides or improper purpose.[25]

While the minister is required to consider the report of the advisory committee on the organisation in question before banning it, he is not obliged to give effect to its recommendations and may declare an organisation unlawful irrespective of, or contrary to, its advice.[26] If he does ban the organisation, any office-bearer of the organisation, by a written request submitted within fourteen days of the publication of the banning in the *Gazette*, may require the minister to furnish reasons for his action together with so much of the information which induced him to issue the banning order as, in the opinion of the minister, may be disclosed; and the minister, in responding to the request for reasons, will have to avoid the vague and general terms in which he has customarily informed security victims of the basis of official action against them.[27] The office-bearer may also request by petition, within the same fourteen-day period, or where reasons have been requested, within fourteen days after the date of the minister's statement setting out the reasons, that the minister submit the declaration of unlawfulness for review.[28] The minister is then obliged, unless proceedings have been brought in a court of law to declare the notice invalid,[29] to refer the papers[30] to the Chief Justice of South Africa for review. The Chief Justice, or a judge of the Appellate Division designated by him (whose decision may not be 'pronounced upon' in a court of law), must then consider the papers and is empowered

---

[22] Section 7(5)(a) employs that standard phrase of subjectively conferred discretion—'is of the opinion'.

[23] See particularly, s 8(7) (prohibiting appearance of a legal representative before an advisory committee), s 8(8) (limiting attendance to authorised persons), s 8(9) (prohibiting disclosure of deliberations or recommendations) and s 8(10) (limiting the right to inspection of records).

[24] Section 8(11).

[25] A committee acting mala fides et cetera can hardly be said to have exercised a function under the Act.

[26] Section 10(1) and (2).

[27] Section 10(3) and (4) and *Nkondo & Gumede v Minister of Law and Order* 1986 (2) SA 756 (A). If the minister furnishes inadequate reasons, the organisation should be entitled to a mandamus or possibly a declaration that the banning is unlawful.

[28] Section 11(1) and (2).

[29] Section 12(3) abolishes the review procedure in such a case.

[30] The notice declaring the organisation unlawful, the statement of his reasons for issuing the notice and the information on which the decision was based, the factual report and recommendations of the advisory committee, the petition and any additional information which the minister deems necessary.

to set the minister's decision aside if satisfied that he has exceeded the powers conferred by the Act, acted in bad faith or based his decision on factors other than those contemplated by the enabling provision.[31]

The provision of a review procedure where an organisation is banned is certainly an improvement; but as a safeguard it is seriously flawed. One of the flaws in this procedure has been rendered less disturbing by the judgment in *Nkondo & Gumede v Minister of Law and Order*.[32] Prior to that decision, ministers were accustomed to giving bald and uninformative reasons for security actions such as banning. In effect, the victims of bans and detentions were told that they had been naughty and, if they were unable to disprove their unspecified naughtiness, the action taken against them could not be challenged. In *Nkondo & Gumede* the court was not prepared to accept vague and uninformative reasons and ministers will have to be more precise and helpful when imposing bans on organisations in the future. Of course, much depends on what the courts will regard as an adequate statement of reasons. It seems that the minister's reasons should be clear and detailed enough to enable the organisation to join issue with him and to rebut his case that there are grounds for banning it. The review judge has to decide whether to uphold or set aside the banning purely on the papers which will contain unverified information submitted to him by the minister. This review will be a farce if the banned organisation is given sketchy reasons and is required to draw up its review petition in ignorance of the minister's real case. It appears to follow that the court has the power to order the minister to provide adequate reasons and to declare the banning invalid if he fails to do so.

Even on the assumption that the minister will in future be required to give precise and detailed reasons for a ban, the review procedure remains unsatisfactory as a safeguard against abuse of power. The probability of the Chief Justice ruling that the minister acted in bad faith or that he exceeded the over-generous grant of powers to him by the Act may be ruled out as fanciful. A finding that the minister based his decision to ban on factors other than those contemplated by the Act (the only other ground of review) is almost equally remote given the wide language of the empowering clause and the fact that the Chief Justice cannot go beyond the papers submitted to him. The limited grounds for upsetting a ban suggest that the review safeguard was not intended to be very effective.[32a]

An organisation that is banned may elect to challenge the banning in a court of law instead of making use of the review procedure just described.[33] The Act imposes a time-limit on court challenge to a banning order and declares that proceedings must be brought within fourteen days of the gazetting of the ban and, unless the party bringing the proceedings

---

[31] Section 11(4) and (6). If the Chief Justice sets the banning aside he must furnish the minister with reasons (s 11(7)). If he confirms the minister's order he endorses the minister's statement of reasons to the effect that no grounds exist for setting the banning aside.

[32] 1986 (2) SA 756 (A).

[32a] In a recent comparative review of the procedure for banning organisations, the South African procedure is found to be inadequate and ineffective: see Gerrit Pienaar 'Die Reg Insake Verbode Organisasies—Regvergelykende Studie' (1986) 1 *SA Public Law* 71, 73–4, 98.

[33] As we have seen s 12(3) makes the review by the Chief Justice and court proceedings strictly alternative.

is not at fault, concluded within twelve months of that date.[34] However, court challenge to a banning is likely to yield as little as the statutory review procedure before the Chief Justice. Since the judiciary, even in *Hurley*, has not altered the doggedly subjective reading that it has given to 'is satisfied' and 'is of the opinion' clauses in the security field, an organisation seeking to reverse its proscription in a court of law faces the insuperable task of showing that the minister acted mala fides, for improper considerations or mindlessly. The only alternative basis of attack on a banning order is procedural irregularity—proof, that is, that the requirements of the Act have not been observed in outlawing the organisation. This alternative basis is likely to be even less fruitful than the other. The authorities usually take care to observe the not very burdensome requirements of the Act for banning. But even where there has been a procedural slip, the possibility of upsetting the ban is remote. Much of the banning process takes place in secret—especially the work of the advisory committee—thereby limiting the chance of discovering procedural errors. The courts themselves have hardly aided the chances of discovery by refusing, in *Real Printing Co (Pty) Ltd v Minister of Justice*,[35] to order the minister to produce documents to show that a reference to an advisory committee had actually taken place. Moreover, it is possible that procedural failures involving the advisory committee are beyond judicial correction since the Act declares that courts of law may not pronounce upon the functions or recommendations of an advisory committee.[36] Finally, even where the luckless organisation does prove a procedural error, it can always be corrected by a subsequent regular banning.

We may conclude that an organisation banned by the minister has a choice between two discouraging alternatives. It may elect to refer the matter to the Chief Justice for review but this procedure, for reasons given earlier, is likely to yield little joy even though it has been improved by the *Nkondo & Gumede* ruling that ministerial reasons must not be in vague and general terms. If the organisation goes directly to the courts, they will put upon it the impossible task of proving that the minister acted mindlessly or dishonestly. The supplicant to the courts faces this crushing burden because the Appellate Division in *Hurley* was not prepared to extend its ruling to grants of power prefaced by phrases like 'is satisfied' or 'is of the opinion'. The organisation does not even have any political recourse since, although the minister must report a banning to Parliament within fourteen days,[37] the iron grip of the ruling party on Parliament deprives this reporting duty of any value.

There is one power which the minister may exercise in relation to unlawful organisations that appears absolute in nature. The Act gives him the power, to be exercised by notice in the *Gazette*, to declare that 'any body, organisation, group or association of persons, institution, society or movement' specified in the notice and which in his opinion exists, or

---

[34] Section 12(1). The operation of a banning notice may not be suspended or postponed by a court pending the outcome of the proceedings (s 12(2)*(b)*).
[35] 1965 (2) SA 782 (C).
[36] Section 8(11).
[37] Or, if Parliament is not in session, within fourteen days of the commencement of the next session.

existed at any time after 7 April 1960, was at all times subsequent to a date specified by him (not being earlier than 8 April 1960) either an organisation declared unlawful under the Act or one which remains unlawful in terms of the provisions of the Act.[38] In short, the minister may legally equate any organisation with an unlawful organisation. The effect of the declaration is that in any criminal proceedings the specified organisation is deemed to exist or to have existed since the specified date and to be (or to have been since the specified date) the unlawful organisation.[39] Any act or omission proved with reference to the specified organisation is deemed to be proved with reference to the unlawful organisation with which it is equated.[40] Office-bearers of the specified organisation, for purposes of criminal proceedings, are deemed to have become office-bearers of the unlawful organisation on the day immediately after the specified date.[41] Apart from the fact that the minister may withdraw such a notice in his absolute discretion,[42] there may be no escape for a person touched by this statutory deeming. The review proceedings applicable to a declaration of unlawfulness are not available in this case.[43] However, it is arguable that since the Act declares that the one organisation is deemed to be the same as the other 'in any criminal proceedings', the deeming order itself may be challenged before a civil court as an improper exercise of power, at least on the ground that it was mala fides or based on improper or irrelevant considerations. If *all* courts are conclusively bound by the ministerial declaration, the possibility of an unjust conviction is real and frightening. Even if they are not, that possibility remains real in view of the limited basis for challenging ministerial orders.

The Consequences of Banning an Organisation

(a) Upon the organisation

Upon a declaration of unlawfulness the organisation in question ceases to have a legal existence. All its property, including rights and documents, vest in a liquidator designated by the Minister of Justice.[44] If the organisation was registered it ceases to be registered and the officer in charge of the register is obliged to remove its name therefrom.[45] The liquidator is required to take possession of all property vested in him, to determine whether the assets are sufficient to pay the debts of the organisation, and thereafter to wind up the organisation either as a solvent or insolvent organisation according to that determination.[46] Any

---

[38] Section 4(2)*(a)*.
[39] Ibid.   [40] Section 4(2)*(b)*.
[41] Section 4(2)*(c)*.
[42] Section 4(3).
[43] Section 11(1). A simple way for the minister to avoid the review procedure is to declare an organisation to be the same as an already banned organisation instead of declaring it unlawful directly.
[44] Section 13(1)*(b)*. The designation of a liquidator is not invalid or ineffective because the organisation was dissolved before his designation or before it was declared unlawful or because it has no assets: s 13(2). Provision for the liquidator's remuneration and the conditions of his appointment by the minister is made in s 13(3). Under s 1(ix) 'liquidator' includes a person acting under the written authority of the designated liquidator.
[45] Section 13(1)*(c)*.
[46] See, generally, s 14.

balance remaining after the payment of debts must be paid into the State
Revenue Fund.[47] For purposes of performing his functions, the liquidator
may exercise the same sweeping powers of investigation that are
conferred[48] upon an authorised officer appointed by the minister prior to a
declaration of unlawfulness.[49] The liquidator is empowered to receive and
retain communications addressed to the organisation and may require the
postmaster to cause all postal articles so addressed to be delivered to
him.[50] If so directed by the minister, the liquidator is required to compile
a list of persons who are, or at any time before the commencement of the
Act were, office-bearers, officers, members, or active supporters of the
organisation.[51]

An unlawful organisation is legally dead not just in the sense that it is
wound up but also in the sense that it is a criminal offence to carry on its
activities or to perform certain prescribed acts which would constitute a
continuation of its affairs.[52] The prohibited acts and activities, in
summary, are the following:

(a) becoming or continuing to be an office-bearer, officer or member of
     the organisation or performing any act in any such capacity;[53] an
     intention to further the aims of the banned organisation is an
     essential part of this crime.[54]

(b) carrying, possessing or displaying anything indicating membership
     of, or the holding of office in, or association with the organisation.[55]
     This prohibition is extremely wide and under the similar provision of
     earlier legislation persons were convicted for retaining in a house
     photographs indicating a role in the ANC in its lawful days[56] and of
     possessing a membership card (and other documents) of the ANC.[57]

(c) contributing or soliciting anything for the direct or indirect benefit of
     the organisation.[58]

(d) taking part in any activity of the organisation or carrying on, in its
     direct or indirect interest, any activity in which it could have
     engaged.[59] The breadth of the prohibition on continuing an activity

---

[47] Section 14(3).
[48] By s 6(3) and (4).
[49] Section 14(12). The powers, in brief, are those of entry, search, seizure and
questioning.
[50] Section 14(11).
[51] Section 14(10). Office-bearers and officers are defined in s 1(xi) and (xii) of the Act.
The significance of the list is discussed below.
[52] Section 13(1)(a) read with s 56(1)(a). This prohibition applies to members (past or
present) and to non-members: S v Mbele 1964 (4) SA 401 (N).
[53] Section 13(1)(a)(i). Proof of membership of, or support for, a banned organisation may
be facilitated by the presumptions in s 69(1) and (4) of the Act. On the similar presumptions
in the Internal Security Act 44 of 1950 (s 12), see S v Matsiepe 1962 (4) SA 708 (A); S v Nkosi
1961 (4) SA 320 (T) and S v Segone 1981 (1) SA 410 (T).
[54] S v Sisulu 1964 (1) PH H58 (T).
[55] Section 13(1)(a)(ii). The court in S v Pase 1986 (2) SA 303 (E) gave a wide meaning to
the prohibition on indicating any association with the banned organisation and held that
words conveying a mental or emotional association with it are covered.
[56] S v Calata 1961 (4) SA 303 (E).
[57] S v Myendi 1962 (4) SA 426 (N). This decision was wrong at the time because possession
was not then prohibited (cf the finding in S v Phiri 1961 (4) SA 348 (T)), but possession has
since been specifically prohibited.
[58] Section 13(1)(a)(iii).
[59] Section 13(1)(a)(iv).

in which the organisation 'could have engaged'[60] is somewhat narrowed by the requirement that the accused must have done this 'in the direct or indirect interest' of the organisation.

(e) promoting or encouraging the achievements of any of the objects of the organisation, *or any similar objects*, or any act likely to further such objects.[61] Before the words 'similar objects' were made part of the prohibition[62] the courts decided in *S v Nokwe*[63] that the independent promotion of the same objects as were pursued by a banned organisation is not a crime. The independent promotion of similar objects is now a crime provided that, as said in *Ndabeni v Minister of Law and Order*,[64] they are similar to objects that are distinctive of the particular organisation in question. (The court correctly decided that the propagation of black consciousness was not an objective distinctive of the banned organisation SASO.) *Ndabeni's* judgment is helpful in delimiting what would otherwise be an excessively wide prohibition. It has also been held that promoting the objects of a banned organisation (advocating, advising, defending or encouraging them) requires *communication* to some audience or readership.[65]

The cumulative effect of all these prohibitions designed to terminate the work and objectives of a banned organisation is staggering in two senses. First, the prohibitions are oppressive because they indiscriminately punish a host of major and minor acts as serious crimes.[66] A single act may constitute a breach of several of the prohibitions and each prohibition covers a large number of specific offences. It was pointed out in *S v Mbele*[67] that one of the prohibitions creates at least nine different offences and decided in *S v Xoswa*[68] that a conviction for two or more offences is possible even if the same evidence is required to establish all. In *Xoswa's* case the court demonstrated that becoming a member, pinning on a badge and soliciting a small donation for a banned organisation could expose the accused to thirty years in prison.[69] Secondly, the prohibitions are far too broad and appear to be aimed not just at terminating the work of the banned organisation but at putting an end to all activity of the same kind. Even though the courts have limited the scope of the prohibitions, they remain menacing as a citizen can never be quite sure that he will not be arrested and charged for some activity that resembles the work of some outlawed group.

(b) Upon Individuals

We have seen that the banning of an organisation has the immediate effect of making it a crime for all persons (whether former members or

[60] There is no indication how the ability of the organisation to have done the act in question is to be judged. Does 'could' mean 'legally could' according to its constitution or 'could' in the sense of physical ability?
[61] Section 13(1)*(a)*(v).
[62] By s 15 of the General Law Amendment Act 37 of 1963 amending s 2*(d)* of the Unlawful Organisations Act 34 of 1960.
[63] 1962 (3) SA 71 (T).   [64] 1984 (3) SA 500 (D).
[65] *R v Adams* 1959 (1) SA 646 (Spec Crim Ct).
[66] The penalty is imprisonment of up to ten years.
[67] 1964 (4) SA 401 (N) 411.   [68] 1964 (2) SA 459 (C).
[69] At 462. If banning were restricted to vicious terror groups there might be some justification for broadly worded prohibitions.

not) to continue its activities in any of the various ways prescribed by the Act. In addition, there may be further consequences, in the form of legal disabilities, for those individuals who did have a connection with the banned organisation. These consequences flow from the 'listing' procedure provided for by the Act. The Director of Security Legislation[70] is required to draw and keep up to date a list known as the consolidated list.[71] Among those who will be entered upon this list are (subject to compliance with the listing procedure described below) all persons whose names appear on a list compiled by the liquidator of an unlawful organisation or on a list compiled by an authorised officer on investigation by him of any organisation prior to its banning. Since these officers will only have compiled such lists if directed to do so by the minister,[72] the appearance of members and supporters of the banned organisation on the consolidated list and the attendant legal disabilities are not inevitable consequences of banning an organisation. However, the power to direct that lists be drawn up rests with the minister and has frequently been exercised by him. Several hundred persons are listed at the present time.

The persons reflected in the lists drawn up by the liquidator or authorised officer, and whose names will be entered upon the consolidated list in accordance with the procedure discussed below, are those who, in the judgment of the liquidator or authorised officer respectively, are office-bearers, officers, members or active supporters of the organisation in question, or who were so at any time before the commencement of the Act.[73] 'Office-bearer' means a member of the governing body or executive of the organisation, or of any of its branches, sections or committees or of any local, regional or subsidiary body forming part of it.[74] An 'officer' of the organisation means any person working for it or for a branch, section or committee of it or for a local, regional or subsidiary body forming part of it.[75] The terms 'members' and 'active supporters' are not specifically defined in the Act. The listing provisions, it is clear, cast a very wide net over persons associated with the unlawful organisation. The definition of 'officer' is wide enough to cover all persons working for the organisation, even in a menial capacity; and the inclusion of all persons who 'at any time' were connected with the organisation means that persons who have dropped out of the organisation before banning, or those who joined it when its activities may have been quite different, will also be entered upon the list. As we shall see below, the disabilities imposed on listed persons are severe.

Before a person whose name appears on the liquidator's or authorised officer's list is entered on the consolidated list (and so becomes liable to the statutory disabilities) he or she must be afforded an opportunity by the minister of showing that his or her name should not be so entered.[76] According to the principle of the decision in *Huyser v Louw NO*[77] the

---

[70] Who is defined in s 1(v) and appointed under s 2(2).
[71] Section 16(1).
[72] Under ss 14(10) and 6(2) respectively.
[73] Sections 6(2) and 14(10).
[74] Section 1(xi).   [75] Section 1(xii).
[76] Section 16(3)(a). This does not apply to persons transferred from the old to the new list in terms of the Internal Security Act of 1982.
[77] 1955 (2) SA 321 (T).

minister is obliged to acquaint that person with the substance of the information on which the listing is based, but not necessarily to allow inspection of the relevant documents. The most likely basis of any representations to the minister objecting to entry on the consolidated list is the absence of any of the specified connections with the banned organisation—that the objector was not an office-bearer, officer, member or active supporter of it. Only one additional ground is envisaged by the Act and that consists of proof by the objector that he or she neither knew, nor could reasonably be expected to know, that the activities, purposes, control or identity of the organisation were of such a nature that it was liable to be declared unlawful.[78] If the minister dismisses the objection, proceedings could be brought in a court of law[79] but would only succeed if the initiator of the proceedings proved either the lack of any connection with the organisation or absence of knowledge that it was liable to be declared unlawful. Proof that the organisation or the person concerned had not constituted a threat to security or to law and order will be legally irrelevant. The grounds for resisting inclusion on the consolidated list are extremely narrow.

The consolidated list drawn up by the director must include the name of every person whose name appeared, on the date immediately preceding the commencement of the Act, on the similar list provided for by the now repealed Internal Security Act of 1950 unless the minister decides that any such formerly listed name should be omitted.[80] Pending entry on to the new consolidated list, the Act preserves all the restrictions, prohibitions and disqualifications which applied to previously listed persons by virtue of the provisions of the 1950 Act.[81] If a previously listed person is not entered on the new consolidated list at the expiration of five years from the date of commencement of the 1982 Act, that person becomes 'de-listed' or 'un-listed' and all disabilities and disqualifications will then fall away.[82] In effect, therefore, the director has been given five years to transfer names from the old to the new list, and pending a decision on transfer, the persons in question remain listed for legal purposes. For some considerable time the bulk of names on the consolidated list will be transferred names—as yet only one organisation has been banned since the Internal Security Act of 1982 was passed. The most recent consolidated list[83] contains the names of over one hundred and twenty persons who have been entered but a number will remain legally listed (though not

[78] Section 16(3)(b).
[79] Such proceedings must be brought by way of action and within twelve months of the date upon which the name was entered on the list: s 17(2) and (3). As under the previous Act, there is nothing to prevent the court from granting an interdict to suspend the effect of a listing pending the proceedings: *Gool v Minister of Justice* 1955 (2) SA 682 (C). It seems that proceedings should be brought against the minister and the Director of Security Legislation. (*Tefu v Minister of Justice* 1953 (2) SA 61 (T) declared that the custodian of the list under the old Act need not be joined but he was not a statutory custodian like the present director.) In any prosecution under the Act, or in civil proceedings arising from its terms, it is presumed, unless the contrary is proved, that the name of a person entered on the consolidated list has been rightly entered—s 17(1). After twelve months the correctness of an entry may not be disputed, unless proceedings were brought in that period and have not been concluded.
[80] Section 16(2)(a).
[81] Section 16(2)(c).
[82] Section 16(2)(b).
[83] GN 1416 of 4 July 1986 (*GG* 10320 of 4 July 1986).

appearing in the consolidated list) until the five-year transition period has expired. There is no provision for representations or a hearing for persons who are transferred from the old to the new list.[84]

Persons who are entered upon the consolidated list by virtue of being on the list compiled by a liquidator or authorised officer need not be notified of the fact of entry by the director. The notification procedure applies only to persons whose entry on the list is due to conviction of certain specified offences or to detention or a personal banning order.[85] It follows that persons transferred from the old to the new list also need not be notified. It seems that the disabilities attendant upon listing take effect when the entry is made by the director, contrary to the common-law principle that the commencement date of an administrative action is the date on which it is notified to the individual.[86] This is so because not all persons appearing on the list have to be notified and the disabilities are made contingent upon the *appearance* of the name of the person in question upon the list.[87] The minister has power, on good cause being shown, to require the director to remove any name from the consolidated list.[88] If the name of a person appears on the consolidated list by virtue of that person's specified association with the unlawful organisation, and the notice declaring it unlawful is withdrawn, the director is required to remove such name from the list.[89] Provision is made for publication in the *Gazette* of the consolidated list, such publication to be made within twelve months of the date of commencement of the Act and thereafter at intervals not exceeding three years.[90] Removals of names must be gazetted.[91]

The Consequences of being Listed   A person whose name appears on the consolidated list is subject to a number of restrictions, disabilities or penalties. In passing, we should note that the consolidated list is not confined to persons who were members or active supporters of a banned organisation but also includes persons convicted of certain offences, who have been detained under s 28 or against whom an individual banning order is in force.[92] All these persons are subject to the pains and penalties to be discussed immediately below.

A person on the consolidated list may not be elected, or if he is elected, may not sit as a member of a house of Parliament unless the prior written approval of the minister or the leave of the house in question has been obtained.[93] Mere acceptance by a disqualified person of nomination for election to these bodies constitutes a criminal offence.[94] Where a person incapable of being elected, is elected as a member and the minister has

[84] Section 16(3)(a) requires that an opportunity for representations shall be given only to those who are entered on the consolidated list in terms of s 16(1)(a).

[85] Section 16(3)(c), which restricts the duty to notify to persons listed by virtue of s 16(1)(b) and (c).

[86] For the common law, see Lawrence Baxter op cit 367.

[87] See, for example, ss 22(1), 33(1) and 34(1).

[88] Section 16(4).   [89] Section 16(5).

[90] Section 16(6)(a).   [91] Section 16(6)(b).

[92] Section 16(1)(b) and (c).

[93] Section 33(2). This applies also to a person convicted of an offence under s 54, 55 or 56 of the Act. Section 97(c) of the Republic of South Africa Constitution Act 110 of 1983 brings the Houses of Delegates and Representatives within the scope of s 33(2).

[94] Section 56(1)(q). The penalty provided is imprisonment for a period not exceeding three years: s 56(1)(ii).

served notice upon the person in question and on the Speaker of the house concerned, his seat shall be deemed vacant.[95] Provision is also made for removal from a house of Parliament, at the instance of a committee of the house, of a sitting member whose name appears on the consolidated list and in respect of whom no circumstances exist justifying removal from the list.[96] Such action may be taken if the house in question approves the report of the committee and does not recommend that no action be taken and if the minister thereafter notifies the disqualified person (and the Speaker of the house) that as from a specified date he or she shall cease to be a member.[97] This procedure for removal of sitting members also applies to any person convicted of specified offences[98] or to a person who at any time, before or after the commencement of the Act is, or has been, an office-bearer, officer, member or active supporter of the Communist Party of South Africa or who has supported the objects of communism in certain specified ways.[99]

A person whose name appears on the consolidated list is disqualified from being admitted to practice as an advocate, attorney, notary or conveyancer and provision is made for the striking off of any such person from the appropriate roll of practitioners.[100] The same disqualification applies to persons convicted of certain offences under the now repealed Internal Security Act of 1950[101] or under certain sections of the present Act[102] unless the minister has signed a certificate that he has no objection to the admission of such person.[103]

Persons whose names appear in the consolidated list, or who are, or at any time before or after an organisation has been declared to be unlawful under the Act were, office-bearers, officers or members of the organisation, may be prohibited by notice published in the *Gazette* at the instance of the minister, even if they are not listed, from being or becoming office-bearers, officers or members of any particular organisation or of an organisation of a nature, class or kind specified in the notice or from making or receiving any contribution of any kind for its direct or indirect benefit or in any manner taking part in its activities.[104] Provision is made for exemption from these prohibitions by the written consent of the minister, the Director of Security Legislation acting under the authority of the minister or a magistrate acting in pursuance of the general or special instructions of the minister.[105] A notice[106] may not be issued by the minister in relation to any registered employers' organisation or trade union except after consultation with the Minister of Manpower.[107] The

---

[95] Section 33(3).
[96] Section 33(1).
[97] Ibid. The seat in question is deemed vacant as from the date of the notice.
[98] Any offence under s 54, 55 or 56.
[99] Section 33(1)(b) and (c).
[100] Section 34(1).
[101] The offences prescribed are those created by s 11(a), (b), (b)bis, (b)ter or (c) of Act 44 of 1950.
[102] Sections 54, 55 and 56.
[103] Section 34(1) and (2).
[104] Section 22(1). This prohibition may also be applied to persons upon whom any prohibition under the Act has been applied by notice (ie to banned persons).
[105] Section 22(1).   [106] Under s 22(1).
[107] Section 21(1).

minister has power to amend or withdraw any notice issued by him by like notice.[108] The Minister of Justice issued notices prohibiting membership, support et cetera of certain specified organisations and of certain organisations of a particular class or kind under the corresponding provision of the Internal Security Act of 1950,[109] and those notices[110] remain in force by virtue of a provision of the present Act.[111] The effect of the ministerial notices is that listed persons are prohibited from being office-bearers, officers or members of a fairly long list of specified organisations, of any organisation which engages in activities which are calculated to promote any of the objects of such specified organisations, or of any other organisation 'which in any manner propagates, defends, attacks, criticises or discusses any form of State or any principle or policy of the government of a State or which in any way undermines the authority of the Government of a State'.[112] The effect is to prevent listed persons from participating in any meaningful form of organisational life except in innocuous bodies of the church bazaar or knitting club type.

It is a criminal offence under the Act to record, reproduce, print, publish or disseminate any speech, utterance, writing or statement (or any extract or statement therefrom) made or produced, or purporting to have been made or produced, at any time by a person on the consolidated list unless the minister has consented thereto or unless this is done for the purposes of proceedings in a court of law.[113] This prohibition applies also to persons prohibited from attending gatherings[114] and to persons to whom it is specifically applied.[115] It follows that listed persons are removed both from the organisational life and the public dialogue of their own society.

A person whose name appears on the consolidated list commits an offence if he or she changes a place of residence or employment and fails forthwith to give notice thereof to an officer in charge of a police station[116] or, if when called upon by a peace-officer[117] to furnish his or her full name and address, fails to do so or furnishes a false name or address.[118]

The minister is authorised by the Act to impose certain restrictions (collectively and popularly known as 'banning') upon a person whose name appears upon the consolidated list.[119] Banning may be imposed on person for a variety of reasons other than the appearance of his or her name on a consolidated list and these restrictions are more appropriately discussed below under the banning of individuals.

[108] Section 21(2).

[109] Section 5ter of Act 44 of 1950.

[110] GN No R2130 (GGE 408 of 28 December 1962) as amended by GN No R1947 (GGE 958 of 27 November 1964), GN No R296 (GGE 443 of 22 February 1963). A person who breaches this prohibition is guilty of a crime and subject to a penalty of imprisonment for a period not exceeding three years: s 56(1)(i) and (ii).

[111] Section 73.

[112] For a detailed discussion of the effect of the ministerial notices, the reader should consult A S Mathews Law, Order and Liberty in South Africa 65–7.

[113] Section 56(1)(p). The penalty is imprisonment for a period not exceeding three years.

[114] Under s 20. The prohibition is more fully discussed below.

[115] Under s 23(1).   [116] Section 56(1)(d).

[117] As defined in the Criminal Procedure Act 51 of 1977.

[118] Section 56(1)(d) and (e). The penalty is imprisonment for a period not exceeding ten years.

[119] See ss 18, 19, 20, 21 and 22.

The foregoing survey of the consequences of being listed indicates that they are indeed severe and have the effect of preventing listed persons from being public representatives at the highest levels of government, from engaging in legal practice and from being active or influential in the public life of the society. This makes it all the more disturbing that listing may occur for reasons unconnected with actual threats to state security and without adequate safeguards for the protection of persons subject to this form of political and personal control.

Organisations—Controls and Restrictions other than Banning

Banning is the most severe of the curbs that may be placed on organisations that are perceived to be a threat to security or public order. A number of statutes impose or authorise less drastic restrictions which are appropriately considered here in conjunction with banning. Though some of these measures are not explicitly part of internal security legislation, they were undoubtedly designed to serve such a function.

The Affected Organisations Act of 1974[120]

This measure is not ostensibly concerned with public safety but it seems to have an underlying rationale of that kind.[121] Its main purpose is to prevent organisations which are declared 'affected' under its terms from receiving financial assistance from foreign sources. The State President is empowered, if he is satisfied that 'politics are being engaged in by or through an organisation'[122] in co-operation with or under the influence of an organisation or person abroad, to declare that organisation an affected organisation by notice in the *Gazette*.[123] Such a declaration may be preceded by an investigation by an authorised officer, appointed by the Minister of Justice,[124] with extensive powers of entry, search, seizure and questioning.[125] It must have been preceded by consideration by the minister of a factual report made by a committee of three magistrates (one of whom shall be a chief or regional magistrate) appointed by him. This factual report is clearly not binding on either the minister or the State President and, according to the decision in *South African Defence and Aid Fund v Minister of Justice*[126] concerning a similar provision in the Internal Security Act of 1950, may be compiled and submitted to the minister without adherence to the audi alteram partem rule. This questionable[127]

---

[120] Act 31 of 1974.
[121] In his second-reading introductory speech, the Deputy Minister of Justice linked foreign funds for local organisations with the terrorist campaign. *House of Assembly Debates*, 22 February 1974, col 1614.
[122] Organisation is widely defined in s 1 to include any kind of body, group or association whether incorporated or unincorporated and whether registered or not. Political parties are prohibited from receiving funds from abroad by the Prohibition of Foreign Financing of Political Parties Act 51 of 1968.
[123] Section 2(1). The words 'is satisfied' again imply, according to the prevailing judicial attitude in security matters, a subjective power of decision which may be challenged only on grounds of mala fides or improper purposes or considerations.
[124] Under s 6(1).
[125] Section 6(2). See also s 7 for the penalties for obstructing or refusing to assist the authorised officer.
[126] 1967 (1) SA 263 (A).
[127] See Lawrence Baxter op cit 572 et seq.

and heavily criticised judgment unfortunately still stands and deprives an organisation declared affected of a right to a fair hearing.

Once an organisation has been declared affected by the State President, it becomes an offence to ask for or canvass foreign money for the organisation, to receive or deal with money from abroad with the intention of handing it over or causing it to be used by the organisation, or to bring or assist in bringing money from abroad with a like intention or purpose.[128] Foreign money in the possession of an affected organisation, whether received before or after the commencement of the Act, may not be disposed of except by donation within one year to a charitable or other organisation designated by the minister.[129] Provision is also made by the Act for an order by the registrar of a division of the Supreme Court, at the request of the Registrar of Affected Organisations appointed by the minister,[130] preventing any person from disposing, except in accordance with a court order, of money in his possession which the registrar suspects is money which has been, is being or is to be dealt with in contravention of the Act.[131] There is provision too for an order of confiscation of such money in favour of the State on application by the Registrar of Affected Organisations to a division of the Supreme Court unless the person in question satisfies the court that the money does not fall under the proscriptions of the Act.[132]

The Registrar of Affected Organisations, or a person acting under his written authority, has power to enter upon the premises of an affected organisation and to inspect or take copies of documents relating to its finances.[133] He may require any person attached to an affected organisation to provide him with particulars of moneys received or paid out and must furnish such particulars to the minister.[134] The registrar is required to fix a financial year in respect of each affected organisation and to report to the minister on the moneys received and paid out by it within six weeks of the close of such financial year.[135] The minister must at least once a year table in Parliament reports and particulars received from the registrar.[136]

Among the organisations declared 'affected' under the Act are NUSAS[137] and the Christian Institute.[138] The most disturbing feature of the Act is that the governing party, itself a participant in the political processes of the country, decides which other groups shall be declared affected without the control of safeguards to ensure a fair, rational and independent judgment.

---

[128] Section 3(2). Money is defined in s 1 to include anything which can be cashed or converted into money. Section 5 prescribes as penalties a fine not exceeding ten thousand rands or imprisonment not exceeding five years (or both) for a first conviction and a fine not exceeding twenty thousand rands or imprisonment not exceeding ten years (or both) for a second or subsequent conviction. As to the meaning of foreign money, see M F Ackermann op cit 214.
[129] Section 3(3). The penalty for a contravention is as set out above (n 128).
[130] Under s 3(1).   [131] Section 4(1).   [132] Section 4(2).
[133] Section 3(2). He may even remove such documents if he thinks this to be desirable for practical reasons.
[134] Section 3(4).   [135] Section 3(3).   [136] Section 3(5).
[137] Proclamations R173, 174, 175 and 176 (GG 4389 of 13 September 1974).
[138] Proclamation No R132 (GG 4728 of 30 May 1975). The Christian Institute was subsequently declared an unlawful organisation.

The Parliamentary Internal Security Commission Act of 1976[139]

This Act establishes[140] a body known as the Parliamentary Internal
Security Commission which consists of not more than ten members of
Parliament appointed by the State President.[141] The function of the
commission is to investigate matters which, in the opinion of the State
President, affect internal security and which are referred to it by the State
President.[142] For purposes of carrying out its function, the commission (or
a committee to which it has delegated power)[143] is vested with extensive
power to summon and examine witnesses and to subpoena books,
documents and other objects.[144] The commission reports to the State
President and he is obliged to lay copies of its reports upon the tables of
the houses of Parliament.[145] However, provision is made for the State
President, after consultation with the Leader of the Opposition, to
dispense with the tabling requirement in respect of a report or a part
thereof.[146] It follows that the work of the commission may be kept secret.
It is a criminal offence to interrupt the proceedings of the commission or
to hinder or obstruct it in the performance of its functions.[147] The State
President is empowered to make regulations assigning additional internal
security duties and powers to the commission, providing for procedural
matters (including a quorum), the preservation of secrecy and providing
generally for the achievement of the purposes of the Act.[148]

If the Act were to be brought into force it could seriously endanger
organisational freedom as happened in the case of similar committees in
the United States in the McCarthy era.

II The Banning of Publications

The power to ban publications outright in the interests of internal
security or public safety is conferred by the Internal Security Act of
1982[149] and by the Publications Act of 1974.[150] The Defence Act of
1957[151] authorises the imposition of general censorship which could
include the outright banning of publications. Restrictions other than
banning on freedom of expression and information are dealt with
elsewhere.[152]

[139] Act 67 of 1976.
[140] Section 2. The history of the Act is briefly discussed by John Dugard *Human Rights and
the South African Legal Order* (Princeton Univ Press 1978) 173.
[141] Section 3(1). The commission has not yet been brought into being by appointment of
members under this section. Provision for the term of office of the commission, the
appointment of a chairman and a vice-chairman, and the like is made in s 3(2)–(7).
[142] Section 4(1). This may include existing or contemplated legislation or administrative
procedures: s 4(2).
[143] Section 6.
[144] Section 6. Penalties are provided for non-compliance or the giving of false evidence.
[145] Section 5(1).
[146] Section 5(2) and (3). The Act requires the tabling to be done by the Prime Minister but
this must now read State President in view of s 102(2)(b) of the Republic of South Africa
Constitution Act 110 of 1983. It seems that the Leaders of the Opposition in each house will
have to be consulted.
[147] Section 9. The penalty is a fine of not exceeding R600 or imprisonment not exceeding
six months.
[148] Section 12. No such regulations have been promulgated as yet.
[149] Act 74 of 1982.   [150] Act 42 of 1974.
[151] Act 44 of 1957.   [152] See chapter 9.

The Internal Security Act of 1982

The minister has the power, by notice in the *Gazette*, to prohibit the printing, publication or dissemination of any periodical publication or the dissemination of any other publication.[153] He may exercise this power *if satisfied* that the publication in question endangers state security or the maintenance of law and order, promotes communism or any of its objects, is (or was) published by a banned organisation or serves (or served) to promote the views of such an organisation, or encourages feelings of hostility between different population groups, or is a substitute for a publication previously banned by the minister.[154] The 'if satisfied' formula for the conferral of the banning power on the minister means, according to the prevailing judicial view, that a decision to ban a publication can be successfully challenged (apart from cases of procedural irregularity) in a court of law only by proving that the minister acted dishonestly, for improper purposes or with reference to improper considerations. The standard judicial response to 'if satisfied' and similar discretion-conferring clauses has already been criticised in the context of detention,[155] and the arguments will not be repeated save to remark that a revised judicial attitude to these clauses is long overdue. Until such a change does take place, the minister's opinion, rather than the presence or absence of the specified grounds, is the decisive factor.

The publications which the minister may ban are broadly defined by the Act. Publication means any 'newspaper, magazine, pamphlet, book, hand-bill or poster';[156] and is regarded as a periodical publication if it is published at intervals.[157] When the minister has banned any such publication, it becomes an offence to be in possession of it without his consent[158] unless the possessor satisfies the court that as soon as practicable after becoming aware of possession, reasonable steps were taken to report or deliver the publication to a police officer. Of course, the act of printing, publishing or disseminating a banned publication is a criminal offence.[159] In passing, we should note that the possession of a publication of a banned organisation is also a crime.[160]

The Act prescribes a procedure, incorporating apparent safeguards, which the minister must follow in banning a publication. This procedure is virtually identical to the procedure which he must follow in banning an organisation and therefore only the basic features will be repeated here. Prior to the issue of a banning order on a publication the minister *may* direct an investigation by an authorised officer[161] who is armed with extensive powers of entry, questioning, search and seizure.[162] The minister *must* have considered, prior to gazetting a banning notice, a factual report and recommendation of an advisory committee[163] set up by

---

[153] Section 5(1).
[154] Ibid. The grounds specified by the Act have been drastically summarised here.
[155] See chapter 7 above.
[156] Section 1(xviii).
[157] Section 1(xiv).
[158] Section 56(1)*(h)*. The penalty is imprisonment of up to three years: s 56(1)(ii).
[159] Section 56(1)*(b)*. The penalty is imprisonment of up to ten years: s 56(1)(i).
[160] Section 56(1)*(c)*.   [161] Defined in s 1(i).
[162] Section 6.
[163] On the appointment and function of such a committee, see s 7(2)–(9).

the State President on the recommendation of the Minister of Justice.[164] Though the minister's notice may be issued 'without notice to any person concerned',[165] the advisory committee is required to call for representations and oral evidence unless it decides that this will not be in the public interest.[166] After the minister has banned a publication, the publisher may have the banning reviewed by the Chief Justice or a judge of appeal designated by him.[167] The grounds upon which a banning order may be set aside are limited to excess of powers, bad faith or regard to considerations not specified by the Act.[168] The major defects of this entire procedure are that it is not absolutely obligatory for the advisory committee to give effect to the maxim audi alteram partem and that the Chief Justice cannot investigate the facts submitted to him by the minister but must take these on trust.

The banning power under discussion has not been used extensively. Under the predecessor[169] of the present provision, five newspapers were banned in the period 1962–1964.[170] In 1977 a further three publications were banned.[171] No bannings have been gazetted yet under the present Act. The reasons for the slight use of this particular banning provision are fairly obvious. First, it is an offence to possess a publication of any banned organisation[172] and this prohibition makes it unnecessary, or less necessary, to ban a great number of publications.[173] Secondly, the Publications Act of 1974, to be discussed below, provides a more expeditious form of banning to which no really effective safeguards are attached.

The Publications Act of 1974[174]

This Act is the chief engine of censorship in South Africa and it deals with many matters, such as indecent, obscene and blasphemous material, which are not relevant to the present study. However, one of the specific grounds upon which material may be banned under the Act is that it is prejudicial to the safety of the state, to general welfare or to peace and good order; and this ground, together with another relating to matters which cause harm 'to the relations between any sections of the inhabitants of the Republic', has facilitated the issue of a spate of banning orders for broadly political reasons.[175] The relevant provisions of the Publications Act will therefore be surveyed briefly here.[176]

---

[164] Section 7(1).   [165] Section 5(1).   [166] Section 7(5).
[167] Section 11.   [168] Section 11(4).
[169] Section 6 of Act 44 of 1950.
[170] These were *Clarion, Advance, New Age, Fighting Talk* and *The African Communist*: see *Annual Survey of South African Law*, 1962 p 55, 1963 p 55, 1964 p 29.
[171] Proclamations R 300–302 of 19 October 1977 (*GG* 3784 of 19 October 1977). The orders brought about the banning of the newspaper *The World*.
[172] Under s 56(1)(c).
[173] Disseminating their publications, moreover, could constitute the crime of furthering the aims of an unlawful organisation under s 13(1).
[174] Act 42 of 1974.
[175] See definition of 'undesirable' in s 47, particularly s 47(2)(d) and (e).
[176] A more extensive analysis will be found in *The Law of South Africa* vol 2 paras 197–212. See also Kelsey Stuart's *The Newspaperman's Guide to the Law* 4th ed (Butterworth, Durban 1986) ch 7 and Strauss, Strydom & Van der Walt *Die Suid-Afrikaanse Persreg* 3 ed (Van Schaik, Pretoria 1976) ch VI. J C W van Rooyen *Publikasiebeheer in Suid-Afrika* (Juta, Cape Town 1978).

Banning under the Publications Act takes the form of a declaration that the publication or object in question is 'undesirable'. Such a declaration may be applied to newspapers (other than those published by a publisher who is a member of the Newspaper Press Union, an exclusion which exempts from the provisions of the Act all the prominent daily and weekly newspapers in South Africa) books, periodicals, pamphlets, posters or other printed matter, writing or typescript that is published or duplicated in any way, drawings, pictures or illustrations, paintings, prints, photographs or engravings, carvings, statues and models, and records or other forms of sound reproduction.[177] So broad is the definition of matter that may be declared undesirable that writing or a drawing on underpants has been held to be covered.[178] The declaration that a publication is undesirable will be made by a committee consisting of not less than three persons drawn from a list compiled by the Minister of Home Affairs.[179] Banning is therefore under the control of the government in power through its nominated committees and through its power to appoint the members of the appeal board to which appeals against committee decisions must be directed.[180] The immediate effect of a declaration of undesirability is that the production of the publication (or object) in question is a crime.[181] Production, in this context, includes the act of printing, publishing, manufacturing, making or producing.[182] The declaration of unlawfulness need not have preceded production and a person may be convicted even though the committee made its declaration after the event.[183] The harsh effects of an ex post facto declaration of unlawfulness are somewhat mitigated by court rulings that a guilty mind (mens rea) is a requirement of the crime, probably in the form of intention.[184] But since intention (or dolus) is satisfied by the foresight of the possibility of a declaration of undesirability, if the producer of a publication realised that it might be banned, and nevertheless proceeded to put it out, he will be guilty. Publications expressing harsh criticism of police action in the townships have been declared unlawful, and it is possible that the publishers of such material in the future will not escape conviction because they lacked a guilty mind, which was the basis on which the accused were acquitted in S v Russell.[185] Guilt seems to depend on knowledge of the elusive vagaries of censorship policy in South Africa; and the better informed you are about such policy the guiltier you are likely to be. For an idyllic but brief period of time a declaration of unlawfulness could be challenged before the court trying the accused for unlawful production and that court, according to S v Moroney,[186] could

---

[177] This is an abbreviation of the definition of 'publication or object' in s 47(1). Though newspapers belonging to the press union are excluded, they may be banned under the Internal Security Act.
[178] Law of South Africa vol 2 para 198.
[179] See ss 4 and 5 dealing with the composition and appointment of committees.
[180] Sections 4, 5 and 35.
[181] Section 8(1). The penalties are prescribed by s 43.
[182] Definition of 'produce' in s 47(1).
[183] S v Moroney 1978 (4) SA 389 (A).
[184] S v Russell 1980 (2) SA 459 (C); S v Roodt 1983 (3) SA 382 (T); S v Potgieter 1985 (4) SA 270 (N).
[185] Supra.
[186] Supra.

make its own finding on the undesirability of the publication in question. This piece of judicial impertinence led to the rapid amendment of the Act so as to make a declaration of unlawfulness *conclusively* binding on the courts.[187]

A further consequence of a declaration of unlawfulness is that once it is gazetted it becomes a criminal offence to distribute the publication in question.[188] 'Distribute' is again widely defined and includes displaying or exhibiting the publication in public or selling, hiring out, or offering or keeping it for sale or hire.[189] Quotations from the banned publication are not specifically prohibited and are therefore not hit by the prohibition unless they are so made as to constitute an offer for sale or hire. It seems that distribution of a part of the banned work will not be criminal unless it is a substantial part. The crime of distribution, as opposed to production, requires a previous declaration of unlawfulness and the publication thereof in the *Gazette*. Both these events must have occurred before the act of distribution with which the accused is charged took place. A guilty mind is a requirement of this crime too but will apparently be satisfied by proof of negligence—that is, a culpable failure to determine whether a gazetting of the work had taken place.[190]

The mere possession of a banned publication may also constitute a crime. Censorship committees are empowered[191] to prohibit the possession of a work found to be undesirable, subject to confirmation by the appeal board.[192] As soon as the prohibition on possession is gazetted, it becomes an offence to possess the publication in question, to distribute it or to possess it with the object of distribution.[193] A guilty mind is also a requirement of this offence in the sense that the accused must be aware of the prohibition on the publication.[194]

There are also criminal prohibitions on the importation of undesirable material[195] and committees under the Publications Act are given the remarkable power of banning the import, except on authority of a permit, of the publications of a specific publisher or those that deal with a specific subject.[196] They also have the power to declare all editions of a periodical publication, both past and future, to be undesirable and where future editions are covered by a declaration of unlawfulness the production or distribution of every subsequent edition is banned.[197] Alternatively, if any edition of a periodical publication has been declared undesirable, future editions may be subjected to permit control.[198]

---

[187] Section 1 of the Publications Amendment Act 44 of 1979.

[188] Section 8(1)(b).

[189] Definition of 'distribute' in s 47(1).

[190] So the court held in *S v Simoko* 1985 (2) SA 252 (E). The court found the accused to be negligent because the publication they distributed dealt with certain 'hot' issues of politics which they should have anticipated could be declared undesirable. This judgment illustrates the insidious nature of political censorship.

[191] By s 9(3).

[192] Section 9(5).

[193] Section 8(1)(d), (dA) and (dB).

[194] *S v Cleminshaw* 1981 (3) SA 685 (C); *S v Ndlovu* 1986 (1) SA 510 (N).

[195] For this purpose the Publications Act must be read in conjunction with the Customs and Excise Act 91 of 1964 (s 113).

[196] Section 9(4) read with s 8(1)(e).

[197] Section 9(1)(a) and (b).

[198] Section 9(2).

Banning orders are likely to take on a political colouring and to interfere with the basic civil right of citizens to information and expression, where they are issued in terms of the power to control publications that are harmful to the relations between any sections of the inhabitants of the country or prejudicial to the safety of the state, the general welfare or peace and good order.[199] A publication bringing the white population into ridicule or contempt has been held to be undesirable in terms of the first of these criteria[200] and an exposé of alleged police malpractices in the townships undesirable in terms of the second.[201] When the courts still had jurisdiction over declarations of undesirability[202] their pronouncements on the two criteria brought little clarity to the law. In *Pillay v Publications Control Board*[203] a play dealing in a satirical manner with race legislation, especially the Immorality Act, was held to be harmful to race relations and to security and good order; but this judgment is best treated as a judicial aberration. In *Buren Uitgewers (Edms) Bpk v Raad van Beheer oor Publikasies*[204] the banning of André Brink's novel *Kennis van die Aand* was confirmed but not on the ground that it endangered state security or good order even though it dealt directly with the ugly side of prison conditions and security police behaviour.[205] In *S v Russell*[206] the court, though acquitting the accused for lack of a guilty mind, seemed to think that severe criticism of the actions of the riot police in the townships would be 'undesirable' if that criticism was untrue but legally innocent if shown to be accurate.[207] Freedom to criticise that is made conditional upon the truth of the facts relied upon will be a very precarious freedom indeed. The burden on the publisher of proving truth in such complex and fast-moving situations as township riots is so great that most are likely to play safe and avoid criticism of the police and therefore the danger of prosecution if the truth cannot be established before a court of law. Professor van Rooyen, the present chairman of the appeal board, has expressed the view that any criticism of the police or defence force members in their law and order capacity, which is likely to bring them into disrepute, is sufficient to justify a finding of undesirability.[208] Whether this principle is still acted upon by the appeal board and the review committee is not clear.[209] It does still apply where the police are portrayed as whites and their victims as blacks.[210] The effect of applying

[199] See definition of 'undesirable', paras *(d)* and *(e)* of s 47(2).
[200] *Law of South Africa* vol 2 para 202.
[201] See, for example, *R v Russell* 1980 (2) SA 459 (C).
[202] Under the Publications and Entertainments Act 26 of 1963 and in criminal prosecutions under the present Act until the enactment of the Publications Amendment Act 44 of 1979.
[203] 1971 (4) SA 208 (D).
[204] 1975 (1) SA 379 (C).
[205] The judges differred on whether it harmed relations between the races because of the picture it presented of Afrikaners.
[206] Supra.
[207] At 468 of the judgment.
[208] J C W van Rooyen *Publikasiebeheer in Suid-Afrika* 131.
[209] Police misbehaviour in the townships is extensively documented in *Report on Police Conduct During Township Protests* (Southern African Catholic Bishops' Conference, November 1984) and this publication has not been banned.
[210] Louise Silver *A Guide to Political Censorship in South Africa* (Univ of the Witwatersrand, Jhb 1984) 145.

such a principle is to suppress political discussion on one of the most crucial issues of contemporary politics—the behaviour and role of the law-enforcing agencies of the society. This is both a denial of political freedom and a dubious policy that is likely to be counter-productive to the very interests of security and order that it is intended to protect. The way in which the criterion of harming relations between sections of the community has been dealt with by censorship committees tends to favour publications which support governing policy (such as the former policy of criminalising sexual relations between blacks and whites) and to disfavour those in which official policy is severely criticised. Professor van Rooyen has written approvingly of the censorship of material which portrays segregation as absurd and wrong[211] but several recent unbannings of satirical works on apartheid suggest this may no longer be appeal board policy.

Though a comprehensive review of trends in the control of publications under the Act discerns a moderate degree of liberalisation,[212] the number of political bannings remains high; according to this review three hundred and thirty-four publications were outlawed under the state security and law and order criteria in 1981. Political works are the hardest hit by bans on possession, the number in 1981 being 336. Though more recent statistics of political bannings under the Act are not available, it does appear that of the 1 805 publications submitted to committees in 1983 and of the 1 808 submitted in 1984, more than half were put forward on the ground of possible prejudice to the safety of the state.[213] Of the material submitted for consideration, over fifty per cent was declared undesirable[214] and a significant proportion of the banned material must have been proscribed on political grounds. Political censorship, even if somewhat more enlightened, is still alive and well in South Africa. Its 'enlightenment', moreover, does not make it acceptable. Board of Appeal rulings have become more progressive but this is not true of committees, especially where they ban on broadly political grounds. Most bannings made by committees are not taken on appeal. Even where the focus falls primarily on appeal findings, one should not be too dazzled by the 'enlightenment' of the system. In the first place, that enlightenment is a qualified one which, for example, does not tolerate severe criticism of defence force activities.[215] Secondly, a censorship that is enlightened remains political censorship and tends to devalue or eliminate many officially unpopular views instead of allowing them to enter the intellectual market place.

There are also serious procedural objections to South Africa's system of prior censorship. Both the work and the composition of publication committees is blanketed in secrecy. Whereas under the previous Act[216] an independent check on bannings was available in the form of an appeal to the regular courts, appeals under the present legislation must go to the

---

[211] J C W van Rooyen op cit 124–5.
[212] Louise Silver 'Trends in Publication Control: A Statistical Analysis' (1983) 100 *SALJ* 580.
[213] 1983 and 1984 *Survey of Race Relations in South Africa* 208 and 882.
[214] Ibid.
[215] Louise Silver *A Guide to Political Censorship in South Africa* 153.
[216] The Publications and Entertainments Act 26 of 1963.

government-appointed appeal board.[217] Appeals are limited to the complainant (the person who referred the publication to the committee) and persons with a direct financial interest—a requirement which was critically examined by the court in *S v Moroney*.[218] The court, in this case, also exposed the difficulty a publisher has in determining whether a publication is likely to be undesirable according to the broad criteria of the Act, and pointed out that even if he decided to submit the matter to a committee for decision, he might already at that stage be guilty of producing an undesirable publication.[219] Though the review powers of the ordinary courts are retained by the Act, the traditional grounds for review—mala fides, improper purpose or considerations and procedural irregularity—are narrow and the Act obliges the reviewing court to refer the matter back to the appeal board for decision unless the court finds that the board acted mala fide.[220] The Publications Act, it is clear, is gravely deficient both procedurally and substantively.

The Defence Act of 1957[221]

Until 1977 this Act authorised general censorship in times of war only. Amendments introduced in that year[222] authorised the State President, by proclamation in the *Gazette*, to impose a general censorship over postal, telegraphic, telephonic or radio services and over certain written or printed matter 'addressed or intended to be delivered or conveyed to any person'.[223] He is empowered to take such action during operations in defence of the Republic or for the prevention or suppression of terrorism or internal disorder. The restriction on the use of the power to times of war clearly falls away. It is not quite clear, however, what the ambit of these censorship powers is in respect of publications. The words 'addressed or intended to be delivered or conveyed to any person' appear to restrict the scope of the power by excluding such matters as books, articles and newspapers, which can scarcely be described as material so addressed. If the power is interpreted broadly, the State President would be able to ban publications under this provision of the Defence Act. As yet no use has been made of this power.

III THE BANNING OF INDIVIDUALS

When a ban is imposed on an individual the victim of the order is crippled in respect of civil liberties and personal freedom. The disabling effect is due to the package of penalties and disabilities contained in the normal banning order. The terms of the order inflicted on the Reverend Beyers Naudé (now happily unbanned) were typical and comprised the following: a prohibition on attending any gathering of two or more persons; as a legal consequence of the ban on attending gatherings, a prohibition on the publication or dissemination of any speech or writing at any time made by him; confinement to the magisterial district of

---

[217] Section 13. The constitution of the appeal board is governed by s 35.
[218] Supra at 404 of the judgment.
[219] By definition, production includes duplication.
[220] Section 39(2).   [221] 44 of 1957.
[222] Section 7 of the Defence Amendment Act 35 of 1977 introducing a new s 101(1).
[223] Section 101(1).

Johannesburg; a prohibition on entering areas designated for blacks, coloureds or Indians; a prohibition on entering the premises of any factory or of any publisher or printer or of various organisations, including broadly political organisations; a prohibition on entering the premises of any educational institution or any court of law (except where personally involved in the proceedings); a prohibition on preparing or assisting in the preparation of any publications; a prohibition on giving educational instruction to any person except his children; a prohibition on taking part in the work of various organisations, including broadly political organisations; a prohibition on communicating with any other banned person; and, finally, an obligation to report to the police once a week.[224] The combination of all these constraints amounts to a civil death, and to a large extent a personal and social death, for the victim of the banning order.

The power to blight the lives of persons in this way is part of the arbitrary authority possessed by the Minister of Law and Order.[225] In every instance where the Act authorises him to impose the restrictions that are comprised by a banning order, the grant of power is expressed in absolute terms[226] or in language which appears to confer a subjective discretion. The conferment of subjective discretion is usually achieved by the use of the expressions 'if the minister is satisfied' or 'has reason to suspect'.[227] These expressions, as already noted,[228] restrict legal challenge to the minister's order to cases where the banned person can prove excess of powers (ultra vires), bad faith (mala fides) or improper purpose. A finding of ultra vires is hardly conceivable since the minister's powers are expressed in sweeping and vague terms. Equally unlikely is a decision that the minister acted in bad faith or for improper purposes. Bad faith (or improper purpose) has to be proved by the person challenging the order and the obstacles to such proof appear to be overwhelming. The courts will not infer bad faith from the apparent unreasonableness of a banning order unless the unreasonableness is so gross that dishonesty is the only reasonable inference.[229] The breadth and vagueness of the minister's powers and the deference of the courts to ministerial judgments in security cases make a finding that he acted with extreme unreasonableness an unlikely event. The majority of South Africans probably regarded the banning of Beyers Naudé as grossly unreasonable but it is unlikely that a court could be propelled towards such a conclusion. Until recently there was a further and equally serious obstacle in the way of a successful challenge to the exercise of the minister's power to ban an individual. The legislature and the courts had surrounded the entire banning process with a veil of secrecy which made it impossible to discharge the onus of proving that the minister had acted in bad faith or for improper purposes when imposing a ban. The Act requires the minister to disclose only so much of

---

[224] These conditions are a summary of those appearing in Dr Naudé's banning orders dated 11 October 1977. The various penalties and disabilities of banning are discussed more fully below.

[225] In terms of the Internal Security Act 74 of 1982 (referred to below as the Act).

[226] As in ss 21 and 22 of the Act.

[227] See ss 18, 19, 20.

[228] See chapter 7 above.

[229] See, for example, *Union Government v Union Steel Corporation* 1928 AD 220.

the information which led to the banning as he deems consistent with the public interest;[230] and, in effect, this authorises him to withhold all the relevant information. The statute does require the minister to provide the banned person with his reasons for issuing the order but this legal duty was almost never adequately fulfilled. When, for example, the minister extended the ban imposed on Beyers Naudé in 1982 his 'reasons' read as follows:

> 'I am convinced that the said Christian Frederick Beyers Naudé is taking part in activities which endanger the safety of the state or the maintenance of law and order or which are calculated to endanger them.'[231]

At the same time the minister declared that in the interests of public safety he could not disclose any of the information on which these reasons and the decision to ban Beyers Naudé were based. What the minister told the banned person in this case was about as helpful as a kick in the pants or a slap in the face. His 'reasons' were no more than a restatement of the statutory ground on which the banning decision was based and that restatement was unsupported by any information. This response is fairly typical of the minister's compliance (or, more accurately, non-compliance) with the provision of the Act dealing with the duty to give reasons and information, and with the similar provision of earlier legislation.

Until recently court judgments fortified ministerial evasions of the kind that took place in the banning of Beyers Naudé. None was more grotesque than *Kloppenberg v Minister of Justice*[232] in which the Natal court appeared to accept the minister's *conclusion* that the banned person was a threat to security as a reason for banning him and decided that, even though the statute does not in any way qualify the minister's obligation to give reasons as it does in relation to information, he need not give reasons either if doing so would involve the disclosure of information that would jeopardise the public interest. The position of the banned person was further aggravated by the Appellate Division in *Minister van Justisie v Alexander*.[233] This was a case in which the minister alleged, in a completely unspecified way, that the banned person, who was restricted immediately after serving a long-term prison sentence, had furthered the objects of communism while a political prisoner in a maximum security jail. The lower court had decided that although it could not force the minister to furnish the information which he was withholding, ostensibly in the public interest, or even inspect that information to determine whether it was being correctly withheld, it did have the power to order the minister to discover (list by description without disclosing the content) the papers and documents on which his decision was based. This rather mild attempt to introduce a modicum of procedural justice into the banning process was rebuffed by the Appellate Division which overruled the lower-court judgment and reaffirmed the rule that the minister's power to ban may be exercised despotically.

Decisions such as these inescapably forced the conclusion that bad faith (mala fides) or improper purposes as viable grounds for an attack on the

---

[230] Section 25 which applies to restrictions imposed under ss 18, 19 and 20.
[231] My translation of the minister's statement of 26 October 1982 issued in terms of s 25.
[232] 1964 (4) SA 31 (N).   [233] 1975 (4) SA 530 (A).

exercise of subjectively worded ministerial powers should be abandoned as an illusion. The effect of such judgments, it has been said, is that the banned person is required by the court to prove his case but illogically denied the means of doing so.[234] In fact, almost all judgments in this field of decision-making appear to be no more than elegant or inelegant variations of the dictum of De Waal JP in *Sachs v Minister of Justice*[235] where he said:

'... and the Minister having informed the court that he acted bona fide throughout, and that throughout he had no other object in view but to exercise his discretion in the proper manner, it is *impossible* for us to say that he acted wrongly, or that he erred in not making further disclosures such as are demanded by the petitioner.'[236]

Deference to executive authority has usually been less candid than that!

The recent judgment of the Appellate Division in *Nkondo & Gumede v Minister of Law and Order*[237] may have improved matters for a banned person who seeks a court review of a banning order. Though this decision concerned a detention order, the court's finding on the extent of the ministerial duty to give reasons is applicable also to banning orders by reason of the similarity of the statutory language in each case. In *Nkondo & Gumede* the court decided that a minister who merely reiterates one of the statutory grounds for detaining a person has not given that person reasons within the meaning of the Act and that general and vague statements (such as the statement that the detainee has created 'a revolutionary climate') do not constitute proper reasons for ministerial action. Since the court found that the minister had not complied with his statutory obligation to provide the detainees with reasons, the court held that the detention orders were invalid. It seems to follow that those banning orders that were accompanied by the usual uninformative ministerial justification (and this probably means all of them) are invalid and goes to show how much a little assertion of due process by the courts can achieve.

What is the likely future impact of the *Nkondo & Gumede* decision on legal challenges to banning orders? In part, this depends on the degree of particularity which the courts demand from the minister when he provides reasons for imposing a ban. If the courts insist on enough detail to enable the victim of the ban to join issue with the minister on whether he is a threat to state security, there is a possibility of establishing that the minister banned on the basis of improper considerations. But even assuming that the judiciary manages to eliminate vagueness from ministerial statements of reasons, several formidable obstacles remain for the victim of a banning order who seeks to set it aside. The decision in *Minister of Law and Order v Hurley*[238] is not applicable to the banning power which may be invoked where the minister 'is satisfied' that the necessary grounds exist and not, as in the detention power dealt with in *Hurley*, where there is 'reason to believe' that they are present. This means that

---

[234] M L Mathews 'Subjective Discretion Clauses and the Jurisdiction of the Court—An Analytical Approach' 1982/1983 *Natal University Law Review* 51, 54–5.
[235] 1934 AD 11, 21.   [236] Emphasis supplied.
[237] 1986 (2) SA 756 (A).
[238] 1986 (3) SA 568 (A).

the court will not enquire into the objective existence of the alleged grounds and that the onus is on the banned person to show that the minister acted improperly. Moreover, the minister has the power to withhold the information on which his decision was based; and without information the banned person may find it impossible to prove ministerial reliance on improper considerations or actual bad faith. This problem will remain so long as the South African judges, unlike their Namibian brethren in *Katofa v Administrator-General for South West Africa*,[239] continue to hold that being 'satisfied' means thinking that one is satisfied, whether or not the grounds for the satisfaction actually exist.

Nevertheless, there are some helpful steps that courts could take short of adopting the *Katofa* ruling. They need not act supinely in the face of a ministerial assertion that he cannot disclose information because to do so would prejudice the public interest. An in camera inspection of the relevant information might be ordered to determine whether it is genuinely sensitive. Though the minister could block such an inspection by invoking the state privilege clause of the Act,[240] the courts should force *him* to close the door on their attempts to reach a factually just decision. While the onus of proving that the minister acted improperly is on the applicant, there is no reason why the courts should not place the so-called temporary onus, or burden of adducing evidence, on the minister where the applicant has responded convincingly to the minister's reasons and demonstrated that his or her activities have been free of subversive colouring. There is no reason why the court, as it cursorily did in *Stanton v Minister of Justice*,[241] should dismiss as irrelevant believable evidence that the applicant's activites have been totally innocuous. Where the burden of adducing evidence is properly placed on the minister, and he does not bring forward convincing evidence to discharge it, the court might well find for the applicant even though the permanent onus remains on the person who seeks a declaration of invalidity. By far the most helpful step the courts could take would be to extend the *Hurley* ruling to 'is satisfied' and 'is of the opinion' clauses,[242] thereby requiring the minister to demonstrate that his belief or opinion had some rational basis in fact.

If a banned person decides to challenge the minister's order before the ordinary courts, he must bring the necessary proceedings within fourteen days of delivery of that order and the proceedings must be concluded within twelve months unless the delay is not the fault of the person launching the challenge.[243] Alternatively, he might decide to take advantage of the review procedure which the Act makes available when the ban includes a prohibition on gatherings or a restriction on movements or on association with specified groups.[244] Since a banning

---

[239] 1985 (4) SA 211 (SWA).

[240] Section 66.

[241] 1960 (3) SA 353 (T).

[242] On this proposal, see chapter 7 above on detention.

[243] Section 42(1). A banning order may not be suspended or postponed by a court pending the outcome of the challenge to its validity: s 42(2).

[244] The review procedure is applicable where restrictions are imposed under s 18(1), 19(1) and (2) or 20. But review is not permitted where proceedings have been instituted to declare a banning order invalid—s 42(3). Periodical review of a banning order will take place at intervals of not less than twelve months from the date of a court judgment confirming the validity of a banning order—s 43(1) and (5).

order invariably includes one or more of these restrictions, the review procedure will generally be operative. This procedure, already discussed in relation to preventive detention, requires the minister to submit the relevant papers to a board of review for consideration and report.[245] While the minister is not bound to give effect to the recommendation of the review board, if his refusal to do so means that the banned person will be subject to stricter measures than those recommended by the board, the matter must be submitted to the Chief Justice for review.[246] The Chief Justice, or a judge of appeal designated by him, has the power to set aside the banning on the basis of excess of powers, mala fides or reference to improper considerations. This entire procedure has already been examined[247] and found to be deficient. Of the shortcomings previously mentioned the most serious are the inability of the banned person to join issue with the minister without knowing the information on which the order was based and the inability of the Chief Justice to investigate the factual basis of the minister's case.

The remaining procedural provisions of the Act relating to banning provide neither safeguards for the victim nor limitations on the minister's powers. The minister may withdraw or relax a banning order[248] but clearly cannot be compelled to exercise this prerogative of mercy. The duty to publish certain forms of restriction[249] in the *Gazette* is a publicity requirement which does not provide the banned person with any remedy.[250] Though provision is made for the minister to warn a person upon whom he is contemplating the imposition of a ban to desist from specified activities,[251] he is not required to do so and, in any event, the warning provision is neither a safeguard nor a limitation of power. The same comment applies to the duty to report bannings to Parliament. The domination of Parliament by the ruling party means that effective political safeguards do not exist.

Nature of the Restrictions Imposed Upon a Banned Person

The normal banning package has already been described in general terms. It is now necessary to unpack that package for detailed analysis of each of the restrictions that may be involved in banning. The restrictions affect all the basic liberties—they curtail drastically freedom of the person, of association, of movement, of assembly and of speech. We now examine each in turn.

The Prohibition on Attending Gatherings

A banned person is invariably prohibited from attending gatherings by written notice from the minister. The enabling provision[252] declares that the minister may prohibit a person from attending gatherings if he is

---

[245] Section 38.
[246] Section 41.
[247] See chapter 7 above.
[248] Section 24.
[249] Those imposed under ss 20 (attending gatherings) and 23(1) (disseminating speeches and writings).
[250] Section 27(3) requires publication at intervals of not exceeding twelve months.
[251] Section 70.
[252] Section 20.

satisfied that the person in question is engaging in, or likely to promote, activities that endanger state security or the maintenance of law and order; or if that person is on the consolidated list or has been convicted of specified offences[253] and the minister has reason to suspect that he will engage in or promote the said activities; or if the minister is satisfied that the person in question is causing, or likely to cause, feelings of hostility between the different population groups (or parts of population groups) in the Republic.[254] Each of the broad grounds upon which the minister may base a prohibition on attending gatherings is comprehensive enough, or vague enough, to constitute a generous grant of power to him. In any event, as we have seen, the courts will not investigate the exercise of the minister's discretion to determine whether it is factually connected to one of the specified grounds.

A prohibition on attending gatherings must take the form of a notice signed by the minister which is addressed and tendered or delivered to the person concerned.[255] It may be made operative at any place or area or during any period or on any day or during any times within any period.[256] In short, its scope and duration are in the minister's absolute discretion. It may be made subject to exceptions contained within the notice itself or to written exemptions granted by the Director of Security Legislation or a magistrate under authority of the minister.[257] It is clear that any deviations from the terms of a ban on attending gatherings are under strict official control.

The gatherings (including 'concourses' and 'processions') which the minister may prohibit the banned person from attending fall into two classes: (a) any gathering and (b) particular gatherings or gatherings of a particular nature, class or kind. Where the prohibition relates to gatherings falling into the first class (any gathering) there is a restriction on attending gatherings in general. Where it relates to gatherings falling into the second class (particular gatherings) the restriction will be on attending a specified gathering or a particular kind of gathering. Taking the case of the Reverend Beyers Naudé as an example, he was prohibited from attending any gathering anywhere in the Republic (that is, gatherings of the first class) and any social, political or educational gatherings (the latter being gatherings of a particular kind or nature falling into the second class).[258] In either case, the gathering which the banned person is prohibited from attending may consist of as few as two persons, including the banned person. This is the effect of the interpretation by the Appellate Division of the words 'any number of persons' in the definition of gathering that appears in the Act.[259] That court, in S v Wood,[260] overruled an earlier judgment[261] which would have required a considerable number of persons, and declared that the meeting together of

---

[253] Those specified in Schedule 2 to the Act or in s 59 or 60. A person convicted of an offence under s 58 'for which he has been sentenced' is also covered.
[254] Section 20. The section has been paraphrased in the text.
[255] Section 20.
[256] Ibid.   [257] Ibid.
[258] Banning order dated 26 October 1982.
[259] In s 1(vii).
[260] 1976 (1) SA 703 (A).
[261] Sachs v Swart NO 1952 (2) PH K137 (T).

the banned person and one other would constitute a gathering for purposes of the Act. However, if the minister's notice is worded so as to prohibit attendance at a gathering already constituted, there will then have to be at least two persons in addition to the banned person.[262] In most cases, it will be illegal for the banned person to have a meeting with one other person. This is a devastating restriction of associational freedom.

The prohibition on attending gatherings in general (gatherings of the first category known as 'any gatherings') carries with it the requirement that the gathering must have a common purpose, whether lawful or unlawful.[263] This requirement excludes from the prohibition those casual or passing meetings which the banned person may have with another or others, such as joining a bus queue or being in a bus with others. As originally interpreted, particularly in *Dudley v Minister of Justice*,[264] common purpose required that the minds of the persons attending the gathering must have been directed towards some common objective which they intended to achieve by concerted action. This implies that the common purpose cannot be sought in the act of gathering itself and that there must be two constituent elements in every case, namely, the act of gathering and an object to be achieved thereby, each with its own requirement of mens rea. These two requirements were insufficiently distinguished, and thereby merged into one, in *S v Zigqolo*[265] in which the court held that the act of gathering to sing or to listen simultaneously satisfies both requirements. The court should have insisted on two separate stages or elements which, although they might occur or be inherent in the same meeting, are quite distinct from each other. If the court, as in *Zigqolo*, fails to distinguish between the common purpose of gathering and the purpose of achieving something by gathering, the banned person will be guilty if he meets someone simply to talk, without thereby seeking to achieve any special objective. Under such an interpretation the requirement of common purpose has virtually disappeared.[266]

Where the prohibited gathering is a particular gathering, or a gathering of a particular class or kind, there is no requirement of common purpose.[267] Mere attendance is sufficient for a breach of the prohibition. It is common for a banned person to be prohibited from attending social gatherings (as a species of gatherings of a particular kind) and a social gathering has normally been defined in the ministerial notice as 'any gathering at which the persons present also have social intercourse with one another'. The definition seems to imply that, apart from the prohibition on pure social gatherings (for example, a dinner party) other

---

[262] *S v Weinberg* 1979 (3) SA 89 (A); *S v Variawa* 1980 (3) SA 720 (T).

[263] Section 1(vii)*(b)*.

[264] 1963 (2) SA 464 (A). The common purpose need not be shared by everyone present or even by the accused: *R v Kahn* 1955 (3) SA 177 (A) 184. In a prosecution, it is not necessary to prove that the banned person actively participated in the meeting or the achievement of the objective: *S v Carneson* 1967 (4) SA 301 (C) 304.

[265] 1980 (1) SA 49 (A). The case concerned 'gathering' as defined in the Riotous Assemblies Act 17 of 1956 but is applicable to the definition in the present Act.

[266] See, further, A S Mathews *Law, Order and Liberty in South Africa* 78–9.

[267] Section 1(vii). The definition of particular gatherings makes inapplicable the finding in *R v Kahn* (supra) that a social gathering without a common purpose is not prohibited.

gatherings,[268] at which some social activity takes place, are also
prohibited social gatherings. The problem is to determine what kind and
what degree of socialising will convert another kind of gathering into a
social gathering. There appears to be sufficient vagueness and uncertainty
about this to render the prohibition void for vagueness but the Appellate
Division decided otherwise in *S v Meer*[269] and overruled a more persuasive
judgment of the Natal Court in the process.[270] Though it is now clear that
social gatherings as ministerially defined are not void for vagueness,[271] the
court did not provide any real clarity on the nature and degree of
socialising needed to convert an innocent into a prohibited social
gathering. It seems safe to say that the socialising must be more than
negligible and, perhaps, even a major or predominant feature of the
gathering.[272] It is also usual for a banned person to be prohibited from
attending a political gathering, usually defined as one at which any form
of state or principle or policy of the government of a state is propagated,
defended, attacked, criticised or discussed—clearly a very broad proscription. Another common prohibition is on attending gatherings of
students for the purpose of instructing or addressing them.

Where the banned person attends a prohibited gathering of either kind
(any gathering or a particular gathering) he or she commits an offence[273]
but the word 'attends' connotes a planned and deliberate activity, and
casual and unpremeditated assemblies are not punishable.[274] The mens
rea requirement for conviction appears to be an intention to attend.[275]

When a banning order includes, as it invariably does, a prohibition on
attending gatherings,[276] a further restriction on freedom of expression
automatically comes into force. According to this additional restriction,
no speech, utterance, writing or statement[277] made or produced (or
purporting to have been made or produced) at any place or time by a
person prohibited from attending any gathering[278] may be recorded,
reproduced, printed, published or disseminated without the consent of the
minister unless it is required for purposes of proceedings in a court of
law.[279] This prohibition (referred to below as the silencing clause) applies
also to persons to whom the silencing clause has been specifically applied
under the Act[280] and to persons whose names appear on the consolidated
list.[281] The silencing clause is applicable to the speeches, writings, et
cetera of any person 'who has been prohibited under section 20 from
attending any gathering' and the question arises whether it continues to

[268] That is, non-social gatherings.
[269] *S v Meer* 1981 (4) SA 604 (A).
[270] *S v Meer* 1981 (1) SA 739 (N).
[271] For criticism of this finding, see (1982) 99 *SALJ* 1 and 7.
[272] The cases on social gatherings are reviewed in the lower-court judgment in *S v Meer* 1981 (1) SA 739 (N) and in (1982) 99 *SALJ* 1.
[273] Section 56(1)(j). The penalty is imprisonment for a period not exceeding three years: s 56(1)(ii).
[274] *S v Arenstein* 1964 (4) SA 697 (N); *S v Carneson* 1967 (4) SA 301 (C).
[275] *S v Carneson* (supra) 305–6.
[276] Under s 20.
[277] Or any extract therefrom or recording or reproduction thereof.
[278] Under s 20.
[279] Section 56(1)(p).
[280] Under s 23(1).
[281] Section 56(1)(p).

be of effect after such a prohibition has lapsed. The Internal Security Act of 1950, as it stood when repealed by the Act, applied the silencing clause to a person 'in respect of whom a prohibition to attend any gathering is in force under section 5 or 9'.[282] This wording, which clearly does not apply to lapsed banning orders, replaced the previous phraseology 'in respect of whom a prohibition . . . has at any time . . . been issued'.[283] Is the effect of the prohibition under the current Act to restore the original position and thereby to maintain the silencing clause in operation after a prohibition on attending gatherings has lapsed or been withdrawn? It seems that the words 'has been prohibited' are not as clearly in favour of retrospective operation as the words 'has at any time . . . been issued', and that by restrictive interpretation the silencing clause should not apply to prohibitions that have fallen away.

We have seen that the silencing clause also affects persons to whom it has been specifically applied. The power to apply it to specific persons is available only in respect of former residents of the Republic who (according to the satisfaction of the minister) have engaged, in the Republic or elsewhere, in activities which endanger, or are likely to endanger, the security of the state or the maintenance of law and order or who have advocated or encouraged such activities in the Republic or encouraged the achievement of any of the objects of communism.[284] The minister's prohibition may be imposed without notice to the person concerned[285] and may at any time be withdrawn.[286] The silencing clause will no longer be operative once a notice has been withdrawn by the minister. So far as persons whose names appear on the consolidated list[287] are concerned, the silencing clause is of effect only while their names remain on the list.[288]

A person who publishes or disseminates et cetera a speech, writing or statement in breach of the silencing clause, is guilty of a criminal offence.[289] 'Publish' or 'disseminate' does not have the same meaning as it does under the law of defamation and it follows that there must be proof that the material has been made generally known or spread abroad.[290] However, a person who sends material out of the country for publication in a foreign newspaper is liable to conviction if the newspaper is one that is imported into South Africa for local distribution.[291] While mens rea is a requirement of the crime, it may consist in negligence.[292] Nobody may be convicted for quoting the speeches or writings of a person prohibited from attending gatherings or a person to whom the silencing clause has

---

[282] Section 11(5)*bis* of Act 44 of 1950.
[283] The amendment was brought about by s 13 of the General Law Amendment Act 57 of 1975.
[284] Section 23(1). The latest Government Notice contains the names of fifty-two persons: GN 1416 of 4 July 1986 (*GG* 10320 of 4 July 1986).
[285] Ibid.   [286] Section 23(2).
[287] For discussion of the consolidated list, see above under the banning of organisations.
[288] See s 56 (1)*(p)*(iii).
[289] Section 56(1)*(p)* read with s 56(1)(ii). The penalty is imprisonment for a period not exceeding three years.
[290] *S v Ravan Press (Pty) Ltd* 1976 (1) SA 929 (T).
[291] *S v Laurence* 1975 (4) SA 825 (A). In this case the accused was convicted of an attempt where the publication in the foreign newspaper was frustrated by the authorities.
[292] *S v Sayed* 1981 (1) SA 982 (C). The onus is on the State to prove mens rea.

specifically been applied unless the prohibition on such persons has been published in the *Gazette* or the names of such persons appear on the consolidated list.[293] Finally, the Act makes provision for a limited exemption from the silencing clause to be granted by the minister to a university or other institution designated by him in the *Gazette*.[294] The exemption covers only the bona fide use in a library of the material in question by members of staff of the university or institution, or by registered postgraduate students of the university.[295] Moreover, the use of the material must be in accordance with regulations made by the minister.[296] Regulations published by the minister[297] provide inter alia for the materials to be locked in a separate bookcase or room, for a catalogue of the material to be kept in the library and for a register of users.

It seems that the silencing clause does not prevent the banned person (the person who is prohibited from attending gatherings, whose name appears on the consolidatd list or to whom the clause is specifically applied) from making a speech[298] or from preparing any material.[299] The clause does, however, prevent the banned person, or any other, from publishing, disseminating, et cetera either the speech or the material which he or she has prepared.[300]

Restrictions Relating to Places or Areas, Communicating with Persons or Performing Acts

A section[301] of the Act authorises the Minister of Law and Order to impose a variety of restrictions upon an individual by written notice signed by him.[302] He may *(a)* prohibit the person in question from being within or absenting himself from any specified place or area, *(b)* forbid the said person from communicating with any person or category of persons specified, *(c)* place a ban on that person receiving visitors and *(d)* prohibit the performing of any specified act by that person. Each of these restrictions, which may be imposed singly or in combination, will be discussed separately below. The first two restrictions *((a)* and *(b))* are inevitable features of a banning order while the third *(c)* is common where banning takes the form of house arrest. The final restriction *(d)*, although astonishingly wide, has been used only to a limited degree.

Under primary power to curb freedom of movement the minister, subject to permitted exceptions,[303] is authorised to prohibit a person, during a specified period, from being within or absenting himself from any place or area specified in the ministerial notice.[304] 'Place' is widely defined

---

[293] Section 56(3).
[294] Section 56(4).   [295] Ibid.
[296] Under s 56(5).
[297] GN No R1986 (*GG* 8383 of 17 September 1982).
[298] Other provisions of the banning order may have this effect, for example, the prohibition on attending gatherings.
[299] The preparation of material for publication is frequently specifically prohibited in a banning order.
[300] On this point, see A S Mathews *Law, Order and Liberty in South Africa* 84.
[301] Section 19.
[302] And addressed and delivered or tendered to the person concerned.
[303] Authorised in writing by himself or, on his authority, by the Director of Security Legislation or a magistrate acting under general or special instructions.
[304] Section 19(1).

so as to include both public and private places and also any premises, building, structure, vessel, aircraft, vehicle or any part thereof.[305] The minister may impose restrictions of this kind if *(a)* he is satisfied that the person in question engages in activities which endanger or are likely to endanger the security of the state or the maintenance of law and order (or is likely to propagate or promote such activities) or *(b)* the said person is listed in the consolidated list or has been convicted of certain specified offences[306] *and* the minister has reason to suspect that he or she engages in, or is likely to engage in, the aforesaid activities.[307] If so satisfied, the minister may either impose the restriction of confinement (for example, to a magisterial district, to a house, flat or even a room)[308] or the restriction of exclusion (for example, by prohibiting the person from being in areas set aside for other racial groups, in educational institutions, printing or publishing houses, the courts, and so on)[309], or both.

There is a secondary power of confinement or exclusion which has application to areas[310] and not to places. A person convicted of an offence connected with a campaign to break any law by way of protest,[311] or who has himself been convicted of an offence committed by way of protest[312] and whom the minister has reason to suspect is likely to commit the former offence,[313] may be prohibited by notice from being within or absent from an area specified in the ministerial notice.[314] The minister also has the power to exclude from a specified area (but not to confine to a specified area) any person who he is satisfied is causing or encouraging (or will cause or encourage) feelings of hostility between different population groups, or parts of population groups, in any area of the Republic.[315]

A person who is by notice confined to or excluded from a place or area, and who breaches the prohibition imposed upon him, is guilty of a criminal offence.[316] The Act declares that a person who has been prohibited from absenting himself from such place or area shall be deemed to have absented himself from such place or area, if at any time after the minister's notice has been delivered or tendered, that person is found elsewhere.[317] Since a guilty mind (mens rea) is a requirement of the offence[318] the effect of this deeming provision is to create a rebuttable

[305] See s 1(xv) for the full definition.
[306] The offences listed in Schedule 2.
[307] Section 19(1). The subjective nature of this discretionary power has been discussed above.
[308] 'House arrest' may take the severe form of a twenty-four-hour order as in *Minister of Justice v Hodgson* 1963 (4) SA 535 (T).
[309] These are some common examples. Such curbs may have the further drastic effect of preventing a person from earning a living or pursuing a chosen vocation: see, for example, *S v Qumbella* 1967 (4) SA 577 (A).
[310] 'Areas' are not defined in the Act and are obviously broader than the defined concept of 'places'. The most common area for purposes of banning is the magisterial district; but both larger and smaller areas might be specified. However, 'area' could not be interpreted to include a house or building, for example.
[311] As defined by s 59 or 60.
[312] Under s 58.
[313] That is, an offence specified by s 59 or 60.
[314] Section 19(2)*(a)*.   [315] Section 19(2)*(b)*.
[316] Section 56(1)*(k)*, *(l)* and *(m)*. The penalties are different according to the nature of the restriction imposed: see s 56(1)(ii) and (iii).
[317] Section 19(5).
[318] *S v Qumbella* 1966 (4) SA 356 (A) 362. Proof of negligence will suffice.

presumption of guilt on a criminal charge. The Act also provides that a person subject to an order of confinement or exclusion from a specified place or area may be arrested and removed from or to such place or area if, when the notice is delivered or thereafter, the person is found elsewhere.[319]

The minister is also authorised, on the same grounds that justify his exercising the primary power to confine or exclude a person from a specified place or area[320] and by the same method,[321] to prohibit an individual from communicating with any person or category of persons or from receiving any visitor or from performing any specified act.[322] A prohibition on communicating with another person or category of persons appears to cover all forms of communication, whether direct or indirect.[323] It also appears to override personal relationships such as that sanctioned by marriage.[324] A banned person has been convicted of communicating with her fiancé'.[325] A prohibition on receiving a visitor does not debar the banned person from being visited by an attorney or advocate who manages his or her affairs and whose name does not appear on the consolidated list and who is not restricted by notice (that is, banned) under the Act.[326] Apart from this exception, the prohibition may be made absolute and include a ban on visits from a doctor.[327] However, a ban on receiving visitors does not preclude other forms of communication with others; and being visited probably includes an element of social or business intercourse.[328] Admitting a person as part of the household of a banned person does not constitute the act of receiving a visitor.[329] Moreover, the banned person must have intended to receive the visitor in question and where the visitor was entertained by the daughter of the restricted person and had no communication with the restricted person, the prohibition was not contravened.[330] The minister's power to prohibit the banned person from performing any specified act is breath-takingly wide. Common forms of prohibited conduct are the giving of educational instruction or taking part in the preparation or publication of certain kinds of documents or papers.

The penalty for breaching a prohibition on communicating with a prohibited person, receiving a visitor or performing a specified act is

[319] Section 19(4).

[320] See the text accompanying n 307 above.

[321] Written notice signed by him and addressed and delivered or tendered to the person in question.

[322] Section 19(1). The prohibition may be made subject to written exceptions.

[323] Communication in writing, by telephonic or other technical means, appears to fall under the prohibition. In *S v Mandela* 1974 (4) SA 878 (A) the court appeared to accept that communicating indirectly through others (eg sending a message) is within the prohibition.

[324] Since banned persons are generally prohibited from communicating with each other, it has been customary, where a husband and wife are both banned, to exempt them from the restriction on communication: see, generally, A S Mathews *Law, Order and Liberty in South Africa* 92.

[325] A S Mathews op cit 92.

[326] Section 19(1).

[327] A specific exemption for doctors is usually made.

[328] *S v Mandela* 1972 (3) SA 231 (A).

[329] *S v Pityana* 1976 (4) SA 823 (E). It seems that very young children cannot be visitors if they could not form an intention to visit the banned person: M F Ackermann *Die Reg Insake Openbare Order en Staatsveiligheid* (Butterworths, Durban 1984) 89n92.

[330] *S v Mandela* 1979 (1) SA 284 (O).

imprisonment for up to three years.[331] There is a presumption that a person charged with communicating with a person whose name appears on the consolidated list or who is restricted under the Act, knew, unless the contrary is proved, that the person was listed or restricted, provided that the listing or restriction has been duly gazetted under the Act.[332]

Restrictions Relating to Membership of Public Bodies or Organisations

As part of the banning powers conferred upon him by the Act the minister may require any person

(1) to comply with such conditions as are prescribed in a ministerial notice, while he is an office-bearer, officer[333] or member of an organisation[334] or public body specified in the notice, or while he holds a specified public office; or

(2) to resign as an office-bearer, officer or member of a specified organisation and to refrain from again so acting or taking part in any of the activities of the organisation; or

(3) to refrain from becoming an office-bearer, officer or member, or from taking part in the activities of any organisation specified in the notice or of any kind of organisation so specified; or

(4) to refrain from becoming a member of a public body or from holding public office or, if already holding such positions, to resign from them within a specified period and not to take them up again.[335]

These powers may be exercised by the minister if he is satisfied that the person in question engages in activities which endanger or are calculated to endanger the security of the state or the maintenance of law and order (or is likely to propagate or promote such activities) or if the said person appears on the consolidated list or has been convicted on certain specified offences[336] and is suspected by the minister either of engaging in, or being likely to engage in, the aforesaid activities.[337] The limited possibility of successfully challenging a finding of that kind by the minister, in the light of court interpretation of subjective discretion clauses, has already been canvassed.

By exercising the power just described, the minister may effectively debar the banned person from participation in the institutional and organisational life of the country. The only limitations on his powers are that he may not make an order in terms of paragraph (1), (2) or (3) above in respect of any person who is a member, office-bearer, or officer of a registered employers' organisation or trade union except after consultation with the Minister of Manpower;[338] and that he cannot derogate from

---

[331] Section 56(1)*(k)* and 56(1)(ii).   [332] Section 69(3).

[333] The terms 'office-bearer' and 'officer' are defined in s 1(xi) and (xii).

[334] As defined in s 1(xiii).

[335] Section 18(1). Such an order is required to be by written notice signed by the minister and addressed and delivered or tendered to the person concerned. Section 27(1) makes provision for an alternative form of service of any notice or document under the Act where personal service cannot be effected. Where a person is ordered to resign from an organisation, he may do so with effect from the date of his banning notwithstanding any contrary rule or agreement of the organisation: s 18(3).

[336] The offences specified in Schedule 2 to the Act.

[337] Section 18(1).

[338] Section 18(2).

or modify the rules governing the removal of provincial administrators and of judges of the Supreme Court.

The minister also has authority under the Act to make general provision for debarring banned persons (or persons who are listed or who were members, office-bearers, et cetera of a banned organisation) from taking part in the activities of particular organisations or of organisations of a specified kind.[339] He exercised this general power under the old Act[340] by proclamations which prevented banned persons from taking part in the activities of a long list of specific organisations and of organisations of certain kinds, such as those concerned with politics in the widest sense. These proclamations[341] remain in force by virtue of a provision of the present Act[342] but there is doubt as to whether they are prospective in operation and apply to persons who were banned after their promulgation. Possibly because of this doubt it is customary to include in a banning order a specific prohibition on being associated with any of the organisations referred to in the proclamations. Such a specific prohibition was made part of the original banning order of Beyers Naudé.[343] Leaving this technical problem aside, the minister is clearly empowered by the Act both to prohibit each banned person separately from taking part in organisational activity and to do so generally by making the prohibition applicable to all banned or listed persons. Since orders of this kind are a regular feature of banning, the banned person is effectively excluded from participation in all significant organisational activity of our society.

Reporting to a Police Station and Notifying Changes of Address

The Act gives the Minister of Law and Order authority, to be exercised by written notice,[344] to order a person whose name appears on the consolidated list or in respect of whom a prohibition imposed by notice under the Act is in force (that is, who is banned), to report[345] to an officer in charge of a police station at such times and during such periods as may be specified in the notice.[346] Failure to comply with such a notice constitutes a criminal offence[347] for which the penalty is imprisonment not exceeding ten years.[348] Mens rea is a requirement of the offence of failing to report to a police station but it may consist of negligence.[349] Banning orders usually require weekly reporting to a police station.

---

[339] Section 22.
[340] Under s 5*ter* of the Internal Security Act 44 of 1950.
[341] GN No R2130 (*GGE* No 408 of 28 December 1962) amended by GN No R1947 (*GGE* No 958 of 27 November 1964) and GN No R296 (*GGE* No 443 of 22 February 1963).
[342] Section 73.
[343] Banning order dated 11 October 1977.
[344] Signed by him and addressed and delivered or tendered to the person in question.
[345] Subject to exceptions granted by the minister or by the director, or by a magistrate acting under the minister's general or specific instructions.
[346] Section 21. Though the power to require reporting to a police station may be exercised only in respect of a restricted person, both notices (i e the reporting and the restricting notice) may be served simultaneously: *S v Joseph* 1964 (1) SA 659 (T).
[347] Section 56(1)(*f*).
[348] Section 56(1)(i).
[349] *S v Arenstein* 1964 (1) SA 361 (A); *S v Jassat* 1965 (3) SA 423 (A). An accused person who was discovered on an 'escape route' from South Africa some time before his day for reporting to the police station was convicted of an attempt to commit the offence in *S v Mtshizana* 1966 (1) SA 169 (E).

A person restricted by notice under the Act (as well as one whose name appears on the consolidated list) is guilty of an offence on failure to give notice forthwith of a change in his or her place of residence or employment.[350] Once the State proves that the accused has changed a place of residence or employment, the onus is upon him or her to prove that notice was given.[351] Mens rea is a requirement of this offence.[352]

A person against whom a prohibition by notice under the Act is in force (or whose name appears on the consolidated list) is required, when called upon to do so by a peace officer[353] to furnish his or her full name and address. Failure to do so, or the giving of a false or incorrect name or address, constitutes an offence.[354]

IV THE BANNING OF MEETINGS

Officials of government have extensive and, in some cases, absolute control over meetings, gatherings, processions and other forms of assembly. The most far-reaching legislation affecting the right of assembly is the Internal Security Act.[355] Other relevant measures are the Demonstrations in or near Court Buildings Prohibition Act of 1982[356] and the Gatherings and Demonstrations Act of 1973.[357] The effect of this legislation is to drive deep inroads into freedom of assembly and to make the government, itself a participant in the political process as ruling party, the arbiter of the right to gather in public or private places.

The Internal Security Act of 1982

This Act confers limited powers over assemblies on magistrates, and more extensive powers on the Minister of Law and Order.

A magistrate, if he has reason to apprehend that the public peace would be seriously endangered either by any gathering in his district or by a particular gathering or any gathering of a particular nature, class or kind at a particular place or area in his district, may prohibit for a period of not exceeding forty-eight hours every gathering in his district or that particular gathering or a gathering of a particular nature, class or kind except in such cases as he may expressly authorise either in the prohibition or at a later stage.[358] Alternatively, the magistrate is empowered to direct that the particular gathering in question, or any gathering with the same purpose, shall be held only in accordance with such conditions as he may determine, including, in the case of a gathering which takes the form of a procession, conditions prescribing the route, preventing the procession (or any part thereof) from entering any

[350] Section 56(1)(d). The penalty is imprisonment for a period not exceeding ten years.
[351] Section 69(2).
[352] S v Naicker 1967 (4) SA 214 (N). Proof of culpa will clearly be adequate.
[353] As defined in the Criminal Procedure Act 51 of 1977.
[354] Section 56(1)(c). The penalty is imprisonment for a period not exceeding ten years.
[355] No 74 of 1982 (hereinafter referred to as 'the Act'). This Act repeals the provisions of the Riotous Assemblies Act 17 of 1956 dealing with gatherings which existed side by side with similar provisions in the Internal Security Act 44 of 1950. The new provisions of the Internal Security Act 74 of 1982 are similar to the repealed provisions of both these earlier Acts and comparisons will be made where relevant.
[356] 71 of 1982.
[357] Act 52 of 1973.
[358] Section 46(1).

specified place or requiring the persons forming the procession to travel in vehicles.[359] In short, the magistrate has power to prohibit absolutely the holding of all or particular gatherings in his district for a period not exceeding forty-eight hours or to impose conditions in respect of particular gatherings to be held within his district.

Where the magistrate prohibits any kind of gathering under the power just described, he must do so either by notice in the *Gazette* or a local newspaper, or by radio announcement, or by the distribution and display of notices in public or by oral notice at the place where the prohibition is to apply.[360] This gives the magistrate a wide discretion to choose any one of the prescribed methods. The decision as to the mode of publication must be exercised by the magistrate himself and cannot be delegated.[361] Where the magistrate imposes conditions on the holding of a particular gathering, he must publish his direction by one of the methods just described and, in addition, unless the identity and whereabouts of the convener or organiser of the meeting are unknown or urgency renders it not feasible, issue the direction in the form of a written notice signed by him and addressed and delivered or tendered to the convenor or organiser of the gathering in question.[362]

The gatherings which the magistrate may prohibit or place under restrictive conditions are defined in the Act. Where the magistrate exercises the power to prohibit any gathering in his district (that is, where he prohibits all gatherings),[363] gathering is defined to mean 'a gathering, concourse or procession of any number of persons having a common purpose, whether such purpose be lawful or unlawful'.[364] That the magistrate does have power to prohibit *all* gatherings of whatever kind, provided they have a common purpose, is clear both from the wording of the Act[365] and from *S v Mtutuzeli*[366] which held that the word 'gathering' in the similarly worded Riotous Assemblies Act[367] did not have a restricted meaning. The requirement of a common purpose is satisfied by proof of common activities such as talking, singing, praying or protesting even if they are inseparable from the act of gathering itself.[368] Where the magistrate exercises his statutory power to prohibit a particular gathering or a gathering of a particular nature, class or kind,[369] the definition of gathering which is applicable is 'any gathering, concourse or procession of any number of persons'.[370] In this case, the requirement of common purpose does not apply and the prohibition will be breached even if there

---

[359] Ibid.

[360] Section 46(1)*(a)*.

[361] *S v Turrell* 1973 (1) SA 248 (C) 258.

[362] Section 46(2)*(b)*.

[363] As contemplated by s 46(1)*(a)*.

[364] Section 1(vii).

[365] Section 46(1)(i).

[366] 1979 (1) SA 764 (T).

[367] 17 of 1956.

[368] *S v Ziqqolo* 1980 (1) SA 49 (A). In this judgment, the appeal court disapproved of two judgments of the Cape court—*S v Morgan* 1977 (4) SA 471 (C) and *S v Riordan* 1979 (4) SA 256 (C)—in which common purpose had been taken more seriously as a substantive requirement. Casual assemblies without any cohesive purpose, such as bus queues, will not fall under the prohibition.

[369] As contemplated by s 46(1)*(b)*.

[370] Section 1(vii).

is no common purpose of any kind; but the magistrate must clearly identify the particular gathering which he is prohibiting.[371] Whether the gatherings prohibited by the magistrate fall into the first class (any gatherings) or the second class (particular gatherings or gatherings of a particular class or kind) two persons will be sufficient to constitute a prohibited gathering, even if it is in the form of a procession or concourse.[372] Moreover, it is irrelevant whether the gathering takes place on public or private property.[373]

The minister has the power to prohibit, by any of the methods prescribed for magisterial prohibitions,[374] either 'any gathering' or particular gatherings or gatherings of a particular nature, class or kind.[375] Both these classes of gathering have the same meaning as described above.[376] The minister's powers are wider than those of the magistrate in two major respects. First, the prohibition may be made for any place or area in the Republic and, indeed for the entire Republic.[377] Secondly, there is no limit as to the duration of the prohibition and the prohibition may be made effective during any period, or on any day or during specified times or periods within any period.[378] The minister may prohibit any of the above-described gatherings if he deems it necessary or expedient in the interests of the security of the state or for the maintenance of public peace or to prevent hostility between the different population groups (or parts thereof) in the Republic.[379]

Where a magistrate decides to prohibit a gathering or impose restrictions on a gathering, he must have 'reason to apprehend' that the evils envisaged by the statute will follow[380] whereas the minister may act 'if he deems it necessary' in the interests of state security et cetera.[381] The question arises whether the difference in wording relating to the exercise of discretion by these two officials is legally significant. It is clear that, at least in the case of the magistrate, a decision to prohibit a gathering or to impose conditions may be challenged in court on the ground that the objective facts do not justify the prohibition or restriction. In other words, the magistrate's finding that the public peace will be seriously endangered by the gathering may be disputed by evidence to the contrary. The words

[371] *S v Turrell* (supra) 259.

[372] The ratio of *S v Wood* 1976 (1) SA 703 (A) is applicable here on account of the similar definition of gathering with which it was concerned.

[373] See the definition of 'place' in s 1(xv). If the minister decided to ban meeting only in public places, then it seems that 'public place' would cover any place to which the public regularly has access: *Bozzoli v Station Commander, John Vorster Square JHB* 1972 (3) SA 934 (W) 940. The judgment goes too far in treating a gathering of persons who are visible from a public place as being a public gathering on the dubious analogy of indecent exposure cases.

[374] See text accompanying n 360 above.

[375] Section 46(3). He must clearly indicate what type of gathering he is prohibiting (ie whether he is acting under s 46(3)*(a)* or *(b)*) and a failure to do so may render the prohibition invalid: *S v Mahlangu* 1986 (1) SA 135 (T).

[376] Section 1(vii).

[377] By GN 582 (*GG* 10157 of 27 March 1986) the minister has prohibited all outdoor gatherings in the Republic, excepting sporting gatherings, for which permission has not been obtained. This is a renewal of a prohibition on such gatherings that has been in force since March 1977.

[378] Section 46(3).

[379] Ibid.

[380] Section 46(1).

[381] Section 46(3).

'reason to apprehend' do not suggest that a subjective test, challengeable only on grounds of mala fides or failure to consider the question at all, was what the legislature intended. So the court held in *United Democratic Front (Western Cape Region) v Theron NO*[382] on the basis that the ground for banning (apprehension of disorder) is a jurisdictional fact open to scrutiny by the court. This judgment was not followed by Kannemeyer J in *Matroos v Coetzee NO*[383] in which it was decided that the mere say so (ipse dixit) of the magistrate is sufficient to create a foundation for issuing the order. The judgment in *Matroos* is clearly wrong,[384] was implicitly rejected by the Natal court in *Metal and Allied Workers Union v Castell NO*[385] and cannot stand in the light of the Appellate Division decision in *Minister of Law and Order v Hurley*.[386] It is noteworthy that the Israeli Supreme Court intervened on the merits of a decision where the enabling language of a provision relating to public processions authorised the District Commissioner of Police to ban a procession 'if in his opinion it is necessary to do so for the maintenance of public security or public order'.[387] Where legislation specifies the grounds upon which the official in question may act (a serious danger to public peace under the South African legislation) the court should investigate the factual basis of the decision even in cases where the statute has used the expressions 'in the opinion of' and 'is satisfied'. The Israeli Supreme Court has set an example which can profitably be followed in South Africa where the courts, by attaching a special magic to particular verbal formulations, preclude themselves from effectively controlling administrative action.

The ministerial power to prohibit meetings, on the other hand, seems beyond challenge except in the hypothetical instances of bad faith, improper considerations or total mental inadvertence to the issues.[388] The relevant discretion-conferring phrase 'if he deems it necessary' will be held, on the relevant South African authorities, to confer a subjective power of decision on the minister. The citizen's right of assembly may therefore be restricted or even abrogated in the minister's sole discretion. It is significant, in relation to both the minister's powers and those of the magistrates, that it relates to gatherings in both public and private places. For a considerable number of years the minister has placed a Republic-wide ban on all open-air meetings other than bona fide sports meetings.[389] The ban has made an incredibly wide range of outdoor gatherings or processions, including protest meetings, illegal unless authorised by the

---

[382] 1984 (1) SA 315 (C). The overruling of this judgment on appeal (1984 (2) SA 532 (C)) was on other grounds. The approach of the lower court has been followed in two cases in Natal and the Transvaal (unreported).

[383] 1985 (3) SA 474 (SE).

[384] The case of *Groenewald v Minister van Justisie* 1973 (3) SA 877 (A), by which the court deemed itself bound, is distinguishable as dealing with an entirely different matter (application for a warrant of arrest).

[385] 1985 (2) SA 280 (D). Though this case dealt with the granting by magistrates of exemptions from a banning order, the line of reasoning is in conflict with *Matroos*.

[386] Supra.

[387] See the case of *Sa'ar et al v Minister of Interior and Police* discussed in (1981) 16 *Israel Law Review* 116.

[388] So the court suggested in *Metal and Allied Workers Union v Castell NO* (supra) 283.

[389] The ban presently in operation was imposed by GN No 582 (*GG* 10157 of 27 March 1986). The prohibition applies to gatherings not held within a building. As to the meaning of building, see *S v Mahlangu* 1986 (1) SA 135 (T).

minister or the magistrate of the district concerned. Protesters have been arrested even when they have stood a considerable distance apart from each other and such arrests have raised the question of what degree of proximity is required between protesters with a common purpose so as to make their protest action a prohibited gathering. In *R v Van Schalkwyk*[390] a conviction under wartime regulations for attending a gathering of more than five persons at which military drilling was taking place, was sustained by the court even though the prosecution could only prove that the accused were in a camp set up for military training and not on the actual parade ground where the training took place. However, it must not be inferred from this case that close proximity is not a requirement of a gathering. The degree of proximity required will clearly depend on the surrounding physical features and whether the gathering takes place in a crowded city or in open spaces. Ten people standing fifty paces apart on an open field may well constitute a gathering but not where they are part of a great throng of people in a city centre. The courts should adopt as a guiding rule the test of whether, regard being had to physical features and the presence of others, the protesters would constitute an entity in the eye of a bystander.

Though on present judicial authority the minister's decision that circumstances justify a ban on meetings is not reviewable on objective grounds, he may render himself susceptible to court challenge by reason of the manner in which he imposes a ban. The three-month ban imposed by the minister on 30 June 1984 on indoor meetings in Cradock[391] appears to be legally vulnerable on account of vagueness. The meetings banned by him in that district[392] are defined in his notice as 'any gathering at which any form of government or any principle or policy or action of the government of any state or the application or administration of any law is propagated, defended, attacked, criticised or discussed, or *which is held in protest against or in support of anything . . .*'. The italicised words in particular appear to be so broad and indefinite that the notice is thereby rendered incurably vague.[393]

Once a gathering has been prohibited by a magistrate or the minister under the powers discussed above, it is a criminal offence *(a)* to convene or promote the gathering in various ways or to preside at it or address it; or *(b)* to print, publish or disseminate in various ways a notice convening it or to advertise it or in any other manner to make it known;[394] or *(c)* to attend it.[395] A person is deemed to have convened a gathering if he has

---

[390] 1943 AD 469.   [391] GN No 1316 (*GG* 9276 of 29 June 1984).

[392] Similar bans were imposed in other areas.

[393] The proclamation constitutes a virtually total prohibition on speech, public or private. The authority to *regulate* something for certain purposes does not include the power to abrogate it: *Landelike Lisensieraad, Krugersdorp v Cassim* 1961 (3) SA 126 (A); *Slambe v Johannesburg City Council* 1951 (4) SA 91 (T).

[394] This includes a newspaper report which draws attention to the proposed gathering as a news item: *S v O'Malley* 1976 (1) SA 469 (N).

[395] Section 57(1). The penalty in the case of *(a)* above is a fine not exceeding two thousand rands or imprisonment not exceeding two years (increased to three thousand rands or three years for a second or subsequent conviction) and in the case of *(b)* or *(c)* above, a fine not exceeding five hundred rands or imprisonment not exceeding six months. Allowing premises or other property to be used for a prohibited gathering is an offence under s 56(1)*(g)* punishable by imprisonment of up to three years; but knowledge that they are to be so used is required for guilt.

caused a written notice to be distributed inviting the public (or a part of it) to assemble at a specified time or place or if he has issued an oral invitation either directly or through another, or if he has taken part in the publication or distribution of such a notice or in the organisation of, or preparations for, such a gathering.[396] It is a defence for the accused to establish that he had no knowledge of the prohibition unless it has been published in the *Gazette*. The *Gazette* is published at the moment when it is first offered for sale anywhere in the Republic.[397] It is also an offence to hold a gathering in contravention of directions issued by the magistrate[398] or to attend a gathering so held or to attend any gathering to which the direction relates where such attendance constitutes a contravention of a condition imposed by the magistrate.[399] A guilty mind is a requirement of all these crimes but proof of negligence by the state will suffice.[400]

When a gathering has been prohibited, a police officer of or above the rank of warrant officer who has reason to believe that it will take place, may cause access to the place where he believes it is to be held, or to any adjacent place, to be closed off for such time as may be necessary to prevent public access.[401] The barring of the place in question must be notified by the police officer at the entrance thereto, or in its vicinity, by the distribution of notices or oral announcements.[402] A person who, without the permission of the police on duty, enters such a place while it is closed off, commits a criminal offence.[403]

The Act confers power on a police officer of or above the rank of warrant officer to cause either a prohibited gathering, or any other gathering[404] at which any person kills or seriously injures another or destroys or seriously damages any valuable property (or attempts to do, or shows a manifest intention of doing, any of these things), to be dispersed.[405] He is required to endeavour to obtain the attention of the persons present by any lawful means and in a loud voice, in each official language, order them to depart from the place of the gathering within a specified time.[406] In view of South Africa's multiracial composition, and the serious consequences which may follow if those present do not disperse, it is disturbing that, where appropriate, an announcement in a language which the officer making it perceives to be the language of the majority of those present, is not required. If they have not dispersed

---

[396] Section 57(3).

[397] *S v O'Malley* (supra). This resulted in the conviction of the accused in Durban who published a report about a prohibited gathering in ignorance of a prohibition gazetted just previously in Cape Town.

[398] Under s 46(1)(ii).

[399] Section 57(2). The penalty is a fine not exceeding two thousand rands or imprisonment not exceeding two years.

[400] *S v Evans* 1982 (4) SA 346 (C). As M F Ackermann op cit 157 points out, proof of an intentional attendance at a gathering is required but a negligent failure to establish that the meeting had been declared illegal will suffice for a finding of guilt.

[401] Section 47(1).   [402] Section 47(2).

[403] Section 57(4). The penalty is a fine not exceeding R250 or imprisonment not exceeding 3 months.

[404] Whether or not it has been prohibited.

[405] Section 48(1). Prohibited gatherings may therefore be dispersed whether they are dangerous or not.

[406] Section 48(1). No explicit warning that force will be used is required. The earlier requirement of *three* warnings has been superseded.

within the specified time, a police officer of or above the same rank, may order the police under his command to disperse the gathering by force, including the use of firearms.[407] No greater force shall be used than the circumstances require and firearms and other harmful weapons shall not be used until either weapons less likely to cause serious bodily injury or death have been used without success or any person present at the gathering kills or seriously injures any person or destroys or does serious damage to any valuable property (or attempts to do, or shows a manifest intention of doing, any of these things).[408] Firearms must be used with reasonable caution, without recklessness or negligence and so as to produce no further injury than is necessary for the dispersal of the gathering.[409] The Act specifically preserves the provision of any other statutes or the common law relating to the duty of the police or a member of the public to assist in the dispersal of riotous gatherings or in the prevention or suppression of riotous and seditious acts.[410] However, common-law rules which render illegal any gathering of persons in the open air without the consent of the authorities are revoked.[411]

Where a local or similar authority's permission is required by any law for the holding or organising of any procession, such permission must in terms of the Act be confirmed by the magistrate of the district where it is to be held.[412] However, the magistrate is permitted to refuse his approval only if he has reason to believe that the holding or organising of the procession may endanger the maintenance of law and order.[413] The effect of this provision is to subject local authority control over processions to central government direction.[414]

The Court Buildings Act[415]

This Act, which came into operation on 1 August 1982,[416] prohibits all demonstrations, and gatherings relating thereto or arising therefrom, in any building in which a courtroom is situated or at any place in the open air within a radius of five hundred metres from such building, on every day of the week except Saturdays, Sundays and public holidays[417] unless the magistrate of the district has granted his written permission.[418] 'Demonstration' is widely defined to include 'any demonstration by one or more persons for or against any person, cause, action or failure to take action', which is connected with or coincides with court proceedings or an inquest.[419] A gathering means any assembly, concourse or procession of any number of persons relating to, or arising out of, a demonstration.[420] The prosecution need not prove that the gathering was previously

---

[407] Ibid.
[408] Section 49(1).   [409] Section 49(2).
[410] Section 51.
[411] Section 52.   [412] Section 53(1).
[413] Section 53(2). It is submitted that there must be objective grounds justifying the magistrate's refusal.
[414] Unless the minister suspends the operation of these provisions of the Act in any particular area in terms of s 53(3).
[415] The Demonstrations in or near Court Buildings Prohibition Act 71 of 1982.
[416] GN No 135 of 1982 (GG 8319 of 30 July 1982).
[417] Section 2(1).   [418] Section 2(2).
[419] Section 1(i). The inquest must be one held under the Inquests Act 58 of 1959.
[420] Section 1(ii).

organised and gatherings which develop spontaneously are covered.[421] A demonstration or gathering falling within these definitions may be dispersed in the same manner as gatherings prohibited under the Internal Security Act.[422]

Various acts connected with demonstrations or gatherings prohibited by this law are made criminally punishable. These include convening, organising, encouraging or promoting such demonstrations or gatherings or presiding at them or addressing them; printing, publishing or disseminating a notice convening or organising them or in any way advertising or making them known; attending or taking part in them; and, finally, demonstrating in a manner prohibited by the Act.[423]

From the preceding account, it will be seen that there are two main classes of act prohibited by this law: demonstrations connected or coinciding with court proceedings and gatherings relating to or arising out of a demonstration. So far as the first class is concerned, this appears to encompass both 'serious' actions such as a violent protest and more trivial actions such as shaking a fist or shouting a slogan. However, it is submitted that 'demonstration' is not wide enough to encompass any act of disapproval, such as a groan, objection or murmuring at a ruling made in court. If it were, even counsel for the accused might contravene the law by protesting against a ruling by the presiding officer.[424] With regard to the gatherings prohibited by the Act, these will only fall within the language of the provision if there is a causal connection between a prohibited demonstration and a gathering. Gatherings formed for the purpose of a prohibited demonstration or gatherings formed as a result of such a demonstration are clearly within the language of the Act. However, a gathering does not become criminal simply because someone present happens to make a demonstration.

The Gatherings and Demonstrations Act[425]

The purpose of this Act is to prohibit both gatherings and demonstrations in the precincts of Parliament which are termed the 'defined area' in the Act.[426] All gatherings and demonstrations (which are defined in the same way as in the Demonstrations in or near Court Buildings Prohibition Act)[427] taking place in the open air are prohibited unless authorised in writing by the Chief Magistrate of Cape Town.[428] The prohibition does not apply to bona fide divine services, funeral ceremonies or processions,

[421] *S v Sithole* 1984 (1) SA 226 (N).
[422] Section 2(3). Dispersal of such gatherings has been dealt with above.
[423] Section 3. The penalty is a fine not exceeding one thousand rands or imprisonment for a period not exceeding one year, or both. According to M F Ackermann op cit 162 guilt depends upon proof of deliberate attendance but a guilty mind in the form of negligence suffices for other elements of the crime.
[424] A protest by a party, a witness or counsel in the usual course of proceedings, can scarcely be prohibited by the Act.
[425] 52 of 1973.
[426] Section 1 and Schedule to Act. A very wide area of the city centre surrounding Parliament is included in the defined area. As to the precise area covered, see M F Ackermann op cit 161 who argues that the streets by which the defined area is bounded are not part of that area.
[427] See text accompanying nn 419–420 above.
[428] Section 2.

official functions or processions or gatherings or concourses of persons who assemble to view any of these specifically excluded events or ceremonies.[429] Certain acts connected with the demonstrations or gatherings prohibited by this law are made criminally punishable. These include convening, organising, encouraging or promoting such gatherings or demonstrations or presiding at them or addressing them; printing, publishing or disseminating a notice convening or organising them or in any way advertising or making them known; attending or taking part in them; and, finally, demonstrating in any manner prohibited by the Act.[430] All the members of a peaceful procession to Parliament to present the government with a petition of concern after the shootings at Uitenhage in April 1985 were arrested and charged with contravening this law.

[429] Ibid.
[430] Section 3. The penalties are a fine not exceeding three hundred rands or imprisonment not exceeding six months, or both. As to mens rea, see M F Ackermann op cit 161.

CHAPTER 9

Speech and Information

A great number of the security-law provisions that have featured in the discussion so far affect freedom of expression and information. Some of these provisions, such as banning and detention, tend to restrict the right of expression indirectly. Even to the extent that it remains possible for a person in detention or under a banning order to continue to write or speak freely, the exercise of that right is likely to be inhibited or 'chilled' by the imposition of a detention or banning order. If, as frequently happens, the victim of a detention or banning order is a journalist, the consequences for free speech are much more serious. There are other provisions of the security laws previously discussed which have a direct effect on speech and information. Examples are the banning of publications and the silencing clause that comes into operation when an individual's name is entered on the consolidated list. In addition, many of the security crimes that we looked at earlier directly curtail freedom of speech. The multifarious restrictions on speech and information, both direct and indirect, that flow from the security provisions already examined do not come near to exhausting the restraints on these rights imposed by the security system. We turn now to a rag-bag of further statutory incursions into the citizen's right to free expression or to receive information about the administration of the society.

The Registration of Newspapers

The notion of a free press in South Africa has strong mythical elements about it. The power to ban newspapers exists and has been exercised, the most significant instance being the outlawing of the influential daily newspaper *The World*.[1] Newspapers, like everyone else, must avoid contravention of our excessively wide security crimes or the publication of speeches and writings by listed persons, to cite but two examples of restraints on the press. In addition to all the other restrictions, there is a security-law restraint on the registration of newspapers which is not widely known and understood within the country, let alone by persons abroad. This restraint, embodied in a provision of the Internal Security Act of 1982,[2] enables the Minister of Law and Order to make the registration of a newspaper conditional upon the deposit with the Minister of Home Affairs of an amount of up to R40 000 as a kind of guarantee of good behaviour. If the newspaper is thereafter banned under the Act,[3] the deposited amount will be forfeited unless the Minister of Law and Order directs otherwise.

---

[1] GN R301 of 1977 (*GG* 5784 of 19 October 1977). *Weekend World* was banned at the same time by GN R302 of 1977 (*GG* 5784 of 19 October 1977).
[2] Section 15 of Act 74 of 1982.   [3] Under s 5 of Act 74 of 1982.

It is illegal to print or publish a newspaper in South Africa unless that newspaper has been registered.[4] The requirement of registration applies to all newspapers published at intervals of not exceeding one month which consist substantially of political or other news or of articles related thereto or to other current topics.[5] Until the security-law intrusion into the registration process, freedom to establish newspapers was guaranteed by obligation imposed on the minister[6] to register a newspaper if the applicant complied with the prescribed formalities and did not choose for the newspaper being registered a name that was the same as an existing one, or so similar as to be calculated to deceive.[7] Registration was therefore mandatory and freedom to publish guaranteed by the Act. Security legislation has limited this freedom drastically.[8] The Internal Security Act of 1982 declares that no newspaper shall be registered unless twenty-one days have elapsed since the submission of the application for registration and unless the proprietor of the newspaper deposits with the Minister of Home Affairs a deposit of not exceeding R40 000 which the Minister of Law and Order may require from that proprietor within the prescribed period of twenty-one days.[9] The latter minister may insist on such a deposit 'whenever he is not satisfied' that a ban on the newspaper 'will not at any time become necessary' under the banning provision[10] of the Act.[11] In less circuitous language, the minister may demand a deposit if he believes that it might be necessary to ban the newspaper at some future date. If the minister does later ban the newspaper, the deposited amount (together with any interest not paid to the proprietor)[12] is forfeited to the State unless the minister decides that a portion of the money should be refunded.[13]

Newspapers already in existence when the deposit requirement was introduced cannot be subjected to this Damoclean form of press control unless their registration lapses. The Internal Security Act of 1982[14] declares that, unless the Minister of Home Affairs with the concurrence of the Minister of Law and Order decides otherwise, the registration of a newspaper will lapse if printing or publishing is not commenced within one month of registration or is suspended at any time for a period exceeding a month[15] or if the newspaper changes hands. If any of these events has occurred, the right of the newspaper to continue publishing may be made subject to a deposit of up to R40 000.

[4] Section 2 of the Newspaper and Imprint Registration Act 63 of 1971.
[5] See definition of 'newspaper' in s 1 of Act 63 of 1971. It is irrelevant that the publication in question is with or without advertisements or illustrations. On the meaning of 'newspaper' and 'published' see *Ritch v Jane Raphaely & Associates (Pty) Ltd* 1984 (4) SA 334 (T) and *S v Davidson and Bernhardt Promotions (Pty) Ltd* 1983 (1) SA 676 (T).
[6] Now known as the Minister of Home Affairs.   [7] Section 4 of Act 63 of 1971.
[8] A further limitation was introduced by s 1 of the Registration of Newspapers Amendment Act 98 of 1982 which in effect gives the minister the power to cancel the registration of a newspaper which does not submit itself to discipline by the Media Council. This change comes into operation on a date to be proclaimed by the State President.
[9] Section 15(1) of Act 74 of 1982.   [10] Section 5.   [11] Section 15(1).
[12] In terms of s 15(3) interest is payable at the expiration of each five-year period.
[13] Section 15(4).   [14] Section 15(5).
[15] Where a newspaper was not distributed to the general public for more than a month, the court held that registration had lapsed even though some copies were printed in that period and delivered to libraries and state institutions: *Argus Printing and Publishing Co Ltd v Minister of Internal Affairs* 1981 (2) SA 391 (W).

The deposit provision affects freedom of the press in two ways. Its first and main impact is on the establishment of new newspapers. A considerable number of proprietors from whom the money has been demanded have been unable or unwilling to provide it and have consequently abandoned their plans to publish.[16] It goes without saying that the poorer black publishers will be the chief victims of this law. Because the established press is mainly white and caters for interests that are predominantly, though not exclusively, white oriented, it is the press freedom of the disenfranchised that is gravely restricted by this law. In the second place, if the proprietor of a newspaper does manage to raise the deposit required by the minister, there will be a continuing apprehension that the newspaper may offend the minister and that a banning will follow with the consequent loss of the deposited money. This constitutes a diabolical way for the government to keep newspaper criticism and revelations in line with its political requirements.

Prisons, Police and Defence

The activities of the prisons, police and defence departments of government are protected in South Africa by a qualified immunity against criticism and exposés. Though it is hardly surprising that military matters should be covered by secrecy legislation, there is no real justification for putting the operations of the prison and police services under wraps. A society cannot be regarded as open and democratic unless there is official accountability for both prison conditions and police activities[17] and even for defence operations with the proviso, in this last instance, that revelations which will bring advantage to the country's enemies should be prohibited. It is an indication of the breadth, indeed meaninglessness, of the concept of 'security' in South Africa, that the everyday activities of the prisons and police departments are protected by legal restraints on disclosure and publication. Though these restraints are not phrased, in the main, as state security provisions, they clearly have a prominent law and order function. We now examine each in turn.

Prisons

A long-standing provision of the Prisons Act[18] makes it a crime to publish any false information concerning the experience in prison of any prisoner or ex-prisoner or relating to the administration of any prison. The publisher will be guilty of this crime if he knew the information to be false or if, believing it to be true, he failed to take reasonable steps to verify its accuracy. It follows that though a guilty mind is a requirement of the crime, it may consist either of the intentional publication of false material or of negligence in the form of a culpable failure to check on its accuracy. The requirement of the crime that the information must have been published will be satisfied by proof that it has been conveyed to one other

---

[16] The government does not provide figures but the number is believed to be in excess of ten.
[17] Subject to necessary, but closely defined, exceptions designed to protect prisoners against humiliating publications or to prevent escapes or break-ins.
[18] 8 of 1959, s 44(1)(f).

person. The state need not establish that it was made known generally.[19] Where the information published refers to the experience in prison of a prisoner or ex-prisoner, it is not necessary to show that it relates to a particular, identifiable prisoner or that it was the personal experience of the prisoner who reveals it; in short, generalised accounts of prison experiences are covered by the prohibition.[20] Moreover, revelations about the behaviour of a particular prison warder (or warders) will be regarded as a reflection on the administration of a prison and therefore within the scope of the prohibition.[21]

While it may be one of the underlying rationales for this prohibition that prisoners should be protected against humiliation and the un- necessary invasion of their privacy,[22] the main purpose is clearly to protect the prison administration against adverse criticism. This is quite unjustified even though it is a requirement of the crime, which the state must prove, that the information published was false. Anyone who has any acquaintance with trials involving unlawful publication will be familiar with the stream of official witnesses ready to swear that nothing uncivilised has ever happened in their prisons and also with the extreme fear and vulnerability of most prisoners or ex-prisoners who are asked to 'blow the whistle' on the prison system. The worse the conditions are the greater will be the reluctance of a prisoner to speak and to risk doing time again under those same conditions and under the control of the very warders that have been exposed. In the leading case on the law against prison disclosures, *S v South African Associated Newspapers*,[23] the prosecution did not have too much difficulty in establishing before the court that things were basically rosy within the prison system, a proposition which acute observers at that time believed to be untrue and which subsequent revelations have stripped of credibility.[24] It is ironic, therefore, that Harold Strachan, one of the chief authors of the exposé which culminated in *S v South African Associated Newspapers*, went back to jail for his pains and that the journalist and editor responsible for publishing the revelations received a suspended sentence and fine respectively.[25] That their courage was rare is evident from the fact that there has not since been a head-on attack on the prison system in any of our newspapers. In any discussion of press freedom in relation to prisons one needs to distinguish between desultory reports of prison maladministration accompanied by routine official denials and hard-hitting, sustained exposés of the kind that led to prosecution in *S v South African Associated Newspapers*. The first does not pose a threat to the authorities and does little more than confuse the general public. The authorities are now sophisticated enough to permit occasional sniping at the prison service followed by a bit of official return

[19] *S v Kiley* 1962 (3) SA 318 (T). This interpretation of the publication requirement is questionable: see A S Mathews *Law, Order and Liberty in South Africa* 216.
[20] *S v South African Associated Newspapers* 1970 (1) SA 469 (W).
[21] Ibid.
[22] This rationale is more evident, however, in the prohibition on making or taking sketches or pictures of prisoners, or on publishing such sketches or pictures: s 44(1)*(e)*.
[23] Supra.
[24] Particularly by Breyten Breytenbach in *The True Confessions of an Albino Terrorist*, loc cit.
[25] The newspaper itself was also fined.

fire.[26] Such exchanges do little harm and the prosecution of the offender will only draw attention to what the administration wishes to hide. A sustained and frontal attack on a sensitive institution like the prison service is another matter. Such exposés are perceived as real threats which cause people, both here and abroad, to sit up and take notice. In short, they are politically embarrassing. Shock exposés of prison conditions have not been published for over a decade and will certainly incur official wrath and reaction should they be revived. Present policy may be summed up as one of tolerating ineffectual criticism.

The actual effect of the prison censorship law, as applied in *S v South African Associated Newspapers*,[27] is to insulate the prison system not just from false criticism but from all hard-hitting criticism, especially in the form of dramatic newspaper exposés. The fact that Breyten Breytenbach's devastating revelations about prison life in South Africa are freely in circulation does not contradict the assertion that the law has immunised the prison administration from exposure and condemnation. The readership of his book is bound to be restricted in view of its style and intellectualism. There is little reason to believe that a more 'popular' piece written by someone other than an international figure who resides abroad would not lead to criminal prosecution. In fact, prosecution may be predicted as a certainty if disclosures of the kind make by Breytenbach were to be published by the press in the form and style adopted by the accused in *S v South African Associated Newspapers*, that is to say, in the style of a hard-hitting, sustained and detailed account of prison iniquities. The irresistible conclusion is that the provision of the Prisons Act now under discussion is a silencing law which limits the accountability of the prison administration. The word 'false' in that provision, requiring proof by the state in any prosecution that the facts alleged are untrue, may be treated as pro non scripto in the light of past experience and present realities. The publishers in *S v South African Associated Newspapers* had taken steps to verify the accuracy of their information but the court, unrealistically in the light of the realities of newspaper publishing and the broader exigencies of South African society, decided that they had not done enough.[28] When a court, as in this case, puts an unnecessarily heavy onus on the publisher by adopting a strict test of what constitutes reasonable steps to verify, it thereby makes publication perilous for anyone who cannot prove the truth

[26] The present policy of the prison administration is to take no official action so long as the information sought to be published has been submitted in full to the administration which is given sufficient time to investigate and offer comment, and the comment of the administration is given the same prominence as the report itself. In the latest edition of Kelsey Stuart's *The Newspaperman's Guide to the Law* 4 ed (Butterworths, Durban, 1986) 150 this policy is described as ending 'the era of an absolute ban on reporting on prisons and prisoners'. Standing alone, this comment is far too euphoric. The new arrangements for the verification of reports on the prisons are a sophisticated form of press co-optation which have ensured, and will ensure in the future, that newspapers will not 'go overboard' on prison conditions, as in *S v SA Associated Newspapers* (supra). An editor who publishes dramatic exposés in breach of the arrangements is likely to be prosecuted; and one who submits to the scheme for verification is unlikely to make shocking revelations. The only acceptable solution is the complete removal of the ban on prison reporting, not the streamlined and insidious form of censorship that is currently being applied.

[27] Supra.

[28] For criticism of this aspect of the judgment, see A S Mathews *Law, Order and Liberty in South Africa* 216–17.

of his disclosures. Given the closed nature of prison systems, and the balance of power enjoyed by the authorities in South Africa, that is a formidable task. A freedom to publish that is made conditional on proof of the truth of what is published, is no real freedom at all.

The legal constraints on revelations about prisons are not strictly security provisions since they refer to all prisons and all prisoners. Nevertheless, these provisions are pregnant with security implications. Each year a considerable number of the victims of security-law enforcement are taken up into the prisons. In addition, a far greater number of persons convicted of violations of the basic laws of apartheid, or of back-up legislation, are inmates of prisons, and the nature of their treatment has immense significance for peace and security. This is true, perhaps to a greater extent, of the treatment of black citizens by the police force, as we shall see when examining the similar restraint on reporting about police activities. No critical review of the South African security system can afford to neglect the law and order implications of provisions which seek to cover up the actions of the prison and police authorities.

Before leaving prisons, brief mention needs to be made of a provision which prohibits the making or taking of a sketch or photograph of a prison or of any prisoner or group of prisoners without written authority.[29] 'Prisoner' is defined to include all persons serving a sentence of imprisonment or sentenced to death.[30] Without analysing these restrictions in detail,[31] they clearly have the effect of preventing the publication of pictorial representations of the treatment of sentenced prisoners. Though it may be necessary to restrict the photography of prisons for security reasons (for example to prevent escapes) and the photographing of individual prisoners to protect their privacy, the provision in question is too broad, and like a related provision of the Police Act to be discussed below, has the effect of preventing the publication of graphic details of the treatment of persons in the prisons. Such treatment is surely a matter of vital public importance.

Police

In 1979 a provision similar to the prisons clause just discussed was introduced to protect the police against the publication of untrue statements about their activities. This provision[32] makes it a criminal offence to publish any untrue matter about the police force, or any part of it, or about any member of the force in relation to the performance of his functions, without having reasonable grounds for believing the statement to be true. The onus of establishing reasonable grounds falls on the publisher who, if he fails to discharge it, becomes liable to a fine of R10 000 or imprisonment for not exceeding five years, or to both the fine and the imprisonment.[33] Before a prosecution is launched, the written

[29] Section 44(e). An exception is made for sketches or photographs made or taken at the time of appearance at court.
[30] Section 1.
[31] For a fuller analysis, see A S Mathews *The Darker Reaches of Government* (Juta & Co, Cape Town, 1978) 149–50; M F Ackermann op cit 204; Kelsey Stuart's *Newspaperman's Guide to the Law* 150.
[32] Section 27B(1) of the Police Act 7 of 1958.
[33] Ibid.

authority of the attorney-general is required. Although there is no authority on the point, publication should be read to mean 'made generally known' and should not include disclosures to one or a few persons, as in the case of the Prisons Act.[34] The wider meaning adopted by the courts in relation to prisons was influenced by the fact that one of the purposes of restricting disclosure under that Act was the protection of individual prisoners against humiliation and invasion of their privacy. No such purpose underlies the similar provision in the Police Act. The Police Act prohibits publication of 'untrue matter' whereas the Prisons Act refers to 'false information' and, on the basis of this distinction, it has been said that the Police Act is wider in the sense that the making of comment, as distinct from the publication of factual material, may be punished at least where the comment is based on allegations of fact.[35] The different phraseology of the Acts does not appear to be significant and by restrictive interpretation both should be confined to allegations of fact.

The scope or reach of the provision protecting the police force and its members from untrue comment is extensive. The actions of individual members of the force are covered so long as they are acting officially; and 'force' includes all ranks and even temporary members or members of the police reserve unless the Commissioner of Police prescribes otherwise.[36] The treatment of detainees by a security police interrogator or any other policeman will fall under the prohibition, as will reports on individual or group police behaviour in the townships. Reports alluding to the single action of a policeman such as an arrest, or to the actions of contingents or detachments of the police, are all caught up in the statutory net. In a nutshell, the performance of all policing functions, whether by individuals or groups in the force, falls within the scope of the law.

As in the case of the Prisons Act, the fact that the onus is on the prosecution to prove that the published allegations are untrue, offers limited comfort and protection to the would-be critic of the police. It is true that police operations generally take place in the open and that, except where police ill-treatment of detainees is alleged, there is a high probability of non-official witnesses being available to the defence. This factor probably accounts for the more regular appearance of critical articles about police behaviour in the press. Nevertheless, there are many contrary factors which reduce the possibility of courts being presented with a powerful statement of the non-official version of events such as police behaviour in the townships. Some of these are the following: (1) The police often seal off areas in which 'sensitive' actions are occurring thereby preventing the more objective evidence of journalists and photographers being available; (2) Journalists who operate in the townships are quite frequently detained or banned—a powerful disincentive to incurring official anger by candid reporting; (3) The victims of police action in the black townships require a high degree of courage to

[34] K W Stuart *The Newspaperman's Guide to the Law* (Butterworth's, 1982) 3 ed 307 does not give a persuasive reason for arguing that 'publish' in the case of the Police Act also has the same meaning as in defamation, that is, disclosure to one other person. (This argument is not repeated in the fourth edition of the book.)

[35] K W Stuart op cit 307. For further possible differences between the two Acts, see K W Stuart, 307–8. (References here to the third edition.)

[36] Definition of 'the force' in s 1.

testify against a force subject to no significant legal restraints and which frequently, judging by the evidence that there is, acts illegally against those perceived to be the enemies of law and order. Just prior to the killing of nineteen blacks by the police in Uitenhage in March 1985, there was a report of the brutal beating at a local police station of a young manacled prisoner; and local residents have claimed that such happenings were quite regular. Where anyone may become the victim of brutal practices, it takes great courage to expose them; (4) Police actions, especially in conditions of disorder, are part of a swiftly moving and changing pattern of events in which hundreds of participants are frequently involved; in such circumstances, finding witnesses to the specific actions reported on can be difficult, and the exact determination of what actually happened even more so; (5) Courts often tend to favour the official witnesses when confronted by unofficial counter-versions of what took place; the police badge is presumptively a badge of credibility.

The contrary factors just mentioned appear to justify the conclusion that, as in the case of prisons, it is not much of a safeguard of press freedom that in a prosecution for publishing untrue matter about the force, the state has the duty to prove the falsity of what has been revealed. Much depends, of course, on how the courts will interpret the words 'without having reasonable grounds ... for believing that that statement is true' which appear in the relevant provision and which cast upon the publisher the duty of showing that his belief was reasonably justified.

There are no court judgments on the point but the relevant Prisons Act decision, *S v South African Associated Newspapers*[37] is hardly encouraging. M F Ackermann in his book *Die Reg Insake Openbare Order en Staatsveiligheid*[38] suggests that the courts should take into account the information function of the press and display a sympathetic attitude towards the situation of the journalist. Such an approach was not adopted in *S v South African Associated Newspapers* and its likelihood will have to be taken on trust by anyone planning to publish a major exposé on police behaviour and practices. It is a fact that allegations of police misbehaviour, and official denials, are fairly common in the press and that such reports have not led to official retribution; yet it remains unlikely that such restraint will continue to be shown if a major press onslaught on the police force were to take place—a kind of Watergate exposé on South African police behaviour. Though the revelations about police misconduct in Namibia by Archbishop Hurley fell short of that, he was brought to court for a violation of the law only to have the charge withdrawn at the last minute; and it is significant that a recent church report on police misconduct during township protests received low-profile press coverage.[39]

The high degree of official protectiveness towards the police in South Africa and of white ignorance of how they act and are viewed in the black townships, makes a gloves-off account of police conduct an urgent necessity. Though such an attack on police behaviour will be seen by many whites as unpatriotic, the opposite is in fact true. Police lawlessness

---

[37] Discussed above under prisons.
[38] Supra at 195.
[39] *Report on Police Conduct During Township Protests* (Southern African Catholic Bishops' Conference, Pretoria, 1984).

is not just bad; it is a deadly poison that is spreading through the body politic thereby creating an incurable hostility between its constituent parts and the certainty of prolonged instability. When asked to explain the bitterness of the Irish toward the English authorities in Northern Ireland, an Irish woman once said that as a child she had vivid memories, while lying in her mother's bed, of the heavy boots of the Black and Tans (English auxiliaries) treading over the bed. Those experiences created a burning and lasting resentment that goes a long way towards explaining the present-day tragedy of Northern Ireland. Tens of thousands of blacks in South Africa have had comparable experiences at the hands of the local police. A South African story, every bit as telling as the Irish woman's explanation, is that of a prominent black woman who, in speaking about the police, stated that from early childhood her reaction on seeing the local Black Maria (police vehicle) was to turn and run for her life. The point of relating stories such as this is not to denounce all policemen as bad or to overlook the difficulty and danger of their role. This familiar smear of liberal-minded critics of the police force misses the central point of that criticism which, although it rightly includes moral condemnation of police misbehaviour, seeks to drive home the crucial lesson that the misuse of the security machine by its operators is converting it into a major engine of divisiveness and strife in South Africa. The most awesome feature of the current unrest in the townships is the seething hatred of the police and other institutions of authority, and of all who collaborate with them. White reaction to the expression of that hatred is frightening in its incomprehension, ranging from the SABC attempts to portray members of resistance groups in the townships simply as savages and barbarians to the government's unwillingness to learn to what extent the unrest is a reaction to present and past misuse of police power. That unwillingness is evident in the terms of reference of the Kannemeyer Commission appointed to report on the shootings in Uitenhage on 21 March 1985. They read as follows:

'To investigate all *the factual circumstances* regarding the *incident itself* on 21 March 1985 at Uitenhage where people were killed and injured and to submit an urgent report.'[40]

The italicised words speak volumes about the government's reluctance to uncover basic grievances and to have objectively examined the terrible dialectic of action, reaction and counter-action between the police and the township residents. Expressed bluntly, what the police may be doing to death in the townships is not just people but the chances of a peaceful political accommodation between blacks and whites in South Africa. There should be no law on the statute book which prevents or inhibits full public discussion of that terrifying possibility.

Another provision of the Police Act[41] prohibits any person, without the written consent of the commissioner, from making a sketch or taking a photograph of a person in custody or a fugitive from custody or from publishing any such sketch or photograph before the relevant trial has

---

[40] GN R726 of 22 March 1985 (*GG* 9674 of 22 March 1985).
[41] Section 27A of Act 7 of 1958. On the question of when a trial has commenced, see *S v Perskorporasie van Suid-Afrika Bpk* 1979 (4) SA 476 (T).

commenced or the person in question has been released.[42] This
prohibition may have legitimate objectives such as the protection of the
accused when an identity parade is to be held or, more dubiously, the
protection of witnesses from intimidation. However, its operation is not
limited to those objectives and its main effect will be to suppress pictorial
representations of police activities in quelling crime and unrest.

The South African Transport Services Act[43] contained a provision[44]
that prohibited the publication of untrue matter in relation to the action of
the Railways Police. This provision was repealed when the Railway Police
were incorporated into the regular police force.[44a]

The Newspaper Press Union of South Africa and the Commissioner of
the South African Police have established an agreement[45] designed inter
alia to protect the informing function of the press whilst preventing
'obstruction of the administration of justice' by the press. Where, as in
South Africa, the police have excessive statutory powers, including powers
of controlling information about themselves, these agreements are even
less likely to ensure full and adequate reporting than in countries abroad
where power is more evenly balanced. As we shall see in relation to
defence reporting, experiments of this kind tend to secure the co-optation
of the press and to keep criticism within bounds set by the authorities
whilst preserving the appearance of freedom to publish.

Defence

A far-reaching provision of the Defence Act[46] prohibits the publication
of three classes of information without ministerial authority. The
prohibited categories are:

(1) Information relating to the composition, movements or disposition of
     the South African Defence Force (including established auxiliary
     services) or of the forces of allied countries and of South African or
     allied ships and aircraft used for naval or military purposes or infor-
     mation relating to services or property commandeered or requisi-
     tioned under the Act.[47]

(2) Statements, comments or rumours relating to a member or activity of
     the South African or a foreign defence force 'calculated'[48] to
     prejudice or embarrass the government in its foreign relations or to
     alarm or depress members of the public.[49]

(3) Secret or confidential information relating to the defence of the
     Republic, including information relating to actual or proposed works
     connected with fortification or defence.[50]

[42] The penalty is a fine of up to R500 or imprisonment of up to twelve months, or both.
[43] 65 of 1981.
[44] Section 45(8). See, also, s 45(7) for prohibitions on photographs, sketches, et cetera.
[44a] By Act 83 of 1986.
[45] For details, see Kelsey Stuart's *The Newspaperman's Guide to the Law* (4 ed) 157.
[46] Act 44 of 1957, s 118.
[47] Section 118(1)(a). A statement, comment or rumour which directly or indirectly
conveys such information is also prohibited.
[48] On a strict interpretation, 'calculated' means intended but the courts are likely to
interpret it as meaning 'reasonably likely to cause': *Minister van Verdediging v John Meinert
(Edms) Bpk* 1976 (4) SA 113 (SWA).
[49] Section 118(1)(b).
[50] Section 118(2). Information relating to the defence of the Republic is presumed secret
or confidential unless the contrary is proved: s 118(5); and information relating to military
equipment is deemed secret unless publication has been authorised: s 118(6).

Any person who has taken part in the unauthorised publication of any information falling into any of these categories is guilty of an offence.[51] It seems that information will not have been published in contravention of these prohibitions unless it has been made generally known.[52]

The general effect of the prohibition on publication of information falling within the three categories is to place a blanket ban on knowledge about defence matters.[53] The extent of the ban is illustrated by the case of *Minister van Verdediging v John Meinert (Edms) Bpk*[54] in which the court decided that a report about a dangerous incursion of guerrilla fighters into South West Africa (Namibia) was one which could reasonably alarm and depress members of the public (second category of prohibited information) but decided that publication of the report was not prohibited only because it related to the calling up of the police reserve which did not fall under the Defence Act.[55] The statutory ban on defence information enabled the government to invade Angola in 1975 and keep its own citizens in the dark until the war was over. The Angolans and the rest of the world knew about the invasion but South Africans, including those whose children, husbands and friends were being killed or maimed in action, or were in danger of becoming battle casualties, were not permitted to know the truth. The same ban, and related official secrets legislation[56] enabled the government to give clandestine support to resistance movements in neighbouring territories (such as Renamo in Mozambique) with incalculable consequences for the future of southern African relations. Secrecy has meant that the government is simply not accountable for drastic, and sometimes rash, actions which affect all its citizens.

In times of actual war it is generally accepted that citizens will be denied information, particularly information about battle strategy and projected military action. It is also legitimate to suppress information of a scientific or technical kind to prevent the enemy learning about weapons and weapon systems. But even when the battle is raging, the government is under a duty to inform its citizens since, as Jefferson once said, 'it is their sweat which is to earn all the expenses of war, and their blood which is to flow in the expiation of the causes of it'.[57] War qualifies the duty of accountability, it does not eliminate it. A serious problem in South Africa is that the reduced obligation to account that is applicable to war situations, is regarded by the government as a permanent state of affairs by reason of the so-called low-intensity conflict in the society. A judicial

[51] Section 118(3). The maximum penalties are a fine of R1 000 or imprisonment for five years, or both. The written authority of the attorney-general, or a person designated by him in writing, is required for a prosecution for publishing information falling into the first two categories: s 118(1A).

[52] See A S Mathews *The Darker Reaches of Government* 145; *S v Du Plessis* 1981 (3) SA 382 (A) 403.

[53] The ban is fortified by another provision (s 118(4)) which prohibits disclosure without authority of secret or confidential defence information obtained by reason of office in government or employment with government. For details, see A S Mathews *The Darker Reaches of Government* 145.

[54] Supra.

[55] M F Ackermann op cit 72 et seq argues, correctly it is submitted, that the correct test is whether the information would alarm and depress the average, reasonable man.

[56] Discussed below.

[57] Quoted by J R Wiggins *Freedom or Secrecy* (Oxford, 1964) 92.

commission of enquiry into the reporting of defence matters in South Africa readily accepted that the wartime balance between secrecy and information was the appropriate one for present and foreseeable conditions in the country. The commission (the Steyn Committee) declared that the 'current and anticipated threat is so serious that the "Supreme Right" of the State must prevail and its defensibility and survival interests must take precedence over the lesser interests of the individual and the group'.[58] This viewpoint envisages the more or less permanent denial of democratic accountability.

The balance which South African law in general, and the Defence Act in particular, strikes between secrecy and the right to know is one that heavily favours news suppression. The Steyn Committee recognised the need to achieve a desirable balance between the two interests but showed little understanding of, or concern for, the way in which the one interest (the right to know) is sacrificed to the other (secrecy) by current law. The Committee quoted with approval a statement to the effect that there 'must be drastic security legislation' and endorsed the accompanying wishful, and even naïve, qualification that this legislation must be used selectively so as not to stifle rightful criticism.[59] It did recommend the amendment of the provision of the Defence Act with which we are here concerned[60] but the Committee's amendment would punish the unauthorised publication of information concerning joint defence and police operations against terrorism and any other information that is calculated to cause enmity between population groups (or parts of them) and the defence force. The Steyn Committee's cure is nearly as bad as the disease at which it is directed; and it would leave virtually untouched the broad legal power to control the content of information that is published about defence. It puts its faith in official/press collaboration as a means of ensuring an informed public—not in a legally guaranteed balance of rights.

There is an agreement between the defence force and the press on defence reporting[61] but both in form and in practice it is precisely the kind of agreement one would expect between two parties that are hopelessly unequal in terms of legal right. It contains a provision that enables the Minister of Defence, when he has decided to gag the press on a military matter, to require the press not to publish the fact of being gagged. K W Stuart, in his discussion of the agreement, says that it is designed to secure the release of as much information as possible 'within the security framework'—a framework which, as we have seen, makes few concessions to the informing function of the press. In an examination of the background to the agreement, G N Addison declares that 'there was every sign that the Defence Committee [the joint official/press committee set up in terms of the agreement] would become the prime agency of collaboration in a system of propaganda'.[62] It is certainly clear that the government would only co-operate with a press which submitted to, even

---

[58] *Report of the Commission of Enquiry into Reporting of Security Matters Regarding the South African Defence Force and the South African Police Force* (RP 52 of 1980 para 277). (See also para 244.) The Commission is referred to below as the Steyn Committee.
[59] Report of the Steyn Committee para 185.   [60] Section 118.
[61] For details of the agreement the reader should consult Kelsey Stuart's *The Newspaperman's Guide to the Law* 4 ed 159.
[62] G N Addison *Censorship of the Press in South Africa During the Angolan War* (unpublished thesis submitted to Rhodes University in 1980) 115.

if it did not share, its assumptions about the nature and origins of the conflict in southern Africa. In recommending a system of government/ press collaboration to secure a flow of information about defence matters, the Steyn Committee assumed that the press would, and indeed should, submit to such assumptions. The Committee says:

> 'Clear guidelines based on an effective communication policy *which will be determined and controlled by the national strategy*, will have to be worked out. In line with such a communication policy the information industry should be harnessed to combat *the psychological onslaught against South Africa.*'[63]

The italicised words demonstrate quite clearly that even a commission headed by an independent judge requires press conformity to assumptions and goals which are not shared by all South Africans. The 'national strategy' and the 'psychological onslaught' are loaded concepts which characterise the conflict in southern Africa in terms of government, or at least white perceptions and interests. It is also implicit in the Commission's report that the government's reform policy is one that should be accepted as satisfying the aspirations of all South Africans and that the press should see that policy in this rosy light.[64] If an independent commission could demand press conformity to national goals, it is obvious that the Defence Department itself will hardly be more tolerant. G N Addison believes that press reporting under the Defence Act is a system of 'covert censorship in which the press plays the role of accomplice'.[65]

We may conclude that the Defence Act, by placing absolute power to control defence reporting at the disposal of the authorities, has enabled the government to conclude between itself and the press an agreement that is ostensibly designed to encourage full information and free reporting and therefore to be in accord with the requirements of a democratic press; whereas in fact, the information and reporting is controlled and directed by the false assumption of a national consensus on the issues of conflict in the society. Relations between the press and the government being conditioned by this false assumption, any defence reporting which radically rejects the 'national strategy' will simply not be tolerated. The government has secured for itself the best of both worlds in the form of absolute power to dictate what may be published and the appearance of respect for press freedom. The result for the press is that it cannot fulfil one of its chief functions—that of presenting radically alternative accounts of political reality. Only a press with legal rights will be in a position to do that. In time it will be realised that the Defence Act and related legislation has done South Africa a great disservice by making the press rightless and therefore unable to confront South Africans in time with those very realities which a shackled press in Rhodesia was prevented from presenting to its citizens.

Official Secrets

The most comprehensive secrecy law on the statute book is the Protection of Information Act of 1982[66] which repeals and replaces the

---

[63] Steyn Committee Report para 233. (Emphasis supplied.)
[64] For example, para 239 *(c)* of the Report.
[65] Op cit 121.
[66] Act 84 of 1982.

Official Secrets Act of 1956.[67] Though such enactments are fundamentally measures to control information and not speech, there is clearly a close link between the freedoms of information and speech; and freedom of expression in relation to public affairs is hardly conceivable in anything but a grossly distorted form unless there is a reasonable degree of access to information. Viewed in this light, the Protection of Information Act makes substantial inroads into both freedom of expression and information since its general effect is to punish the unauthorised disclosure of virtually the whole range of official government information.

Since the Protection of Information Act is a wide-ranging statute which creates numerous offences, all of which cannot be examined in detail here,[68] the ensuing analysis will focus on the anti-disclosure section[69] of the new law and the new crime of espionage.[70]

The anti-disclosure clause

The anti-disclosure provision makes it a crime to deal in various specified ways (which will be discussed below) either with any secret official code or password or with any document, model, article or information[71] falling into any one of five different categories. The categories of protected information, (excluding secret codes and passwords but including documents, models or articles) are the following:

(1) Information which the accused knew, or reasonably should have known, is related to a prohibited place (defined to include military establishments or installations but also to extend to such things as factories, docks , ships, aircraft and radio telegraph or telephone installations[72]) or to armaments, the defence of the Republic, a military matter, a security matter[73] or the prevention or combating of terrorism.[74] *Any* information relating to *any* of these matters is covered so long as the accused knows or should appreciate that it is so related. In view of the laws in force in South Africa, security matters or matters relating to terrorism have a vast spread and extend to all of the multifarious security activities of the state;

(2) Information which is made, obtained or received in contravention of the Act.[75] If the passing of information involves a contravention of any provision of the Act, including the provision presently under discussion,[76] that information becomes 'quarantined' and no one may deal with it in any of the ways examined below;

---

[67] Act 16 of 1956. This Act was substantially a local enactment of the notorious British Acts of 1911 and 1920: see A S Mathews *The Darker Reaches of Government* 138–9.

[68] The reader who requires more detailed analysis is referred to A S Mathews *The Darker Reaches of Government* chs VI & VII; M F Ackermann op cit 50 et seq and *The Law of South Africa* vol 6 para 421.

[69] Section 4.

[70] Section 3.

[71] The terms 'document' and 'model' are both defined in wide terms in s 1.

[72] Section 1(ix). The State President has the power under s 14 to declare other places to be prohibited places. This power, it has been said, enables the State President to cast an 'impenetrable blanket of secrecy' over any area in the Republic: John Grogan, 'News Control by Degree' (1986) 103 *SALJ* 118, 129.

[73] Defined in s 1(ix).   [74] Section 4(1)(*b*)(i).

[75] Section 4(1)(*b*)(ii).

[76] That is, s 4(1).

(3)   Information entrusted to the accused in confidence by a government official.[77]

(4)   Information which the accused obtained by virtue of holding office in government or by virtue of a contract with the government and which the accused knows, or reasonably should know, should be kept secret by reason of the security or other interests of the Republic.[78] As already observed, the concept of a 'security' interest is excessively broad in South Africa but not as broad or as vague as the additional concept of 'other interests of the Republic' that has been incorporated into this provision. If the accused should have realised that *any* interest of the Republic requires that the information be kept secret (by what criteria, it is not at all clear), the information is protected and may not be disclosed.

(5)   Information possessed by the accused which he knows, or should know, was obtained in the manner described in paras (3) and (4) above (that is, in confidence from an official or by virtue of office in government or a contract with government) and the unauthorised disclosure of which he knows, or reasonably should know, will be an offence under the Act.[79]

If the information (including any document, model or article and any secret official code or password) falls into any of the above five categories, it is protected and it will be an offence to deal with it in any of the following ways:

(a)   to disclose[80] it to any other person other than a person to whom the accused is authorised to disclose it or to whom it may be lawfully disclosed or to whom, in the interests of the Republic, it is his duty to disclose it.[81] What is punished by this provision is unauthorised disclosure and the offence may be committed either by an official who discloses what he is not permitted to reveal[82] or by a private person[83] who passes on secret information. If the government decides that protected information should not be disclosed, that is the end of the matter and it will be no defence to argue that it is desirable that the information should be available. If the courts decided to interpret liberally the authority granted by the Act to reveal where there is a duty to disclose 'in the interests of the Republic', the position would be different and the accused could escape liability by showing that, although disclosure was unauthorised, the revelation thereof (say of maladministration) was in the interests of the Republic.[84] Unfortu-

---

[77] Section 4(1)(b)(iii).

[78] Section 4(1)(b)(iv). This provision has been heavily paraphrased in the text.

[79] Section 4(1)(b)(v).

[80] Presumably 'disclose' means to convey the content of the information to another person. In *S v Du Plessis*, 1981 (3) SA 382 (A) 394 the court decided that 'communication' implies conveying the content of the information to someone else; merely showing military documents to another without conveying what is in them is not an offence.

[81] Section 4(1)(aa).

[82] When an official is authorised to disclose is extremely difficult to say. Presumably 'high-up' officials have a discretion to authorise disclosure but not subordinate officials. On the concept of authorisation, see A S Mathews *The Darker Reaches of Government* 110.

[83] A private person who reasonably believes that disclosure was authorised will not be guilty since mens rea is an element of the offence: see A S Mathews op cit 110.

nately, neither the British nor the South African courts have ever made use of this possibility. In the absence of a liberal interpretation by the courts, government maladministration in the security field (for example) may not be disclosed unless the government itself has sanctioned the revelation of such information.

(b) to publish it in a manner or for a purpose prejudicial to 'the security or interests of the Republic'.[85] Case authority makes it clear that if something is objectively speaking prejudicial to the security or interests of the Republic, the accused will be guilty even if his purpose in making the disclosure was not to prejudice such interests.[86] There is more dubious authority that the interests of the state are identical with the interests of the government of the day.[87] There is once again no indication of any criterion by which prejudice to the 'interests of the Republic' is to be judged. Various statutory presumptions assist the prosecution in proving prejudice to these interests by requiring the accused, in effect, to disprove prejudice in specified circumstances.[88]

(c) to retain the information[89] without right or contrary to duty or not to comply with lawful directions for its return or disposal.[90]

(d) to neglect or fail to take care of the information or to act so as to endanger its safety.[91]

If a prohibited dealing with protected information in any of the four ways described above is proved against the accused, he is guilty of an offence and liable to punishment of a fine of up to R10 000 or imprisonment of up to ten years, or both the fine and imprisonment.[92] If the revelation was made for purposes of disclosure to a foreign state of hostile organisation[93] the penalty becomes imprisonment of up to twenty years.[94] This is certainly drastic for information that need not be specially sensitive.

A writer on security law has welcomed the new anti-disclosure provision[95] as an improvement on the earlier provision[96] which it

---

[84] On this line of argument, see A S Mathews op cit 110–1. As Lawrence Baxter op cit 57 points out, the general interest of the public is not identical, except in simplistic terms, with the interests of the public authority in question.
[85] Section 4(1)*(bb)*. It seems that the word 'other' should appear before 'interests' in this subsection.
[86] *S v Du Plessis* (supra) 396.
[87] *Chandler v Director of Public Prosecutions* (1964) AC 763. Not all the judges in *Chandler* subscribed to this proposition and for criticism of this judgment, see A S Mathews *The Darker Reaches of Government* 104.
[88] Sections 8 and 10.
[89] This probably has application only to information recorded in some tangible form such as on a document or tape.
[90] Section 4(1)*(cc)*. Section 4(2) also provides for the punishment of those who unlawfully receive protected information.
[91] Section 4(1)*(dd)*.
[92] Section 4(1). The offence of communicating protected information requires a guilty mind either in the form of intention or negligence (a culpable failure to appreciate that the information is protected or that it should be kept secret in the interests of the Republic). The offence is absolute in the sense that the accused's motive or purpose in releasing it is irrelevant: see A S Mathews *The Darker Reaches of Government* 109–10.
[93] For the definition of a hostile organisation, see s 1(vi) which includes all unlawful organisations.
[94] Section 4(1).   [95] Section 4(1).
[96] Section 3(1) of Act 16 of 1956.

replaced.[97] He relies particularly on the requirement that the accused must be proved to have known, either actually or constructively, that secrecy was required in terms of the security or other interests of the State. This requirement, however, does not apply to all the categories of protected information (for example it is inapplicable to 'security' information) and, in any event, the expression 'other interests of the Republic' is so wide and vague that virtually anything could be found to be undisclosable because harmful to such interests. Unless the courts demonstrate an unaccustomed tolerance of leaks of official information and distinguish very sharply between the interests of the government of the day and those of the state, the improvement is likely to be marginal and to exclude from the ambit of the Act only trivial information such as the numbers of cups of tea drunk in civil service departments every day. It seems unlikly that the disclosures of the kind revealed in *S v Marais*[98] (that the security police had set up a secret section to monitor the telephone calls of certain opposition members of parliament) could be made with impunity under the new law. Marais was acquitted on appeal only because the court found that the information had already become generally known. In *Minister van Polisie v Marais*[99] he had been interdicted provisionally from publishing what was apparently the same information and it seems certain that the courts will treat similar information as protected under the present Act. This means that information which points towards the abuse of police power remains protected because it relates to a security matter. Only if the totally unexpected occurs, and the courts declare such disclosures to be excused by reason of a duty to reveal in the interests of the Republic of South Africa, will revelations about the use and abuse of security power become legal.

In *S v Du Plessis*[100] the accused was convicted under the old Official Secrets Act[101] of handing a book containing information of a military character to his publisher. The Appellate Division confirmed this conviction even though the accused envisaged the vetting of the book by a lawyer and the removal by the publisher of material likely to offend the Act.[102] The court's judgment does not indicate what the information was but an 'enlightened guess' suggests that it concerned South Africa's military adventures in the neighbouring states of Angola and Mozambique. Revelations of clandestine support for resistance movements operating in neighbouring countries, and the pursuit of a dangerous policy of southern African destabilisation, would clearly fall under the proscriptions of the new law and the leaking of information about such activities, however detrimental they may be to South Africa's interests, would be criminal. In seems too that the disclosure to the press of an official document which proved government complicity in the abortive Seychelles coup of November 1981,[103] would offend the anti-disclosure provisions of the Protection of Information Act. Whether there was such an involve-

---

[97] M F Ackermann op cit 55.
[98] 1971 (1) SA 844 (A).
[99] 1970 (2) SA 467 (C).
[100] Supra.
[101] 16 of 1956, s 3(2)(a).
[102] See pp 401–3 of the judgment.
[103] For the facts found by the trial court see *S v Hoare* 1982 (4) SA 865 (N).

ment was canvassed in the press but the relevant parts of the trial of the
mercenaries who took part in the coup attempt were held in camera. It
should not be a crime, assuming that the government was involved in this
stupid and dangerous piece of opportunism, to disclose official documents
and thereby make public the involvement of government officials. While
such disclosure remains criminal, there is no real government accountability to the public and no disincentive to avoid future acts of irresponsible
military or foreign policy adventurism.

An interesting test of the scope of the anti-disclosure clause of the
Protection of Information Act is to ask whether that clause would inhibit
disclosure of a new scandal of the kind now known as Muldergate or as the
'information scandal'. At the centre of that scandal was the use of secret
government funds to the tune of R32 million[104] to establish and fund a
pro-government English language newspaper. It is clear from the
character of that newspaper, *The Citizen*, that its purpose was to promote
government policy, whatever may have been said at the time about the
need to have an 'objective' newspaper in the English language. On this
point the Erasmus Commission was quite unequivocal and declared in its
report that the newspaper was required to 'support the party policy in
regard to separate development' and that 'it is indisputably clear that the
newspaper positively encouraged voters to vote for the ruling party'.[105] It
is a gross irregularity and act of mismanagement for a government to
devote public funds for party political gain; and this misconduct was
compounded by the secrecy which surrounded the operation and the
unauthorised transfer of funds from other government departments into
the secret account of the Department of Information.[106] The question that
now concerns us is whether such irregularities, if they occurred again,
could be revealed without fear of contravening the anti-disclosure clause
of the Protection of Information Act. Though the answer to that question
is not at all clear, there are a number of considerations which suggest that
disclosure might well contravene the Act. An honest government servant
who learns of the irregularities will have obtained access to the
information by virtue of his office (category (4) of the classes of protected
information) and may not disclose it if he knows, or should know, that
secrecy is required by the security or other interests of the Republic. Can
we be sure that the courts will decide that a secret plan conceived to
counter the so-called psychological onslaught on the Republic is not in the
'interests of the Republic'? The Erasmus Commission said that the
'purpose' of the secret fund, to counter anti-South African propaganda,
'had all the attraction of a lovely fresh apple' but conceded that lack of
clarity in 'existing statutory control' constituted 'a germ which could
cause complete rot to set in'.[107] This suggests a rather equivocal judicial
attitude to the misconceived scheme to further the 'interests of the
Republic'. A more serious difficulty is that schemes of this kind are

[104] The exact amount at the time of the report of the Erasmus Commission was R31 907
732: see *Report of the Commission of Enquiry into Alleged Irregularities in the Former Department of
Information* (RP 113/1978) para 9.298 (referred to below as the Erasmus Commission
Report).
[105] Ibid para 9.263.
[106] On the source of the funds, see Erasmus Commission Report, para 2.26.
[107] Erasmus Commission Report, para 3.36.

frequently a compound of legitimate and illegitimate plans and activities, and that the disclosure of irregular aspects could involve disclosure of everything. A study of the Muldergate affair shows that this was precisely the problem that faced civil servants at that time:

> 'As anxious as they are to clear themselves of any involvement, they will not be seen to be identified with any exposure that could be harmful to the country. They are frightened of contravening the Official Secrets Act and point out that if the probe is to reach any material conclusion, many legitimate current operations would have to be exposed at great cost to the country.'[108]

In the absence of court rulings that the disclosure of secret schemes of mismanagement is in the interests of the Republic, the fears described in this quotation are not irrational. In the recent British trial of Clive Ponting, a senior official in the Department of Defence, for releasing to a member of the British parliament information that disclosed that parliament had been deceived about the exact circumstances of the sinking of the *Belgrano*, the judge equated the 'interests of the State' with 'the policies of Government Ministers at any given moment'.[109] A rebellious British jury saved Clive Ponting from conviction; but for the South African civil servant who leaks information there is no such jury to come to his rescue.

Even a private citizen who learns of irregularities of the kind that occurred in Muldergate, may hesitate to blow the government's cover. Apart from fears of illegal retribution,[110] the terms of the Protection of Information Act are not reassuring for the private citizen either. If he has received the information in confidence from an official of government (category (3) of the classes of protected information) or suspects that it has been passed on in contravention of the Act (category (2) of the classes of protected information) he clearly risks prosecution and conviction unless his disclosures are found by the court to be in the interests of the Republic—a finding, we have seen, that is unlikely in the light of past precedents. It is significant that the government's cover in Muldergate was effectively blown only when Judge Mostert decided to make public the information which he had received in the course of his investigation into exchange control irregularities. In releasing the information, he was able to rely on his powers to disclose testimony under the Commissions Act,[111] a legal justification that is not available to the ordinary citizen (or to a civil servant) who leaks information. Judge Mostert provided the press with 'hard' information—with information that, unlike speculation based on rumour, the government was unable to deny.[112] The terms of the Protection of Information Act remain ominous for anyone who provides the public with hard information of government mismanagement. Such a person runs the risk, which Mostert did not face, of the material being deemed by a court to be protected (under the broad category of security,

[108] Mervyn Rees & Chris Day, *Muldergate* (Macmillan, Jhb, 1980) 46.
[109] See report in *The Observer* 17 February 1985,10–11 and 1986 *Crim L Rev* 491, 497.
[110] As to which, see Mervyn Rees and Chris Day *Muldergate* passim.
[111] 8 of 1947. For text of Judge Mostert's statement on releasing the information, see Mervyn Rees and Chris Day op cit 96.
[112] On the concept of 'hard' information and on the risk of prosecution for releasing it, see A S Mathews *'The Erasmus Commission Report'* (address published by the South African Inst of Race Relations Durban, 1979) 2 et seq.

for example) against disclosure in the undefined 'interests of the Republic'. The Act is therefore no great improvement on its predecessor.

Before we take leave of Muldergate, it is important to record that this shameful episode did not prompt the government to open the channels of communication with the general public. Instead, it secured the passage through parliament of a body of laws that have the opposite effect of restricting the public's right to know. This is partly due to the inexplicable failure of the Erasmus Commission to recommend the narrowing of existing secrecy laws or the introduction of a positive right to information along the lines of freedom of information legislation that is becoming increasingly common in the Western world. One of the first measures to be introduced by the government (in response to the imminent eruption of the information scandal) was the Secret Services Account Act of 1978.[113] This Act provides for the creation of a fund, out of moneys appropriated by parliament, to support secret government schemes and activities. Transfers may be made from this fund, by agreement between the Minister of Finance and the minister of the department concerned, to secret accounts established by legislation in the departments of Defence, Foreign Affairs, Security Services, Information and Police.[114] In addition, by similar agreement, money may be transferred from the fund to any other department for 'services of a secret nature'.[115] In a nutshell, the Secret Services Accounts Act authorises a secret fund in any or every department of state. In many Western societies it is common for the intelligence services to be funded by secret appropriations but permitting clandestine funds right across the board is an unusual and alarming extension of the principle. It is also alarming that the auditing of secret accounts by the auditor-general, and his access to vouchers, may be limited by the minister of the department concerned;[116] and the minister may also limit the auditor-general's report to parliament in respect of such accounts.[117] One of the Acts which establishes a departmental secret account, the Information Service of South Africa Special Account Act,[118] authorises the use of the money in the fund for promoting the image of the Republic and averting psychological attacks upon it.[119] The Muldergate scandal illustrated how easily members of the government confuse the government's image with that of the Republic and how readily attacks upon the government are equated with attacks on the Republic. The establishment of the *Citizen* newspaper with public money was *par excellence* an example of that kind of confusion. Similar confusions may be influencing the use of secret funds at this very moment and the new legislation appears to have created a machinery for regularising and concealing such behaviour rather than exposing it. Irregularities of the

[113] Act 56 of 1978.
[114] Section 2(2). The legislation establishing departmental secret accounts consists of the Foreign Affairs Special Account Act 38 of 1967, the Security Services Special Account Act 81 of 1969, the Information Service of South Africa Special Account Act 108 of 1979, the Defence Special Account Act 6 of 1974 and the South African Police Special Account Act 74 of 1985.
[115] Section 2(3).
[116] Section 42(7) of the Exchequer and Audit Act 66 of 1975.
[117] Section 45(1A) of the Exchequer and Audit Act 66 of 1975.
[118] 108 of 1979.
[119] Section 2(2).

kind that characterised Muldergate may never again be uncovered unless they take the form of actual embezzlement and fall under the provisions of the Advocate General Act of 1979.

The Advocate General Act[120] is the only piece of legislation that has any claim to being a legislative corrective to the evils of Muldergate. It provides for the appointment of a specialist 'ombudsman' to investigate and report to parliament on the dishonest use of public moneys or on the misappropriation of public moneys in an unlawful or improper manner.[121] Legislatively, therefore, the role of the advocate-general is restricted to financial corruption in the public service and related bodies.[122] The fundamental evil of Muldergate, however, was not corruption in the narrow sense (though there was evidence of that) but the mismanagement of state funds.[123] As a remedy for that problem the Act is misdirected and misconceived. Since his appointment, the advocate-general has managed to broaden his mandate and to report on matters such as improper telephone tapping.[124] In a recent investigation concerning the possible enrichment of persons involved in South Africa's oil purchases, the advocate-general did investigate the question whether too much had been paid for crude oil and answered this question negatively.[125] These tentative extensions of jurisdiction have taken the advocate-general into the area of mismanagement and it could be argued that he has fashioned his office into one which might deal with and expose irregularities of the Muldergate type. Unfortunately, such an argument is an unduly optimistic one. The chief hindrance to the use of his powers as a counter to maladministration in a broad sense is the requirement of the Act that complaints must be placed before him on affidavit.[126] Civil servants who are aware of acts of mismanagement are hardly likely to put on affidavit complaints about colleagues or superiors, including any minister that may be involved. Public servants are simply not given to such suicidal conduct even on the assumption (and it is a large one) that they are likely to be offended by departmental policy and practice. Failing acts of 'treachery' by members of the government service, there is unlikely to be anyone else who will be in a position to reveal mismanagement. We have seen that the minister of a department may limit the audit of secret funds and the access of the auditor-general to relevant vouchers. Though the advocate-general may initiate an investigation[127] he will not normally see the accounts and vouchers of secret funds and is certainly not likely to use his powers under the Act[128] to conduct a general fishing expedition into the management of secret accounts. Even if the impossible were to happen, and an act of mismanagement relating to a secret fund were to be investigated, the Act would still not operate as a disclosure law by reason of a clause[129] authorising the advocate-general to prohibit publication of a report in the interests of state security. The exercise of this discretion to

---

[120] 118 of 1979.   [121] Section 4.
[122] See definition of public moneys in s 1 of the Act.
[123] See A S Mathews 'The Erasmus Commission Report'.
[124] Lawrence Baxter Administrative Law 291 and Reports of the Advocate General, Report 2 (1980).
[125] Reports of the Advocate General, Report 7 (1984) pp 42–3.
[126] Section 4(2).   [127] Section 5(5).
[128] Section 7 relating to production of documents.   [129] Section 5(2).

suppress publication is highly likely where secret accounts are concerned. We may conclude that the most promising law enacted in response to Muldergate is not an effective disclosure law, especially where secret accounts are concerned. It is disconcerting, too, that several other anti-disclosure laws were enacted after Muldergate; but these will be discussed separately below since they were not legislative reaction to the information scandal.

The espionage clause

Having examined the anti-disclosure provision of the Protection of Information Act, we now turn attention to the new espionage clause[130] of the same Act. The understanding that most people have of espionage, or spying as it is more commonly called, is that it involves the passing of military secrets to the enemies of the country. The word 'spying' conjures up the names of people like the Rosenbergs or Fuchs who passed atomic secrets to the Russians; or of Burgess and Maclean who systematically provided the Russians with sensitive information before defecting to the East. The espionage clause of the Protection of Information Act, while providing for the punishment of such people for such acts, extends so far beyond the conventional conception of spying as to make the crime almost unrecognisable as an anti-espionage measure. It is, more accurately, an anti-disclosure law which catches up espionage and about a hundred other things in its generous but sinister embrace.

A remarkable feature of the espionage clause is that it does not directly punish the most common example of spying - the passing of sensitive information to a foreign state. Instead of focusing on the act of passing information it deals with the prior stage of *gathering* information for that purpose. In addition, it is not limited to sensitive military information but to a whole range of information that need have no connection with defence and may not even be specially sensitive. It is these two features of the crime that give it the quality of a broad concealment statute. In the ensuing analysis of the offence, a distinction will be made between the *actions* prohibited (the gathering aspect) and the *nature of the material* that must be so dealt with (that is, gathered for purposes of passing).

Beginning first with the nature of the material that is protected by the espionage provision, we find that information falling into four categories is covered, these being:

(1) a secret official code or password. No objection can be taken to protecting such information as it is clearly sensitive;
(2) information (and any document,[131] model or article) relating to a prohibited place, or to armaments. As noted earlier 'prohibited place' extends well beyond military installations and covers all industries and a large part of the infra-structure of the country;[132];
(3) information (including any document, model or article) relating to military or security matters or to anti-terrorist operations. The broad scope of security matters and of terrorism has been stressed in relation to the anti-disclosure provision of the Act;

---

[130] Section 3.   [131] Widely defined in s 1.
[132] 'Prohibited place' is defined in s 1.

(4) information relating to any other 'matter or article' (including any document, model or article). This final blanket category is obviously both vague and far-reaching.

The first category of information (para (1) above) is absolutely protected while the next three (paras (2), (3) and (4) above) are protected if the accused knew or should have known that the information in question would be of direct or indirect benefit to a foreign state or hostile organisation[133] and that the security or other interests of the Republic require its non-disclosure. Though these two requirements are clearly meant to set outer limits to the information covered by categories (2), (3) and (4) above, only a small degree of reflection is needed to recognise that the narrowing effect of the statutory limitations is insignificant. There is a vast amount of information (both sensitive and non-sensitive) that will be directly or indirectly useful to a foreign state or hostile organisation; and it will not be too difficult to find a security interest or *any other interest of the Republic* that will require non-disclosure of that information.

Various forms of dealing with information falling into any of the four protected categories are made criminal offences by the Act.[134] No person may receive or obtain any such information or prepare, compile or produce it for the purpose of disclosure to any foreign state or institution (or inhabitant or member thereof) or to any hostile organisation (or member, officer, office-bearer or active supporter thereof).[135] In brief, the crime consists of receiving, preparing or producing protected information for foreign transmission. Actual transmission is not an element of the crime, only intended transmission. Though the prosecution is required to prove the intention to transmit, its task may be made easier by a number of presumptions in the Act. If the prosecution shows that the accused communicated or attempted to communicate with an 'agent' or that the accused is an 'agent' or that he is reasonably suspected of being used (directly or indirectly) by a foreign or international body or institution, or that he entered the Republic in contravention of any law, he is presumed to have received, prepared or disclosed the information in question for the purpose of foreign communication unless he proves the contrary.[136] 'Agent' is widely defined to include present or past agents of a foreign state or hostile organisation or any person reasonably suspected (by the accused?) of being used by a foreign state or hostile organisation for the purpose of committing any act prejudicial to the security *or other interests* of the Republic or reasonably suspected of having committed (or attempting to commit) any such act in the interests of a foreign state or hostile organisation.[137] A further presumption facilitates proof that the accused has communicated with an agent and such communication will be presumed where, for example, he has visited the address of an agent (or

---

[133] Defined in s 1 to mean any banned organisation or any organisation declared to be hostile under s 14.

[134] The penalty is imprisonment for up to twenty years: s 3.

[135] The prohibition on dealing with protected information extends to dealing with parts of it and the prohibition on obtaining it includes copying it: s 1(2). The same subsection makes it clear that disclosing something includes transmitting or transferring it; disclosure of the content is not necessary for guilt.

[136] Section 8(1).

[137] Section 1.

suspected agent) or the address of such a person is found in his possession.[138] What these presumptions mean is that it will be fairly easy for the prosecution to shift the onus on to the accused so that he will have to disprove an intention to communicate rather than the state being required to prove it. If you have visited a foreigner, or have a foreigner's address in your address book, you may end up by having to prove that you are not a spy, especially if that foreigner has connections with a foreign government or institution. Another presumption facilitates proof that information which the accused received, compiled or prepared is in fact information which is directly or indirectly of use to a foreign state or hostile organisation. If the accused is an agent (as defined above) or is reasonably suspected (by the authorities?) of having been used by a foreign or international body or institution, then it is presumed that the information in question was of direct or indirect use to a foreign state or hostile organisation.[139] Where all the presumptions operate, there is very little that the prosecution has to prove, and a great deal that the accused has to disprove to avoid conviction.

The foregoing analysis of the crime of espionage demonstrates that people could be condemned as spies for some pretty innocent activities. An economic researcher who prepares a paper on South Africa's vulnerability to sanctions and who sends it to a colleague at a foreign university appears to be guilty because the paper was compiled for disclosure to 'an employee ... of [an] institution ... in any foreign state' and is of such a kind that it will 'directly or indirectly be of use to any foreign state'. The prosecution will have little difficulty in establishing that *some* interests of the Republic requires non-disclosure of such a research paper. A fortiori, there will be guilt where the paper is sent to a foreign journal for publication. Since the information does not have to be official,[140] many other examples of the transmission of material abroad will constitute spying: an analysis of the government's programme to combat 'terrorism'; the conduct of the military and the police in township disturbances, acts of military or foreign policy adventurism and the like. None of these examples can be excluded with confidence from the reach of the crime of espionage. The only real limiting factor is that the attorney-general may decline to give his written authority for a prosecution;[141] but the attorney-general is statutorily under the control of the Minister of Justice.[142]

Key Points, 'Goods and Services', et cetera

The South African statute book abounds with anti-disclosure laws and a systematic account of these would require a separate book. In this concluding section brief reference will be made to some of the more notable of these provisions.

---

[138] Section 8(2).
[139] Section 9. This presumption applies to protected information referred to in s 3*(a)* and 3*(b)*(1) and (2); it is not applicable to information referred to in s 3*(b)*(iii).
[140] As it would for a prosecution under the anti-disclosure provision (s 4) of the Act.
[141] This is required by s 12.
[142] Section 3(5) of the Criminal Procedure Act 51 of 1977.

The National Key Points Act[143]

This law is designed to protect places or premises deemed to be of strategic interest against sabotage or other forms of attack. It authorises the Minister of Defence to declare any place (meaning any premises, building, installation or industrial complex[144]) or any area (meaning any soil or water surface, with or without structures thereon[145]) to be a National Key Point.[146] The minister may also declare two or more National Key Points to be a National Key Points Complex if he believes that joint action by the owners will contribute to their security.[147] The declaration by the minister does not require any formality except that he is required to give written notice to the owner.[148] It seems that the minister need not publicise the declaration in any way. Various consequences following a declaration of any place or area as a National Key Point (or Key Points Complex), such as the duty to take steps to the satisfaction of the minister for the security of the place or area affected by the declaration.[149] The consequences that are relevant in this discussion are those that prohibit the disclosure of information. The first of these is embodied in a provision which makes the provisions of the Protection of Information Act relating to prohibited places applicable to National Key Points.[150] This means that in general the disclosure of information relating to a National Key Point or the gathering of such information with a view to foreign communication carries the penalties provided for by the Protection of Information Act. This extension is disturbing for two reasons. First, the disclosure of information about almost anything from bare ground to buildings (of any kind) may become subject to the drastic penalties of the Protection of Information Act. It is hard to imagine anything other than movables that cannot be given key point status. Second, the declaration of a place or area as a National Key Point may be done in secret with no one knowing about it except the owner who is himself under a duty of non-disclosure under the Act.[151] A journalist, for example, who writes about a key point is guilty if he should reasonably have known that it was one—but what steps he should have taken to avoid a court finding that his ignorance was unreasonable is something of a mystery. Another anti-disclosure provision of the Act makes it a crime to 'furnish' without legal obligation or right, or without the authority of the minister, any information relating to the security measures applicable at a key point or relating to any incident that occurred there.[152] 'Incident' means 'any occurrence arising out of or relating to terroristic activities, sabotage, espionage or subversion'.[153] This drastically curtails the right to report on the nature and extent of the campaign of political violence in

---

[143] 102 of 1980. For more detailed accounts of this Act, see M F Ackermann op cit 126.
[144] Definition of 'place' in s 1.
[145] Definition of 'area' in s 1.
[146] Section 2.
[147] Section 2A.
[148] Sections 2 and 2A.
[149] Section 3. The owner who fails to take the required steps is guilty of an offence and the minister may cause the necessary steps to be taken at the owner's expense.
[150] Section 10.   [151] See ss 4 and 10.
[152] Section 10(2).
[153] Section 1.

South Africa. It enables the authorities to keep the public in the dark about the kind of place that is becoming dangerous and the direction and magnitude of that campaign. Even if the authorities do not wholly cut off the supply of such information, they are in a position to control its content and emphasis. There are some restrictions on disclosure which are more precise and justifiable—for example the publication of information about security measures in force at a key point[154] or concerning the composition, duties, movements and methods of security personnel who operate there.[155] If the legislature had restricted itself to such prohibitions instead of putting a blanket ban on disclosures, the intrusion on freedom of speech and information would be negligible and defensible.

The National Supplies Procurement Act[156]

This Act offers another fine example of the crude shotgun method of information control in South Africa. The main purpose of the Act is to grant vast powers to the Minister of Industries, Commerce and Tourism to manufacture, produce or acquire goods and services, to control or even prohibit the manufacture, production, acquisition, supply or even possession of goods and services by any person, or to requisition goods and services for the state.[157] The minister may take such action whenever he deems it necessary or expedient for the security of the Republic; and his actions may relate to any goods or services, these terms being undefined by the Act. When the minister has taken action in terms of these vast powers (for example, has taken over production and supply, prohibited it or requisitioned goods and services) it becomes a criminal offence to disclose to any person any information relating to the affected goods or services unless the minister (or a controller authorised by him) has authorised disclosure or unless it has been made as a witness in a court of law, for purposes of the Act itself, or to a person to whom there is a duty to make it.[158] The prohibition on disclosure extends also to any 'statement, comment or rumour calculated directly or indirectly to convey such information or anything purporting to be such information'.[159] The Act goes even further and, in another prohibition, authorises the minister to prohibit generally the disclosure of any information relating to any goods or services (or statement, comment or rumour calculated to convey it directly or indirectly) if he deems such prohibition to be necessary or expedient for the security of the Republic.[160] This prohibition authorises secrecy in relation to goods or services even if the minister has not exercised his powers under the Act in relation to them. What are we to make of a law which empowers an official to make a state secret of the whole of commerce and industry? The grant of such power appears to be as stupid as it is awesome.[161] That grant moreover took place in 1979,[162] a fact which illustrates how well lessons of Muldergate have been learnt!

[154] Section 10(2).
[155] Regulation 19 in GN R1731 of 13 August 1982 (*GG* 8338 of 13 August 1982).
[156] 89 of 1970.   [157] Sections 2, 2A and 3 of the Act.
[158] Section 8A. The penalty is a fine of up to R7 000 or imprisonment of up to seven years, or both.
[159] Ibid.   [160] Section 8B. The penalties are those indicated in n 158 above.
[161] On the technical requirements for guilt, see M F Ackermann op cit 61.
[162] Sections 8A and 8B were introduced by s 1 of Act 73 of 1979.

Miscellaneous anti-disclosure provisions

Concealment clauses similar to those relating to key points and goods and services appear in a large number of the statutes but in general do not have quite the same boundless application as those already discussed. Only some of the more relevant of these will be mentioned. Heavy penalties[163] are provided in the Petroleum Products Act of 1977[164] for the unauthorised publication[165] of wide range information relating to petroleum products, including crude oil. A similar provision in the Armaments Development and Production Act of 1968[166] prohibits *disclosure to any person* of a broad range of information relating to armaments. Then again the Nuclear Energy Act of 1982[167] prohibits every conceivable type of disclosure relating to nuclear materials and energy. Though in each of these cases there is a legitimate interest to protect, the concealment clauses prohibit disclosures in such an indiscriminate way that everything, both sensitive and non-sensitive, is protected. Thus in *S v Marais*[168] the accused was convicted of contravening the relevant clause of the Petroleum Products Act by alleging in a speech at a public meeting that there was no shortage of petrol in South Africa and that the government was in fact supplying petrol to neighbouring black states. An Act which criminalises this type of broad political criticism of the government makes unnecessary inroads into political freedom. It is noteworthy that Marais was not accused of revealing information that was genuinely sensitive, such as the sources and location of South African crude oil stocks. In the course of his judgment, Spoelstra J said that the purpose of the law was to enable the government to control the nature of information published about petroleum products. On this interpretation, the government may control criticism of itself and criminally punish those who do not conform to its prescriptions.[169]

State privilege

This is a doctrine of the law of evidence which entitles the executive branch of government to assert that information (usually documentary) in its possession is privileged from disclosure in court or similar proceedings on the ground that the public interest would be jeopardised by its production. The effect of a successful assertion of state privilege is to deny the information to the litigant and the court even though it may have a direct bearing upon the issues being tried. Therefore, although state privilege is not an anti-disclosure law, by preventing a litigant and the courts of justice from access to certain kinds of information, it functions as

[163] A fine of up to R7 000 or imprisonment of up to seven years, or both: s 12(1A).
[164] Act 120 of 1977, s 4A.
[165] Although the word 'publish' in the Act means to make generally known, it is not a defence to show that the information was previously disseminated without authority by some other person: *S v Marais* 1983 (1) SA 1028 (T).
[166] Section 11A of Act 57 of 1968. The maximum penalties are a fine of R15 000 or eight years' imprisonment, or both.
[167] 92 of 1982 ss 68, 69 and 70.
[168] 1983 (1) SA 1028 (T).
[169] Since the decision in *S v Marais* (supra), the Act has been amended and the prohibition on publication is now dealt with by regulations (GN R1614 *Reg Gaz* 9846 of 19 July 1985). However, the prohibitions in the regulations are as wide as before and would justify Marais' conviction.

a secrecy law which also deprives the general public of information about the conduct of executive government. Information produced in court or other judicial proceedings is normally available to the public by reason of the public character of justice in open political systems.

In some countries, the privilege of the executive to withhold information is a broader doctrine which transcends the law of evidence. In the United States, for example, it has been asserted to deny information to Congress and its committees about the functioning of the executive branch of government. An American court upheld a claim to executive privilege against an investigating committee of the senate in *Senate Select Committee on Presidential Campaign Activities v Nixon*[170] on the ground that the information being sought by that committee was only tangentially related to its functions. The final decision on the right to withhold the information significantly rested with the court in this case. In South Africa, executive privilege is known only in its evidential form since parliament is not in the habit of asserting an investigative power over the executive which in practice controls it. We shall not therefore be discussing the wider doctrine of executive privilege in this section[171] but rather the more traditional state privilege rule under which the executive may deny evidence to judicial bodies.

Some of the leading cases on state privilege dramatically illustrate the conflict of interests that lies behind this doctrine and the suppression of evidence for which it is authority. In the war-time English case of *Duncan v Cammel Laird & Co Ltd*[172] the plaintiff in an action for damages arising from the death of a crewman in a submarine which sank with almost total loss of life, was denied access to documents relating to the construction of the submarine in the attempt to prove negligence on the part of the contractors who built the submarine. The state interest in keeping the design of its submarines secret in times of war was preferred to the litigant's interest in a fair and just resolution of the dispute. The litigant also lost out in the similar case of *United States v Reynolds*[173] in which the plaintiff was denied investigative reports on the crash of an airforce plane in which her husband had been killed. These reports would have revealed information about the electronic equipment in the aircraft. The conflict of interests in these cases is somewhat more complex than a clash between the public interest in protecting certain secrets and the individual interest in justice. The rendering of justice is not simply an interest which the particular individual has in a particular case but also a general public interest in the proper and equitable resolution of disputes. There is also a clash between two institutions of government (the executive and the judicial) each of which is concerned about the harm that will be done to its own functioning should the privilege to withhold information be upheld or denied.[174] Finally, upholding a privilege to suppress information has the

---

[170] 498F 2nd (D C Cir 1974).
[171] For a more detailed discussion of executive privilege in the broader sense see A S Mathews *The Darker Reaches of Government* 52.
[172] [1942] 1 All ER 587 (HL).
[173] 345 US 1 (1953) 97 L ed 727.
[174] On the conflict of interests in state privilege cases, see S J van Niekerk et al *Privilegies in Die Bewysreg* (Butterworths, Durban, 1984) 240 et seq.

effect of denying the general public knowledge about important matters of government administration.

The vital interests that are at issue in state privilege cases make it important that the resolution of the conflict between the state, when it asserts the privilege, and a litigant who seeks access to the officially withheld information, should be under the control of independent courts. As we have seen, these interests transcend those of the nominal parties to the dispute and their importance demands a judicious weighing-up of the respective claims of each in the context of the relevant facts. The courts are best equipped to balance the conflicting interests in a dispassionate and fair-minded way and to decide in particular cases which interest should prevail. For a considerable time in England, *Duncan v Cammel Laird & Co Ltd* [175] was taken as authority for the proposition that the executive had the final say in state privilege cases and that the courts had no power to override a clear assertion of privilege by an appropriate executive official.[176] The matter was reconsidered by the House of Lords in *Conway v Rimmer*[177] and court subordination to the executive was rejected in that case.[178] In the later judgment of *Burmah Oil Co Ltd v Bank of England* [179] the court declared that *Conway v Rimmer* had laid the *Duncan* doctrine finally to rest. The position seems to be the same in the United States where the courts have assumed authority as the final arbiter in executive privilege cases. In *United States v Reynolds*[180] the Supreme Court reserved the power, even in national security cases, to determine how far it should 'probe in satisfying itself that the occasion for invoking the privilege is appropriate'. The court also clearly assumed the function of arbiter in *United States v Nixon*[181] and ordered the Nixon tapes to be produced for inspection. In some of these judgments the courts have expressed reservations about the power of the courts where national security is involved; but it is submitted that these reservations do not imply a total submission to executive authority when the privilege is asserted in the interests of national security. At most, they imply that the courts, while exercising the final decision on whether to uphold or reject a claim of state privilege, will be more deferent to the executive view in a national security case. Clearly, then, in both Britain and the United States, state privilege has been subjected to rule-of-law requirements. What is the position in South Africa? The common law appears to be favourable to the proposition that the final judgment on concealment versus disclosure in state privilege cases rests with the courts. This was the effect of the decision in *Van der Linde v Calitz*[182] even though the court reserved its opinion on the proper resolution of national security cases.[183] The common law has been modified by statute, initially by the General Law Amendment Act of

---

[175] Supra.
[176] The Privy Council had held otherwise in *Robinson v State of South Australia* [1931] All ER 333 (PC).
[177] [1968] 1 All ER 874 (HL).
[178] See particularly, the judgments of Lord Reid at 888 and Lord Morris at 898 and 900.
[179] [1979] 2 All ER 461, 472 (CA).
[180] Supra at 735.
[181] 418 US 683 (1974); 41 L Ed 2nd 1039.
[182] 1967 (2) SA 239 (A).
[183] Even where national security is involved, the courts, it is submitted, will make the final decision but with much more deference to the claims of the executive.

1969.[184] That Act transferred the decision to withhold information to the executive in respect of information which, if released, would prejudice public security or the interests of the state—a formulation which appeared wide enough to encompass all assertions of state privilege and therefore to replace the common law. However, in *Geldenhuys v Pretorius* [185] the court interpreted the law strictly by confining the expression 'interests of the state' to matters that affected the state as a whole with the result that the common-law power of the judiciary to make the final decision was preserved in all non-security cases that did not affect the state as a whole. Criticism of the 1969 law, and consideration of it by the Potgieter Commission, led to its amendment in 1972.[186] In its amended form, the Act removed the jurisdiction of the courts only where injury to national security was the basis for an assertion of state privilege to withhold information. The amended 1969 law has since been replaced by a provision of the Internal Security Act of 1982[187] and this provision is now the governing enactment on the subject of state privilege.

The relevant provision of the Internal Security Act authorises the responsible minister, or the administrator of a province, to claim privilege for information on the ground that its production to a court or commission of enquiry will prejudicially affect state security. Such a claim, if made in proper form[188] is conclusive and no court may order or permit the information to be given as evidence. This outcome—that in security cases the executive has the final word whereas in non-security cases the courts retain their ultimate common-law jurisdiction—was considered satisfactory by both the Potgieter Commission[189] and the Rabie Commission.[190] Both commissions put their faith in the requirement of the law that the minister and administrator are personally required to consider the matter and sign the affidavit in which privilege is asserted. The truth is that the present law is gravely deficient and ripe for further reform. The chief problem is once again the breadth and vagueness of the concept of national security in South Africa. The relevant laws and the practices of the security authorities indicate that security in this country is an indeterminate concept. The minister and administrator, moreover, have the absolute power under the Act to expand the concept of security as far as they wish. Once an affidavit is filed, the court cannot look into the issue and must accept the official declaration that security will be prejudiced by production of evidence as if that declaration were engraved on a holy tablet by the Almighty. If the court cannot fix the boundary between information touching security and non-security matters, there is no effective control and government officials have full power to give expression to their bizarre conceptions of national security. Even where

---

[184] 101 of 1969 s 29.
[185] 1971 (2) SA 277 (O).
[186] By s 25 of the General Law Amendment Act 102 of 1972.
[187] Section 66 of Act 74 of 1982.
[188] By the appropriate minister or administrator on affidavit after personal consideration of the matter.
[189] *Report of the Commission of Enquiry into Matters Relating to the Security of the State* (RP 102/1971) 71.
[190] *Die Verslag van die Kommissie van Ondersoek na Veiligheidswetgewing* (RP 90/1981) para 8.5.3.

the minister has correctly classified the matter as one of security, there is the further problem that the court is also bound by his belief that production of the information will actually prejudice security interests. South African ministers are prone to confusing the interests of the government with those of the state and in many cases in which they have refused to provide information about security-law operations there is a strong suspicion, if not certainty, that the government is protecting itself (and not state security) against political embarrassment. There is little doubt that the reason for embarrassment in many instances is that release of the information will show conclusively that the government has misused its security powers; in other words, non-production of information is a device for concealing the bankruptcy of its case against security-law victims. The convenience of being able to mask security actions in this way is certainly attractive to those who exercise power but that convenience is no reason for invoking the doctrine of state privilege and thereby denying the individual justice in the particular case and depriving the public of knowledge of how government powers are being exercised and frequently misused.

The courts' jurisdiction over state privilege in both security and non-security matters should be restored notwithstanding the readiness of judges Potgieter and Rabie to abdicate to the executive. The judiciary will know what secrets are worthy of protection; after all, the courts had no hesitation in protecting military secrets in the *Duncan* and *Reynolds* judgments. If granted the necessary power, the judges will also curb the executive by denying a claim of state privilege where it is put forward for improper reasons—but that, surely, is why free societies have independent judiciaries. The removal of judicial control in state privilege cases has simply provided the executive with a licence to abuse the noble purposes that underlie the doctrine.

CHAPTER 10

Surveillance, Entry, Search and Seizure

The ever-watching eye of big brother is a phenomenon not just of the totalitarian East but also of the 'free' West. Modern techniques of police snooping are highly sophisticated and most victims of it in the West are probably unaware that they are being monitored. The sophistication of surveillance is complemented by advanced systems of information storage and retrieval which put computer-based political and security profiles of thousands of citizens at the instantaneous disposal of the authorities. These Orwellian practices are regarded as a serious threat to freedom even in those societies in which citizens enjoy the basic political and civil liberties. The information gained and stored through clandestine surveillance is untested information and it is therefore liable to be wrong, inaccurate or distorted; and, as a British writer has said, it 'may be used as a basis for a decision crucially affecting someone's life'.[1] This same author gives as a telling example of the unreliability of covert information gathering the case of a woman who was recorded in British Special Branch files as having a connection 'with terrorists in Europe' only because a Dutch café owner had mistakenly reported that her husband looked like a member of the Baader-Meinhof group involved in a shooting in Amsterdam.[2] The couple had been on holiday and had visited this café at the time. The mistake was discovered because the woman's father was a former member of Scotland Yard and was therefore able to identify the source of the false story. Persons who are not fortunate enough to have well-connected relatives will usually not discover even the *existence* of unreliable information that has prejudiced their life chances by, for example, leading to denial of an appointment.

If the consequences of uncontrolled surveillance may be dire for British subjects, they can only be described as potentially catastrophic for South African citizens. In this country secret information is almost always the basis for decisions to ban or detain people, to deprive them of passports or to inflict other arbitrary penalties upon them. As in other countries, there is a high likelihood that information gathered for security purposes will be false or distorted. In at least two cases of banning in South Africa, information disclosed subsequent to the imposition of the order has demonstrated that the authorities relied on incorrect or distorted facts. In 1966, the Minister of Justice, in the course of defending in Parliament the banning of the then president of NUSAS, Mr Ian Robertson, gave as reasons inter alia the activities of Robertson during a visit to Swaziland and his membership of the Defence and Aid Fund. It was then revealed that Mr Robertson had never visited Swaziland and that he had never

---

[1] Patricia Hewitt *The Abuse of Power* (Martin Robertson, Oxford, 1982) 48.
[2] Op cit 49.

attended a meeting of Defence and Aid, his membership of it being ex officio his presidency of NUSAS.[3] The second case relates to Dr Manas Buthelezi who was issued with a banning order in December 1973. Shortly thereafter a government front newspaper stated in an editorial that the government ought to have revealed the reasons for the banning since these reasons would have silenced critics of the order. According to the editorial the reasons were that Dr Buthelezi had made inflammatory and revolutionary speeches. In an ensuing libel action against the newspaper, the court found that the allegations about Dr Buthelezi were unfounded and defamatory. The banning was withdrawn two months after Dr Buthelezi challenged the newspaper allegations.[4] In most cases of banning or other arbitrary restrictions no information is given and there is no opportunity to test the reliability of the 'facts' upon which the authorities have relied. When no information is revealed there is the further danger (apart from inaccuracy) that the material relied upon by the authorities is irrelevant in the sense that, if known, it would become clear that the facts could not possibly justify the restriction on liberty imposed in the particular case. There must be many South Africans who have been banned or detained on information which proves that they are political rather than security threats. In a nutshell, covert information gathering is far more menacing in a society in which the authorities possess arbitrary power to take away basic rights.

In the light of these dangers it will be instructive to take a close look at police powers of surveillance in South Africa and at the controls upon such powers. As might be expected, there are powers a-plenty but a dearth of mechanisms of control. Big brother powers will be discussed below under several separate headings of which the chief are interception of communications, bugging (including entry), search and seizure and undercover operatives (human 'plants').

Interception of communications

The Post Office Act[5] has long contained a provision authorising the 'detention' of postal articles or telegrams reasonably suspected of being linked in various prescribed ways to the commission of any offence. The clause in question[6] authorises the officer in charge of any post office or telegraphic office to 'detain' such an article or telegram and provides that it may be referred by the Postmaster to an attorney-general, or to a prosecutor if the attorney-general so requests. The power to intercept under this provision is limited in a number of ways. It can only be exercised over postal articles[7] and telegrams and does not apply to telephone conversations. Furthermore, intervention is possible only on reasonable suspicion that the article or telegram will afford evidence of an offence, has been sent to further an offence or to prevent the detection of one. Though this last limitation is somewhat weakened by the existence of

---

[3] A full account of the Robertson banning and subsequent revelations appears in *A Survey of Race Relations in South Africa* (1966) 39 et seq.

[4] The Buthelezi case is summarised by Lawrence Baxter, op cit 743n477 and in *A Survey of Race Relations in South Africa* (1974) 68.

[5] 44 of 1958.

[6] Section 118.

[7] As defined in s 1.

numerous broad and vague political crimes in South Africa, it remains an important restriction on the use of the power.

Prior to 1972 the Post Office Act did not authorise interception of communications in the interests of state security (unless a crime was suspected) and it did not authorise telephone tapping for any purpose whatever. In 1971 a government-appointed commission of enquiry into security matters (the Potgieter Commission) recommended that there should be statutory authority to intercept communications for state security purposes[8] and thereafter the Post Office Act was amended in 1972 by the introduction of an appropriate section.[9] The matter was again considered by the Rabie Commission and in its report[10] of 1981 this commission recommended a number of 'improvements' to the provision introduced in 1972. The present provision[11] remains unsatisfactory despite its being the product of two intensive investigations by commissions of enquiry.

As it now stands, the law authorises the interception either of any 'particular article' or 'particular communication' which has been or is being or is intended to be transmitted by telephone or in any other manner over a telecommunications line; or of all such postal articles or communications to or from any person, body or organisation for periods not exceeding six months at a time.[12] In brief, the interception may relate to a particular article or communication or to all articles or communications to or from a person, body or organisation. The definitions in the Act[13] ensure that the possibility of interception extends to all the modern forms of communication made available by the Department of Posts and Telecommunications.

The interception may be authorised by the minister who administers the National Intelligence Service, the Minister of Law and Order or the Minister of Defence (in each case with the concurrence of the Minister of Posts and Telecommunications) or by the Minister of Posts and Telecommunications or an officer (not being below the rank of Deputy Postmaster General[14]) authorised by him. An interception[15] may be ordered by any one of those persons only if a request to that effect has been made by a state official designated[16] for this purpose by the State Security Council and holding a rank no lower than that of Deputy-Director General in the public service.[17] The person making such a request must believe that the interception is necessary for the maintenance of the

---

[8] 'Report of the Commission of Enquiry into Matters Relating to the Security of the State' (RP 102/1971) paras 207–12.

[9] Section 118A.

[10] 'Die Verslag van die Kommissie van Ondersoek na Veiligheidswetgewing' (RP 90.1981) paras 13.2.1–13.2.36.

[11] That is, s 118A.

[12] Section 118A(1). Various sections of the Act make it a criminal offence to open mail or intercept communications, or to divulge the content of either, without lawful authority: see, particularly ss 96 and 105.

[13] That is, of 'postal article', 'telecommunications' and 'telecommunications line' in s 1 of the Act.

[14] Section 118A(7).

[15] Which includes the power to examine the article or listen to and record the communication: s 118A(5).

[16] Under s 118A(2)(a).

[17] Section 118A(7) prescribes the rank of the requestor.

security of the Republic and must specify the grounds for that belief.[18] A request not initially made in writing must be put into writing as soon as possible thereafter.[19] The person who orders the interception in response to the request must be satisfied that the action is necessary in the interests of the security of the Republic.[20] Where the interception is general (that is, not relating to a single message or article) the same persons who are empowered to order the initial interception may order extensions of up to six months at a time on the same specified grounds.[21] Though provision is made for the return of intercepted postal articles and telegrams to the department for transmission to the addressee, non-return and disposal is authorised if the interests of security so require.[22]

The legislature, on the recommendation of the Rabie Commission and the advocate-general, has affected an attempt to control the awesome power of surveillance possessed by the postal and telecommunications department of government by confining both requests and authorisations for interception to senior and 'responsible' officials. No doubt, the criterion specified in the Act—the interests of security—is also meant to be a restraining factor; but in the light of the vagueness of the term 'security' and the breadth of the security laws of the Republic, the criterion is unlikely to operate as a significant restraint. We are left, then, with the 'safeguard' that interception may be ordered only by responsible officials of government. The problem about this limitation is that it is purely internal and that we have therefore to rely on members of the ruling party and their subordinates not to abuse the power by invoking it against their opponents without adequate justification. The temptation to misuse powers of surveillance against political opponents has proved too strong for government members and officials even in societies where there is far more political accountability than in South Africa. Though the officials empowered to order an interception in South Africa are responsible in the sense of being senior, they are not as accountable as public officials in the open democracies. President Nixon was the most senior member of government at the time of Watergate but, as the subsequent revelation showed, this did not prevent him from putting opponents under surveillance. If responsibility in both senses of the word (seniority and accountability) has not prevented misuse in full democracies, it is hardly likely to be an effective restraint in South Africa.

Adequate control over interceptions can be secured only by some form of *external* supervision. External control was rejected by the Rabie Commission primarily because it is not practicable to afford the proposed victim of the interception a hearing before the judge or tribunal charged by law with sanctioning that interception; if the victim knows about the proposed interception, that will defeat the whole purpose of surveillance.[23] The reasoning of the commission is curious since it

---

[18] Section 118A(2)*(b)*.   [19] Section 118A(5).
[20] Section 118A(3)*(a)*.   [21] Section 118A(3)*(b)*.   [22] Section 118A(6).
[23] Rabie Commission Report, para 13.2.25. The commission failed to appreciate the nature of the clash of interests involved in surveillance, particularly in its comment that the security interests of the state clash with the interest of the individual in protecting his privacy (paras 13.2.20 and 13.2.31). The commission completely overlooks the broad social interest in maintaining equal advantages for all participants in the political process. Telephone tapping for political purposes will give the governing party an unfair advantage over the others.

expresses the surprising proposition that if full due process is not possible there should be no due process at all. The commission does not convince when it denies that half a loaf is better than no bread. The reform of the law governing interception of communications is certainly practicable and also necessary to ensure greater adherence to rule-of-law principles. Reform should be based upon two basic principles—the principle of independent supervision (without the right of a hearing) and the principle of precise criteria according to which that supervision should be exercised. As we shall later record, such reforms have already been brought about in Canada.[24]

An important point to record in passing is that the Post Office Act does not authorise the tapping of telephones for non-security crimes. One can only assume that this happens in a completely unregulated and uncontrolled way.

Bugging

Surveillance in the modern state is not restricted to the interception of communications conveyed through the agency of public institutions such as the Posts and Telecommunications Department. Advanced technology has made it a simple matter for the authorities to 'bug' premises or vehicles and thereby gain access to private conversations and discussions. Though bugging usually involves the placing of listening, recording or transmitting devices into premises, access to private conversations may be gained without entry to premises by such techniques as wall-microphones and laser-beam listening devices. Long-distance microphones are also available to record conversations of people in the open. The security authorities of today have ample means to invade the privacy of the home or work-place and to discover and record the goings-on in what used to be a safe and protected retreat for private citizens. What are the legal rules which govern such intrusions?

There is no statute providing for the controlled use of bugging devices as there is for the interception of communications transmitted through the agency of the Post and Telecommunications Department. Such statutory regulation as there is seems to prohibit bugging and related practices outright. Provisions of the Radio Act of 1952,[25] which subject broadcasting (both radio and television) to licensing control, appear to be wide enough to prohibit the interception of private conversations by radio apparatus. One such provision prohibits unlicensed persons from transmitting or receiving by radio 'any sound, image, sign or signal';[26] and the definitions of 'radio'[27] and 'radio apparatus'[28] bring some bugging devices within the scope of the prohibition. However, bugging by the secretion of a tape recorder or by laser-beam[29] devices are not within

---

[24] See ch 12 below.
[25] Act 3 of 1952.
[26] Section 5.
[27] 'Radio' is defined in s 1 as 'electromagnetic waves of frequencies lower than 3000 GHz propagated in space without an artificial conductor'.
[28] 'Radio apparatus' covers 'any radio receiving or transmitting set which is capable of receiving or transmitting by radio any sound, image, sign or signal' and includes any article specially declared to be radio apparatus by the minister: s 1.
[29] Which employ frequencies outside the limit of 3000 GHz.

the statutory definitions. While the statutory prohibitions are not comprehensive (and not very clear) the common law in South Africa clearly makes bugging without the consent of the victim an actionable delict. The leading authority on the law of privacy in South Africa regards non-consensual eavesdropping on private conversations as an invasion of privacy.[30] There is no reason why this should not apply to agents of the state who carry out bugging practices for state security reasons. While such agents could invoke certain principles of legal justification for their actions, such as necessity and emergency, such defences are construed narrowly by the courts and would not authorise a general snooping on suspects.[31] The claim that security police surveillance is in the public interest[32] will not provide a legal excuse in the absence of statutory authorisation of the acts in question. As noted earlier, such authorisation exists in the case of telephone tapping and the interception of postal articles, but there appears to be no statutory warrant for bugging carried out for security reasons. The Criminal Procedure Act does authorise police officers to enter premises with a warrant (or without a warrant in circumstances of urgency) for the purpose of 'carrying out such investigations and of taking such steps as such police official may consider necessary for the preservation of the internal security of the Republic or for the maintenance of law and order or for the prevention of any offence'.[33] Wide though this language may be, it was not intended to authorise surveillance for which a more specific legislative sanction is clearly required. The broad powers of investigation granted to authorised officers and liquidators by the Internal Security Act of 1982 equally do not confer a power to bug premises.[34] It is sometimes suggested that the prerogative provides authority for intrusions into privacy in the interests of state security but the better view is that prerogative powers cannot be used to invade private interests without statutory authorisation.[35] In the British case of *Malone v Metropolitan Police Commissioner*,[36] in which the power of the state to tap telephones without specific legislative authority was canvassed, the Crown did not even raise the justification of prerogative power; and the prerogative is at best a dubious source of authority for the invasion of private rights.[37] The prerogative can scarcely be given such a broad application in a modern state founded upon the principle of constitutionalism and legality. Where bugging involves entry into private premises, the entry itself constitutes an actionable delict unless there is a legal justification for the intrusion. The relevant statutes which authorise entry, particularly the Criminal Procedure Act of 1977,[38] do not permit invasions of private property in order to plant bugs and it

---

[30] J Neethling *Persoonlikheidsreg* 2 ed (Butterworths, Durban, 1985) 219. See also D J McQuoid-Mason *The Law of Privacy in South Africa* (Juta & Co, Cape Town, 1978) 147.
[31] On the scope of these defences, see J Neethling op cit 103 and 198 et seq.
[32] On this defence, see J Neethling op cit 241.
[33] Section 25(1) of Act 51 of 1977.
[34] Sections 6(3) and (4) and 14(12) of Act 74 of 1982.
[35] Lawrence Baxter op cit 613 and the case of *Sachs v Dönges NO* 1950 (2) SA 265 (A) cited there.
[36] (1979) 2 WLR 700.
[37] See for example, John Lambert 'Executive Authority to Tap Telephones' (1980) 43 *Modern Law Review* 59.
[38] Sections 20, 21 and 25 of Act 51 of 1977.

follows that the victim of such action will have a remedy for invasion of privacy and for trespass.[39] The entry as such entitles the aggrieved party to damages for an iniuria; and if actual damage is caused during the course of the entry such damage would be recoverable under the *Lex Aquilia*. The victim should also be entitled to an interdict to prevent further intrusions into his home. Finally, entry into premises without consent or legal justification is punishable as criminal trespass under the Trespass Act of 1959.[40]

Search and Seizure

In general, police officials who are investigating security crimes and subversion have to comply with the 'ordinary law' in conducting search and seizure operations. The ordinary law is contained in the Criminal Procedure Act[41] and is briefly examined below. However, there is a large number of special laws which confer very extensive powers of entry, search and seizure and which could be used by the security arm of the police force. For example,[42] a provision of the Arms and Ammunition Act[43] permits entry, search and seizure without a warrant upon reasonable suspicion of the possession of an article[44] used in the commission of an offence under the Act or of any arms or ammunition required for the investigation of any offence (whether under the Act or not). Again by way of example, search of premises without a warrant is permitted on reasonable suspicion of illegal possession of liquor or other contraventions of liquor legislation.[45] Searches without warrant are freely permitted within ten kilometres of any border with a foreign state under a provision of the Police Act.[46] The creation of numerous independent homelands within the Republic gives this exemption a broad application. Many other examples could be given of warrantless entry and search powers but their full recitation is not necessary to make the simple point that the controls over search and seizure in the Criminal Procedure Act are substantially undermined by unrestricted powers of the same kind conferred by other Acts. Simply exprssed, a police officer who has not complied with the limitations imposed by the Criminal Procedure Act, may escape liability by claiming that he had entered to look for illegal liquor or weapons.[47] There are so many statutory justifications for warrantless searches that only a stupid policeman could fail to find one appropriate to the occasion. If a police intrusion into premises is challenged in a court, the presiding officer will investigate the basis of the policeman's belief that he had a right to enter for a legitimate purpose; but with so many statutory exceptions to ordinary law the chances of a judicial finding adverse to the authorities is remote.

---

[39] J Neethling op cit 217; D J McQuoid-Mason op cit 137.
[40] Act 6 of 1959.   [41] Act 51 of 1977, ch 2.
[42] For a more extensive review of these special laws, see Lansdown and Campbell *South African Criminal Law and Procedure* vol 5 (Juta & Co, Cape Town, 1982) 152 et seq.
[43] 75 of 1969, s 41.
[44] 'Article' is undefined in the Act and clearly has a broad meaning.
[45] Section 177(1) of the Liquor Act 87 of 1977.
[46] Section 6(4) of Act 7 of 1958.
[47] Or to investigate a drug offence under s 11 of the Abuse of Dependence-Producing Substances and Rehabilitation Centres Act 41 of 1971.

Unfortunately even the 'ordinary law', contained within ch 2 of the
Criminal Procedure Act,[48] is deficient in the protection that it offers to
citizens against unjustified search and seizure. The first of the relevant
provisions[49] authorises the search of premises and the seizure of articles
under a search warrant issued by a magistrate or justice of the peace. If
the magistrate or justice is satisfied by information on oath that there are
reasonable grounds for believing that an article reasonably believed to be
concerned in the commission or intended commission of an offence, or to
afford evidence of such an offence, is in the possession of any person or
upon any premises, he may authorise a warrant for the search of such
person or for entry into the premises and seizure of the article. A warrant
for such a search and seizure is not necessary, however, if the person
concerned consents or if a police officer believes on reasonable grounds
that a search warrant would be issued to him by a magistrate or justice if
he applied for one but that the delay in obtaining it would defeat the
object of the search.[50] In summary, a legal warrant is usually required for
entry, search and seizure but in cases of urgency, or where the victim
consents, the police may act without a warrant on reasonable apprehension that the facts would justify the issue of a warrant. Standing
alone, this power of search and seizure is not unreasonable even though it
is marred by at least three defects. First, it authorises *any* policeman to
enter *any* premises in search of an article connected with *any* offence.[51]
Second, the warrant required is not necessarily a judicial warrant since a
justice of the peace (an office that includes any commissioned police
officer)[52] may grant it. This means that the police are self-authorising in
respect of warrants. Third, if the person issuing the warrant honestly
believes that reasonable grounds exist, the court will not investigate
whether or not they actually do exist.[53] Despite these defects, the
provision in question is arguably one that is necessary for the investigation
and prevention of crime.

Unfortunately, the search and seizure power just discussed does not
stand alone but is complemented by a much wider provision of the
Criminal Procedure Act. This provision[54] authorises a magistrate or
justice to issue a warrant for entry on to premises if satisfied by
information on oath that there are reasonable grounds for believing either
that internal security or law and order is likely to be endangered by a
meeting to be held in the premises or that an offence has been committed
or is being committed in the premises, or that it is likely to be committed
there.[55] The warrant may authorise the police to enter the premises, to
carry out such investigations or to take such steps as they believe
necessary to preserve internal security or law and order, or to prevent the

---

[48] 51 of 1977.
[49] Section 21, read with s 20.
[50] Section 22.
[51] John Dugard *South African Criminal Law and Procedure* vol IV (Juta & Co, Cape Town,
1977) 66.
[52] Justices of the Peace and Commissioner of Oaths Act 16 of 1963, s 4 and First Schedule.
[53] *Divisional Commissioner of SA Police, Witwatersrand Area v SA Associated Newspapers Ltd* 1966
(2) SA 501 (A); *Ndabeni v Minister of Law and Order* 1984 (3) 500 (N) 512.
[54] Section 25.
[55] Or that preparations for its commission are being made there.

commission of an offence. The warrant may also authorise the police to search the premises or any person in them for any article reasonably believed to be present and connected to an offence or to afford evidence of an offence. However, all these actions may be taken by the police without a warrant if they reasonably believe that a warrant would be granted if applied for and that the delay in obtaining it would defeat the purpose of their entry, search, seizure or other appropriate action.

This second and wider provision of the Criminal Procedure Act is susceptible to all the criticisms directed at the first, in particular that the police are once again self-authorising and that the extensive powers conferred by it are applicable to the investigation of any offence whatever. More alarming than these defects is the dangerous extension of power to enter private premises which the second provision confers. Entry and search may take place if there is a reasonable apprehension that internal security or law and order is likely to be threatened by a meeting in the premises. The expressions 'internal security' and 'law and order' have no clear meaning and are made more obscure by the breadth and vagueness of South African internal security legislation. Once the police have entered the premises they are authorised, over and above the normal search and seizure powers, to 'take such steps' as they believe necessary for the preservation of internal security, the maintenance of law and order or the prevention of crime. It hardly seems necessary to underline the folly of placing such ill-defined powers in the hands of a policeman.

There is a final and more circumscribed power of entry available to a police officer who is investigating an offence and who suspects that a person who can furnish information about it is on any premises. He may enter such premises without a warrant for the purpose of interrogating the person and obtaining a statement from him.[56] This provision does not authorise entry into a private dwelling without the consent of the occupier.[57]

Considered as a whole, the powers of search and seizure conferred by the Criminal Procedure Act invade the rights of the citizens too broadly and deeply. Where the power-conferring language of the statute is loose and unspecific, it is only of limited assistance to make a policeman who acts contrary to a warrant, who searches without a warrant contrary to the requirements of the Act or who gives false information under oath to secure a warrant, guilty of a criminal offence.[58] Such prosecutions will be rare in view of the generous grant of search and seizure authority to the police under the Act and the authority for warrantless searches under numerous other acts. For the same reasons, the chances of a successful civil action in consequence of police search and seizure operations are equally remote. The courts could be of some assistance by requiring strict adherence to the requirement of the reasonable apprehension of an offence where the police enter to search for and seize articles. In *Ndabeni v Minister of Law and Order*,[59] a case involving police seizure of political pamphlets

---

[56] Section 26.   [57] Ibid.

[58] Section 28. The penalty is a fine of up to R200 or imprisonment of up to six months. Provision is also made for an award to compensate the victim for damage caused during an illegal search.

[59] 1984 (3) SA 500 (D). Unfortunately, the strict attitude of the court in *Ndabeni* is not evident in the recent appeal court ruling in *Control Magistrate, Durban v Azanian Peoples Organisation* 1986 (3) SA 394 (A).

alleged to further the aims of an unlawful organisation because they propagated black consciousness, the court found that the police, on an objective test, did not have reasonable grounds for believing that an offence had been committed and it therefore ordered return of the seized pamphlets. By confining broad security crimes in this way, the courts can deter gross invasions of citizens' rights under search and seizure powers; and they might achieve the same result by giving a strict and narrow reading to expressions like 'internal security' and 'law and order' which figure in one of the search and seizure provisions of the Act.[60] Another opportunity for judicial restriction of the search and seizure powers conferred by the Criminal Procedure Act is provided by the obscurity of the meaning of the word 'premises' used in the relevant provisions. In 1984 members of the security police were discovered in the Electrical Engineering building of Natal University in Durban with equipment which they were using to monitor a United Democratic Front meeting in a nearby but separate building. Such actions raise the important legal issue of whether the Act authorises entry only into the building in which the suspected article is situated or in which the apprehended crime or breach of security is being planned or committed; or whether the police may enter adjacent buildings of the same owner or occupier, or even those of a different owner or occupier. The definition of 'premises' in the Act[61] is unhelpful on this point. The court should not permit the police to invade the premises of one occupier in order to gather evidence of what is happening in another occupier's premises. In short, the courts can restrict search and seizure powers by reading 'premises' narrowly so as to mean a place that is separately occupied.[62] The court might also play a restraining role when there is a legal challenge to the massive house-to-house searches that are becoming common in the black townships. The Criminal Procedure Act manifestly does not give the police the right to enter and search every house in a township because it is apprehended that articles connected with crime or security law offenders might be present in *some* of them. A township owner or occupier who does not consent to the search of his premises appears to have a clear case against the police authorities who have no reasonable grounds for entering and searching the particular house in question but do so as part of an indiscriminate search operation throughout the township. There are, therefore, several ways in which the courts could curtail the use of search and seizure powers but, at best, they can only restrain the grosser excesses of the police. The real answer is a legislative narrowing of the Criminal Procedure Act.

Before concluding the discussion of search and seizure, brief mention needs to be made of the unrestricted powers conferred upon an 'authorised officer' appointed to investigate an organisation prior to banning and upon a liquidator appointed to wind up a banned organisation. The authorised officer[63] may 'without notice at any time

---

[60] Section 25 discussed above.

[61] In s 1.

[62] On this interpretation, premises refers to occupational entities and the entry power could not cut across such entities.

[63] Appointed under s 6(1) of the Internal Security Act 74 of 1982.

enter upon any premises whatsoever' for the purpose of making any
investigation he deems necessary; and he may also seize, examine and
copy documents related to his investigation.[64] The liquidator of a banned
organisation is vested with the same broad powers of entry, search and
seizure.[65]

Undercover Operatives

This expression was used by the McDonald Commission[66] in Canada
to describe persons who are more colloquially referred to as spies,
informers or secret agents. Surveillance through the use of undercover
operatives takes various forms which range between information passed to
the authorities by casual informers through information acquired from
paid informers to spying by means of secret police agents. Most societies
employ these practices in the fight against crime, especially consensual
crimes; and they are certainly useful in uncovering such things as illegal
drug trafficking or illicit diamond and gold buying. The McDonald
Commission explicitly recognised the value of undercover operatives for
anti-crime and anti-espionage activities.[67]

While undercover operatives have their advantages, there is also a
variety of dangers in their employment. Among these are the danger that
the operatives will act illegally (for example, by encouraging the
commission of crimes as *agents provocateur*) that they will be used to spy on
perfectly legitimate political activities and that they will pass on
inaccurate and unreliable information.[68] The last two dangers are
particularly worrying in South Africa. The statutory definition of
subversion and the official understanding of what constitutes subversive
activity are so broad that many groups that are involved in ordinary
political activities are regularly spied upon by undercover operatives. Any
member of the English-speaking universities in South Africa knows that
spies and informers abound to monitor and report on routine campus
activities. It is not surprising that the McDonald Commission concluded
that undercover operatives can have a serious impact on civil liberties and
inhibit the basic rights of political association and free speech.[69] This
danger is clearly more serious in South Africa where the information
transmitted by informers may result in arbitrary bans, detentions or
passport refusals—actions that are not competent in free societies like
Canada. The inhibiting effect on the exercise of basic rights like speech
and association is far greater in South Africa. Also greater, is the danger of
the passing of false or distorted information. As the McDonald Commission said: 'Mechanical recording devices do not lie or exaggerate or
distort; human sources can and do.'[70] Although the authorities in the
open democracies undoubtedly do receive false or distorted information

---

[64] Section 6(3).
[65] Section 14(12).
[66] Report entitled *Freedom and Security Under the Law* being the Second Report of the
Commission of Enquiry Concerning Certain Activities of the Royal Canadian Mounted
Police (Canadian Govt Publishing Centre, Ottawa, 1981) vol 1 295 et seq (referred to below
as the McDonald Report).
[67] McDonald Report 328.
[68] For a general review of the dangers, see McDonald Report 295 et seq and 536 et seq.
[69] McDonald Report 538.   [70] Ibid 536.

from undercover operatives, their power to use it to the disadvantage of the victim is restricted. In South Africa, such information can result in the unjustified loss of liberty by banning, detention and the like. The cases of banning based on inaccurate information described at the beginning of this chapter were almost certainly cases in which liberty was lost as a result of information supplied by undercover operatives.

In the light of the dangers just alluded to, it is disturbing that informing and spying are so prevalent as to have become a disease in South Africa. Police spies and informers have been uncovered on university campuses, in political organisations, in black communities and in churches. The extent of the penetration is well illustrated by the discovery that several police informers were simultaneously members of the student representative council at the University of the Witwatersrand, thereby making the police component of the council a substantial voting block if not a majority.[71] It is not just the prevalence of undercover operatives that disturbs but also the nature of their mandate which requires them to report on political dissent irrespective of whether it relates to crime of either a subversive or non-subversive kind. They have been used, for example, to monitor the activities of the eminently respectable Lawyers for Human Rights organisation. A large part of their general business is to monitor anti-government opposition. Sometimes the information so gathered is used for crude intimidation, as when parents of dissenting students are anonymously given information about the 'dangerous' political activities in which these students are indulging on the campuses. Information of a similar kind passed on to employers has resulted in the firing of workers. Even such limited freedom as the law permits in South Africa is being sapped away by the pernicious use of undercover operatives.

There is a total absence of both legal and political control over the use of spies and informers in South Africa. The common law is unlikely to be of much assistance to a victim of undercover operations. While the persistent shadowing of a person may be actionable as an invasion of personal rights,[72] undercover operatives do not usually follow or observe the victim in an obvious way. If confidential papers and documents are removed or copied there may be an action;[73] but removal of papers is not an inevitable feature of informing or spying. Is the act of spying itself an actionable invasion of personal rights? Where the informing involves reports on what is said in a university classroom or open meeting, there seems to be no invasion of personal rights such as privacy. It is possible, however, that persons who participate in confidential meetings may have an action if their private discussions are carried elsewhere.[74] But even if there is a common-law remedy, its scope is presently unclear and, in any event, it does not provide a really effective method of controlling

---

[71] This incident is briefly reported in *A Survey of Race Relations in South Africa* 1980 p 550.
[72] J Neethling op cit 221; D J McQuoid-Mason op cit 154.
[73] See for example *Goodman v Von Moltke* 1938 CPD 153, 157 and the comment thereon of J Neethling op cit 183.
[74] One of the complicating factors is that the informer will usually have become a member of the organisation which he has penetrated. It is conceivable that a member who has a right to receive information at meetings may nevertheless act illegally if he conveys it outside the organisation. There seems to be no direct authority on the point.

unjustified spying. What is needed in South Africa is some kind of official or public authority control over the use of undercover operatives. The McDonald Commission, after extensive investigation, found that judicial warrants were an inappropriate form of control and did not recommend them for Canada.[75] The Commission recommended that a set of ministerial guidelines, along the lines of those laid down by the attorney-general in the United States in order to ensure that 'individual rights are not infringed and that the government itself does not become a violator of the law', should be adopted in Canada and published for general information.[76] Officially enforced guidelines are clearly needed in South Africa and should specify the criteria for the use of undercover operatives as well as the kind of conduct that will not be tolerated of the part of such persons. The criteria should seek to exclude the possibility of political snooping and the code of conduct should prohibit informers from encouraging the commission of crime (as *agents provocateur*) or intimidating persons who are spied upon. Without controls of the kind suggested, there is likely to be total corruption of politics in the society.

[75] McDonald Report 538.
[76] Ibid 539.

CHAPTER 11

Emergency Powers

Introduction

It is both common and respectable for modern states, even democratic ones, to adopt permanent statutes which empower the government of the day to take swift and effective action in times of crisis or emergency. While the situations with which such legislation deals often include natural disasters (such as earthquakes) and serious economic depression, our present concern is with those emergencies that threaten the safety of the state or the maintenance of peace and order. The extreme danger that insurrectionary groups may pose to the stability and welfare of societies is tragically illustrated by the destruction of the Weimar Republic by the Nazi movement. Such historical precedents remind us of the importance of giving governments the means of protecting the institutions of state and the people against insurrection, riot, disorder and revolution. Although the source may be dubious, no objection can be taken to the sentiment of Machiavelli's statement that 'those republics which in time of danger cannot resort to a dictatorship will generally be ruined when grave occasions occur'.[1]

There is also the danger, much more common in our times, that societies may be ruined not by 'grave occasions' which threaten peace or stability but by their manner of responding to them. This is particularly the case when the government makes the emergency permanent, no doubt a contradiction in terms but one which is regularly encountered in practice. Though democracies may well be undermined by riot or revolution, they are just as susceptible to destruction by being converted into permanent dictatorships on the pretext of the need to cope with a continuing crisis or emergency. David Bonner, in his recent work on emergency powers, draws attention to the danger of crisis government leading to the installation of an authoritarian regime and shows that, while this is typical of the Latin American experience, there are instances of it occurring in Europe as well.[2] For this very reason, an expert on emergency government has said that 'it is temporary and self-destructive' and that 'when the crisis goes, it goes'.[3] When the citizens of a country are 'made to live as if in a perpetual state of emergency'[4] we can be sure that the government is caught up in a legitimacy crisis on account of such factors as the denial of political rights, discrimination and repressive

[1] Quoted by Bernard Crick *In Defence of Politics* (Penguin 1964) 179.
[2] David Bonner *Emergency Powers in Peacetime* (Sweet & Maxwell, London 1985) 15.
[3] Clinton L Rossiter *Constitutional Dictatorship: Crisis Government in the Modern Democracies* (Princeton Univ Press 1948) 8.
[4] *African Conference on the Rule of Law* Report of the Conference of the International Commission of Jurists held in Lagos, Nigeria 3–7 January 1961 (Geneva 1961) 16.

policies. A legitimacy crisis is not a true emergency but rather a
fundamental social malaise requiring political responses from those in
power. Emergency rule by definition qualifies or removes the basic
freedoms of an open society; and when a government seeks to avoid
thorough-going reform by instituting crisis government, the destruction of
democracy is assured. In countries like South Africa where the roots of
democracy are shallow and its realisation only partial, the regular use of
crisis powers may turn political development decisively in the direction of
authoritarianism and thereby undermine the prospects of a democratic
resolution of conflict.

The security legislation discussed and analysed in preceding chapters
has put South Africa into a state of permanent emergency. Under that
legislation citizens may be banned or detained by official decree or
prosecuted for contravening vague security crimes. The legislation also
provides for extensive censorship, the arbitrary control of meetings and
assemblies and the proscription of organisations. While some of these
powers are typical of emergency rule, the crucial difference in South
Africa is that they have become a normal part of political life. Moreover,
in addition to the security powers previously discussed, there are others
that contribute formidably to the reality of permanent crisis rule. The
Defence Act of 1957 provides that the South African Defence Force, or any
portion or member of it, may be employed on service for the prevention or
suppression of terrorism and internal disorder in the Republic.[5] Both the
Permanent Force and the Citizen Force may be so employed[6] and the
State President is given the power to mobilise the defence force, or any
branch of it, for the purpose of combating terrorism or internal disorder.[7]
He may effect mobilisation either by proclamation in the *Gazette* or 'in
such other manner as he may deem expedient'.[8] The power to employ the
defence force for the suppression of terrorism or internal disorder may be
exercised at any time without a declaration of emergency and without the
observance of formalities. Members of the defence force who are used in
this way have all the powers and duties, and are entitled to the same
immunities, as are enjoyed by, or imposed upon, the police under the
Police Act.[9] The Defence Act also confers other extensive powers which
may be exercised without a declaration of emergency. These include the
power to impose tight controls on access to harbours and airports,[10] to
commandeer property,[11] to impose rigorous censorship[12] and to commandeer transport systems.[13] These powers, normally associated with war,
may be activated by the State President at any time for the prevention or
suppression of terrorism and internal disorder. In addition, the Minister
of Defence has the power to take control of a ten-kilometre strip along the
borders of the Republic in order to combat terrorism[14] and to order the

[5] Section 3(2) of Act 44 of 1957.
[6] Section 90.   [7] Section 92.
[8] Ibid.
[9] Section 3(4).
[10] Section 99.
[11] Section 100.
[12] Section 101.
[13] Section 102.
[14] Section 99A.

evacuation of persons from any building, premises or area anywhere in the Republic, or to order their assembly in any such place.[15] This order may be made effective for no longer than four days and may be issued also by any officer acting under the minister's authority. Finally, a provision of the Defence Act confers an extensive indemnity against civil and criminal liability on members of the force for actions done in good faith in the prevention or suppression of terrorism[16] and empowers the State President to stay legal proceedings instituted against himself, the state, the Minister of Defence or a member of the force if in his opinion the proceedings arise out of good faith actions for the prevention of terrorism and it is in the national interest that they shall be stopped.[17] A certificate was issued in terms of this last-mentioned power in order to stay legal proceedings brought in Namibia by persons who alleged that they had been illegally detained by the authorities. In the ensuing court case, *Kaluma v Minister of Defence*,[18] the court decided that the State President's opinion that the actions in question (the detentions) were good faith acts committed within the scope of operations for the prevention of terrorism, and his opinion that the national interest required that legal proceedings arising out of them be stayed, was binding on the court which could not itself investigate whether there were adequate grounds for such opinion. This means that the State President has absolute power to deny the victims of 'anti-terrorist operations' redress in a court of law. In July 1986 the trial of four soldiers on a charge of murdering a civilian was stopped by the use of this power.[19]

The cumulative effect of the entire corpus of permanent security legislation in South Africa, including the provisions of the Defence Act just discussed,[20] is to vest the government indefinitely with many of the powers normally associated with martial-law or crisis rule. There are some martial-law powers, it is true, which the government does not possess permanently, such as the power to place the citizens under general curfew, the power to try security-law offences before military courts, and the power to evacuate or concentrate citizens for periods longer than four days. But the exceptions are minimal and do not detract much from the reality of permanent emergency government in South Africa. This reality explains why the only true emergency law on the statute book, the Public Safety Act of 1953, has been used to a limited extent since its enactment despite South Africa's growing and virtually unbroken law-and-order crisis of the past three decades. An emergency was first declared in April 1960 and lifted approximately five months later.[21] Twenty-five years lapsed before the powers of the Act were again employed by the proclamation of an emergency in July 1985.[22] This emergency lasted until

---

[15] Section 103*bis*.   [16] Section 103*ter*(1), (2) and (3).   [17] Section 103*ter*(4).
[18] 1984 (4) SA 59 (SWA).   [19] *The Natal Witness* Friday 25 July 1986.
[20] For a discussion of other permanent emergency-type laws, see the chapter entitled 'Public Safety' in *Law of South Africa* vol 21 paras 350–3.
[21] For a discussion of the 1960 emergency, see *A Survey of Race Relations in South Africa 1959–60*, 73 et seq and A S Mathews *Law, Order and Liberty in South Africa* 224.
[22] Thirty-six magisterial districts were put under emergency rule by Proclamation No R120 of 1985 (*Reg Gaz* 3848 of 21 July 1985). On 24 October 1985 the emergency was lifted in six of these districts by Proclamation No R199 of 1985 (*Reg Gaz* 3890 of 24 October 1985) but extended two days later to a further eight districts by Proclamation R200 of 1985 (*Reg Gaz* 3891 of 26 October 1985). The emergency was finally withdrawn from all areas on

7 March 1986 but was rapidly followed by a new emergency declared on 12 June 1986,[23] this time for the entire Republic in contrast to a much more limited scope of application on the previous occasion. The 1986 emergency (which is still in operation at the time of writing) should be called the inadvertent emergency since it was promulgated only because the rapid passage of amendments to the Public Safety Act, which authorise the Minister of Law and Order to declare mini-emergencies in local areas, was frustrated by the Houses of Delegates and Representatives. Mini- or micro-emergencies are likely to play a prominent part in unrest control in the future mainly because, unlike macro-emergencies declared by the State President, they are perceived to have less damaging consequences for political and business confidence and foreign relations. The power to declare emergencies by stealth, and to free the security authorities from almost all legal controls and from public accountability in local emergency areas, will finally bring the Public Safety Act off the shelf where it has gathered dust for so long and place it alongside the Internal Security Act as a prime instrument of repression and control. The Public Safety Act, thus extended and rejuvenated, has become the unexpected instrument of the abolition of the remaining vestiges of the rechtsstaat as an institution of South African society. We turn now to its terms.

THE PUBLIC SAFETY ACT OF 1953[24]

In view of the introduction of the concept of micro-emergencies by amending legislation in 1986,[25] the terms of the Public Safety Act will be discussed under the separate headings of Macro-emergencies (those declared by the State President) and Micro-emergencies (those declared by the Minister of Law and Order).

Macro-emergencies

The Act empowers the State President to declare by proclamation in the *Gazette* that a state of emergency exists within the Republic or South West Africa (Namibia) or within any area thereof.[26] He may issue such a proclamation if in his opinion there is, on account of action or threatened action within the Republic of South Africa (or Namibia), a serious threat to the safety of the public or the maintenance of public order which cannot be brought under control by the ordinary law of the land.[27] The power to declare a state of emergency, and to withdraw a proclamation establishing it, is entirely within the discretion of the State President, and is not subject to legal challenge in the absence of proof of bad faith.[28] It is a mind-

---

7 March 1986 by Proclamation No R39 of 1986 (*Reg Gaz* 3930 of 7 March 1986) having lifted from eight districts on 3 December 1985 and a further seven on 7 February 1986 (see Proclamation No R220 of 1985 (*Reg Gaz* 3906 of 3 December 1985) and Proclamation No R13 of 1986 (*Reg Gaz* 3923 of 7 February 1986)).

[23] Proclamation No R108 of 1986 (*Reg Gaz* No 3963 of 12 June 1986).
[24] Act 3 of 1953.   [25] The Public Safety Amendment Act 67 of 1986.
[26] Section 2(1).   [27] Ibid.
[28] *Stanton v Minister of Justice* 1960 (3) SA 353 (T) 357. Though the declaration of state of emergency is usually a matter for executive discretion, judicial control on objective grounds is not unthinkable. See 'Note, The Internal Security Act of 1950' 51 (1951) *Colum L Rev* 406, 646–57 in relation to a declaration of an 'internal security emergency' by the United States President under legislation now repealed. British courts have always been unwilling to review the necessity for the declaration of an emergency: D Bonner op cit 64.

boggling thought that the courts were therefore precluded from questioning the State President's belief that 'ordinary law' (including extreme measures for banning, indefinite detention and the like) were 'inadequate' to contain the unrest that led to the 1985 and 1986 declarations of an emergency. An emergency may be made retroactive for up to four days prior to the proclamation[29] but this will not nullify the 'nullum crimen sine lege' maxim and an activity which was not a crime when it was committed, will not become criminal on account of the retroactive operation of the emergency.[30] The proclamation of a state of emergency may not remain in force for longer than twelve months but it may be followed by another or other proclamations of emergency.[31]

The State President is authorised to proclaim regulations for any area in which a state of emergency has been declared and for as long as the existence of the emergency remains in force.[32] The enabling provision declares that he may make such regulations as appear to him to be necessary or expedient for maintaining public safety or public order and terminating the emergency or dealing with circumstances pertaining to the emergency.[33] Except for certain express limitations on this power prescribed in the Act,[34] the State President's power to promulgate emergency regulations is expressed in the broadest terms though it goes too far to say, as the court did in *R v Maphumulo*[35] that his authority is equal to the legislative power of Parliament. This statement has since been repudiated by the Transvaal court in *Momoniat & Naidoo v Minister of Law and Order*[36] in which Goldstone J pointed out that it was clear that although legislation passed by Parliament otherwise than bona fide is not susceptible to a declaration of invalidity, this does not apply to subordinate legislation even if made by the State President under the ample powers conferred by the Act. In two recent judgments[37] of the Natal Court, certain provisions of the emergency regulations relating to the making of subversive statements and the seizure of newspapers were struck down as invalid, thereby laying to rest the notion that the State President is on a par with Parliament when he legislates under the powers conferred upon him by the Public Safety Act. On what grounds may the validity of regulations made by the State President be impugned before the courts? In *Momoniat & Naidoo*, bad faith was postulated as a basis for a declaration of invalidity but since the notion of legislating in bad faith (as

---

[29] Section 2(1).

[30] Section 3(2)*(b)*; *R v Manthutle* 1960 (4) SA 827 (C).

[31] Section 2(2).

[32] Section 3(1). The regulations must be promulgated in the *Gazette*. The words 'for as long as the emergency remains in force' do not prohibit a prosecution after withdrawal of the emergency for an offence committed during the emergency: *R v Sutherland* 1961 (2) SA 806 (A).

[33] Section 3(1).

[34] The regulations may not create retrospective crimes, impose compulsory military service or affect the laws relating to the membership, powers and sessions of the President's Council, Parliament or a provincial council: s 3(3).

[35] 1960 (3) SA 793 (N). See also *Ex parte Hathorn: In re OC Durban Prison Command* 1960 (2) SA 767 (D).

[36] 1986 (2) SA 264 (W).

[37] *Metal & Allied Workers Union v State President of the Republic of South Africa* 1986 (4) SA 358 (D) and *Natal Newspapers (Pty) Ltd v The State President* (as yet unreported judgments of the Natal Provincial Division delivered on 4th September 1986).

opposed to giving a decision in bad faith) is an awkward one, the court adopted as an alternative to mala fides the proposition that subordinate legislation is invalid if the legislature could 'never have contemplated that such a measure be countenanced'.[38] The test for determining what the legislature could not have contemplated was unrelated, the court said, to the subjective state of mind of the authority in question but was an objective one to be determined according to the facts. This approach is in reality the test of unreasonableness but, in view of the wide powers to legislate conferred upon the State President, it has to be unreasonableness in so gross a form that it is beyond the intended powers of the subordinate legislator.

In the first of the two Natal cases referred to above, *Metal & Allied Workers Union v State President of the Republic of South Africa*, Didcott J acted on the basis that subordinate legislation which is vague and uncertain (aspects of the definition of subversive statements) or which goes beyond the objectives for which the State President may legislate (the ban on seeing a legal adviser without permission) is void and unenforceable. In either case, the ground of invalidity is the ultra vires doctrine in terms of which subordinate legislation is invalid if it is too unclear to be understood or if it strays beyond the objectives specified in the enabling legislation. If a regulation is ultra vires it will not be saved even by the new ouster clause[39] introduced in 1986 and designed to prevent legal challenges to regulations issued by the State President or Minister of Law and Order.

Subordinate legislation could be made subject to a further limitation in the form of a presumption that Parliament is deemed, in the absence of a contrary indication, to have preserved established constitutional principles and the fundamental values of the common law. The effect of this limitation would be to create a kind of implied bill of rights[40] enforceable against subordinate law-making authority; but the court in *Momoniat & Naidoo* was not prepared to go that far since it held that the State President could deprive detainees of a *prior* right to a hearing (audi alteram partem) even though the legislation did not expressly authorise withdrawal of this basic right. The court did express the view that had the State President abolished the right to a hearing after confirmation of a detention order, the regulation so providing would be ultra vires as a grossly unreasonable exercise of power that Parliament could not have contemplated.[41] It is arguable, however, that the right to a hearing *prior* to being detained is so fundamental to our legal and constitutional tradition that it should give way only in the face of a clear and irresistible statutory intention to abolish it. The following passage from H W R Wade's book on administrative law is pertinent in this context:

'One of the law's notable achievements has been the development of the principles of natural justice, one of which is the right to be given a fair hearing *before being penalised in any way*. These principles are similarly based upon implied statutory conditions: it is assumed that Parliament, when conferring power, intends that power to be used fairly and with due consideration of rights and

---

[38] *Momoniat & Naidoo v Minister of Law and Order* (supra) 273.
[39] Section 5B introduced by s 4 of the Public Safety Amendment Act 67 of 1986.
[40] See D Bonner op cit 52.
[41] At p 276 of the judgment.

interests adversely affected. In effect, Parliament legislates against a background of judge-made rules of interpretation, which place the necessary restrictions on governmental powers so as to ensure that they are exercised not arbitrarily but fairly and properly.'[42]

This passage shows that courts could go further than the judges in *Momoniat & Naidoo* subject only to the condition that to afford a hearing would not frustrate the exercise of the admitted power to detain persons without trial. It seems clear that recognition of the right of a detainee to make written representations (as distinct from an oral hearing), while involving the authorities in more work and inconvenience, would not cause a breakdown in the administration of the institution of preventive detention. In *Omar v The Minister of Law and Order*[43] Friedman J brusquely (and correctly, it is submitted) dismissed the inconvenience argument by saying that if fourteen days was too short to consider representations from detainees, the State President should provide for a longer period. Didcott J, in the *Metal & Allied Workers Union* case, came close to basing the court's decision on the invalidity of the regulation excluding the right to see a lawyer without permission on the fundamental nature of that right in our legal system. Unfortunately, the finding is not explicit on the acceptance of the notion of an implied bill of rights and the regulation dealing with access to lawyers foundered on the rock of overbreadth.

The possible grounds of a declaration of invalidity reviewed above all appear to be expressions of the ultra vires principle. A subordinate lawgiver such as the State President may be said to act ultra vires when he makes regulations which are vague or meaningless, grossly unreasonable, contrary to the fundamental principles of the legal system or executed in bad faith. There is persuasive authority for the view that all the traditional grounds of review may be subsumed under ultra vires;[44] and an important practical consequence of so doing is that the ouster clause contained in the Public Safety Act[45] will not protect anything that is found to be beyond the powers conferred upon the State President.

If a declaration of emergency is made retroactive, emergency regulations may likewise be made retroactive to the date from which the emergency has been declared to exist;[46] and although regulations are normally applicable only in declared emergency areas, the State President may specifically declare that they are to be applicable outside such areas if he deems this necessary for dealing with the state of emergency.[47] Without prejudice to the generality of the power to make regulations conferred on the State President, the Act specifically declares that he may delegate authority to make orders, rules and by-laws,[48] provide for the imposition of penalties for breach of regulations or directions issued thereunder,[49] and make different regulations for different areas or classes of person.[50] In

---

[42] H W R Wade *Administrative Law* 5 ed (Oxford 1982) 38–9 (emphasis supplied).
[43] 1986 (3) SA 306 (C) (minority judgment).
[44] Lawrence Baxter *Administrative Law* 307 et seq; *Natal Newspapers (Pty) Ltd v The State President* (supra).
[45] Section 5B.
[46] Section 3(2)*(b)*—subject to the aforementioned prohibition on retrospective crimes.
[47] Section 3(1)*(b)*.
[48] Section 3(2)*(a)*(i). This includes the authority to prescribe penalties.
[49] Section 3(2)*(a)*(ii). The power of confiscation is specifically authorised as a penalty.
[50] Section 3(2)*(c)*.

regard to delegation, the courts have recently held that the power to delegate may not be sub-delegated except to specified persons and the regulation authorising the Commissioner of Police to delegate the authority to make orders to any person authorised by him was declared invalid.[51] The State President immediately thereafter overcame these judgments of the courts by the retroactive promulgation of an amended regulation which provided for delegation to commissioned officers of the security forces.[52] It is possible that the specification of delegates in the amending regulation is still not specific enough. Regulations may further make provision for the summary arrest and detention of persons[53] and for such persons to be held anywhere in the Republic, whether within or without an emergency area.[54]

The extreme power of the State President to qualify or nullify the basic rights of citizens under emergency rule shines through the regulations promulgated in all three emergencies declared since the enactment of the Public Safety Act in 1953. The 1960 emergency regulations have been extensively surveyed in the literature[55] and will not be discussed here. The regulations promulgated under the emergency declared on 21 July 1985[56] provided for detention without trial and access, conferred legal immunity on officials (including the police and defence forces) for bona fide actions taken during the emergency, authorised extended powers of search and seizure, made provision for censorship over emergency reports, created a broad crime of threatening to inflict harm, hurt or loss upon any person, and authorised the use of such force as an officer 'deemed necessary' to remove or otherwise act against persons who had failed to respond to an order to proceed to any place or to desist from specified conduct. Rules made in terms of delegated authority granted by the regulations provided inter alia for the treatment of detainees, curfews in prescribed areas, control of movement into areas and the prevention of educational boycotts. When the third emergency was declared on 12 June 1986, the regulations[57] promulgated by the State President sought to vest the state and its agents with totally lawless power. The 1985 emergency regulations were substantially re-enacted but they were beefed up by a mind-blowing criminal prohibition on the making of 'subversive statements', by a prohibition on the making without permission of visual or sound reproductions of unrest activities or security force actions to contain them, and by conferring on the Minister of Law and Order the arbitrary power

[51] *UDF v Die Staatspresident* (as yet unreported judgment of the Witwatersrand Local Division of the Supreme Court delivered on 28 July 1986) and *The United Democratic Front v The State President* (as yet unreported judgment of the Eastern Cape Division delivered on 30 July 1986). In the first judgment the court was prepared to uphold the subdelegation to unspecified persons of administrative acts as opposed to rule-making authority.
[52] Proclamation No R140 of 1986 (*Reg Gaz* 3986 of 1 August 1986).
[53] Section 3(4). The names of detainees held for longer than thirty days must be tabled in Parliament within fourteen days after the expiration of such period, or if Parliament is not in session, within fourteen days of the commencement of the next session.
[54] Section 3(4)*bis*.
[55] See, for example, A S Mathews *Law, Order and Liberty in South Africa* 224; *A Survey of Race Relations in South Africa 1959–60* 73 et seq.
[56] Proclamation No R121 of 1985 (*Reg Gaz* 3849 of 21 July 1985) (amended by Proclamation Nos R199, R201, R207 and R208 of 1985).
[57] Proclamation No R109 of 1986 (*Reg Gaz* 3964 of 12 June 1986) (amended by Proclamation Nos R110, R121, R125, R131 and R140 of 1986).

to seize publications and to abolish the right to publish. The discussion that follows will focus on selected aspects of the 1986 emergency regulations, with occasional reference to those that were promulgated during the 1985 and 1960 emergencies.

Detention

Under all three emergencies, the security forces have been given the power to detain without trial. During each emergency the authorities employed this power to detain on a mass scale. Over eleven thousand persons were detained during the emergency in 1960,[58] eight thousand during the 1985 emergency[59] and a number believed to be in the region of eight thousand for the first two months of the current emergency.[60] Massive detentions have been facilitated by the arbitrary nature of the detention power. The latest regulation[61] provides for an initial detention of fourteen days at the instance of any member of the police or defence forces and thereafter, by written notice signed by the Minister of Law and Order, for further detention for as long as he may determine. Following a decision by the courts that the corresponding regulation of the 1985 emergency required the minister to afford the detainee a hearing before extending detention,[62] this 'obstacle' was swiftly removed by retrospective amendment and the 1986 regulation also puts the matter beyond doubt by declaring that the minister may extend detention without giving notice to the detainee and without affording a hearing. According to *Momoniat & Naidoo v Minister of Law and Order*[63] the detainee is entitled to be heard *after* the extension of his detention and any regulation purporting to deny or frustrate the exercise of that right would be invalid. The court in *Cameron-Bill v Minister of Law and Order*[64] followed this ruling and amplified it by declaring that the detainee, for purposes of making written representations to the minister, is entitled to consult a lawyer, to demand an outline of the reasons for his detention and to adequate time to prepare his submissions. To the extent that the regulation empowers the authorities to refuse access to a lawyer for purposes of preparing written representations, it is ultra vires the authority of the State President and therefore invalid.[65] The recognition of the right to make submissions after the

---

[58] *A Survey of Race Relations in South Africa* 1961, 52.

[59] *The Weekly Mail* 14–20 March 1986.

[60] *The Weekly Mail* 1–7 August 1986. At the resumption of the adjourned session of Parliament in August, the minister tabled eight and a half thousand names: *The Natal Witness* 18 August 1986.

[61] Regulation 3 of the regulations published as Proclamation No R109 of 1986 (*Reg Gaz* 3964 of 12 June 1986). The regulations are referred to below as 'the regulations'. Similar provision for detention was made during the 1985 emergency by reg 3 of the regulations promulgated in Proclamation No R121 of 1985 (*Reg Gaz* 3849 of 21 July 1985) (referred to below as the 1985 emergency regulations).

[62] *Nkwinti v Commissioner of Police* 1986 (2) SA 421 (E).

[63] Supra.

[64] As yet unreported judgment of the Witwatersrand Local Division delivered on 4 August 1986: see *The Natal Witness* 5 August 1986.

[65] Though the Cape court in *Omar v Minister of Law and Order* 1986 (3) SA 306 (C) upheld the validity of the regulation making access to the detainee, including access by lawyers, subject to official permission, Didcott J in *Metal & Allied Workers Union v State President of the Republic of South Africa* (supra) declared the regulation (and the corresponding rule made by the Minister of Justice) to be ultra vires to the extent that it covered access to lawyers.

minister has decided to extend a detention is no doubt better than having no right at all; but, as suggested earlier, there are persuasive arguments for the proposition that the State President does not have the power to abolish the prior right to a hearing and this proposition should prevail before the Appellate Division.

The language of the regulation conferring the power to arrest and detain, and authorising the minister to extend a detention, is subjectively phrased and this means, according to the prevailing dogma, that the courts will not generally investigate the merits of the decision to arrest and detain or to extend detention. Discretion that may be exercised subjectively cannot be challenged on the basis that it is unsupported by relevant facts; it may only be challenged on the ground that it was influenced by bad faith, improper motives or legally irrelevant considerations. In *Krish Naidoo v Minister of Law and Order*,[65a] Jennett J upheld a detention order which he conceded was based on facts that were open to doubt because 'it has been established that Petzer (the police officer) held the requisite opinion, whether rightly or wrongly'. A detainee who seeks to have a detention order set aside by the courts on the ground that there was no justification for it therefore has a formidable and perhaps hopeless mission, especially where the detaining authority provides plausible reasons for linking the detainee with unrest or disorder and has not disclosed an improper motive or purpose in effecting the arrest or detention. Where detainees have managed to secure their release by court order, the arresting official has generally acted so as to proclaim a reliance on improper or irrelevant considerations. This is true of the arrest and detention of a nun after she had objected to a police assault upon a young man in a black township and of the detention of a journalist whose professional occupation appeared to be the sole reason for the decision to take him into custody.[66] Does the detainee have any chance of success where the detaining authority has not acted ineptly or with obvious inadvertence to the purposes for which detention was authorised? The answer to this question depends largely on judicial attitudes to the onus of proof and to how that onus is discharged. It has frequently been said that there is an onus on those who arrest and detain to justify the deprivation of liberty, and this principle was reaffirmed by the court in *Minister of Law and Order v Hurley*.[67] It seems equally well established that a person who alleges bad faith or reliance on improper considerations in the exercise of statutory powers carries the burden of proving the allegation. These two propositions appear to be in conflict but they may be reconciled in the following way:

1. If the exercise of a subjective power to arrest and detain is challenged, the detaining authority is required in law to establish a justification for the arrest and detention by adverting to relevant reasons which warrant the deprivation of liberty. This does not involve proof that actual grounds for detention exist, only an

---

[65a] As yet unreported judgment of the Eastern Cape Division (Case No 978/86).

[66] *Dempsey v Minister of Law and Order* (unreported judgment of the Cape Provincial Division delivered on 9 July 1986) and *Radebe v Minister of Law and Order* (unreported judgment of the Transvaal Provincial Division delivered on 7 July 1986).

[67] 1986 (3) SA 568 (A).

indication of grounds which would justify the detention if they did exist.[68]

2. If the detaining authority does advert to (without proving the existence of) grounds which would justify its opinion that the detention is justified by the enabling regulation, the onus will clearly lie upon the detainee to establish that the opinion in question was (i) held in bad faith or (ii) either not held at all (because the authority did not apply its mind to the matter) or alternatively, if so held, was arrived at by reference to legally irrelevant or improper considerations. The detainee may show, for example, that because the detaining authority did not consider obvious alternatives to a detention order, the opinion held by that authority was not the kind of opinion contemplated by the Act.[68a]

3. The discharge by the detainee of the onus of proving bad faith or irrelevant considerations will be greatly facilitated if the arresting official, by his own words and conduct, has revealed an improper basis for acting (as in the case of the nun and journalist referred to above). In the absence of such evidence, can the detainee discharge the onus by showing that his or her activities have been innocuous and that those activities have no connection with the unrest or disorder that the emergency is meant to contain? In *Stanton v Minister of Justice*,[69] a detention case decided under the 1960 emergency regulations, the detainee put forward evidence of a blameless life which the court proceeded to treat as irrelevant even though the detaining authority had refused to provide any reasons for the detention. *Stanton's* case should not be followed since it demands the impossible of a detainee by requiring refutation of a case which the detainee is not allowed to know. If the detainee puts forward believable evidence that his or her conduct has been innocent, the burden of adducing evidence is cast upon the detaining authority. If that authority declines or fails to put forward relevant reasons for the detention (as in *Stanton*) the court is entitled to find for the detainee. The arresting official cannot be forced to place information before the court but, as Goldstone J said in *Radebe v Minister of Law and Order*, 'his failure to do so may have the consequence that his defence to the application turns out to be abortive'.[70]

4. The presumption of good faith in reg 16(4) does not affect the onus of proof of bad faith which is in any event cast upon the applicant who alleges the absence of it.[71]

[68] This distinguishes the onus which falls upon the authorities where, as in *Minister of Law and Order v Hurley* (supra) the discretion is not subjective but must be based on objectively present jurisdictional facts. In such a case, the onus is on the arresting or detaining authority to prove the existence of those facts.
[68a] *The Bishop of the Roman Catholic Church of the Diocese of Port Elizabeth v Minister of Law and Order* (unreported judgment of the Eastern Cape Division of 1 August 1986 (Case No 1101/86)).
[69] 1960 (3) SA 353 (T).
[70] Supra. See also *Greyling & Erasmus (Pty) Ltd v Johannesburg L.R.T.B.* 1982 (4) SA 427 (A) 448.
[71] See the judgment of Marais J in *Dempsey v Minister of Law and Order* (supra) at p 7 of the typed judgment.

If the courts follow these rules as to onus, the detainee will at least be able
to join issue with the state over the basis of the detention but, as suggested
above, the evidential onus upon the detaining authority is to put forward
justifiable grounds for the deprivation of liberty, not to prove their
existence as in cases where the law requires the presence of objectively
established facts as a prerequisite for detention. Though the court is not
concerned with facts which bear upon the merits of the decision to detain,
it can (and should) investigate and pronounce upon facts relevant to the
issues of good faith and possible official reliance upon improper or
irrelevant considerations. Where the discretion to detain is a subjective
one, as under the emergency regulations, that discretion is still controll-
able by the courts but not to the degree that objective discretionary power
(for example, detention under s 29 of the Internal Security Act) is cribbed
and confined by the obligation to prove the actual existence of
jurisdictional facts.

Detention under the emergency regulations might also be challenged on
procedural or technical grounds rather than a substantive attack upon
propriety of the decision to detain. An essentially procedural argument
was put forward in *Kerchoff v Minister of Law and Order*[72] in which the
detainee was already in detention under s 50 of the Internal Security Act
1982 when it was decided to hold him under the emergency regulations.
The argument was that the arrest which must precede a detention under
emergency law had not taken place (the detainee already being in
custody) and that the minister's extension of the detention was invalid
since it was not preceded by the arrest contemplated by the regulation.
The court emphatically rejected this argument. In *Tsenoli v The State
President*,[73] the court had to consider whether the detention regulation was
invalid because it purported to confer wider powers on the detaining
authority than the State President was granted by the Act. The relevant
provision[74] of the Act empowers the State President to make regulations
for 'the safety of the public *or* for the maintenance of public order' *and* 'for
terminating such emergency'. However, the power to arrest for detention
may be premised on the belief that such action is necessary for 'the
maintenance of public order or the safety of the public . . . *or* for the
termination of the state of emergency'.[75] The effect of the substitution for
the conjunction '*and*' in the Act of the word '*or*' in the regulations is to
assign to the arresting officer a power that is wider than the State
President's power of legislating. It was also argued in this case that the
detention regulation is invalid because, while specifying the grounds for
arrest, it fixes no criteria for the subsequent detention and the extension
thereof by the minister. In *Tsenoli* a full bench upheld the argument that
the words of the enabling Act should be read conjunctively and that the
substitution of 'or' for 'and' in the regulation rendered it invalid.

---

[72] As yet unreported judgment of the Natal Provincial Division delivered on 15 August
1986 (Case No 1912/86). In *Suttner v The State President* (unreported judgment of the
Transvaal Provincial Division of 8 August 1986) the court rejected the argument that the re-
arrest of a person already in custody was a prerequisite for a valid detention.

[73] As yet unreported judgment of the Durban and Coast Local Division delivered on 8
August 1986 (Case No 4988/86).

[74] Section 3(1)*(a)*.

[75] Regulation 3(1).

However, in *Kerchoff* another full bench in a judgment delivered a few days later rejected the *Tsenoli* ruling even though the issue of validity had not been raised or properly argued by the applicants. The matter now awaits resolution by the Appellate Division. The *Tsenoli* judgment appears to represent a more sensible interpretation of the Act since it would prevent detention (or other restrictive action) for reasons unconnected with the emergency (for example, of a group of soccer hooligans who clearly constitute a threat to public safety but whose activities have no connection with emergency unrest) and, in addition, emphasises the need for a constrained power to regulate as opposed to the largely unfettered one supported in *Kerchoff*.

The regime provided for detainees by the regulations,[76] read with the rules for the treatment of detainees promulgated by the Minister of Justice,[77] is one of exceptional severity. The detention is incommunicado and visits may only take place with official permission.[78] There is a specific right to interrogate detainees[79] and this probably explains why there have been so many allegations of ill-treatment and torture since the promulgation of the 1985 and 1986 emergencies. Where assault, torture or other forms of maltreatment are alleged, the court may grant a restraining order on the authorities and did grant a provisional order against the security forces in the Eastern Cape in October 1985 following the startling revelations made by a young district surgeon, Dr Wendy Orr, who placed her observations on the condition of detainees examined by her before the court on affidavit. Dr Orr was shortly thereafter prevented from seeing detainees and similar applications to court could founder because there are few Wendy Orrs in strategic positions in the government service. Several such applications have succeeded, however, before the Natal court. The rules governing detention also provide for strict control over communications with outside persons by letter[80] and make detainees guilty of an offence if inter alia they sing, whistle, or make unnecessary noise, cause discontent or agitation among fellow detainees or are insolent or disrespectful towards prison employees, official visitors or the police.[81] These prohibitions make it surprising that the fact of the detainee's existence has not been declared criminal and punishable. Finally, it is an offence to disclose the names or identities of detained persons without the consent of the minister or a person authorised by him.[82] If the authorities so decide, detentions could be kept secret until the names of detainees are tabled in Parliament in terms of the Act.[83] The prohibition on disclosing the identities of detainees has introduced into South Africa the phenomenon of 'los desaparecidos', surely one of the marks of a police state.

---

[76] Regulation 3.
[77] GN No 1196 (*GG* 10281 of 12 June 1986) referred to below as the 'detention rules'.
[78] Regulation 3(10). Visits by lawyers have been dealt with above.
[79] Regulation 3(5).
[80] Rule 6.
[81] Rule 21.
[82] Regulation 13. Once the authorities have disclosed the name and identity of a detainee to any person, the prohibition appears to fall away.
[83] See s 3(4).

The Indemnity Provision

The 1986 emergency regulations incorporate a provision which seeks to indemnify the security forces and certain named officers of state from criminal or civil liability for actions taken in good faith in the course of their emergency duties and functions.[84] The combined effect of this regulation (if valid) and the censorship regulations to be considered below is to free the security forces *in advance of action taken by them* from both legal and public accountability. Such immunity is disturbing in the light of the ominous development in the Eighties of an increasingly lawless police power in the state. There appears to be enough evidence to convince an objective observer of the recent unrest in South Africa that the police 'eliminate' troublemakers by shooting, that they support or turn a blind eye to vigilante attacks on activists[85] and that torture is widely practised on detainees. The growth of official lawlessness makes the scope and validity of the indemnity regulation an issue of the highest importance. The validity of a similar indemnity enacted as part of the 1960 emergency regulations was questioned before the court in *Mawo v Pepler NO*[86] but it was unnecessary for the resolution of the case to pronounce on this question. Although the presiding judge declared obiter that he was 'far from holding' that the indemnity clause was invalid, it is arguable that it is a grossly unreasonable exercise of rule-making authority. Whether this is so depends on the scope of the indemnity provision as determined by judicial interpretation; and the first point to be made is that it is not as wide as it is generally assumed to be. The indemnity covers only acts 'in good faith advised, commanded, ordered, directed or performed' in the carrying out of duties, the exercise of powers or the performance of functions *'in terms of these regulations'*. It follows that it does not exempt members of the police or defence forces, or the other persons specifically mentioned, from legal liability for actions performed under the authority of any law other than the emergency regulations. If, for example, the police have acted in terms of the general powers derived from the Police Act of 1958, the indemnity is not applicable. Moreover, only bona fide acts are covered and the indemnity will be inapplicable if the official in question is proved to have acted in bad faith. It is by no means clear, however, what bona fide means in this context. Does an official who knows that his actions are illegal but honestly believes that they are necessary to deal with the unrest situation, act in good faith? Can an official be said to act in good faith if what he has done is strictly not necessary for the suppression of the unrest? There is English authority for the proposition that there is a general presumption against the indemnification of acts not necessary for the suppression of rebellion but also for the proposition that an indemnity may be wide enough to protect acts which an official knew to be illegal but which he genuinely believed were necessary to cope with the emergency situation.[87] Though the

[84] Regulation 16(1). A similar regulation was enacted for both the 1960 and 1985 emergencies.
[85] See, particularly, Nicholas Haysom *Mabangalala: The Rise of Right-Wing Vigilantes in South Africa* (Centre for Applied Legal Studies, Jhb 1986) 137.
[86] 1961 (4) SA 806 (C).
[87] P O'Higgins 'Wright v Fitzgerald Revisited' (1962) 25 *MLR* 413.

indemnity regulation enacted for the 1986 emergency is framed in wide terms, courts should insist on the requirement that the official in question should have entertained the honest belief that his actions were lawful. If this is not made a requirement for the operation of the indemnity clause, the torture of a detainee to discover the location of a cache of weapons would be protected if the interrogator genuinely believed that his actions were necessary to ensure the safety of the public or to bring the unrest situation under control.

There are several other factors which appear to limit the invocation of the indemnity provision. It has been suggested, for example, that it affects only criminal prosecutions of the authorities and delictual actions against them, and that actions in contract or to determine the ownership of property are left untouched by its provisions.[88] The indemnity could not be invoked, moreover, in criminal prosecutions of individuals under the emergency regulations.[89] Moreover, only actions falling within the scope of official duties are protected. Finally, the indemnity could not operate so as to bar an inquiry into the validity of the regulations themselves.[90]

Notwithstanding these apparent limitations on the potential scope of the indemnity clause, it might have the effect of legalising extreme invasions of citizen rights. The Commissioner of Police was granted the power under the emergency regulations to issue orders inter alia 'relating to any other matter the regulating, control or prohibition of which in his opinion is necessary or expedient with a view to the safety of any member or members of the public or the maintenance of public order, or in order to terminate the state of emergency . . .'.[91] Prior to the shootings at Langa investigated by the Kannemeyer Commission, all Divisional Commissioners of Police received a telex which contained the following instruction:

'When acid and/or petrol bombs are thrown at police vehicles, private vehicles and houses, efforts must be made in all circumstances to eliminate those who are guilty.'[92]

If this instruction had been issued as an order by the Commissioner of Police prior to the declaration by the court in *Natal Newspapers (Pty) Ltd v The State President*[92a] that the conferral upon him of the blanket power to make regulations was invalid, it seems that it would have been protected by the indemnity (together with any action taken under it) since the commissioner at that stage could have genuinely believed that such an order was necessary for the protection of the public or the maintenance of law and order and that it fell within the wide powers accorded him by the regulations. Moreover, if the regulations are amended so as to grant the commissioner a narrower power to make orders for the protection of the

---

[88] See *Brief on the Legal Regime Operative in Areas Subject to a Proclamation of a State of Emergency and Areas Declared to be Unrest Areas under the Public Safety Act 3 of 1953* (Faculty of Law, Univ of Cape Town, June 1986) 25. Referred to below as 'Cape Town Law Faculty Brief'.
[89] Ibid.   [90] At 27.
[91] Regulation 7(1)(d).
[92] *Report of the Commission Appointed to Enquire into the Incident Which Occurred on 21st March 1985 at Uitenhage* (RP 74–1985) 95. This instruction, in the original Afrikaans text read: 'Wanneer suurbomme en/of petrolbomme na polisievoertuie, privaatvoertuie en geboue gegooi word moet daar onder alle omstandighede gepoog word om die skuldiges te elimineer.'
[92a] Supra.

force or the public against terroristic acts, he might again form the bona
fide belief that an order for the elimination of throwers of petrol bombs is
both necessary and lawful. There are strong grounds for believing that an
indemnity that purports to immunise such conduct is ultra vires either on
the ground that it is a serious interference with court jurisdiction[93] or on
the ground that its enactment is unreasonable conduct which could not
have been anticipated by the legislature as a valid exercise of subordinate
law-making authority. The effect of indemnity clauses (as distinct from
ouster clauses which are inoperative where an official has acted illegally)
is to validate conduct that would otherwise be illegal and, being only
indirectly related to the task of restoring law and order, their creation
should generally be a matter for Parliament and not for inferior law-
making authorities to whom Parliament has not clearly delegated this
specific power. The nature of indemnity clauses cautions against a judicial
policy of inferring parliamentary delegation of the power to enact them.
Dicey wrote as follows on the subject of Indemnity Acts:

'. . . of all laws which a Legislature can pass an Act of Indemnity is the most
likely to produce injustice. It is on the face of it the legalisation of illegality; the
hope of it encourages acts of vigour, but it also encourages violations of law and
of humanity. The tale of Flogging Fitzgerald in Ireland, or the history of
Governor Eyre in Jamaica, is sufficient to remind us of the deeds of lawlessness
and cruelty which in a period of civil conflict may be inspired by recklessness or
passion, and may be pardoned by the retrospective sympathy or partisanship of
a terror-stricken or vindictive Legislature.'[94]

Considering that Dicey was discussing a retrospective indemnity law, and
not one which sought to free the authorities *in advance* from liability for
illegal actions, our courts should insist that indemnities are a matter for
the highest legislative authority (as in the case of s 103*ter*(2) of the Defence
Act 44 of 1957).[95] The Public Safety Act does not clearly and
unequivocally delegate the power to create indemnities to the State
President and his attempt to do so should be declared to be ineffective.

Censorship

The combined effect of a number of emergency regulations, considered
on their face, is to impose a news and information black-out on matters
connected with the unrest situation or with measures taken to counter it.
These regulations, in brief, prohibit the making, possession of, distribution, display or even utterance of a subversive statement,[96] authorise the
minister or his nominee to seize a publication which contains a subversive
statement or one detrimental to public safety or order,[97] empower the
minister by notice in the *Gazette* to prohibit the production, publication,
dissemination or possession of a publication (or future editions of a
periodical publication) which he believes to be of a subversive nature,[98]

[93] Cape Town Law Faculty Brief, 25.
[94] Quoted by P O'Higgins (1962) 25 *MLR* 413 at 422.
[95] It has been pointed out that prospective indemnities frustrate parliamentary scrutiny
and are contrary to parliamentary and democratic government: see Cape Town Law Faculty
Brief 24.
[96] Regulation 10 read with the definition of 'subversive statement' in reg 1.
[97] Regulation 11.
[98] Regulation 12.

prohibit the making or distribution of films (or other like forms of visual representation), photographs, drawings and sound recordings of unrest incidents or security force actions to counter or control them without the permission of the Commissioner of Police,[99] and authorise the Commissioner of Police to issue orders to regulate or prohibit comment or news relating to the law-and-order functions of the security forces.[100] It is no exaggeration to say that press freedom in relation to the security situation has been brought to an abrupt end by these measures in that they have made it impossible for the media to present independent information and comment about unrest and disorder in the country and about the activities of the security forces. The State President has through subordinate legislation done what Parliament itself has been unwilling to do by statute. This raises the question whether the regulations so destructive of press freedom, or at least some of them, are not invalid because outside the rule-making authority of the State President. In *Natal Newspapers (Pty) Ltd* the court freed the press from the seizure and banning powers conferred upon the minister or his delegate but upheld the regulations which authorise the prohibition on visual or sound material and news or comment on unrest and security force actions to counter it. The detailed implications of this judgment are indicated below.

According to the regulations, it is an offence to make, write, print or record a subversive statement, to possess such a statement, to disseminate or circulate it among the public or a section of the public or to dispatch, supply or offer it to any person, to display it in any place to which the public has access, to utter it or to play it by means of any apparatus in the hearing of any person.[101] Severe penalties in the form of a fine not exceeding R20 000, or imprisonment not exceeding ten years (without the option of a fine, if so decided by the court) are provided for persons convicted of commission of the offence just described.[102] The court may declare confiscated any 'goods, property or instrument by means of which or in connection with which the offence has been committed'. Even though the prohibition on possession was declared invalid in *Natal Newspapers (Pty) Ltd*, the reach of this crime in relation to news gathering and dissemination is quite stunning. The reporter who writes a subversive statement on a note pad or who repeats it to his editor is guilty of the crime; and if it is run off on the newspaper's printing presses they may be declared forfeited to the state. These prohibitions are the stuff of the siege society and the police state.

If the range of persons affected by the crime is stunning, the scope of the definition of a subversive statement can only be described as stupefying. It includes statements that are calculated or likely to have the effect of promoting *any* object of any unlawful organisation, of inciting the public, a section of it, or any person, to 'resist or oppose' the government in connection with any measure relating to the administration of justice, of

---

[99] Regulation 9.
[100] Regulation 7(1)*(c)*.
[101] Regulation 10. In several instances, the regulation punishes both the person who does the act (for example, makes or records a subversive statement) and the person who causes it to be done.
[102] Regulation 14.

engendering feelings of hostility between sections of the public or individuals, of weakening or undermining confidence in the termination of the state of emergency and of encouraging or promoting foreign action against the Republic.[103] These prohibitions are so bizarre or meaningless that the full bench of the Natal Supreme Court unanimously declared them to be ultra vires and void.[104] The prohibitions that still stand, and remain enforceable according to the Natal judgment, are those relating to statements calculated or likely to have the effect of inciting the public or section of the public or any person—

(a) to take part in unlawful strikes, gatherings or demonstrations or in acts of civil disobedience;

(b) to take part in or support any boycott action;

(c) to discredit or undermine the system of compulsory military service;

(d) to resist or oppose[105] the government or any of its officials in connection with emergency or law-and-order measures;

(e) to commit any act or omission which endangers or may endanger the safety of the public, public order or the termination of the emergency;

(f) to encourage or promote disinvestment or sanctions.

Though these prohibitions (*(a)*–*(f)* above) survived challenge, at least two of them may be unenforceable in terms of the subsequent judgment of the Natal court in *Tsenoli v The State President* if this judgment (and not the contrary one in *Kerchoff*) is affirmed by the Appellate Division.[106] The two that appear to be affected by *Tsenoli* are *(d)* and *(e)* above, since in each case the prohibited conduct is not linked to the statutory requirement that regulations must be directed to the termination of the emergency. Leaving aside the *Tsenoli* judgment which in any event can easily be nullified by amendment, there is no doubt that the enforceable parts of the definition of subversive statements are extraordinarily wide. They are aimed at resistance or protest politics and cover a large part of the field of extra-parliamentary opposition.

The regulations also provided that the Minister of Law and Order, or a serving commissioned officer of the force, if of the opinion that any publication contained a subversive statement or other information detrimental to the safety of the public, the maintenance of public order or the termination of the state of emergency, could order the seizure of one or more or all of the copies of such publication.[107] The minister was granted the further power, without giving notice or affording a hearing, to ban publications, including future editions of periodical publications such as newspapers, if of the opinion that the publication in question contained any matter of a subversive nature.[108] After an order of this kind had been issued it would become an offence to make, write, import, print, publish, distribute or possess the publication, or to be in any way involved in such activities. In addition, the minister (or a commissioned officer) could

---

[103] Regulation 1.

[104] *Metal & Allied Workers Union v The State President of the Republic of South Africa* (supra).

[105] The Natal court expressed the view in the *MAWU* case that oppose means something akin to resist, and does not mean to criticise.

[106] Supra.

[107] Regulation 11.

[108] Regulation 12. The ban must be imposed by notice in the *Gazette*.

order the seizure, forfeiture and disposal of publications affected by the banning order. In a nutshell, the minister was granted the power (to be exercised according to his subjective discretion) to shut down newspapers and, indeed, the entire press in the Republic. These regulations authorising the seizure and banning of publications were declared ultra vires and invalid by the court in *Natal Newspapers (Pty) Ltd v The State President*.[109] The court found that the regulations in question were beyond the powers of the State President, grossly unreasonable in their consequences and too vague to afford a clear guide to newspapers as to how to avoid the drastic consequences of ministerial action. The court, having declared the regulations invalid, did not consider the issue of whether the delegation of powers to commissioned officers was a permissible delegation of authority.[110]

There is, as we have seen, a provision in the regulations which prohibits persons, without official permission, from making, taking, recording, reproducing, publishing, broadcasting, distributing or sending any film, photograph, drawing or sound recording of unrest incidents, the persons involved in them, and of the conduct of the security forces or their members in the exercise of public safety or law-and-order functions.[111] This prohibition may fairly be described as a total ban on visual and aural material concerned with unrest or disorder. Though the very breadth of this regulation appears to undermine its validity (it appears to cover unrest which has occurred at any time or place) it was upheld in *Natal Newspapers (Pty) Ltd*. The court confined the prohibition to public disturbances 'arising after the promulgation of the regulation and conceivably to the publication of past disturbances etc which have present relevance'. Even though rescued by the court, the regulation remains obscure as to coverage of past unrest.

The final censorship regulation that requires brief consideration is one that authorises the Commissioner of Police or a divisional commissioner to issue orders inter alia to regulate, control or prohibit news or comment concerning the conduct of the security forces or its members 'regarding the maintenance of the safety of the public or the public order or the termination of the state of emergency'.[112] Acting under this power, the commissioner issued an order on 16 June 1986 prohibiting, without prior permission, the 'announcement, dissemination, distribution, taking or securing within or from the Republic' of any such news or comment. The commissioner, acting under another provision of the regulation empowering him to make orders,[113] also issued an order banning newsmen from

---

[109] Supra.

[110] The wording of reg 11 (and of certain other regulations) was changed following the judgments in *UDF v Die Staatspresident* (unreported judgment of the WLD delivered on 28 July 1986) and *The United Democratic Front v The State President* (unreported judgment of the ECD delivered on 30 July 1986) in which the court declared improper a subdelegation to a person authorised by the delegate. It is submitted that Coetzee J's reservations about the rule against subdelegation in respect of administrative acts (as opposed to rule-making authority) are not warranted in relation to reg 11 which contemplated a delegation to commissioned officers of a duty involving a substantial element of discretion and judgment. In other words, the power of delegation is not purely ministerial.

[111] Regulation 9. This regulation has been paraphrased in the text. Its breadth, vagueness and severity is quite startling even for a regular reader of South African security statutes.

[112] Regulation 7(1)*(c)*.   [113] Regulation 7(1)*(d)*.

black areas or unrest areas for the purpose of reporting on the conduct of
the force or its members in the exercise of their law-and-order functions
unless prior written permission was granted.[114] The effect of the first order
is to extend to the written word the prohibition in the regulations on the
making or use of visual or aural material about security force activities;
and of the second, to prevent the gathering of such material. Together
they seek to diminish drastically the public accountability of the security
forces by preventing the public from knowing what they are doing. In
Natal Newspapers (Pty) Ltd the state conceded that these two orders were
invalid for lack of proper promulgation and they have since been replaced
by more carefully worded orders having the same effect and promulgated
in the *Gazette*.[114a] The new orders appear to be valid in terms of the
enabling regulation[114b] and like their predecessors they prohibit, without
official permission, (i) the announcement, dissemination, distribution or
the taking or sending of news concerning security force action concerned
with unrest and (ii) the presence of journalists, cameramen et cetera at
places of unrest. The orders are not retrospective and therefore appear to
refer to news or comment about security force actions which occur after
promulgation. Furthermore, the definition of 'security action' is not wide
enough to cover the conduct of the security forces which cannot be
regarded as action to terminate or control unrest, such as gratuitous
assaults or property damage which have reportedly been inflicted on
township dwellers. There appears, therefore, to be some limited scope for
exposing abuse of security powers in unrest areas if despite the banning of
journalists from such places, the news leaks out.

Promulgation of Orders

The power of the Commissioner of Police and of divisional commissioners to make orders has been partially considered in relation to censorship.
Except for the blanket delegation of authority declared invalid in *Natal
Newspapers (Pty) Ltd*, the delegation of the power to make orders appears to
be within the competence of the State President and was upheld in that
case.

Use of Force

The right to use force, including lethal force, is freed from virtually all
controls or restraints by a provision of the emergency regulations[115] which
authorises a commissioned, warrant or non-commissioned officer who has
formed the opinion that the presence or conduct of any person or persons
at any place may endanger the safety of the public or the maintenance of

[114] This order was originally issued on 16 June 1986 and then replaced by an order of 21
June 1986.
[114a] GN No 1881 of 3 September 1986 (*GG* No 10429 of 3 September 1986).
[114b] Regulation 7(1)(b) and (c) the validity of which was upheld in *Natal Newspapers (Pty)
Ltd*.
[115] Regulation 2. There are prerequisites for the validity of the use of force and they appear
to be that an opinion is held by the designated officer that the circumstances are such as to
endanger public safety et cetera and that the necessary order must have been properly
announced and not obeyed forthwith by those present. These are jurisdictional prerequisites
and, in their absence, the use of force will be illegal and not protected by the indemnity in
reg 16.

public order, to order the person (or persons) in question in a loud voice in both official languages to move elsewhere or to desist from the conduct in question and, if the order is not obeyed forthwith, to use such force as he under the circumstances may deem necessary to prevent the suspected danger. The most disturbing feature of this clause is the subjective nature of the discretion conferred on what may be a low-ranking member of the police or defence force. The right to order persons to leave or to desist from specified conduct is conditional upon the *opinion* that they may constitute a danger, not upon their actual conduct and its context. Once that order has been given and disobeyed, the extent of force that may be used depends upon the subjective judgment of the officer in question, not upon the nature and extent of the threat. This may be contrasted with the right to use force in non-emergency situations where the law requires a degree of correspondence between the extent of the force that is used and the objective to be achieved.[116] The use of force under emergency law is legally divorced from the surrounding circumstances and conditioned entirely on belief, however little that belief may correspond to reality. A further disturbing feature of the law is that in a multilingual country the announcement preceding the use of force is required to be in the official languages, and not in the language or languages of the majority of persons in the area concerned.

There appears to be little doubt that the force which may be used under the emergency regulations includes the killing of persons. For this reason, the courts should be willing and even ready to judge the bona fides of an officer's use of lethal force by the external facts. Where killing appears to have been clearly unnecessary to ward off the suspected danger, a finding that force was used in good faith should not be made. Though good faith is presumed[117] unless the contrary is shown, the proof of facts that throw serious doubt on the good faith of the officer in question should generally be sufficient to discharge the onus. Assuming that the indemnity clause of the regulations is valid, it will only validate a use of force which complies with all the conditions of the regulations and which the court finds to have been used in good faith.

General

Emergency regulations also provide for a power to enter premises, to search such premises or any person, and to seize property therein.[118] This power may be exercised without warrant at any time and the officer effecting an entry is given the very broad power to take such steps as he deems necessary for the maintenance of order, the safety of the public or the termination of the emergency. The subjective power to determine the steps that are taken is of questionable validity. The regulations also create a sweeping crime of threatening, whether directly or indirectly, to cause hurt, harm or loss to any person or his property.[119] This special crime goes well beyond the offence of intimidation created by the Intimidation Act of 1982. An offence under the Intimidation Act is committed if the

---

[116] Sections 48 and 49 of the Internal Security Act 74 of 1982.
[117] Regulation 16(4).
[118] Regulation 5.
[119] Regulation 4.

threat is made with the purpose of inducing someone to act or to refrain from acting or to assume or abandon a particular standpoint. The emergency crime consists of threats simpliciter without reference to their purpose. Depending on how the words 'harm' and 'hurt' are interpreted, and particularly on whether they encompass non-physical hurt or harm, the scope of the emergency crime may be far broader than intimidation which is confined to physical injuries. Finally, the emergency crime specifically covers threats to a person's relatives or dependants.

The 1986 emergency regulations were extended on 13 July 1986 by the enactment of some special regulations for black schoolchildren.[120] In brief, they deny education to black children unless they are registered for attendance at their school, require all pupils to reapply for registration for the second part of 1986, authorise the arbitrary rejection of an application for registration, empower education officers to override the principal's decision as to placement of a child in a class or standard and provide for the expulsion of a child who is not prepared to accept such placement. These regulations do not deal directly with public safety or law and order but do so indirectly through controls in the educational system, presumably on the rationale that much of the disorder is centred on black education and has involved pupils and schools. On this rationale, the State President could apply restrictions to many other institutions (for example, trade unions) and it is not surprising that the regulations have been challenged as being ultra vires.[121] Certainly some of the regulations go too far, particularly those which allow for arbitrary refusal of registration or arbitrary placements.

Prior to the 1986 amendments to the Public Safety Act an inadequate measure of parliamentary control over the nature and scope of emergency regulations was incorporated into its provisions. The relevant clause required regulations to be tabled within fourteen days of promulgation or, if Parliament was not in session, within fourteen days of the commencement of the next ordinary session. The regulations would lapse if not approved by the end of the session or if disapproved by resolution of Parliament, whichever occurred earlier. The executive domination of modern parliaments weakened the possibility of a restraining influence being imposed by Parliament. This control has been attenuated even further by amendments to the Public Safety Act. These amendments[122] ensure that the regulations will remain valid and enforceable until all three Houses of Parliament have adopted a motion annulling them in whole or part. Any single House is therefore able to block legislative challenge to the regulations. The Natal court held in *Metal & Allied Workers Union v The State President of the Republic of South Africa*[123] that a failure to table regulations did not invalidate them and that such a failure is remediable by parliamentary and not judicial action.

The Minister of Law and Order, if of the opinion that urgent necessity so requires, may exercise the powers granted to the State President by the

---

[120] Proclamation No R131 of 1986 (*Reg Gaz* 3976 of 13 July 1986).

[121] The application in this case (as yet unreported) was dismissed for lack of *locus standi* and the substantive issue remains undecided.

[122] See the new s 3(6)(a) introduced by s 2 of the Public Safety Amendment Act 67 of 1986.

[123] Supra.

Act.[124] The minister is required to exercise such powers by notice in the *Gazette* and any such notice will be valid only if no proclamation for the area in question is in force under the Act. The minister's powers will be valid for a maximum period of ten days and will be ipso jure superseded if a proclamation is issued by the State President within that period.

Micro-emergencies

The main purpose of the Public Safety Amendment Act of 1986 was to introduce a 'no hassle' emergency power. As the memorandum accompanying the preceding bill frankly admits, the declaration of a state of emergency by the State President 'has far-reaching consequences for the Republic'. The amending Act aims to eliminate or to mitigate the impact of these consequences, which have hitherto constituted the most effective restraint on the use of emergency powers, by authorising the Minister of Law and Order (who replaces the Minister of Justice as the responsible minister under the Act) to declare areas to be unrest areas and to apply in these areas such regulations as he may deem necessary to control the situation.[125] The declaration will be effective for three months (unless withdrawn at any prior time by the minister) but may be renewed with the consent of the State President. The minister is granted a power to make regulations for unrest areas which is broadly equivalent to the State President's legislative authority under the Act. Both the declaration of an area as an unrest area, and the framing of regulations for such area, are stated to be within the subjective discretion of the minister, the exercise of his powers being made dependent in the first instance on his opinion and in the second on what appears to him to be necessary or expedient. In an attempt to limit further the jurisdiction of the courts over emergencies, a provision of the Act now declares that the courts are to have no jurisdiction over declarations of emergencies or states of unrest or over regulations made pursuant to them.

It appears to have been the objective of the 1986 amendments to make the State President an absolute despot in respect of national emergencies and the Minister of Law and Order a lower-ranking but equally absolute despot over micro-emergencies. Although the courts, as shown earlier, have never demonstrated any eagerness to question the proclamation of the emergency itself and are equally unlikely to pronounce on the decision to proclaim an unrest area, the ouster clause does not appear to take the matter any further and the courts will continue, as they recently have under macro-emergencies, to test regulations for compliance with the ultra vires doctrine, either in its pure form or in the form of its prohibition on vague or grossly unreasonable subordinate legislation. As the Eastern Cape court said in *United Democratic Front v The State President*,[126] its jurisdiction to decide whether a regulation has been lawfully made in terms of the Act is not extinguished by the ouster clause. Of course, the extent of court involvement depends on general judicial attitudes and the outcome of the recent conflict between an emphasis on power, as represented by the Natal full bench in *Kerchoff*, and an emphasis on the

---

[124] Section 4.
[125] Section 5A introduced by s 4 of the Public Safety Amendment Act 67 of 1986.
[126] Supra.

limitation of power, as expressed by the full bench in *Tsenoli*, is crucial to the future role of the courts in emergency government whether of the macro or micro type.

Other Emergency Legislation

In terms of the Civil Defence Act[127] provincial councils could make ordinances relating to civil defence for the purpose inter alia of combating civil disruption during a state of emergency declared under the Public Safety Act.[128] All four provinces have enacted ordinances in terms of this power.[129] The Minister of Defence also has the power under the Civil Defence Act to declare a state of disaster for the purpose of adopting extraordinary measures to protect the public and to combat civil disruption. A disaster is defined in the Act as including the consequences arising out of terrorism.[130] The declaration of a state of disaster does not appear to confer any further emergency powers on the authorities but rather to have the effect of activating the provisions of civil defence ordinances and of putting civil defence organisations on the alert. It does, however, enable the Minister of Defence to take over powers or duties imposed or conferred by the Act and the ordinances.[131] Finally, the State President has extensive powers of legislation over black areas and these have often been used to impose emergency rule within such areas.[132]

---

[127] Act 67 of 1977. For a more detailed description of this Act, see *Law of South Africa* vol 21 para 350.
[128] Section 3 of Act 67 of 1977. Such ordinances may not make provision for armed action or the combating of crime.
[129] The Civil Defence Ordinance 20 of 1977 (T); The Civil Defence Ordinance 10 of 1977 (OFS); The Civil Defence Ordinance 8 of 1977 (C); The Civil Defence Ordinance 5 of 1978 (N). The four ordinances are almost identical and empower the Administrator to activate civil defence programmes, inter alia by giving directions to local authorities.
[130] Section 1.
[131] Section 5.
[132] See *Law of South Africa* vol 21 para 353.

PART III

General Evaluation

Introduction

The body of laws that constitutes the state security system in South Africa has been described and analysed in Part II. Though that analysis was in no sense uncritical, the larger and more comprehensive judgments that can be made about the security system have been reserved for this part. Detailed study of laws and their application has prepared the ground for their overall assessment and evaluation in terms of relevant criteria. The main yardstick will be the concept of the rule of law that was expounded in the first part of this work. After a rule-of-law assessment of the security system, it will be judged in political and moral terms. The political evaluation will seek to determine the role and function of the security apparatus in the governing of South Africa and thereafter to judge it by the normative criteria of democracy. The moral critique of the security system will draw on the basic standards of humanity and decency that are part of all civilised cultures. Finally, the security apparatus will be assessed according to its own implicit criterion of justification—its supposed contribution to the maintenance of peace and order in South Africa.

This functional and normative evaluation of the South African security system is intended to pave the way for a final chapter on reform proposals. The reforms suggested there will be directed towards the goal of the establishment of a rule-of-law state in South Africa in which both freedom and order are secured through law. However, in formulating specific reform proposals account will be taken of the social and political realities of the country and of the awesome problem of maintaining stability during a process of modernisation and of change towards a non-discriminatory system.

CHAPTER 12

The Security System and the Rule of Law

The preferred theory of the rule-of-law state that was expounded and adopted in Part I distinguished between the substantive and procedural aspects of the doctrine. If we now bring these two aspects together, and simplify them for purposes of application to specific security-law provisions, the rule of law may be described as a doctrine which requires

(a) that laws touching on the basic rights of citizens shall be narrowly and precisely drafted so as to constitute a clear guide to official action and citizen conduct;[1] and

(b) that the application and interpretation of such laws shall be under the control of impartial courts operating according to fair procedures.

In the course of applying this simplified version of the rule of law to specific security laws, account will be taken of the security legislation of other relevant countries. The main purpose of the comparison will be to illustrate that security threats may be countered by measures that conform more closely to rule-of-law requirements. The comparison will also reveal that security systems may differ greatly in terms of underlying philosophy and strategy and that the survival of the rule of law is crucially related to the models which particular governments have adopted to deal with security threats.

Security Crimes and the Rule of Law

The earlier discussion of present-day security crimes[2] was confined to statutory offences and the common-law crimes aimed at preserving the integrity and authority of the state or its organs of government were not examined. Even though the common-law offences fall outside the confines of this study, it is worth passing mention that certain of these crimes, particularly treason and sedition, are alarmingly elastic in character and have a scope of application that potentially includes robust political opposition. Treason, for example, may consist of any act 'however innocent it may seem to be when viewed objectively';[3] and the hostile intent which must accompany the act to make it treasonous 'may take the form of attacking the authority of the executive and thereby coercing it

---

[1] It also demands that restrictions on fundamental rights shall not erode their basic essence; but this question—whether the basic essence of civil rights has been preserved—will be discussed in the political evaluation of the security system below.

[2] See ch 6 above.

[3] C R Snyman *Criminal Law* (Butterworths, Pretoria 1984) 259.

220 GENERAL EVALUATION

into a change of policy'.[4] The employment of force, actual or envisaged, is not a requirement of treason.[5] The crime of sedition, which consists of the act of unlawfully and intentionally gathering to challenge, defy or resist the authority of the state, has a forbidding range of application, depending on how it is interpreted. In a recent judgment that has been academically criticised but not overruled, it was held that the gathering may consist of as few as two people, that actual or intended violence is not an essential element of the crime and that assailing the authority of any of the organs of the state, whether central, regional or local, is tantamount to resisting the authority of the state itself.[6] The proposition that violence is not an essential part of the offence of sedition is supported by a leading authority on criminal law.[7] Until the courts limit the scope of these crimes by a stricter interpretation of their basic requirements, their elasticity will make them a serious threat to persons who engage in extra-parliamentary political opposition. If the judiciary continues to regard non-violent coercion of the executive (or any of its organs or departments) in order to bring about a change of policy as treason, and gathering for non-violent purposes as sedition, it will in effect countenance the drastic limitation of democratic rights by the common law. It is bad enough that the court, in the recent case of *S v Hogan*,[8] has deviated from the important principle that guilt in criminal law is personal. The accused was convicted of treason for essentially non-violent activities carried out on behalf of the banned African National Congress. In one part of its judgment, the court appears to have ruled that a person can never support the ANC without being guilty of treason even if that person's actions are lawful social activities that were not intended to further the ANC policy of overthrowing the present government of South Africa. This passage reads:

'By joining the ANC, and thereafter performing the specific acts[9] which have been proved to have been performed by her, she signified by her conduct her agreement *with all the aims of the organisation* and has therefore made herself guilty of a conspiracy to commit treason.'[10]

This pronouncement calls to mind the insistence of the Supreme Court of the United States that guilt is personal and that the judiciary should guard against the danger that 'one in sympathy with the legitimate aims of such an organisation (one dedicated to the violent overthrow of government) but not specifically intending to accomplish them by resort to violence, might be punished for his adherence to lawful and constitutionally protected purposes, because of other and unprotected purposes which he does not necessarily share'.[11] Though this finding was constitutionally based, we surely do not need constitutional authority for the principle that guilt is personal and that all the requirements of the

[4] J R L Milton *South African Criminal Law and Procedure* 2 ed (Juta and Co, Cape Town 1982) 8. See also Snyman op cit 261.
[5] J R L Milton op cit 27.
[6] *S v Twala* 1979 (3) SA 864 (T).
[7] Milton op cit 41; cf Snyman op cit 265, who requires violence or a threat of violence.
[8] 1983 (2) SA 46 (W).
[9] All non-violent.
[10] At 66 of the judgment (emphasis supplied).
[11] *Noto v United States* 6 L Ed 2nd 836, 842–3 (1961). See also *Scales v United States* 6 L Ed 2nd 782 (1961).

crime must be established against the accused personally. It follows that unless there was cogent evidence of a substantial link between Hogan's activities and the violent goals of the ANC,[12] she should have been found guilty at most of furthering the aims of an unlawful organisation. Such a verdict would not have justified the drastic ten-year sentence of imprisonment imposed in this case.

If common-law security crimes fail to meet the rule-of-law requirement of a clear guide to prohibited conduct, the statutory crimes can only be described as totally destructive of this principle. The major security crimes of subversion and sabotage to a high degree, and other security crimes to a lesser degree, violate the basic principle of the rule of law that penal prohibitions should be clear and understandable. Considered singly, each of the major crimes has as great a penumbra or outer circle of uncertainty as an inner core of certainty. Though examples of the obscure contours of these crimes have already been given,[13] one more will be considered here to illustrate the point about obscurity. This example will be expressed in the form of a question: Does an advocate of change in South Africa who speaks either locally or abroad about the advisability of economic sanctions against the country commit the crime of subversion or sabotage? The definition of subversion makes it an offence to perform any act in the Republic or elsewhere which could have resulted in prejudice to any industry or undertaking in South Africa, or industries or undertakings in general, with a view to bringing about constitutional, political, industrial, social or economic changes.[14] Whether speech or writing advocating sanctions constitutes subversion is unclear and depends upon such factors as whether the words in question constitute an 'act' for purposes of the section and whether they 'could have' caused prejudice to an industry or undertaking. The answer to the latter question depends on issues of causality and these are notoriously difficult in law. The crime of sabotage is defined so as to make the giving of encouragement or advice to any person to commit an act, with intent to prejudice an industry or undertaking, or industries and undertakings in general in South Africa, criminally punishable.[15] On the face of it, this covers a recommendation to implement sanctions but conviction of an accused person will again depend on court interpretation of the statutory words and phrases that constitute the crime. If boycotts and sanctions are within the reach of the crimes of subversion and sabotage, then many other activities that are considered lawful in free societies are liable to be punished as serious crimes in South Africa, depending on how the sections of the Act are expanded or contracted by judicial interpretation. In the mean time, no citizen can truly know precisely what the law commands or forbids, and this uncertainty undermines the first principle of the rule of law. In fact, the cumulative effect of all security crimes (particularly the effect of subversion, sabotage, espionage, intimidation and furthering the aims of

---

[12] The court's judgment appears to vacillate between the holding that the accused did share the violent aims of the ANC and the finding that by supporting the ANC she must be assumed to have shared them.

[13] See chapter 6.

[14] Section 54(2)(b), read with s 54(2)(i), of the Internal Security Act 74 of 1982.

[15] Section 54(3)(e), read with s 54(3)(iv), of the Internal Security Act 74 of 1982.

communism) is to bring our political justice into line with the article of the Russian Criminal Code which punishes anti-state agitation and propaganda.[16] What the communists have achieved in a single obscure provision we have brought about by the separate enactment of a variety of penal statutes which collectively prohibit an ill-defined range of 'anti-state' activities.

In two societies with a law and order problem at least as severe as ours—Northern Ireland and Israel—the phenomenon of the dragnet and loosely defined political code of criminal law is unknown. In each of these countries there are some security crimes which lack rule-of-law precision; but these are unusual and where they do exist are virtually dead-letter law. There is certainly nothing in either country that remotely approaches the indiscriminate criminalisation of political and anti-state activities that is characteristic of South Africa and the Soviet Union. In Northern Ireland, the prosecution of security-law offenders takes place mainly under the common law or under statutes dealing with the unlawful possession or use of firearms and explosives. In the recent Baker Report on Northern Ireland security legislation,[17] a statistical table of prosecutions that followed upon the detention of suspects indicates that charges fell into the following categories: murder and attempted murder, firearms and explosives offences, theft, arson, hi-jacking, petrol bombing, unlawful imprisonment, assisting offenders, witholding information, hoax bombs and ordinary crime. The statutory security offences in Northern Ireland, apart from those relating to firearms and explosives, are contained in the Northern Ireland (Emergency Provisions) Act 1978 and the Prevention of Terrorism (Temporary Provisions) Act 1984. The chief offences created by the former Act are the following: belonging to, or supporting in various ways, a proscribed organisation[18] (these being the terrorist organisations prescribed in Schedule II to the Act);[19] gathering various kinds of information that could assist the terrorists in identifying human targets or carrying out violent attacks;[20] training any person, without lawful authority, in the making or use of firearms or explosives;[21] failing to disperse after a meeting, considered by a police officer to be threatening, has been ordered to disperse;[22] dressing or behaving in public so as to arouse the reasonable apprehension of membership of a prohibited organisation;[23] wearing hoods, or masks or other disguises without lawful authority in a public place.[24] The main offences created by the second Act (The Prevention of Terrorism (Temporary Provisions) Act 1984) are providing, receiving or soliciting material support for the commission or preparation of acts of terrorism;[25] and witholding information which is

[16] See chapter 2 above.
[17] 'Review of the Operation of the Northern Ireland (Emergency Provisions) Act 1978' (Cmnd 9222, April 1984) 162 (referred to below as the Baker Report).
[18] Section 21 of the Northern Ireland (Emergency Provisions) Act 1978 c 5.
[19] Judge Baker received no recommendations from any source to the effect that any of the scheduled organisations should be removed from the list: Baker Report 116 et seq. This seems to indicate that the scheduled organisations are widely accepted as being terrorist.
[20] Section 22.   [21] Section 23.   [22] Section 24.
[23] Section 25.   [24] Section 26.
[25] Section 10 of the Prevention of Terrorism (Temporary Provisions) Act 1984 c 8. 'Terrorism' is defined in s 14 as the use of violence for political ends, including its use for putting the public, or any section of it, in fear.

known or believed to be of material assistance in preventing an act of terrorism or in securing the apprehension of terrorists.[26] Though one or two of these offences are a little vague and capable of too wide an application (for example, dressing as a member of a terrorist organisation), they are generally narrow in range and reasonably precise in meaning. There has certainly been no attempt, as in South Africa, loosely to criminalise a vast range of political activity.

The British legacy in Israel, in the form of the Defence (Emergency) Regulations 1945,[27] has provided the Israeli security authorities with an arsenal of security weapons, including some wide-ranging security crimes. Among these crimes is a category of serious security offences which are triable exclusively before military courts. The most serious offence in this group is the capital offence of discharging firearms at persons, throwing bombs, grenades, et cetera at persons or property or carrying firearms, ammunition, grenades, et cetera without a lawful permit.[28] Though these provisions are both reasonably clear and justified in a security crisis, the capital offence is also committed by a person *who is a member of a group* in which anyone has discharged a firearm, thrown a bomb or unlawfully carried firearms or explosives in contravention of the regulation in question. It is not clear whether membership of such a group constitutes an offence only if it is a group specifically formed for the purpose of an attack (such as a terrorist commando) or whether membership of an organisation of which any member has at any time been guilty of the acts described, is also covered. The offence created by this regulation is therefore both obscure and potentially far reaching. According to the attorney-general's office in Jerusalem the membership crime is no longer employed.[29] However, it is disturbing that it remains in force as a capital offence. The remaining crimes that are exclusively triable by military courts are the following: (1) unlawful possession or manufacture of firearms, explosives or dangerous weapons; destroying, damaging, endangering or interfering with a variety of vehicles, aircraft, installations, transport equipment or basic services;[30] (2) wearing military uniforms without lawful authority[31] or wearing other prohibited forms of dress;[32] giving or receiving military or armaments training, or being present at such training;[33] (3) using a disguise in circumstances likely to prejudice public safety or order;[34] (4) assisting or harbouring persons who have been engaged in activity prejudicial to public safety or public order or who have committed any of the above offences.[35] The offences relating to disguises and to harbouring or assisting are a little unclear in scope and

[26] Section 11.
[27] Promulgated by the British mandatory authority in 1945 in terms of the Palestine (Defence) Order in Council of 1937 and still in force at present.
[28] Regulation 58 of the Defence (Emergency) Regulations 1945.
[29] In a conversation with Mrs Judith Karp, the Deputy Attorney-General, in June 1984, I was informed that she had no recollection of any prosecutions under the membership clause of the regulation.
[30] Regulation 59.
[31] Regulation 60.
[32] Regulation 61.
[33] Regulation 62.
[34] Regulation 63.
[35] Regulation 64.

capable of wide-ranging application; in general, however, these military
crimes are not unreasonable or excessively vague. Apart from the offences
triable exclusively by military courts, there are several falling under the
jurisdiction of the civil courts that appear to violate the clear definition
requirement of the rule of law. The most serious cases of infringment are:
the crime of influencing public opinion 'in a manner likely to be
prejudicial to public safety, defence or the maintenance of public order'[36]
and threatening persons with injury to their person, reputation and
property in order to alarm them or to compel them to do, or not to do, any
act.[37] It seems that these offences are presently in abeyance in Israel.[38]

Israel has also enacted a Prevention of Terrorism Ordinance[39] which
has been in force since 1948 as an emergency law. The main crime created
by this law is that of belonging to, or actively managing or participating
in, a terrorist organisation which the ordinance defines 'as a body of
persons resorting in its activities to acts of violence calculated to cause
death or injury to a person or to threats of such acts of violence'.[40] The
conduct made punishable by this offence is reasonably clear. However, a
further provision makes it criminal inter alia to do any act in public places
manifesting sympathy with a terrorist organisation,[41] and the range of
activities prohibited by this offence is potentially limitless. It has been
used, for example, to punish persons for singing a nationalist song.[42]

The position in Northern Ireland and Israel may be summed up as
follows: In Northern Ireland there are no sweeping security crimes of the
kind found in South Africa—most prosecutions are for relevant common-
law offences such as murder or arson. The few statutory crimes that exist
are reasonably narrow in scope and justifiable responses to security
threats. In Israel there are some security crimes that are loosely drawn
and broad in scope; but these are more closely related to actual security
threats than in South Africa. There is nothing either in Northern Ireland
or Israel remotely approaching the dragnet criminal prohibitions such as
subversion and sabotage that are found in South Africa.

The second requirement of the rule of law in the criminal justice field is
that the trial of offenders should take place before independent courts
applying fair-trial procedures. The prosecution of security-law offenders
in South Africa takes place before the regular courts according to
procedures that, by and large, conform to those in trials of ordinary
criminal offenders. However, there are a number of deviations from
standard procedure of which one is serious and the others less disturbing.
The less serious deviations are those relating to withdrawal of the right to
bail, to the joint trial of offenders and to the venue of security trials. These
lesser deviations from standard procedure will be considered before
turning to the major threat to fairness in security trials arising from the

---

[36] Regulation 142(1).
[37] Regulation 143(1).
[38] The Department of Justice in Jerusalem has informed me that no prosecutions under
the first of these two crimes have occurred in the past five years.
[39] No 33 of 5703—1948 amended by the Prevention of Terrorism Ordinance (Amendment) Law 5740—1980.
[40] Sections 1, 2 and 3.
[41] Section 4(g).
[42] See *Amnesty International Annual Report* (1982–3) 312.

use in those trials of detainee evidence and detainee confessions and admissions.

The power of the attorney-general to prevent the release of a security-law accused on bail has already been considered.[43] In a judgment delivered in April 1985 in the case of *S v Ramgobin* (1)[44] the court, for the first time since the enactment of the 'no-bail' clause, subjected the provision to sharp strictures and described it as a serious inroad into the 'traditional role of the courts'. These critical remarks were carried further by the Judge President of the Natal Provincial Division who declared that the age of the no-bail clause was 'its sole claim to respectability'.[45] The strong judicial reaction to the denial of bail in *Ramgobin* resulted in the withdrawal of the attorney-general's certificate prohibiting bail and to the grant of bail by the court under agreed conditions. While courts do, and clearly should, have the power to deny bail for appropriate reasons (the danger that the accused will abscond or interfere with witnesses, for example) the arbitrary withdrawal of bail by a non-judicial authority violates both personal freedom and the right to a fair trial. Discussions about the right to bail tend to emphasise the effect of its denial on fair-trial requirements far less than the personal liberty aspect; but in political trials, especially complex ones, the right to bail is directly related to the right to a fair hearing. Political trials, especially major ones, tend to be a contest for legitimacy and to involve the discrediting of opponents. As a result the prosecution, on behalf of the state (more realistically, the government of the day), tends to marshall all possible resources to establish the guilt of the accused. Frequently, political trials are factually and legally complex and involve multiple charges relating to long periods of complicated human political activity. Both of these features are true of the *Ramgobin* case (the UDF treason trial in Natal) just mentioned. The prosecution in this case, which subsequently collapsed, was far more than a test of the guilt or innocence of the accused; it was more importantly a government attempt to discredit and de-legitimise the UDF and for this purpose there was a massive deployment of prosecution resources. The complexity of the trial is evident just from the indictment which ran to six hundred pages. Now it is clear that where the accused remain locked up from the time that charges are brought to the conclusion of the trial, the ability of the defence to marshall its own resources is gravely impaired. The accused will have a restricted ability to consult regularly with legal advisers on the highly complex indictment against them and to find witnesses and organise counter-evidence and, as a result, the contest between the state as the prosecuting authority and the individuals in the dock will be more unequal than ever. The possibility of a fair trial under an adversary system of justice may be substantially reduced if one of the adversaries is prevented by arbitrary incarceration from presenting an adequately prepared case.

The chances of a fair trial could also be affected by the provision of the Internal Security Act which empowers the prosecution to charge together persons alleged to have committed offences under that Act at the same time and place, or at the same place at approximately the same time.[46] In

---

[43] Chapter 7 above.   [44] 1985 (3) SA 587 (N).
[45] *S v Ramgobin (2)* 1985 (4) SA 130 (N).

a nutshell, the provision authorises the joint trial of separate offenders for separate offences provided that the offences are reasonably concurrent in respect of place and time. The most obvious danger of the joint trial procedure is to increase the difficulty and complexity of defending the accused persons. The task of disentangling the threads of evidence and relating each to the appropriate accused and the relevant charge will be formidable where the accused are defending themselves. It takes a singularly clear mind to sort out charges, issues and evidence in a mass trial. But even if the accused are represented, the task of defence will remain formidable where one or two lawyers are representing a large number of defendants. An extraordinary ability for skilful legal juggling, which many lawyers do not possess, will be essential to ensure that an effective defence is presented in respect of each and every accused. A less obvious but real danger of the joint trial procedure is that the judicial officer will fail to discern different degrees of guilt or involvement among a mass of defendants and, in giving judgment or imposing sentence, tar them all with the same brush. It is not unknown for the prosecution to charge a hardened subversive together with a group of political innocents; and where this occurs skilful advocacy is required to prevent the cases of the 'innocents' being tainted by the evidence presented against their more notorious co-accused.

The most notorious deviation from standard procedure in security trials is the regular use by the prosecution of the evidence of persons who have been detained and interrogated in isolation (frequently for long periods) or of confessions and admissions made by accused persons who have been held or interrogated in such circumstances. The reasons why the acceptance of any such evidence undermines the fairness of the trial procedure have been reviewed earlier.[47] That review indicated that the use of detainee evidence and statements constitutes so fundamental a threat to fair-trial procedure that the security trial is thereby deprived of legitimacy in the minds of its victims and those who identify with them and indeed more widely in the thinking of fair-minded lawyers throughout the world. A large factor in the low repute of political justice in South Africa is the spectacle of the pitiful victims of interrogation in isolation being paraded in court as witnesses for the prosecution. This is a matter above all others which our courts should address urgently if the growing gulf between them and the black community in South Africa is to be narrowed.[48]

Since the institution of Diplock courts in Northern Ireland there have been deviations from standard procedures in security trials in that country. Diplock courts were created following the report[49] of the Diplock Committee set up by the British government to investigate the legal procedures for dealing with terrorism in Northern Ireland. Following the

[46] Section 67 of the Internal Security Act 74 of 1982.
[47] See chapter 7 above.
[48] The extent of Black alienation from the system of justice in South Africa was one of the remarkable features of the papers presented by black lawyers to the seminar on *Legal Aspects of Apartheid* held in Washington DC on 6 and 7 July 1985 under the auspices of the Lawyers' Committee for Civil Rights Under Law. (Proceedings not yet published.)
[49] *'Report of the commission to consider legal procedures to deal with terrorist activities in Northern Ireland'* Cmnd 5185 (London 1972).

submission of the report in 1972, its chief recommendations became law in 1973 in the form of the Northern Ireland (Emergency Provisions) Act 1973. This law was replaced in 1978 by the Northern Ireland (Emergency Provisions) Act of 1978 which retained Diplock courts and which is still in force at present, though a new Act is now being drafted following the report[50] of the Baker Committee. The Baker Committee supported the retention of Diplock courts with minor modifications and the British government has declared its intention of accepting this recommendation.

The philosophy that underlies the Diplock Report and the creation of Diplock courts is that terrorism in Northern Ireland should be dealt with as far as possible through normal criminal procedure and with minimum reliance on special measures such as internment.[51] The reliance on the normal criminal process therefore carries with it the corollary that terrorism should not (and probably could not) be effectively countered by the wholesale suspension of basic rights that is characteristic of the South African approach. However, on account of the pressures and stresses to which the criminal process is subject in a society plagued by terrorism (such as the intimidation of witnesses and jurors) the standard procedures of the criminal courts require some modifications in security trials. The Diplock committee recognised that these modifications should be kept to a minimum in order to retain the basic features of a fair trial and the legitimacy of the criminal process. It is these limited modifications which give Diplock courts their special character in the trial of security offences which are technically designated as 'scheduled offences' in Northern Ireland. In a nutshell, Diplock courts are the ordinary High Courts in Northern Ireland operating according to modified procedures in the trial of scheduled offences. A full understanding of the operation of Diplock courts requires an explanation of the concept of a scheduled offence and of the special procedures which the law has mandated for the trial of such an offence.

Scheduled offences are 'broadly all those crimes regularly committed by terrorists and their supporters'.[52] Among those declared to be scheduled[53] are murder and other serious offences against the person, robbery and aggravated burglary (involving the use of firearms, explosives or weapons), arson and other specified offences against property, certain offences created by the Prevention of Terrorism (Temporary Provisions) Act of 1984 and the Northern Ireland (Emergency Provisions) Act of 1978 and almost all firearms and explosives offences. Trials of scheduled offences are centralised in Belfast[54] and take place in accordance with the modified procedures to be described below. Since many of these offences may be committed by persons who are not involved in terrorism, there is provision for some of them to be de-scheduled or 'certified out' by the Attorney-General for Northern Ireland and where this is done the trial will be conducted in accordance with the ordinary criminal process.

[50] 'Review of the Operation of the Northern Ireland (Emergency Provisions) Act 1978' Cmnd 9222 (London, 1984).
[51] Boyle, Hadden and Hillyard Law and State: The Case of Northern Ireland (Martin Robertson, London 1975) 78–9.
[52] Boyle, Hadden and Hillyard Law and State: The Case of Northern Ireland 95.
[53] See Schedule 4 to the Northern Ireland (Emergency Provisions) Act 1978.
[54] Section 6 of the Northern Ireland (Emergency Provisions) Act 1978.

Following criticism that many non-terrorist cases were being tried by the modified procedure, the Baker Report[55] recommended that the power of the attorney-general to de-schedule offences should be extended and the government has decided to accept this recommendation with minor modifications. The extended power of certifying out should help to ensure that the special trial procedures are not employed in non-terrorist cases.[56]

The modified procedures for the trial of scheduled offences affect the right to bail, the right to trial by jury and the rules governing the acceptance of admissions and confessions by the accused.[57] Because it was felt that magistrates were granting bail too freely in terrorist cases, the Northern Ireland (Emergency Provisions) Act of 1978 restricts the right to grant bail for scheduled offences to a judge of the Supreme Court.[58] Moreover, the judge is directed not to grant bail unless satisfied that the accused will comply with bail conditions, not interfere with witnesses and not commit any offence while on bail. This means that stricter conditions for the granting of bail apply in scheduled cases and that the onus of satisfying the court is on the accused. One result of the new bail rules is that the discrimination in bail decisions in favour of Protestant accused persons has been virtually eliminated.[59] The Baker Report recommended that bail in scheduled cases should continue to be under Supreme Court jurisdiction but that the initial onus should be on the prosecution.[60] Whether or not this recommendation becomes law, it is clear that the modified rules as to bail do not seriously prejudice the right to a fair trial. Unlike the position in South Africa where court jurisdiction over bail has been removed in certain security trials, in Northern Ireland the power to grant bail remains with the courts where it belongs. The Baker Committee found that judges had interpreted the bail provision 'liberally and sensibly'.[61] The Northern Ireland bail rules in scheduled cases do not seriously derogate from criminal due process as do the rules in South Africa.

The second procedural modification to the criminal process in Northern Ireland is one which requires scheduled cases to be tried by a judge without a jury.[62] The main reasons for removing the right to a jury trial where the offence is a scheduled one is the intimidation of jurors and the danger of partisan verdicts or hung juries in a divided community. The Baker Report finding[63] that intimidation remains a serious threat to the proper functioning of jury trials is convincing. The other threat—of partisan verdicts or hung juries—is equally still applicable; in fact, it seems that the elimination of jury trials has removed pro-Protestant bias

---

[55] Baker Report paras 130–151.
[56] It has been suggested that 'certifying in' instead of out is more likely to produce an acceptable result: David Bonner *Emergency Powers in Peacetime* (Sweet & Maxwell, London 1985) 150.
[57] There are certain other minor procedural changes which will not be dealt with as they do not impinge on the right to a fair trial.
[58] Section 2. This does not apply to summary trials or to the trials of persons under 14 years of age.
[59] Boyle, Hadden and Hillyard *Law and the State: The Case of Northern Ireland* 108.
[60] Baker Report paras 63–81.
[61] Baker Report, para 75.
[62] Section 7 of the Northern Ireland (Emergency Provisions) Act 1978.
[63] Baker Report para 107.

in terrorist cases.[64] The case for the return of juries in these trials rests mainly on alleged case-hardening of judges with an attendant lower acquittal rate.[65] The Baker Committee was unconvinced by the case-hardening argument[66] and, in any event, the risks inherent in restoring the jury system are clearly far greater than those attendant upon trial by judge alone.[67] The criticism that procedural justice has been undermined by withdrawing the right to jury trials in scheduled cases has simply not been sustained.

The third procedural modification relating to admissions by the accused is the most controversial since it is one which arguably prejudices the fairness of the trial in scheduled cases. The provision in question[68] relaxes the rules governing the acceptance by the court of admissions or confessions made by the accused. The court is directed by this provision to admit a confession or admission as evidence unless satisfied that the accused was subjected to torture or to inhuman or degrading treatment in order to induce him to make the statement in question.[69] Normally confessions or admissions that are induced by any form of coercion, including an oppressive set-up, are inadmissible as not being voluntary; and the effect of the change is to exclude only those confessions or admissions which are induced by grosser forms of coercion while admitting those which are extracted by a 'moderate degree of physical maltreatment'.[70] The provision therefore tries to make a distinction between acceptable and unacceptable forms of coercion and to exclude statements by the accused only where they were induced by coercion that is unacceptable. The main justification for the relaxation of the normally strict rules governing the admission of statements by the accused is that the intimidation of witnesses frequently makes it impossible to bring forward any evidence other than an admission or confession;[71] and if these could be excluded by the court because the robust interrogation of the accused was a form of coercion rendering them admissible because involuntarily made, the policy of dealing with terrorists through the criminal justice system would fail.

The idea that the prosecution should be entitled to rely on a statement made after moderate physical abuse—a few cuffs and kicks, as it were—or by threats of violence to the accused or close family, is certainly revolting to a civilised legal mind. It was judicial distaste for the notion that such statements are acceptable evidence that led the judges in Northern Ireland to the conclusion that they had a discretion (apparently not conferred by the statute) to exclude statements obtained by treatment that fell short of torture or inhuman or degrading treatment. The Baker Committee found that the courts would not tolerate 'physical violence of

[64] Boyle, Hadden and Hillyard *Law and State: The Case of Northern Ireland* 96.
[65] Boyle, Hadden and Hillyard *Ten Years On in Northern Ireland* (The Cobden Trust, 1980) 80.
[66] Baker Report paras 122–6.
[67] For a review of some alternatives to trial by a single judge, see David Bonner op cit 149.
[68] Section 8 of the Northern Ireland (Emergency Provisions) Act 1978.
[69] The onus is on the prosecution to show that he was not so induced.
[70] Baker Report para 192.
[71] For other difficulties in obtaining direct evidence in Northern Ireland security trials, see David Bonner op cit 100.

any degree'.[72] However, even though the judiciary had made the necessary adjustment to the provision in question, Judge Baker recommended that the section be amended to make it clear that the courts retain their normal discretion in relation to admissions and confessions, and that statements induced by physical violence or the threat thereof should be excluded.[73] The British government has declared its acceptance of this recommendation and it follows that, upon the enactment of the necessary amendment, the courts will be entitled to admit statements induced by coercion that fall short of torture, inhuman or degrading treatment, physical violence or the threat thereof; but that even in such cases they may exclude the statement if satisfied that its admission would be unfair to the accused or prejudice the interests of justice. The practical effect of the change is that interrogation in itself, even if persistent and vigorous (in the non-physical sense) will not preclude the use of statements made by the accused on account of such questioning.

In evaluating the special rules governing the admission of statements by the accused in scheduled cases, several factors must be borne in mind. First, the maximum period for detention for interrogation is seven days — there is no such thing as indefinite pre-trial detention as in South Africa. Secondly, the short period of detention for interrogation in Northern Ireland is subject to the stringent controls imposed following the Bennett Committee report, including the use of closed-circuit television to monitor the interrogation visually. Thirdly, the modified trial procedures have been introduced so as to minimise reliance on arbitrary controls such as detention without trial. These factors make the amended rule governing the acceptance of statements by the accused an acceptable one *in the conditions prevailing in Northern Ireland*. By contrast, the South African programme which combines changes to the procedural justice system (including indefinite detention of witnesses for interrogation) with the general abrogation of basic civil rights, is indefensible and even abhorrent.

By reason of the use of military courts in Israel,[74] departures from standard procedures in security trials in that country are serious. As noted earlier certain offences under the Defence (Emergency) Regulations 1945 are exclusively triable by military courts while other offences created by these regulations may be tried either by military courts or before the ordinary criminal courts. Even in respect of the offences exclusively triable by military courts, the prosecution may have a choice of tribunal since terrorist-type offences will frequently constitute offences both under civil and military law and the tribunal that tries a particular accused will depend on how the charge is framed. This creates a danger of discrimination as between different offenders. The Israelis recently charged and convicted of anti-Arab terrorist offences were brought before the ordinary criminal courts whereas Arabs charged with anti-Israeli terror are usually tried by military tribunals. There appears to be no rational or defensible criterion on which the choice of tribunal — military or civil — is made.[75] An accused person brought before a military tribunal

---

[72] Baker Report para 193.   [73] See Appendix J to the Baker Report.
[74] Such courts operate in Israel proper and in the occupied territories.
[75] In discussions with the Deputy Attorney-General in Jerusalem in June 1984 I was unable to discover any such criterion.

appears to be at a grave disadvantage. In the first place, it is questionable whether members of the military, who are themselves active in anti-terrorist operations, either have, or will be seen to have, the necessary detachment for the fair trial of a security offender. Secondly, the judges in military tribunal trials may not be legally qualified or trained. Then again, military tribunals are empowered 'in the interests of justice' to admit otherwise inadmissible evidence against the accused.[76] According to the Department of Justice in Jerusalem, military courts sitting in Israel proper, as distinct from the occupied territories, as a matter of practice apply the rules of evidence applicable to trials before the ordinary courts.[77] Moreover, military tribunals are given a wide discretion as to trial procedure.[78] Finally, the death penalty, which is otherwise abolished in Israel, may be imposed by a military court for certain offences.[79] It is surprising that the military trial model introduced in Israel by the British in 1945 has not been abandoned for Israel proper, as opposed to the occupied territories.

The preceding account of security trial procedures in the three societies under review has sought to determine how far each measures up to the second requirement of the rule of law in the criminal justice field—the requirement that security-law offenders be tried by ordinary courts applying fair-trial procedures. How do each of the three countries come out in this assessment? But for the use of evidence and statements from solitary confinement detainees, South African political justice would fare well in the comparison. However, the qualifying 'but' is a serious one and the use of such evidence and statements undermines the credibility of the political trial in South Africa. Political justice in Northern Ireland is in far better shape and the departures from standard procedure there, though unfortunate, are not serious enough to destroy the legitimacy of security trials. The use of military courts in Israel[80] is a major deviation from criminal justice for which their English ancestry can no longer be pleaded as an excuse.

Detention and the Rule of Law

On the surface, there appears to be little sense in discussing detention in relation to the rule of law since these two institutions are usually seen as mutually destructive opposites—the recognition of one implies the annihilation of the other. Their incompatibility is underlined by the fact that detention and the suspension of habeas corpus are synonymous whereas both historically and conceptually the rule of law and habeas corpus are indissolubly linked to each other. Yet the discussion will not be as pointless, for example, as the exercise of attempting to reconcile chastity and promiscuity. Detention laws are certainly not all of a piece and different models of detention may be compared with each other for the precise purpose of determining the degree of departure from rule-of-

---

[76] Regulation 20 of the Defence (Emergency) Regulations 1945.
[77] Letter from the Department of Justice dated 20 March 1986.
[78] Regulation 21.
[79] Though appeals were initially not permitted, internal appeals may now be brought.
[80] The use of military courts in the occupied territories is understandable but their retention in Israel proper seems unfortunate.

law standards. The purpose of such a comparison is not simply one of satisfying academic curiosity. A detention system which violates rule-of-law requirements at every point is infinitely more dangerous to human freedom and, indeed, to the survival chances of its victims, than one in which deviations from legality are kept to a minimum. The approximately sixty or seventy deaths in detention in South Africa, many or most of which occurred in circumstances suggestive of illegal treatment, are directly attributable to the lawless character of the detention power in this country.[81] If there are some rule-of-law-type controls which can save lives, they are certainly worth investigating.

The degree of departure from rule-of-law standards is extreme in the case of South African detention laws. For purposes of assessing the seriousness of the deviation, the rule of law will again be expressed in the form of the requirements of *(a)* clear and reasonably precise guidelines for official conduct and *(b)* external control over the application of these guidelines. External control is important both as to the decision to detain and the subsequent treatment of the detainee. Finally, the procedures applicable to detention will require examination to determine the extent to which procedural fairness has been expelled from the system.

Preventive Detention

Preventive detention laws are notorious for their tendency to confer on executive authorities a broad and vaguely worded power to detain subjects and in this respect South African laws are no exception. The most far-reaching form of preventive detention in South Africa (s 28 detention)[82] authorises the Minister of Law and Order to order indefinite detention if he has reason to apprehend that the victim of this order will commit the vaguely defined offences of terrorism, subversion or sabotage or if he is satisfied that the detainee will endanger the security of the state or the maintenance of law and order. The statutory guidelines provided by this language are cloudy because they do not indicate what kind of conduct will be regarded as a danger to state security or law and order. It is certainly not impossible to specify such conduct[83] but the legislature has chosen to leave this unstated. The guidelines for the decision to detain are therefore unsatisfactory but the degree of cloudiness that surrounds them depends on whether the courts interpret the empowering language subjectively or objectively. A subjective interpretation makes the minister the sole judge of what endangers security or law and order[84] whereas an objective approach requires a rational link between the facts (the conduct of the detainee) and the statutory grounds for decision. South African courts have unfortunately given the discretion-conferring language of s 28 a subjective interpretation; even the seminal judgment of Leon J in *Hurley*

---

[81] While by no means the only factor this is an important one. The prevailing standards of civilisation and the political culture are also crucial.

[82] See chapter 7 above.

[83] For example, the employment of force or violence against persons or property, or any threat thereof or incitement thereto, with a view to achieving political goals.

[84] In technical language, this decision can be challenged only by proving that he did not apply his mind to the question at all or that he acted in bad faith or for improper considerations. In practice, the subjective approach has made the minister the absolute judge of the propriety of his own actions.

v Minister of Law and Order,[85] in which s 29 detention was put on an objective basis, stopped short of giving s 28 a similar reading. This is true also of the appeal court judgment in *Minister of Law and Order v Hurley*[86] in which Rabie CJ limited the court's ruling to s 29 detention. The position at present, therefore, is that the power to detain preventively under s 28 is viewed subjectively by the courts and in practice this means that the minister can detain as and when he wishes. Legally speaking there are no guidelines for the exercise of the preventive detention power. It is possible that the duty to give meaningful reasons, following the decision in *Nkondo & Gumede v Minister of Law and Order*,[87] may lead to the development of guidelines but this will depend on vigilant and strict supervision by the courts.

Israel's new and 'progressive' preventive detention law is also vague in the specification of the grounds for detention. This law, the Emergency Powers (Detention) Law of 1979,[88] empowers the Minister of Defence to authorise a detention if he has reasonable cause to believe that 'reasons of state security or public security' require it.[89] But, as we shall see in a moment, every detention order in Israel must be reviewed by the courts and this provides judges with the opportunity to make more specific the broad language employed by the legislature. This was in fact done by the District Court of Haifa in the case of *Gemayel Bathish v Minister of Defence*[90] during the course of reviewing a detention order by the minister. The court declared that the expression 'security of the public' meant that 'the public should not be injured by means of physical violence' and it set aside the detention order because there was no evidence that the detainee had taken part in such activities.[91] Judicial control over detentions can therefore be used to further the rule-of-law requirement of clear and specific guidelines for official conduct by assigning a narrowing interpretation to sweeping statutory language.

The most important feature of Israel's preventive detention law is that it *requires* independent external control over every detention order issued by the Minister of Defence. Prior to the enactment of the 1979 law, detentions in Israel took place in terms of the Defence (Emergency) Regulations 1945, enacted by the British mandatory power and subsequently 'absorbed' into Israeli law after independence in 1948.[92] While such detention orders could be challenged before the ordinary courts, there was no prospect of thereby securing a review on the merits of the detention; but the courts did intervene to ensure a strict compliance with procedural requirements.[93] There was, however, a non-judicial form of external control exercised through an advisory committee which in

[85] 1985 (4) SA 709 (D).
[86] 1986 (3) SA 568 (A).
[87] 1986 (2) SA 756 (A).
[88] No 5739—1979.
[89] Section 2.
[90] AAD 18/82.
[91] See Harold Rudolph *Security, Terrorism and Torture: Detainees' Rights in South Africa and Israel—a Comparative Study* (Juta & Co Ltd, Cape Town 1984) 124–6.
[92] For a brief history of this absorption process, see Harold Rudolph op cit 61 et seq.
[93] See Amos Shapira 'Judicial Review without a Constitution: The Israeli Paradox' (1983) 56 *Temple Law Quarterly* 405 and Harold Rudolph op cit 75 et seq.

practice operated as a significant check on the detention power. As Harold
Rudolph points out, the advisory committee was always chaired by a
judge of the Supreme Court and its recommendations were accepted and
followed in every case.[94] Nevertheless this system was considered
unsatisfactory in a democratic state, even though that state was faced by
formidable law and order problems, and the 1979 law provided that every
detention order had to be brought for review before the President of the
appropriate District Court within forty-eight hours failing which the
detainee was entitled to immediate release.[95] The President of this court
has the power, moreover, to confirm or to set aside a detention order
brought before him. The effect of the law is to subject preventive detention
in Israel to the control and supervision of the ordinary courts. Initially the
courts responded somewhat tentatively to their new responsibility and in
the case of *Rabbi Kahane v Minister of Defence*[96] the Supreme Court declared
that while it was the function of the court to review the considerations
which prompted the minister to issue a detention order, the 'court may
not substitute its own considerations for those of the Minister of
Defence'.[97] Although in the later case of *Quawasma v Minister of Defence*[98]
the court set aside a detention order on appeal from the decision of the
President of the District Court to confirm it, it acted on the traditional
ground of review that the minister had used the detention power for an
improper purpose. As already mentioned, the passive role of the court in
these two cases was replaced by a more interventionist attitude in *Gemayel
Bathish v Minister of Defence*[99] and while the judgment in this case was one
of a District Court as opposed to the Supreme Court (the Court of Appeal)
in *Rabbi Kahane* and *Quawasma*, there is persuasive academic authority for
the view that the courts' function in the detention process was intended to
be the active one of determining for itself whether grounds for detention
exist.[100] But even if the courts maintain or revert to a more deferent
approach in the exercise of their new powers under the 1979 detention
law, the simple fact of their involvement constitutes a significant check on
the Minister of Defence. The value of bringing the court into the process is
that the presiding judge sees all the evidence on which the minister has
relied in issuing the order and that he does review the detention on the
merits. The knowledge that professional and independent judges will
examine the case for detention is in itself an inhibitory factor on the
exercise of the minister's power; and even a deferent court will intervene
where it believes that a reasonable man could not have concluded that
detention was justified in the circumstances of the case. The subdued

[94] Op cit 73–4. See also Baruch Bracha 'Restrictions of Personal Freedom without Due
Process of Law According to the Defence Emergency Regulations, 1945' (1978) 8 *Israel
Yearbook on Human Rights* 296, 308.
[95] Emergency Powers (Detention) Law 5739—1979, s 4*(a)*.
[96] 35(2) PD 253.
[97] Harold Rudolph op cit 115.
[98] 36(1) PD 666.
[99] Supra.
[100] Harold Rudolph op cit 119 et seq citing Professor Y H Klinghoffer. Another influential
commentator, while not accepting Professor Klinghoffer's views, argues that a wide form of
judicial intervention was contemplated by the Act: Shimon Shetreet 'A Contemporary
Model of Emergency Detention Law: An Assessment of the Israeli Law' (1984) 14 *Israel
Yearbook on Human Rights* 182, 201–2.

approach of the courts in the earlier cases does not mean that they have viewed the decision to detain as one for the subjective decision of the minister; rather it implies that after reviewing the decision on the merits (that is, objectively) the courts will be reluctant to nullify it unless it seems clearly wrong. There is great value in an objective independent assessment of the exercise of executive power even if it is undertaken with caution.

External control over preventive detention under s 28 in South Africa is ineffective and limited in contrast to the mandatory judicial review that exists in Israel. As already indicated[101] s 28 detentions are only referred to the ordinary courts (in the form of a review by the Chief Justice of the Appellate Division) if the advisory board which reviews such detentions is in disagreement with the minister over the exercise of the detention power. Review by the ordinary courts is therefore conditional and not mandatory as in Israel. Moreover, when the matter does reach the Chief Justice he is not authorised to review it on the merits but is restricted to the traditional grounds of bad faith, excess of powers or improper considerations in deciding whether to set the decision aside. The review powers of the Chief Justice in South Africa are more circumscribed than those exercised by the Israeli courts. Furthermore, since preventive detention orders in South Africa are frequently issued for a period of six months, and since the Act[102] does not specify any time limit for the completion of the hearing by the board of review, the detainee will frequently have been released or detained under a new order before the matter can be referred to the Chief Justice.[103] By the simple device of detaining persons for limited periods, the need to put the matter before the Chief Justice can be avoided. Finally, the right to an initial review by the advisory board, and to referral of the matter to the Chief Justice thereafter, lapses if the detainee challenges the validity of his detention before the ordinary courts.[104] The barriers which the legislature has placed between the detainee and the effective review of his detention by the courts are discouraging in the extreme. The South African legislature, in contrast to the Knesset in Israel, has done its best to avoid proper review of preventive detention orders.

The limited form of advisory board review available to s 28 detainees is deficient in another major respect—there are grave deficiencies in the procedural rules governing a review. The main deviations from procedural justice requirements have already received attention[105] and will only be summarised here. The detainee does not have the right to legal representation at his hearing but only in the preparation of written representations; he can be denied the right to give oral evidence; and, finally, if review does take place before the ordinary courts by way of referral of the matter to the Chief Justice, he carries out his review on the papers without any independent power of investigation.

From a procedural point of view the great virtue of the Israeli system of

---

[101] See chapter 7 above.

[102] Sections 38 and 41 of the Internal Security Act 74 of 1982.

[103] The requirement of periodic six-monthly reviews applies only after the board of review has made its decision in the initial review: s 43(1).

[104] Section 42(3). As previously noted, the chances of success on challenge before the ordinary courts are minimal unless there has been a serious procedural failure.

[105] See chapter 7 above.

review of preventive detention decisions is that it takes place before the
ordinary courts which are largely in control of their own procedures. The
courts' power to determine how the proceedings should be conducted
appear to be shackled in two respects only. First, all review hearings must
be heard in camera.[106] (As in the case of statutory review in South Africa.)
Secondly, though the detainee has a right to legal representation his
choice of counsel may be restricted by the power of the Minister of Justice
to limit representation to those who have the right to act as defence
counsel in courts martial.[107] Apart from these two instances, the
authorised deviations from standard procedure are under the control of
the courts. Though the detainee has a right to be present at the hearing,[108]
the President of the District Court may accept evidence in the absence of
the detainee or his representative, and without disclosure of the evidence
to them, if he is satisfied that disclosure may impair state or public
security.[109] The President of the District Court may also deviate from the
normal rules of evidence if he is satisfied that this will be conducive to the
discovery of truth and the just handling of the case.[110] While there can be
no doubt that these two provisions authorise substantial departures from
the normal requirements of procedural justice in criminal trials, the great
virtue of the Israeli system is that such departures are in the discretion of
the presiding judge who will only permit them when they are considered
to be necessary. The courts can moderate their effect by, for instance,
providing the detainee and his legal representative with the gist of
evidence received in their absence.[111] Since the preservation of intelligence sources and methods is vital in dealing with modern terrorism and
subversion,[112] such departures are lamentable necessities in societies
faced by formidable security threats. However, the Israeli government
deserves credit for giving the independent courts of the country the power
to control their own review procedures and thereby to prevent abuse of the
right to a fair hearing by the executive authorities.

The rule-of-law requirement of independent external control of
detention has been discussed thus far in relation to the decision to detain.
We now turn briefly to court control over the treatment of the detainee. In
both South Africa and in Israel the conditions under which detainees are
held in preventive detention are prescribed by regulation. The regulations[113] governing s 28 detainees are purportedly binding on South
African courts which are expressly prohibited from pronouncing on their
validity.[114] No such prohibition appears in the Israeli legislation. Court
access to detainees is not specifically prohibited in South Africa and the
'no-access clause' lists judges among those who are exempted from the
prohibition on visits to the detainee.[115] There appears to be no reason why

---

[106] Section 6 of the Emergency Powers (Detention) Law 5739—1979.
[107] Section 8(b).   [108] Section 8(a).
[109] Section 6(c).
[110] Section 6(a). He is required by s 6(b) to record the reasons for the deviation.
[111] This is apparently the practice in the review of detentions: see Harold Rudolph op cit
99.
[112] Paul Wilkinson Terrorism and the Liberal State (Macmillan, London 1977) 132 et seq.
[113] See chapter 7 above for details.
[114] Section 28(7).
[115] Section 28(8).

South African courts should not order production of a detainee before them in hearings alleging ill-treatment of the detainee. The judgment[116] declaring that the court had no such power related to detention for purposes of interrogation in isolation where different considerations were held to apply. Judges in Israel regularly visit detainees and hear their complaints.[117] Nothing in Israel prevents the courts from exercising their ordinary powers, including habeas corpus orders, where maltreatment of a detainee is alleged. Finally, it is worthy of note that the Israeli regulations governing the conditions of detention[118] are, by and large, more favourable to the detainee than the South African counterpart.

The power to detain preventively (or to intern) has long been used in Northern Ireland. That power remains on the statute book though it has not been used since 1975. In the most recent investigation into Northern Ireland security laws, Judge Baker recommended the repeal 'without qualification' of the preventive detention provisions of the relevant Act[119] but in its reaction to this recommendation the British government has declared that it intends to keep detention on the statute book for possible use in conditions of extreme emergency. This dormant detention power is part of the Northern Ireland (Emergency Provisions) Act 1978[120] and may be activated for periods of up to six months by order issued by the Secretary of State.[121] Current British policy on detention accords with Lord Gardiner's view that its prolonged use is likely to have dangerous social consequences[122] but that the conditions in Northern Ireland require that it be retained as a reserve power for extreme occasions. Before subjecting this reluctantly retained power to rule-of-law analysis, the previous detention (or internment) laws will be briefly surveyed.

In the early part of this century, internment[123] was authorised in Northern Ireland in terms of regulations published under the Civil Authorities (Special Powers) Act (NI) 1922. The relevant regulation authorised internment on the broadly worded ground that it appeared expedient to the detaining authority for securing the preservation of peace or the maintenance of order. Court decisions[124] have shown that the decision to detain was effectively beyond judicial control and, as an influential commentary on security laws in Northern Ireland has concluded, 'there were no cases in which the effective release of a person detained or interned under the Special Powers Act was secured by legal action . . .'.[125] An advisory committee system did operate and, while

---

[116] *Schermbrucker v Klindt NO* 1965 (4) SA 606 (A).   [117] Harold Rudolph op cit 107.

[118] Reviewed in detail by Harold Rudolph op cit 160 et seq.

[119] *'Review of the Operation of the Northern Ireland (Emergency Provisions) Act 1978'* (Cmnd 9222, April 1984) 71 (referred to below as the Baker Report).

[120] Section 12 and Schedule I.   [121] Section 33(3)(c).

[122] *'Report of the Committee to Consider, in the Context of Civil Liberties and Human Rights, Measures to Deal with Terrorism in Northern Ireland'* (Cmnd 5847, 1975) 43 (referred to below as the Gardiner Report).

[123] The expression favoured at that time for long-term preventive detention. Internment and detention are essentially similar phenomena and were so treated by the Baker Report para 233.

[124] In particular *R (O'Hanlan) v Governor of Belfast Prison* (1922) 56 *ILTR* 170 and *Re James McElduff* (Queen's Bench Division of High Court of Northern Ireland, 1971).

[125] Boyle, Hadden and Hillyard *Law and State: The Case of Northern Ireland 39*. See also David Lowry 'Internment in Northern Ireland' (1976) 8 *Univ of Toledo Law Review* 169, 186. This article provides a useful short history of internment in Northern Ireland.

recommendations for release of detainees were usually accepted,[126] the practice certainly cannot qualify as a rule-of-law restraint on internment. After direct rule from Westminster was imposed in 1972, a new system of detention with judicial features was introduced by order and subsequently incorporated into the Northern Ireland (Emergency Provisions) Act of 1973. This system provided for detentions for periods of longer than twenty-eight days to be reviewed by a detention commissioner operating according to a procedure that incorporated a number of rule-of-law elements. The chief of these were (i) the statutory specification of suspicion of involvement in any act of terrorism[127] as the ground for ordering a detention; (ii) a full hearing before the detention commissioner in which the detainee was entitled to a statement of the nature of the terrorist activities alleged, to legal representation and to the right to call witnesses; and (iii) an appeal to a Detention Appeal Tribunal.[128] There were two significant departures from procedural justice requirements: the normal rules of admissibility relating to evidence were not applicable and the detention commissioner was empowered in the interests of security or the safety of persons to exclude the detainee and his representative from parts of the hearing. Otherwise the hearing was conducted according to the standard requirements of an adversarial process of investigation.

Surprisingly, this semi-judicialised procedure for reviewing detention orders was almost universally unpopular in Northern Ireland and was pronounced a failure in the Gardiner Report.[129] The following statement from that report forcefully expresses the reasons why the committee condemned the procedure:

> 'The most cogent criticism was that the procedures are unsatisfactory, or even farcical, if considered as judicial. The adversarial method of trial is reduced to impotence by the needs of security. The use of screens and voice scramblers, the overwhelming amount of hearsay evidence and the in camera sessions are totally alien to ordinary trial procedures. The quasi-judicial procedures are a veneer to an enquiry which, to be effective, inevitably has no relationship to common-law procedures.'[130]

The Gardiner Committee condemned the independent review system because it was imperfectly judicial: it contained rule-of-law elements but did not adhere fully to the criminal trial model of procedural justice. This criticism is the product of excessively high and unrealistic expectations. When security threats require the use of preventive detention[131] it follows ex hypothesi that due process principles will *to some extent* be qualified by the requirements of state security. The construction of an enquiry procedure for detentions must involve a delicate balancing of conflicting security and rule-of-law interests and the resultant compromise should be one in which departures from legality are kept to a minimum. Given the need for preventive detention, it is fanciful to expect full adherence to

---

[126] Boyle, Hadden and Hillyard *Law and State: The Case of Northern Ireland* 58.
[127] Terrorism being defined as the 'use of violence for political ends' and including 'any use of violence for the purposes of putting the public or any section of the public in fear'.
[128] Section 10(5) and Schedule I of the Northern Ireland (Emergency Provisions) Act 1973.
[129] Gardiner Report paras 150–8.
[130] Gardiner Report para 152. See also Boyle, Hadden & Hillyard op cit 74.
[131] This is a policy matter requiring political rather than legal judgment.

'ordinary trial procedures'. The enquiry procedure rejected by the Gardiner Report resulted in a detainee release rate of about one-third following the initial enquiry, of about one-tenth after appeal and up to one-half after subsequent periodic reviews.[132] If, as found by the Report, there was an 'almost complete lack of worthwhile material available to the Commissioners in the conduct of a review',[133] the answer is surely to appoint tougher-minded commissioners who will reject flimsy cases and thereby increase the percentage of releases from detention. Instead the Gardiner Report recommended that detention should once again become a matter for pure executive discretion and its proposals (somewhat modified) were carried into law by the Northern Ireland (Emergency Provisions) (Amendment) Act of 1975 and later re-enacted as Schedule I of the Northern Ireland (Emergency Provisions) Act 28 of 1978. Though this law remains in force, its detention provisions are presently dormant and require an order from the Secretary of State to activate them. As observed earlier, British policy since 1975 has rejected the use of preventive detention in Northern Ireland.

The Gardiner model of preventive detention requires the Secretary of State personally to take the decision to detain. He is empowered to make an 'interim custody order' where it appears to him that there are grounds for suspecting that the person in question has been concerned in the commission or attempted commission of an act of terrorism or in directing, organising or training persons for the purpose of terrorism.[134] If before the expiry of fourteen days from the date of the interim order, the Secretary of State has not referred the case to an adviser, the order lapses and the detainee must be released.[135] Detention for longer than fourteen days therefore depends upon referral of the matter to an adviser with legal training[136] and upon consideration of the case by him. If the matter is referred to an adviser, the Secretary of State is required to provide the detainee with a statement of the nature of the terrorist activities of which he is suspected[137] and to convey to the adviser any written representations which the detainee submits together with the detainee's request (if any) to be seen personally by the adviser.[138] Though the adviser is empowered to gather his own information, either oral or written,[139] the investigation conducted by him is essentially informal and inquisitorial and excludes the calling of witnesses, cross-examination and legal representation.[140] The adviser is required, after consideration of the case in this way, to report to the Secretary of State whether in his opinion the detainee has been concerned in terrorist activities and whether detention is necessary for the protection of the public.[141] After receiving the adviser's report, the

---

[132] Boyle, Hadden & Hillyard op cit 70.
[133] Gardiner Report para 157.
[134] Paragraph 4(1) of Schedule I to the Northern Ireland (Emergency Provisions) Act 1978.
[135] Paragraph 5(1).
[136] Paragraph 2.
[137] Paragraph 6(1).
[138] Paragraph 6(2).
[139] Paragraph 7(2).
[140] Paragraph 7(3) provides for the private interviewing by the adviser of persons who provide him with information.
[141] Paragraph 7(1).

Secretary of State may issue a detention order 'if he is satisfied' of the detainee's involvement in terrorism and that detention is necessary in the interests of the public.[142] If not so satisfied the detainee must be released. Once a detention order is issued its duration is in the discretion of the Secretary of State[143] but provision is made for periodic review of the case by an adviser.[144]

Conformity to rule-of-law requirements was not intended by the author of this system and has certainly not been achieved. There are a few positive points. The grounds for detention are clearly specified and require the detaining authority to be satisfied of the detainee's involvement in terrorism. This is in strong contrast to the grounds for preventive detention in South Africa which are more broadly and vaguely stated as the involvement in activities which endanger state security or the maintenance of law and order. It is arguable that the grounds specified in the Gardiner model constitute objective jurisdictional facts and that the court may set aside a detention if persuaded that a reasonable person could not have concluded from the detainee's conduct that he was involved in terrorism. Intervention by the court appears to be permitted by the line of reasoning adopted in *Inland Revenue Commissioner v Rossminster*[145] and *Attorney-General of St Christopher v Reynolds*[146] which together with the decision in *Secretary of State for Education and Science v Tameside Metropolitan Borough Council*[147] are authority for the proposition that the words 'appears to the Secretary of State that there are grounds for suspecting' and 'the Secretary of State . . . is satisfied' do not necessarily confer a purely subjective power of decision-making. If these arguments are correct, the current detention law for Northern Ireland will conform more closely to the rule of law. However, the Gardiner model was intended to be an executive-dominated system of detention and it remains to be seen whether the boldness of the Privy Council in *Attorney-General of St Christopher v Reynolds*[148] will be given local (rather than foreign) application by the British courts. From a rule-of-law point of view the only other positive feature of detention in Northern Ireland is that the detainee is entitled to a statement of his alleged involvement in terrorism.

Court control over the conditions under which detainees are held in Northern Ireland does not appear to be a problem. The Act does not contain the no-access clause that is so familiar a feature of detention in South Africa and requires that the detainee, subject to directions from the Secretary of State, shall be 'treated as nearly as may be as if he were a prisoner detained in a prison on remand . . .'.[149] Maltreatment of detainees could be remedied by a court order and there is nothing in British law to prevent an order for the personal appearance of the detainee in court if abuse of the detainee is apprehended. British courts have recently

---

[142] Paragraph 8(1).
[143] Paragraph 10(2).
[144] Paragraph 9.
[145] [1980] 1 All ER 80 (HL).
[146] [1980] AC 637 (PC).
[147] [1977] AC 1014 (HL).
[148] Supra.
[149] Paragraph 11(3) of Schedule I to the Northern Ireland (Emergency Provisions) Act 1978.

adopted a sharply positive approach to prisoners' rights and this includes the right of 'unimpeded access to the courts'.[150]

Before turning to pre-trial detention, the shorter forms of preventive detention authorised by ss 50 and 50A of the South African Internal Security Act of 1982 require brief discussion. Section 50 authorises fourteen-day detention, initially at the instance of a police officer and thereafter upon the order of a magistrate if the period of detention is to exceed forty-eight hours.[151] There is limited conformity to the rule of law in the case of s 50 detention. The grounds for detention are specified and consist of a suspected contribution to public disturbance, disorder, riot and the like. After forty-eight hours the detainee must be released unless a magistrate confirms the order. Adherence to the rule of law fades rapidly once the matter reaches the magistrate. He need not afford the detainee a hearing before extending the detention (presumably because the legislature thought that he should not be confused by contrary arguments or facts) and his order is not reviewable before the courts except on that chimerical ground of bad faith or improper purpose. Detention under s 50A (180-day detention) was designed to avoid each and every requirement of the rule of law and in this its framers appear to have been successful.[152] It constitutes a totally lawless detention power.

Pre-trial Detention

The ill-repute which South Africa has gained for its security system is due primarily to a succession of notorious pre-trial detention laws. Of those that remain in force we shall examine two in the light of rule-of-law principles: indefinite detention for interrogational purposes (s 29 detention) and the detention of witnesses (s 31 detention).[153] Both forms of detention are potentially of extended duration, both authorise the isolation of the detainee and permit his interrogation while so held, and both are subject to minimal safeguards and controls. Of all of the victims of repression in South Africa, the plight of pre-trial detainees is the most woeful. The large number of deaths under pre-trial detention and evidence of torture is proof enough of their grievous situation.

The most basic requirement of legality is that the statute authorising detention should clearly specify the grounds upon which it may be ordered. The empowering language of s 29 does specify grounds in the form of a reasonable belief on the part of the detaining authority that the detainee has committed, or intends to commit, the crimes of terrorism or subversion (or certain related crimes) or that he has information about the commission of such crimes. On the surface this is a clear enough statutory specification of grounds but in reality it is not since the crimes of which the detainee must be suspected, or in respect of which he is believed to have information, range obscurely across a wide spectrum of human activity. If, however, the courts can investigate these grounds and pronounce upon their existence, there is the possibility of a judicial specification of what

---

[150] Dirk van Zyl Smit 'The Legislative Entitlements of Security Detainees and Prisoners' Rights' (1985) 1 *SA Journal of Human Rights* 160.
[151] See chapter 7 above for full discussion of fourteen-day detention.
[152] See the discussion in chapter 7 above.
[153] See chapter 7 above for a detailed discussion of these provisions.

the legislature has left vague. In *Minister of Law and Order v Hurley*[154] the court asserted the right and power to examine for itself the grounds of detention but the judgment did not lead to a narrowing construction of the statutory language because the minister declined to make the grounds for the detention known to the applicants or the court, and the detainee was released because no basis for detention was revealed by the detaining authority. Although the judgment has not invested the empowering legislation with rule-of-law precision,[155] it does bring s 29 detention into conformity with a second important requirement of legality—that of external control over executive action in the civil rights field. The case illustrates the value of that control even when it lacks the direction afforded by clear statutory standards. In a number of cases following the judgment, the authorities have released detainees immediately on receiving notice of their intention to approach the court. One of the benefits of external court control is that where the authorities act for flimsy or non-existent reasons, or for reasons which they are unwilling to submit to court scrutiny, the detainee will secure his freedom. It would be better, of course, if court control was guided by clear legislative standards or criteria; but even in their absence there is value in requiring the authorities to account to independent judicial officers. Unwillingness to do so confirms what many have always suspected—a pathetic official case for invoking the detention power.

Section 31 detention (i e of witnesses) is authorised if the detaining authority, the attorney-general, is of the opinion that the detainee is likely to give material evidence for the state in a criminal prosecution for certain offences and that if not detained, the detainee may abscond or be subjected to interference or intimidation. Once again, this appears to be a precisely specified ground for detention until we discover that the offences which the detainee must be thought to have witnessed include a number of vague common-law and statutory crimes such as sedition, subversion and sabotage. The attorney-general could conceivably order my detention if it is reported to him that I heard somebody advocating sanctions against South Africa (which is possibly a contravention of the section creating the crimes of subversion or sabotage) or that I heard two persons gathered together in a street verbally defy the authority of the government (sedition). The provision for the detention of witnesses is further aggravated by the unwillingness of the court to pronounce upon the reasons for a detention ordered by the attorney-general. It refused to do so in *Singh v Attorney-General, Transvaal*[156] by holding that the attorney-general's *opinion* is the pre-condition for his exercise of the detention power over witnesses and that if he bona fide holds that opinion the court will not be prepared to second-guess his decision. While this judgment is open to criticism, it is not affected by the ruling in *Hurley* and still stands as the authoritative interpretation of the statutory power to detain witnesses. It follows that this form of detention denies the basic rule-of-law requirements of clear standards and external judicial control.

---

[154] supra.
[155] Nor does it purport to assert any control over the decision whether or not to release the detainee after a valid detention.
[156] 1967 (2) SA 1 (T); See also *Thuntsi v Attorney-General, Northern Cape* 1982 (4) SA 468 (NC).

Section 29 detention is supposedly controlled by a number of procedural safeguards which, in brief, require the detaining authority to notify the Commissioner of Police and the Minister of Law and Order of any detention, make detention for longer than a month conditional on the written authority of the said minister, and for longer than six months on referral of the matter to a review board with advisory powers only.[157] The due process deficiencies in this scheme are the absence of any provision requiring delivery to the detainee of a statement of the grounds for his detention, the lack of independent stature on the part of the ministerially appointed review board and the fact that the review board is not required to conduct a full hearing or empowered to make binding decisions. In any event the requirement of referral to a review board applies only after six months in detention by which time the need for protection may already have passed. Prior to that the 'safeguards' consist simply of *internal* reporting or confirmation requirements. Section 29 clearly makes a mockery of the procedural requirements of the rule of law. The detention of witnesses under s 31 does not envisage any official compliance with procedural justice. The legislature has provided in this instance for an entirely arbitrary procedure which does away with the fundamental principles of natural justice, including the right to a hearing before being adversely affected by official action.

We may conclude that while *Minister of Law and Order v Hurley*[158] imposed a measure of rule-of-law control over the decision to detain under s 29, the departures from legality remain serious for both s 29 and s 31 detention. The reassertion by the court of jurisdiction over s 29 detention is manifestly a welcome step in re-establishing the rule of law. This important gain should not blind us to the rule-of-law denials that remain, in particular the vagueness of the statutory grounds for s 29 and s 31 detention, the absence of external control over s 31 detention, and the arbitrary nature of the *discretion to release* the detainee under both forms of detention. External control is also deficient in respect of the important matter of the treatment of the detainee during detention. By reason of the isolation imposed on s 29 detainees by the 'no-access' clause, the court's power (partly due to its own finding in *Schermbrucker v Klindt NO*)[159] to prevent illegal treatment of detainees is severely circumscribed. The courts do issue orders interdicting the authorities from maltreating detainees and requiring the statutory visitors to the detainees (magistrates and district surgeons) to investigate allegations of abuse of rights. What is missing, however, is the effective policing by the courts of their own orders. Proper policing of court orders requires regular judicial visits to detainee cells and the restoration of court power to demand the production of the detainee in court so that the nature of his or her treatment can be determined from physical appearance and direct testimony.

The institution of extended pre-trial detention is not part of Israeli law[160] but in Northern Ireland pre-trial detention of limited duration has

---

[157] See chapter 7 above for a detailed discussion of these procedures.
[158] Supra.
[159] 1965 (4) SA 606 (A).
[160] Israel, in this context, refers to Israel proper and not to the occupied territories.

been at the disposal of the security authorities for a considerable time. Regulations published under the Civil Authorities (Special Powers) Act (NI) 1922 authorised police officers, acting in the interests of the maintenance of peace and order, to arrest and detain persons for up to forty-eight hours for purposes of interrogation. At present there are three pre-trial detention provisions in Northern Ireland, each of strictly limited duration. They are:

   (i) A provision of the Northern Ireland (Emergency Provisions) Act 1978[161] which authorises any constable to arrest any person whom he suspects of being a terrorist. The person so arrested may be held for up to seventy-two hours and, although the enabling provision does not say so, interrogated by the police.

  (ii) A provision of the same Act[162] which authorises a member of the armed forces to arrest and detain for not longer than four hours any person whom he suspects of committing, having committed or being about to commit any offence. The arresting official is not required to state the ground of arrest and may simply inform the arrested person that he is acting as a member of the armed forces. The purpose of this provision is clearly to give members of the armed forces a brief period in which to obtain information about suspects prior to invoking other powers of arrest or detention.

 (iii) A provision in the Prevention of Terrorism (Temporary Provisions) Act 1984[163] (which is applicable throughout the United Kingdom including Northern Ireland) authorising any constable to arrest any person whom he has reasonable grounds for suspecting to be a person who has committed certain offences under the Act or who is or has been concerned in acts of terrorism.[164] A person so arrested may be detained for up to forty-eight hours but the period may be extended by order of the Secretary of State for a further period not exceeding five days. Detention under this provision (referred to below as 7-day detention) is also clearly for purposes of interrogation although it could be used for the more limited purpose of obtaining information (such as identity) about a suspect.

The Baker Committee investigation into the Northern Ireland (Emergency Provisions) Act 1978 has recommended that 72-hour detention (under (i) above) and 7-day detention (under (iii) above) be fused for Northern Ireland in such a way that the police would initially be able to arrest and detain *on reasonable suspicion* of involvement in terrorism[165] for up to forty-eight hours with the power to extend the period for a further period not exceeding five days by order of the Secretary of State for Northern Ireland.[166] Since this is likely to be the

       [161] Section 11.   [162] Section 14.
       [163] Section 12. This form of detention was part of an anti-terrorist package introduced in 1939: see Owen G Lomas 'The Executive and the Anti-Terrorist Legislation of 1939' 1980 *Public Law* 16.
       [164] The section also empowers arrest of persons subject to exclusion orders, that is, orders excluding the person from the United Kingdom or some part of it. Such orders most commonly provide for the exclusion from Great Britain of persons who came to it from Northern Ireland.
       [165] Or the commission of certain security offences.
       [166] Baker Report para 304.

new model of pre-trial detention for Northern Ireland, the discussion that follows will be confined to 7-day detention with reference, once again, to the requirements of the rule of law.

Does 7-day detention comply with the requirement of legality that the grounds for official action should be clearly specified by law? This question may be answered affirmatively in the light of the clear requirement of the statute that the arresting official must have reasonable grounds for suspecting that the arrested person has committed certain offences[167] or that he has been concerned in the commission, preparation or instigation of acts of terrorism. Terrorism is defined with reasonable clarity as 'the use of violence for political ends, and includes any use of violence for the purpose of putting the public or any section of the public in fear'.[168] The statutory definition is perhaps too broad and could be improved by confining terrorism to the use of 'serious violence'; but even without being so limited the kind of activities to which it refers is indicated clearly enough. The rule of law also requires that there should be independent external control over the decision to arrest and detain. Because the enabling section of the Act[169] declares that the constable effecting the arrest must act on reasonable grounds, the court is empowered to judge the reasonableness of the suspicion on which he acts.[170] The initial decision to detain is therefore reviewable before the ordinary courts according to objective criteria. (In contrast, 72-hour detention may be ordered if a constable 'suspects' that the person in question is a terrorist[171] and this wording appears to invest the detaining official with a subjective power to act which the courts may not review on the merits. It was precisely to avoid this exclusion of an objective review power that Judge Baker recommended the requirement of reasonable suspicion.)[172] It seems, however, that the decision of the Secretary of State to extend detention beyond forty-eight hours for anything up to five days is not subject to external court control except on the hypothetical basis of proof that he acted in bad faith or for improper purposes. The language of the relevant section, which declares simply that the secretary of state 'may' extend detention by up to five days, appears to give him a power that will be absolute in practice. For two reasons this is less serious than it appears at first sight. If the initial arrest and detention is illegal because it is not based on proper grounds, any extension thereof by the Secretary of State would also be illegal. In the second place, the entire period of detention cannot exceed seven days and an absence of court control over the decision to extend an initially valid detention from two to a maximum of seven days is hardly alarming. We may conclude that the rule-of-law requirements of clear standards for administrative action and the external control thereof are substantially met by the system of 7-day detention. The fact that there have been no legal challenges to detention decisions before the ordinary courts is probably due to the fact that detainees or

---

[167] These offences (created by s 1, 9 and 10 of the Prevention of Terrorism (Temporary Provisions) Act 1984) relate mainly to membership of, or support for, proscribed terrorist organisations or to acts which further the commission of terrorism.
[168] Section 14(1) of the Northern Ireland (Temporary Provisions) Act 1978.
[169] Section 12(1).   [170] Baker Report para 280.
[171] Section 11(1) of the Northern Ireland (Emergency Provisions) Act 1978.
[172] Baker Report paras 280–3.

their relatives and friends know that the detention *must* terminate at the end of seven days with the release or formal charging of the person held.

The shortness of the period of pre-trial detention in Northern Ireland has not precluded the ill-treatment of detainees. Soon after the opening of two new interrogation centres in Belfast and Armagh in 1977, complaints began to pour in about the maltreatment of detainees who were processed there.[173] In 1975 there were 180 such complaints and by 1977 the number had reached 671.[174] An Amnesty International investigation in 1977 and report in 1978 led to the appointment by the British government of a committee (the Bennett Committee) to investigate interrogation procedures in Northern Ireland.[175] Although the Committee was not authorised to investigate individual complaints of ill-treatment, its report accepted that there was prima facie evidence of abuses and that medical evidence of injuries sustained by detainees during police custody indicated that the injuries were not self-inflicted.[176] The Bennett Report proposed a package of recommendations designed to eliminate malpractices and these proposals have been accepted and applied by the British government. The chief recommendations were for closed-circuit television screening of interrogation sessions, for limits on the duration of such sessions and on the number of officers who conduct them, for an interrogational code of conduct and for an absolute right of access to a lawyer after the first 48 hours of detention. The implementation of the Bennett recommendations has virtually eliminated malpractices with the result that Judge Baker was able to find in 1984 that 'no physical violence of any degree would now be tolerated . . .'[177] and that complaints in that year referred only to verbal abuse by interrogators.[178]

The Bennett Committee remedy for the maltreatment of detainees was essentially one of internal controls and sanctions. What must not be overlooked, however, is that internal controls are effective in the case of 7-day detention partly because external court control has not been removed, as it has in South Africa. There is no clause prohibiting access to the detainee and no exclusion of court jurisdiction. In practice, access to a solicitor is discretionary in the first forty-eight hours but at the end of that period the detainee has an unconditional right of access to a solicitor and this right may be exercised every forty-eight hours thereafter.[179] Judge Baker was not prepared to recommend an unqualified right in the first

[173] Boyle, Hadden and Hillyard *Ten Years On in Northern Ireland: The Legal Control of Political Violence* 39.

[174] Ibid.

[175] These investigations were not the first to be undertaken into allegations of maltreatment of detainees in Northern Ireland. Following the re-introduction of internment in 1971, allegations of torture and ill-treatment of internees led to the appointment of the Compton Committee which in its report (Cmnd 4823, London 1971) declared that interrogation 'in depth' of suspects had occurred. A subsequent committee (the Parker Committee) produced a divided report on the use of interrogation in depth (involving the use of wall-standing, hooding of internees, noise bombardment and food and sleep deprivation) but the government accepted Lord Gardiner's minority report (Cmnd 4901, London, 1972) to the effect that such methods were intolerable in a civilised community.

[176] *'Report of the Committee of Inquiry into Police Interrogation Procedures in Northern Ireland'* (Cmnd 7497, London 1979) para 404(16) (referred to below as the Bennett Report).

[177] Baker Report para 193.

[178] Baker Report paras 308–313.

[179] Baker Report paras 320–3.

forty-eight-hour period of custody as this might interfere with the process of interrogation.[180] Lord Shackleton had earlier found in his investigation into the Prevention of Terrorism (Temporary Provision) Act 1974 and 1976 (the precursor of the present Act) that access in the early stages of interrogation could have dangerous consequences where the police had caught only some members of a terrorist group.[181] Other forms of access (for example, to friends and relatives) are permitted if the process of investigation is not likely to be harmed. All these forms of access, particularly access to a solicitor, make it possible to invoke external judicial control, at least after forty-eight hours, in order to prevent maltreatment of the detainee. Courts could issue an injunction and exercise the power, which the legislation does not remove, to take evidence from the detainee. The fact that this procedure has not been followed in Northern Ireland is due to several factors but, particularly, the shortness of detention, the government's clear disapproval of inhuman treatment backed up by effective internal control measures, and the pressure of public opinion on the authorities in the United Kingdom.

The factors just outlined have made 7-day detention a tolerable although hardly welcome institution for the combating of terrorism. Published opinion is divided and ranges over a broad spectrum of viewpoints. Professor Harry Street accepts the necessity of detention but wants its conditions liberalised.[182] Other commentators reject it outright as a Draconian instrument of injustice.[183] In one influential commentary, the improvements following the Bennett Report are welcomed but also criticised for not going far enough.[184] From a South African perspective, one may note with wry amusement the extent of controversy that surrounds a strictly limited form of detention that is subject to significant rule-of-law and internal controls, and from which the use of torture or inhuman treatment has been expelled. This controversy throws into relief the complete indefensibility of extended and poorly controlled pre-trial detention in South Africa from which torture and barbarous treatment have certainly not been expelled.[185]

Banning and the Rule of Law

The word 'banning' was used earlier[186] to describe inter alia the proscription of organisations, the imposition of restrictions on individuals and the prohibition of meetings and processions. The ensuing rule-of-law analysis of these three procedures will again focus on the requirements of clear standards, external control and due process.

---

[180] Baker Report para 323.

[181] 'Review of the Operation of the Prevention of Terrorism (Temporary Provisions) Act 1974 and 1976' (Cmnd 7324, London 1978) 27 (referred to below as the Shackleton Report).

[182] Harry Street 'The Prevention of Terrorism (Temporary Provisions) Act 1974' 1975 Criminal Law Review 192, 198.

[183] David R Lowry 'Draconian Powers: The New British Approach to the Pre-trial Detention of Suspected Terrorists' (1976–7) 8–9 Columbia Human Rights Law Review 185.

[184] Boyle, Hadden and Hillyard Ten Years On in Northern Ireland: The Legal Control of Political Violence, 51 et seq.

[185] Don Foster & Diane Sandler A Study of Detention and Torture in South Africa. Preliminary Report (Inst of Criminology, Univ of Cape Town 1985).

[186] See chapter 8 above.

Proscription of Organisations

There are various statutory grounds upon which the Minister of Law and Order may ban an organisation. While some of these grounds are reasonably specific (for example, that the organisation was formed to carry on the affairs of an unlawful organisation) others are broad and imprecise. Since each of the grounds constitutes a separate and substantive basis for proscription, the entire section authorising banning is flawed by vagueness. The minister is empowered to ban an organisation if he is satisfied that it engages in activities which endanger the security of the state or the maintenance of law and order. He may also act if satisfied that the organisation in question in furthering any of the objects of communism, and 'communism' is itself a rather elastic term in the definitional clause of the Act. What makes these broad grants of authority even vaguer, is the subjective sense in which they have been interpreted by the courts.[187] That interpretation means that if the minister thinks that an organisation is endangering state security, then the court will assume that it does without investigation of the relationship of the actual facts to the statutory criteria. Banning depends on ministerial will, not on rationally determined grounds or criteria. Non-intervention by the courts has rendered the already imprecise statutory standards for banning both irrelevant and meaningless.

The Act does provide a weak form of external control by empowering an office-bearer of the organisation to have the proscription reviewed by the Chief Justice of the Appellate Division of the Supreme Court. This form of review has a number of serious deficiencies of which the most significant, for present purposes, is that the Chief Justice may set aside the banning only if satisfied that the minister acted in bad faith, outside his powers or for improper considerations. The invocation of these standard review powers will do nothing to clarify the broad language of the Act. The Chief Justice does not give a public judgment when he either affirms or sets aside the proscription of an organisation—he merely informs the minister of his decision and provides him with reasons when he decides to set a banning aside.[188] The secrecy of the review process militates against its use as a device for clarifying or narrowing vague statutory criteria. Even without the secrecy, review of the minister's decision on the traditional grounds of bad faith et cetera is hardly likely to invest a vague grant of power with meaningful precision. Though a review may involve interpretation, it is much more likely to turn on whether the facts submitted to the Chief Justice on paper point towards an absence of good faith or a reliance on improper considerations. The interpretative aspect of the judicial function will not be prominent in an enquiry of that kind. We may conclude that review before the Chief Justice will not bring any rule-of-law precision to the sweeping power to ban under the Act.

The process for banning organisations in South Africa also violates the requirements of procedural justice. Since these violations have already been canvassed,[189] attention is directed here only to the most serious

---

[187] Ibid.
[188] Section 11(7) of the Internal Security Act 74 of 1982.
[189] See chapter 8 above.

departures from due process. Because the minister is empowered to withhold from the banned organisation all the information on which he acted, that organisation will generally have to present its case to the advisory committee, and through it to the Chief Justice, without knowing the factual basis for the declaration of unlawfulness. This is the problem, so familiar to the victims of ministerial bans of all kinds, of having to argue a case in the dark. The court ruling in *Nkondo & Gumede v Minister of Law and Order*,[190] requiring the minister to provide detainees with meaningful reasons, is clearly applicable to the ministerial duty to give reasons for the banning of organisations. Depending on how assertive the courts are in demanding detail in the ministerial statement of reasons, the organisation's due process rights may be enhanced. If the courts do not insist upon a full outline of the minister's case, the papers which reach the Chief Justice (who has no independent power of investigation) are unlikely to confront him with a proper joinder of issues. Finally, the power of the Chief Justice to intervene is restricted to the standard grounds of review and a referral of the matter to him without the grant of an independent power of investigation is likely to be pointless.

Security law in Northern Ireland makes provision for the proscription of organisations. The Northern Ireland (Emergency Provisions) Act 1978 outlawed seven terrorist groups on both sides of the Protestant/Catholic divide[191] and vested the Secretary of State with authority to add to or subtract from the list of organisations banned by the Act. (There is corresponding provision for banning in Great Britain under the Prevention of Terrorism (Temporary Provisions) Act 1984 and the IRA and the Irish National Liberation Army are currently banned under this law.)[192] The banning of organisations in Northern Ireland is not new and was exercised earlier by regulation under the Civil Authorities (Special Powers) Act (Northern Ireland) 1922. It was under the authority of this Act that the Secretary of State in 1967 made his notorious addition to the then list of banned groups by declaring as proscribed:

> 'The organisations at the date of this regulation or at any time thereafter describing themselves as "Republican Clubs" or any like organisations howsoever described.'

The House of Lords gave an almost equally notorious judgment in *McEldowney v Forde*[193] when this broad and vague proscription was subjected to legal challenge. The court upheld the proscription as valid over two strong dissenting judgments from Lords Diplock and Pearce. In his dissent Lord Pearce gave laconic expression to an important principle of government under law. 'A man', he said, 'must not be put in peril on an ambiguity under the criminal law.'[194] The minority view in *McEldowney* appears to have been more influential than the majority, and the Secretary of State has not since attempted to proscribe in such general terms.

How do the legal provisions for banning organisations in Northern Ireland and Great Britain measure up to the requirements of the rule of

---

[190] 1986 (2) SA 756 (A).
[191] Section 21(3) and Schedule 2 to the Act. Organisations passing under the same name are also proscribed.
[192] Section 1 and Schedule I to the Act.
[193] [1969] 2 All ER 1039 (HL).   [194] At 1064.

law? The answer to this question is a little more complex for the United Kingdom where all groups currently banned have been proscribed by Act of Parliament whereas in South Africa all except one (the Communist Party of South Africa) have been banned by executive order. In Britain and Northern Ireland the groups currently banned are all known terrorist organisations dedicated to securing political change by criminal acts. (This is not true of the banning of the Communist Party of South Africa which at the time it was outlawed was a political party with lawful aims.) Judge Baker received no representations that any of the organisations banned in Northern Ireland should come off the list,[195] a fact which underlines the almost universal acceptance in the United Kingdom of the justification for the bans imposed. The banning list has even been criticised for under-inclusiveness.[196] Independent and objective investigations into security legislation in Great Britain have recognised that the banning of organisations may make inroads into basic rights which we associate with the rule of law. Lord Shackleton said in his report that

> 'We have in this country a tradition that the freedom of association and the expression of support for any group or cause are not restricted under the law. These are essential freedoms and not something we should lightly abrogate or infringe.'[197]

Lord Jellicoe later expressed the same views[198] but both reports concluded that, being restricted to groups that are terrorist by any definition, the proscriptions did not seriously curtail basic liberties and were necessary on balance to counter terrorism in Great Britain. Judge Baker came to a similar conclusion for Northern Ireland.[199] Though the bans have been criticised as being cosmetic and for punishing people for their beliefs and associations rather than their actions,[200] they do not constitute serious infringements of freedoms associated with the rule of law because of their restricted scope. It is noteworthy that Sinn Fein, which openly supports violence in Northern Ireland and has been described as 'the IRA in drag', is not currently banned. The UDA, which appears to have links with Protestant military groups, is also not on the banned list.

The power of the Secretary of State to add to the list of banned organisations has not been exercised for some while, but it nevertheless requires assessment in terms of rule-of-law principles. Though now dormant, this power could be exercised at any moment. The legal basis for any such action by the Secretary of State is specified clearly by the relevant legislation which declares that he may add organisations to the banned list if they appear to him to be concerned in terrorism or to be promoting or encouraging it.[201] As observed earlier, terrorism is defined

---

[195] Baker Report para 410.
[196] David Bonner op cit 186.
[197] Shackleton Report para 29.
[198] *'Review of the Operation of the Prevention of Terrorism (Temporary Provisions) Act 1976'* (Cmnd 8803, London 1983) paras 210 and 212 (referred to below as the Jellicoe Report).
[199] Baker Report para 416.
[200] See, for example, Patricia Hewitt *The Abuse of Power: Civil Liberties in the United Kingdom* (Martin Robertson, Oxford 1982) 165–6.
[201] Section 1(4) of the Prevention of Terrorism (Temporary Provisions) Act 1984 and s 21(4) of the Northern Ireland (Emergency Provisions) Act 1978.

as the use of violence for political ends and includes threats of violence intended to put the public in fear. The criterion for banning is therefore specified precisely by law. *McEldowney v Forde*[202] is, on the face of it, discouraging as to court involvement in banning decisions. Closer analysis suggests that the judgment need not be an obstacle to external court control over the power exercised by the Secretary of State. In *McEldowney* the banning of Republican clubs was effected under broad powers to introduce measures necessary for the preservation of peace and order whereas under present law the Secretary of State is granted the much more limited power to proscribe organisations involved in terrorism. If, as occurred in *McEldowney*, he proscribes organisations that are non-subversive, it is likely that the courts will not stand aside. While it is true that the empowering language authorises him to act if it 'appears to him' that the group in question is involved in terrorism, recent judgments of the British courts reviewed earlier[203] indicate that this language does not preclude court investigation of the facts, particularly where the statutory criterion for official action is spelt out so clearly. In the absence of a clear relation between the action taken by the Secretary of State and the purposes of the law, the courts should intervene. Finally, some comment is appropriate on the proscription of organisations by the Secretary of State and the requirements of procedural justice. The Acts in question do not envisage, and almost certainly do not require, notice to the organisation in question of an intention to outlaw it or the opportunity to present arguments as to why proscription should not be imposed. This omission is not as serious if, as argued above, the ordinary courts have authority to review the basis of the action taken by the proscribing authority. Moreover, if bans are limited to terror groups either by the necessary restraint of the part of the Secretary of State or by court intervention when he goes too far, the omission of hearing procedures is understandable even if unfortunate in terms of due process principles. However, if the courts stand aloof as in *McEldowney*, and do not confine executive action against groups to the prescribed statutory purposes, the absence of procedures would be a serious rule-of-law failing.

In Israel, legal provisions concerning unlawful organisations appear in the Defence (Emergency) Regulations 1945[204] and in the Prevention of Terrorism Ordinance of 1948.[205] The relevant provision[206] of the Defence (Emergency) Regulations 1945 declares organisations having certain objectives, or carrying on certain activities, to be unlawful simply by reason of those objectives and activities and makes further provision for any organisation (without reference to aims and activities) to be declared unlawful by order of the Minister of Defence. The organisations which are automatically unlawful by reason of their objectives or activities are those which aim to overthrow the government by force or violence, or to bring it into hatred or contempt (or to incite disaffection against it), or to destroy

---

[202] Supra.
[203] See chapter 7 above.
[204] Regulations published by the British mandatory authority under the Palestine (Defence) Order in Council of 1937 and still in force (with amendments) at present.
[205] No 33 of 5703—1948 amended by the Prevention of Terrorism Ordinance (Amendment) Law 5740–1980.
[206] Regulation 84.

or injure the property of the government or to commit acts of terrorism
against its servants. Various forms of support for any such organisation
are made criminal offences by the regulations.[207] The Minister of Defence
has the power, as we have seen, to declare any organisation to be
unlawful. The effect of such a declaration is to make supporting activities
for such an organisation illegal and criminally punishable[208] and to bring
about an official winding-up of its assets.[209] The Prevention of Terrorism
Ordinance of 1948 makes it a criminal offence to be a member of, to
manage or direct, or to engage in various supporting activities for, an
organisation that is terrorist in terms of the statutory definition.[210] The
relevant definition declares a body of persons which resorts to 'acts of
violence calculated to cause death or injury to persons' or to 'threats of
such acts of violence' to be a terrorist organisation.[211] When a charge is
brought against any person under the Ordinance, the issue of whether the
organisation in question is terrorist will be determined by the court and a
government declaration of unlawfulness is not binding upon the court but
merely has the effect of placing the onus of disproving the terrorist nature
of the group upon the accused.[212] The Ordinance declares that property
belonging to a terrorist organisation is confiscated in favour of the state.[213]
The question whether a group is terrorist, and its property therefore liable
to confiscation, is determined by the District Court having jurisdiction.[214]

The foregoing account of the Israeli laws governing unlawful organisations shows that provision is made in that country for unlawfulness to
arise by declaration (as in South Africa and Northern Ireland) and also
for unlawfulness as a consequence of the objectives or activities of the
body in question. The latter process (which we shall call automatic
unlawfulness) is not a feature of security legislation in Northern Ireland or
South Africa. Unlawfulness by declaration in Israel appears to violate all
the requirements of the rule of law. The power to ban is unconfined by a
structure of legislative purposes or objectives[215] and there is accordingly
no statutory specification whatever of the grounds for official action. The
grant of authority to ban is stated in such arbitrary terms that court
intervention is unlikely. Israeli courts have steadfastly declined to
investigate the merits of decisions under the Defence (Emergency)
Regulations 1945.[216] The principles of procedural justice are also nullified
since a declaration of unlawfulness is a unilateral and arbitrary official
act. The only thing that can be said in favour of banning by declaration is
that it is very rarely used. There have been three bannings in Israel

---

[207] Regulation 85(1).
[208] Ibid.
[209] Regulation 85(2).
[210] Sections 2, 3 and 4.
[211] Section 1.
[212] Section 8. There are also presumptions as to membership of an organisation that is
terrorist: s 9.
[213] Section 5.
[214] Ibid.
[215] It does not seem possible to limit this power by reference to the grounds upon which
organisations are automatically unlawful since it was meant to be an alternative to the
automatic banning procedure.
[216] See the authorities cited in n 93 above and the case of *Alyubi v Minister of Defence* 1950 4
PD 220.

proper—the El Ard movement in 1965, the Arab Congress in Nazareth in 1980 and the National Co-ordinating Committee in 1981.[217] The process of automatic unlawfulness coincides more closely with the rule of law. The statutory criteria are specified, although some are rather broad and vague;[218] the courts retain control over prosecutions for managing, belonging to or supporting the organisation and this includes the determination of whether it is unlawful according to the prescribed criteria; and, finally the court procedures, although modified by some excessively broad statutory presumptions, are in accordance with normal trial procedures.[219]

The banning process in all three societies is characterised by significant departures from the principles of the rule of law. The position is least disturbing in Northern Ireland where banning is limited to the real terror groups that operate in that society. The same is true of the organisations banned in Great Britain. In both instances, bans have been imposed with restraint because they are the responsibility of a representative Parliament which is sharply conscious of the need to preserve freedom of expression and association. Though few organisations have been banned in Israel, proscription there has more of a political flavour and has been used to counter the growth of Arab nationalism. The banning process in Israel violates all the requirements of the rule of law. In South Africa the proscription of organisations has been both indiscriminate and politically based. Over thirty organisations remain banned at present and of these most were manifestly not terror groups at the time of their proscription. The characteristic that is almost universally present in the banning of organisations in South Africa is that they were effective anti-apartheid groups operating in the extra-parliamentary arena of politics. This appears to be true also of the latest banning imposed on the Congress of South African Students (COSAS)[220] which appears to have organised opposition to official education policy and practices for black students by means which included boycotts and demonstrations but not violence or terror. We may conclude that the banning of organisations in South Africa has gravely prejudiced the basic rights of association and expression and that it undermines the principles of the rule of law.

The Banning of Individuals

The process for banning individuals violates the legality principle in the same way as ministerial proscriptions of organisations. In brief, the criteria for banning an individual are broad and unspecific (activities which endanger the security of the state or the maintenance of law and order), the possibility of court intervention is negligible (because of the current judicial attitude to subjective discretion clauses), and the

[217] This was confirmed to me in letters from the Ministry of Justice dated 26 June and 22 November 1984.
[218] For example, the criterion of bringing the government into hatred or contempt or of inciting disaffection against it, in reg 85(1) of the Defence (Emergency) Regulations 1945.
[219] Military courts have concurrent jurisdiction with the ordinary courts over offences created by reg 85(1) and trials before military courts do not accord with rule-of-law requirements.
[220] COSAS was banned on 28 August 1985 by GN No R1977 (*GG* 9914 of 28 August 1985).

procedure for reviewing banning orders is ineffective mainly because the Chief Justice, to whom the matter will be referred when a review board disagrees with the minister's decision, has a strictly circumscribed power to interfere. The case of *Nkondo & Gumede v Minister of Law and Order*[221] has introduced an important due process element into the banning procedure since, in terms of that decision, meaningful reasons will in future have to be given for banning an individual. Past banning orders which were not accompanied by a proper statement of reasons appear to be invalid. Nevertheless, the due process violations remain disturbing despite the improvement just mentioned and the possibility of a court reviewing the grounds for a banning order is remote.

The power to ban individuals is another of the dubious blessings conferred upon Israel by the British under the Defence (Emergency) Regulations 1945 and most regrettably accepted by the state of Israel as a necessary measure for dealing with subversion. Banning orders in Israel may take the form of a restriction order[222] or a police supervision order[223] issued by a military commander. Under a restriction order a person may be excluded from specified areas, required to notify the authorities of his movements, prohibited from possessing or using specified articles and subjected to specified restrictions in respect of his employment or business, his association or communication with other persons or his freedom of expression. Under a police supervision order a person may be required to reside in a particular area, not to leave his town or village without written authority, to report to the police when called upon to do so and to remain indoors at night. Extensive inroads into personal freedom and basic rights are made possible under restriction or police supervision orders.

Military commanders are empowered to issue an order of either kind if of the opinion that it is necessary or expedient for securing public safety, the defence of the state, the maintenance of public order or the suppression of mutiny, rebellion or riot.[224] The statutory criteria are broad and, in some instances, vague and imprecise. The courts have been of no assistance in lending precision to the loose language of the legislation. In the leading case of *Alyubi v Minister of Defence*[225] the court stated that its jurisdiction in respect of restriction and police supervision orders was limited 'to examining whether the authority exceeded its power under the law by virtue of which it was empowered to act, if the said authority paid attention to the factors stated in the same law, and whether the authority acted in good faith'. The court specifically declared that it 'will not scrutinise the reasons prompting the competent authority to issue the given order'. However, while the Israeli courts will not pronounce on the substantive grounds for a banning order, there is one

---

[221] 1986 (2) SA 756 (A).
[222] Under reg 109.
[223] Under reg 110.
[224] Regulation 108.
[225] (1950) 4 PD 220, 227. In a later judgment, however, that court did declare that it would examine the exercise of the banning power with due diligence and that it 'no longer uses the self-restraint and self-limitation which characterised the parallel English judgments examining the exercise of similar powers in England': *Sallah Baraaseh v OC Central Command* 1 Sup Ct cases 36 IV 242, 251 (1981).

extremely important function which they do exercise and which distinguishes their involvement in banning from the practice of the South African judiciary. The judiciary has the power in Israel to make the final decision on whether information which the authorities claim to be privileged should be withheld on that account from the court and the litigants. It has exercised this power in reviewing restriction orders and in one case reported on by Amnesty International the court, having examined the secret information relied upon by the military authorities in imposing a ban, ordered 90 % of it to be released to the restricted person and his lawyer.[226] The court itself is entitled to see all the information on which the authorities rely. The knowledge that restriction and police supervision orders may be challenged, and that the evidence supporting them may be examined and even released by the courts, acts as a powerful inhibiting factor on the authorities. The attorney-general who acts for the military authorities when restriction orders are challenged will not support poor cases;[227] and legal challenge to banning orders has often led to their non-renewal.[228] From a procedural justice point of view, court supervision of banning powers in Israel is more acceptable than in South Africa. In practice, banning orders in Israel limit mainly freedom of movement and do not subject the victim to the civil death that is characteristic of bans in South Africa. On the other hand, audi alteram partem (the duty to afford a hearing) does not apply prior to the issue of orders either in Israel or in South Africa.

There is no procedure comparable to individual banning orders in Northern Ireland but exclusion orders might be said to have a remote resemblance to them. Exclusion has been described as 'a system of internal exile by executive order';[229] but exclusion orders do not have an exclusively internal application since they can be used to exclude persons who are not British citizens from the United Kingdom. The system of exclusion has been used mainly to exile persons of Northern Ireland origin from Great Britain. The power to issue an exclusion order is vested in the Secretary of State who must be 'satisfied' that the person to be excluded has been concerned in acts of terrorism designed to influence public opinion or government policy with respect to affairs in Northern Ireland.[230] Though the grounds for exclusion are stated with reasonable clarity, the process is an administrative one which the courts are unlikely to review on the merits.[231] There is an internal review procedure which entitles the excluded person to make representations to an adviser appointed by the Secretary of State and where practicable to have a personal interview with the adviser.[232] Adherence to due process requirements is clearly minimal under this review procedure. The person affected is not entitled to a statement of the case upon which his exclusion

[226] *Amnesty International Report* dated 1 February 1983.
[227] This was emphatically stated to be the position in an interview with the Deputy Attorney-General in June 1984.
[228] Information supplied by Ms Ruth Gavison, Faculty of Law, University of Jerusalem.
[229] Patricia Hewitt op cit 168.
[230] Part II of the Prevention of Terrorism (Temporary Provisions) Act 1984, especially ss 3, 4, 5 and 6.
[231] See David Bonner op cit 192.
[232] Section 7.

is based; the 'hearing' conducted by the adviser is no more than an informal interview; and, in any event, the Secretary of State is not required to follow the recommendation of the adviser.

Because the exclusion power may result in drastic curbs on the civil liberties of British subjects (particularly on freedom of movement) and because deviations from procedural justice in the exercise of that power are substantial, it is the most heavily criticised provision of the Act. The Jellicoe Committee, which recommended its retention with important modifications, was frank on the Draconian nature of the power and declared that it affected civil liberties more severely than any other power under the Act; and that the departure from the normal criminal process was more extensive than in the exercise of any other powers permitted by the legislation.[233] The committee recommended the retention of the power to exclude with reluctance on the ground that it had been effective in the fight against terrorists and their support groups. The Jellicoe Committee, in line with the thinking of the earlier Gardiner Report, also decided that the introduction of more due process elements into the review procedure 'would in practice constitute no more than a parody of due legal process and would thus contribute to a loss of public confidence in the legal system'.[234] This is the most questionable of the committee's recommendations and is best answered by the following comments of Professor Harry Street:

> 'I do not accept the unshakeable view of the Administration that no issue of security is ever to be justiciable in Britain, that legal representation must always be denied if the Administration incants the magic words "national security"—in short that security is inconsistent with anything that constitutes a fair hearing. I will not accept the conclusion that what the United States does as of course is impossible in this country.'[235]

This refreshingly robust view is relevant to all the forms of banning discussed in this chapter.

The Banning of Meetings

The most extensive controls in South Africa over meetings, processions and assemblies are in the Internal Security Act of 1982[236] which authorises both the minister and a magistrate to impose bans. In the case of ministerial bans, the Act drives the proverbial coach and horses through the rule of law. The grounds on which the minister may act are nebulously stated—he must deem it necessary or expedient to act in the interests of state security, the maintenance of public peace or order or the prevention of inter-group hostility. The wording of the Act seems designed to ensure that the courts have no power to review the grounds upon which a ban is imposed,[237] and the procedure by which the order is made is simply one of ministerial fiat. Not a single principle or procedure of the

---

[233] Jellicoe Report para 193.
[234] Jellicoe Report para 193.
[235] Harry Street 'The Prevention of Terrorism (Temporary Provisions) Act 1974' 1975 *Criminal Law Rev* 192, 196.
[236] See chapter 8 above for a discussion of these controls.
[237] Even the more enlightened and activist Natal court has baulked at the idea of controlling the minister's power: *Metal and Allied Workers Union v Castell NO* 1985 (2) SA 280 (D) 283–4.

rule of law is left intact by this provision for ministerial banning. This is all the more alarming because there is no limit on the scope of the minister's power and he is virtually authorised to abolish the right of assembly on public and private premises in South Africa.

At the magisterial level, the banning power is more circumscribed. The magistrate may act only if he has reason to apprehend that the public peace will be endangered by the meeting or assembly in question. In this instance the basis for the prohibition is specified with reasonable clarity. However, while some courts have been prepared to review the magistrate's reasons for acting, others have decided that a bona fide decision by the magistrate made without ulterior purpose is not subject to challenge in the courts. If this second approach is adopted by the Appellate Division, rule-of-law controls will in practice fall away even in respect of magisterial bans. While magistrates can ban only in their own districts, this absence of external control would be disturbing in view of the frequency of such bans in all the metropolitan areas of the Republic. Magistrates do not enjoy independent status and are civil servants subject to instructions from the government.

Neither in Northern Ireland nor in Israel is there power to abrogate the citizens' right of assembly at the stroke of an official pen. In Northern Ireland there are some limited provisions touching the right of assembly. If a senior military or police officer is of the opinion that any assembly of three or more persons may lead to a breach of the peace or to public disorder, or that it may make undue demands upon the security forces, that officer or any member of the force acting on his instructions may order the assembly to disperse.[238] A person who fails to disperse or thereafter joins the assembly is guilty of a criminal offence.[239] A senior police officer who forms the opinion that a funeral may have the same specified results (breach of the peace, public disorder or undue demands on the security forces) may impose conditions on the conduct of the funeral, including conditions prescribing its route, prohibiting it from entering certain places and requiring it to travel in vehicles.[240] In both instances, the grounds upon which the officer may act are specified with satisfactory precision and a person charged before a court with the offence of failing to disperse or of breaching prescribed conditions relating to funerals is entitled to raise as a defence the absence of any grounds for the dispersal order or the imposition of conditions. Judge Baker noted in his report that there had been no prosecutions under the first provision in recent times but supported its retention.[241] One further measure in Northern Ireland requires comment. Sectarian marches and counter-marches have long been a source of provocation and disorder in that country. There is accordingly legal provision[242] for controlling the routes of marches or for the outright banning of such marches. Even though the authorities are given wide powers over marches by this law, a critical

---

[238] Section 24(1) of the Northern Ireland (Emergency Provisions) Act 1978.

[239] Section 24(2). The penalties are imprisonment for not exceeding 6 months or a fine of not exceeding £400.

[240] Regulation 4, Schedule 2 of the Act. The penalty for non-compliance is again imprisonment of up to 6 months or a fine of up to £400: s 27(2) and (3).

[241] Baker Report, para 434.

[242] The Public Order Acts (NI) 1951–1971.

study of security policy in Northern Ireland does not condemn the power itself but rather the partisan manner in which it has been used.[243] We may conclude that intrusions into the right of assembly in Northern Ireland are limited and closely tailored to the actual requirements of security.

In Israel, district police commanders are given limited power to control meetings or processions within their districts.[244] For purposes of this law, a meeting must consist of fifty or more persons assembled to hear a speech or address on any topic of political interest, or to discuss any such topic.[245] A procession must also consist of fifty or more persons but it need not be one concerned with a political topic.[246] If a district police commander is of the opinion that the maintenance of public order or public security so requires, he may order persons intending to convene, organise or hold a meeting or procession to apply to the District Commissioner, not less than five days (or such other period as may be specified) before the proposed date of the meeting or procession, for a licence.[247] Unlicensed meetings are deemed to be unlawful assemblies and it is an offence to take part therein.[248] Israeli courts have not been deterred by the subjective flavour of the empowering language from investigating bans on an objective basis[249] and the power to ban meetings is therefore more limited and less arbitrary than in South Africa.

Miscellaneous Security Measures and the Rule of Law

Deviations from the principles and procedures of the rule of law have been examined so far in relation to security crimes, detention and banning. It would be tedious to extend this analysis to each and every provision of security legislation. In this section the emphasis will be on the more flagrant violations of the rule of law by other provisions of security legislation, with occasional reference to helpful material from foreign countries.

I Speech and Information

Security legislation touching upon speech and information exemplifies all three of the basic types of rule-of-law violation—lack of clear standards, absence of independent control and procedural injustice. We deal with each in turn.

Clear standards. The power of the Minister of Law and Order to make the registration of a newspaper conditional on a forfeitable deposit of up to R40 000 may be invoked when the minister forms the opinion that it might become necessary to ban the newspaper in the future.[250] The grounds for banning a newspaper are both broad and vague (in brief, an apprehension of prejudice to state security or law and order or a belief that the newspaper is furthering any of the objects of communism or

---

[243] Boyle, Hadden and Hillyard *Law and State: The Case of Northern Ireland* 29.
[244] Police Ordinance (New Version) 5731—1971.
[245] Section 83.
[246] Ibid.
[247] Section 85.
[248] Section 89.
[249] *Sa'ar v The Minister of Interior and Police* (1980) (II) 34 PD 169. This judgment related to a similarly worded earlier provision and is reviewed in (1981) 16 *Israel Law Rev* 116.
[250] See chapter 9 above.

encouraging inter-group hostility) and it follows that the power to demand a deposit is conditioned upon criteria that are about as clear as mud. Restrictions on speech and information under the Defence Act of 1957 and the Protection of Information Act of 1982[251] are characterised by overbreadth and imprecision. The Defence Act, for example, punishes the publication of statements, comments or rumours calculated to embarrass the government in its foreign relations or to alarm or depress members of the public. This puts a critic or commentator at risk of criminal punishment for the failure to appreciate what the law has deliberately made obscure. The range of information which it is illegal to communicate under the Protection of Information Act is boundless. Excessive breadth is a special class of vagueness since it is impossible to predict when the authorities will prosecute for an offence that has universal coverage.

External control. The possibility of independent court supervision and control is either remote or non-existent in a number of instances. When the Minister of Law and Order makes registration of a newspaper conditional on a deposit, he acts under a power that appears to be quite arbitrary. He has a subjective power of decision-making which is beyond court challenge unless the newspaper proprietor concerned achieves the impossible and obtains proof that the minister acted dishonestly or for improper considerations. Court intervention is clearly a theoretical possibility, not an actual one. Censorship decisions under the Publications Act of 1974[252] are made by government-appointed committees and boards and the possibility of a more objective assessment by the judiciary is precluded except on grounds of procedural irregularity. Where a decision to withhold information from the courts is taken on the ground that the information is privileged for national security reasons, court jurisdiction is absolutely excluded and the executive decision is final and binding.[253] This absolute power to deny the court and the litigant relevant information has ramifications throughout the area of state security. It gives executive officials absolute and unsupervised authority to blanket security-law decision-making under total secrecy.

Procedural justice. In some instances official action may be taken without any adherence whatever to the requirements of procedural justice. This appears to be the case where the minister demands a deposit prior to registration of a newspaper. He is not required to disclose his reasons or to afford a hearing. In other cases procedural due process is merely modified. In the area of speech and information, the most serious modifications are those in which the accused charged with a crime is required to disprove elements of the crime in order to avoid conviction. Examples of this shifting of the onus are the obligation on the accused to prove that reasonable steps were taken to verify the accuracy of material published about the police and prisons departments[254] and some very broad presumptions of guilt, which the accused must displace, under the Protection of Information Act of 1982.[255]

---

[251] See chapter 9 above.   [252] See chapter 8 above.   [253] See chapter 9 above.
[254] As shown in chapter 9 above, the court has cast an unnecessarily heavy burden on the accused.
[255] See chapter 9 above.

Commentary and comparisons. There is no system of political censorship in Northern Ireland but in Israel the Defence (Emergency) Regulations of 1945 make provision for extensive censorship by the security authorities. These provisions include the power to prohibit the publication of material regarded as prejudicial to public safety and order, control over the importation of publications, and a prohibition on the printing and publishing of newspapers without the authority of a permit.[256] In general, there are no clear statutory guidelines for the exercise of this power by the censor and the possibility of intervention by the courts is remote in the extreme.[257] Censorship law in Israel and the rule of law are not reconcilable. However, Professor Amos Shapira has said that the gap between the enacted law and the law in action is conspicuously wide in the field of security censorship and that military censorship has been 'superseded by the realities of Israeli democracy'.[258] In a general study of secrecy in Israel, Dina Goren concluded that 'despite the longevity of military censorship in Israel, it has not had a decisive impact on the reporting of security information in the press'.[259] These views are substantially confirmed in a recent evaluation of press freedom in Israel, subject to some reservations about political censorship applied to Arab newspapers in East Jerusalem and the West Bank.[260] Though it appears to be true that the alarming potential of the Defence (Emergency) Regulations for suppressing free discussion about political and security matters has never been realised, the freedom that exists is a consequence of consensus and accommodation rather than the constraints of law.

In 1968 Israel took a step of crucial importance to the re-establishment of the rule of law in the security field. By the enactment of the Evidence (Amendment) Law 1968 the Israeli judiciary was vested with the final decision as to whether a minister could withhold from the court information alleged to be privileged from disclosure.[261] The court has the power to overrule a minister even when he declares that the disclosure of information will prejudice state security. South African experience has demonstrated that the court's supervisory function, in cases where it still exists, is gravely impaired by inability to examine the state case for the imposition of security restrictions. Absolute executive power to withhold the relevant information undermines the central rule-of-law requirement of external control over decisions affecting the liberty of the subject. The Israeli reform is one that could be followed in South Africa without jeopardising important state secrets since there is no reason to believe that our judges cannot act responsibly in protecting genuinely sensitive information.

[256] Regulations 86–101 of the Defence (Emergency) Regulations 1945.
[257] In the case of *El-Asad v The Minister of the Interior* (1980) 34 (1) PD 505 the court did set aside the decision of a District Commissioner to refuse a permit for the publication of a newspaper but it did so only because the District Commissioner, while not legally obliged to do so, volunteered the information on which he had acted which the court found to be inadequate.
[258] Amos Shapira loc cit.
[259] Dina Goren *Secrecy and the Right to Know* (Turtledove Publishing, Israel 1979) 130.
[260] Ze'ev Chafets, 'Press and Government in Israel' (1984) 14 *Israel Year Book on Human Rights* 134.
[261] The provision now appears in the Evidence Ordinance (New version) 5731—1971: see Harold Rudolph, op cit 85, 90 and 117.

The wide-ranging protection of official secrets is an English institution which was transmitted as a rather dubious inheritance to many of the British colonies. While several of the former colonies (for example, Canada, Australia and New Zealand) have modified the range of official secrets legislation by introducing access to information measures, attempts to narrow the Official Secrets Acts in the mother country, and to introduce a positive right to information, have been conspicuous by their failure. As a result, the broad restrictions on the communication of information that are found in the Official Secrets Acts are operative also in Northern Ireland. The fact that a comprehensive study of the maintenance of security in Northern Ireland makes no reference to the Official Secrets Acts[262] suggests that they have not been significant in security operations there. Nevertheless, as the McDonald Commission in Canada has said, Acts of this nature are an anachronism by any standard and are particularly objectionable on account of their catch-all quality.[263] It is the catch-all nature of official secrets legislation which violates the rule-of-law requirement of clear criteria for guilt under the criminal law.

In Israel, the British mandatory authority enacted official secrets legislation along the lines of the English legislation in 1932. This legislation has been replaced and the latest consolidation of penal law in Israel contains measures on espionage and official secrets that are more limited in scope and more consonant with democracy and the rule of law than the British model.[264] The provisions on official secrets[265] deal mainly with disclosures by public servants and government contractors and do not include a general prohibition on the disclosure of official information.

II *Surveillance, Search and Seizure*

The South African laws, such as they are, that regulate the interception of telephonic communications and the use of bugging devices, were examined earlier and found to be hopelessly inadequate.[266] The statutory ground for the interception of telephonic communications is the belief that the maintenance of security requires such action, and the relevant legislation lacks any definition of security or any provision for external supervision over the invocation of the power to order an interception. Bugging is widely practised but almost totally unregulated. There is no statutory law which prescribes criteria or requires external control. Interception and bugging are both insidious threats to freedom but neither is subject to rule-of-law control in South Africa. Search and seizure is regulated by statute, and as we have already noted,[267] the presence of a broad power to enter premises and investigate apprehended threats to security, and also of numerous statutes authorising warrantless searches, mars the otherwise reasonable state of the law on this question. The problem, once again, is that the existence of almost limitless security

---

[262] Boyle, Hadden and Hillyard *Law and State: The Case of Northern Ireland* do not anywhere refer to the Acts.

[263] *Freedom and Security Under Law: Commission of Enquiry Concerning Certain Activities of the Royal Canadian Mounted Police* (Supply and Services, Ottawa, Canada 1981) Second Report, vol 2 99 et seq. (referred to below as the McDonald Report).

[264] Chapter 7 of the Penal Law 5737—1977.   [265] Sections 117–120.

[266] See chapter 10 above.

[267] See chapter 10 above.

crimes provides a readily available justification for entering premises on the basis that the persons present there are endangering state security or law and order; and because an apprehension of such dangers can so easily be formed, the statute in effect provides no clear guidelines for the right to invade private property. To sum up, surveillance and search and seizure practices in South Africa violate the rule of law either because the law provides no criteria for official action or because it fails to require external control of such action. In some instances both are lacking.

Though it may not be possible to subject powers of surveillance, search and seizure to full rule-of-law control, the McDonald Commission in Canada has shown that a substantial adherence to the requirements of legality is possible and consistent with the maintenance of security. That Commission's report,[268] and the legislation that has been enacted in response to it,[269] demonstrate that the security interests which the government seeks to protect by means of these powers may be defined with reasonable precision and that external judicial control is feasible if complete adherence to procedural due process is not demanded.[270] Canadian law now subjects the interception of communications (including bugging) and search and seizure operations for national security reasons[271] to a system of judicial control. The main features of this system, which was given statutory expression in the Canadian Security Intelligence Service Act of 1984, may be summarised as follows:

(a) The interception of a communication (broadly defined to include bugging) or the entry into premises for purposes of searching for and obtaining information, requires a warrant issued by a judge of the federal court.[272]

(b) An application for a warrant must be accompanied by an affidavit setting out the facts relied upon to justify the investigation of a threat to the security of Canada and deposing that other investigative procedures have failed, are unlikely to succeed or cannot be employed for reasons of urgency.[273]

(c) The judge, who hears the application in private,[274] may issue a warrant to investigate a security threat by means of interception or entry into premises, for a period not exceeding sixty days.[275] Renewals may be granted by the judge if he is satisfied by application on oath that the statutory grounds for its issue are still present.[276]

---

[268] McDonald Report vol 1 Part V Chapter IV.

[269] The Canadian Security Intelligence Service Act of 1984. This Act does not follow the McDonald Report to the letter and permits surveillance on somewhat wider grounds than the report recommended.

[270] For example, a judicial order for the interception of communications cannot be preceded by a full hearing without frustrating the entire purpose of the interception. Moreover, security interests clearly require in camera decisions by the courts on requests for interception orders.

[271] When such activities are planned for purposes of criminal investigation, judicial authorisation is required by the Canadian Criminal Code.

[272] The Canadian Security Intelligence Service Act of 1984, s 21.

[273] Ibid.

[274] Section 27.

[275] Section 21(3). Warrants authorising the investigation of non-Canadian citizens for counter-intelligence or like purposes may be issued for one year.

[276] Section 22.

(d) A warrant may be issued on two grounds only: the investigation of a
threat to the security of Canada or the collection of intelligence or
information relating to foreign states or non-Canadian citizens or
residents.[277] A threat to the security of Canada is defined so as to
encompass espionage or sabotage, foreign-influenced activities that
are clandestine or deceptive and detrimental to Canadian interests,
activities that involve the use or threat of serious acts of violence for
achieving a political objective and activities aimed at the destruction
or overthrow by violence of the constitutionally established system of
government in Canada.[278]

The rule-of-law gains achieved by this system appear to be impressive.
The most significant is the introduction of independent judicial control
over the clandestine and intrusive activities of the security authorities.
This reform makes Canada one of the few countries to allow the judiciary
to supervise and control mail interception, bugging, telephone tapping
and search and seizure operations by the security authorities. Judicial
control, moreover, is not of a 'lawless' nature—it functions according to
statutory criteria which govern all the activities of the security service and
constitute its legal mandate. The effect of the statutorily imposed criteria
is to limit the security authorities to the investigation of espionage,
sabotage, foreign intelligence activities, political terrorism and subversion
and to place lawful opposition, protest and dissent beyond their
jurisdiction.[279] In so far as these criteria refer to security crimes (for
example espionage and sabotage) it is relevant that such crimes have a
limited reach in Canada and that some of them are in the process of being
narrowed even further.[280] We may conclude that the statutory mandate of
the security authorities in Canada is reasonably narrow and reasonably
clear,[281] and that significant aspects of its operations are now subject to
independent control.

Prior to 1985, the interception of postal and telephonic communications
in the United Kingdom was 'governed by administrative practices rather
than by express legal rules'.[282] Interception took place under warrant
from the Home Secretary and the issue of such warrants, while subject to
a number of internal checks, was regulated neither by precise legal
standards nor by independent external control. These practices were
attacked unsuccessfully before a domestic forum in *Malone v Commissioner
of Police (No 2)*[283] and later before the European court which vindicated
the applicant's challenge in *Malone v United Kingdom*.[284] In declaring the

---

[277] Section 21 read with s 16.
[278] This is a summary of the definition of 'threats to the security of Canada' in s 2.
[279] See J LL J Edwards 'The Canadian Security Intelligence Act 1984: A Canadian
Appraisal' (1985) 5 *Oxford Journal of Legal Studies* 143.
[280] The McDonald Commission recommended a substantial narrowing of the crime of
espionage: McDonald Report vol 2 939. This is presently being undertaken by a criminal-
law revision committee.
[281] This opinion is not shared by all informed Canadians. Mr Alan Borovoy, director of
the Canadian Civil Liberties Association, and Professor Michael Mandel of the Osgoode
Hall School of Law, both expressed to me the view that the statutory criteria are too wide
and that intrusive techniques of surveillance should be used only to investigate actual crime.
[282] Istvan Pogany 'Telephone Tapping and the European Convention on Human
Rights—I' (1984) 134 *New Law Journal* 175.
[283] [1979] 2 All ER 620 (Ch).   [284] (1985) 25 *European Human Rights Reports* 14.

warrant procedure to be contrary to certain articles of the European
Convention on Human Rights, the European court identified the two
basic rule-of-law requirements to which the domestic law should conform.
Declaring that 'it would be contrary to the rule of law for the legal
discretion granted to the executive to be expressed in terms of an
unfettered power', the court held that 'the law must indicate the scope of
any such discretion conferred on the competent authorities and the
manner of its exercise with sufficient clarity' and that the individual
affected by it should be afforded 'adequate protection against arbitrary
interference'.[285] Following the European court judgment in *Malone*, the
British Parliament passed the Interception of Communications Act 1985.
This Act deals only with the interception of communications through a
postal or telecommunications system and other forms of surveillance
(such as bugging) are not covered.[286] It does require a warrant for
interceptions but this will be issued by the Secretary of State.[287] The
Canadian model of external judicial control has been rejected and
traditional British repugnance for court involvement in security matters
reaffirmed. One of the grounds on which a warrant may be issued by the
Secretary of State is described simply as 'the interests of national
security'[288] without any further specification of those interests as in the
Canadian legislation. On the positive side the Act does establish a
tribunal to which individuals may complain if they believe that an
unjustified interception has taken place and the tribunal has the power to
order remedial action.[289] However, the effectiveness of the tribunal for the
protection of individual rights is seriously in doubt.[290] The rule-of-law
achievements of the British legislation appear to be limited.

Broad powers of entry, search and seizure for security purposes have
been enacted in Northern Ireland and Israel. The legislation applicable in
Northern Ireland authorises designated security officers to enter premises
for the specific purposes of searching for munitions, explosives and
transmitters[291] and of rescuing persons who may be detained in
circumstances that endanger life.[292] These limited search powers are
complemented by one which empowers any member of the armed forces
or any constable, if he is authorised to do so by or on behalf of the
Secretary of State or if he considers it necessary in the course of operations
for the preservation of peace or the maintenance of order, to enter any
premises whatsoever.[293] This power is of a general nature, unconfined by
narrowing criteria, expressed in subjective language and unreviewable by
the courts except on very limited grounds. Nevertheless, the Baker
Committee received no representations for its repeal or modification[294]
and it accordingly appears that the general power of entry is being used

[285] At 41. The court did not rule on the applicant's contention that United Kingdom law
provided him with no adequate domestic remedy for breaches of his rights.
[286] Ian J Lloyd 'The Interception of Communications Act 1985' (1986) 49 *MLR* 86, 93.
[287] Section 2.
[288] Ibid.
[289] Section 7.
[290] Ian Leigh 'A Tappers' Charter?' 1986 *Public Law* 8.
[291] Sections 15 and 16 of the Northern Ireland (Emergency Provisions) Act 1978.
[292] Section 17.
[293] Section 19.
[294] Baker Report para 397.

with restraint.[295] In Israel, the Defence (Emergency) Regulations of 1945 empower designated military or police officers to enter premises and conduct searches if there is reason to suspect that the premises are being used, or have been used, for purposes prejudicial to public safety, the maintenance of order, the defence of the country or in connection with inciting rebellion or riot.[296] The exercise of this broad power is premised upon a 'reason to suspect' certain activities and this language appears to make it subject to review before the courts. In both Northern Ireland and Israel, the more general powers of entry, search and seizure are too broad to measure up to rule-of-law requirements.

III *Emergency legislation*

There is something decidedly artificial about discussing emergency legislation and the rule of law in South Africa. 'Ordinary' and permanent legislation has already brought about a ninety-per-cent destruction of the rule of law and put the country into a permanent state of emergency. When, on top of this, an emergency is declared under the Public Safety Act of 1953,[297] the tattered remnants of the rule of law are stripped away for the duration of the crisis. Under the 1985 emergency, the security authorities assumed a number of additional powers, in particular, the power to detain with greater freedom on a mass scale, to impose curfews and drastic limitations on movement, and generally to act as they wished without being answerable to the courts for anything that could not be proved to have been done mala fide.[298] This last power, brought into effect by the indemnity provision of the regulations, has enabled the police and military authorities, in the language of the notorious instruction sent to the Port Elizabeth police prior to Uitenhage, to 'eliminate' the law-and-order troublemakers. When the law enables the security forces to mete out their own version of street justice, it seems bizarre to talk about the requirements of the rule of law.

Under the nation-wide emergency declared on 12 June 1986, the State President promulgated regulations which purported to strip away the last vestiges of security force legal and public accountability that remained under the previous emergency. In a regulation subsequently held to be partly invalid, the publication of subversive statements was prohibited, such statements including those that are expressed to one other person and have the effect of causing hostility towards 'any section of the public or person or category of persons' or of 'weakening or undermining the confidence of the public or any section of the public in the termination of the state of emergency'.[299] Other regulations[300] imposed a system of total

---

[295] The frequency of house searches has declined dramatically since the beginning of the current emergency in Northern Ireland: Boyle, Hadden and Hillyard *Ten Years On in Northern Ireland: The Legal Control of Political Violence* 27–8.

[296] Regulation 75. Entry and search is also permitted if an offender against the regulations, or goods liable to seizure, are suspected to be in the premises.

[297] As happened on 21 July 1985 and again on 12 June 1986.

[298] See chapter 11 above for a more detailed description of the 1985 emergency regulations.

[299] Definition of 'subversive statement' in reg 1 of the regulations published in Proclamation No R109 (*Reg Gaz* No 3964 of 12 June 1986). These particular aspects of the definition were struck down by the Natal Supreme Court on 16 July 1986.

[300] Particularly, regs 7(1)(c), 7(3), 9, 11 and 12.

censorship over the emergency, including the conduct of the security forces. Most newspapers published little more than the 'ministry of truth' announcements that came from official sources. The methods used by the security forces thereafter ceased to be part of public knowledge but occasional private reports and court judgments (such as the one ordering the release of a nun from a detention that took place when she attempted to prevent a member of the security forces from assaulting a young man) suggest that advantage is being taken of the charter for lawlessness and secrecy that is ironically known as emergency *law*. The Minister of Law and Order now has the power to declare emergencies on a local basis and to make regulations similar to those that were put into effect in the 1985 and 1986 emergencies.[301] The exercise of his power will signal the final interment of the principle of government under law in South Africa.

In the free countries of the West, emergencies are understood to be short-term dictatorships which free the authorities of some of the restraints of the rule of law so as to enable them to deal with a temporary crisis.[302] These dictatorships are none the less *constitutional* dictatorships which operate *within a legal framework*, though it is one in which the constraints of law are considerably slackened. In its recent investigation of emergency powers in Canada, the McDonald Committee underlined the need when drafting emergency regulations 'to ensure that proper attention will be paid to civil liberties'[303] and stressed that certain of the requirements of legality were so fundamental that they should not be withdrawn even during emergency rule. It recommended, for example, that detentions should not be of indefinite duration and that all detentions should be subject to review board control.[304]

A modern development that has posed the most serious contemporary threat to the rule of law is that of the regularly extended emergency. Emergency powers of some kind or another have been in operation in Northern Ireland for at least as long as living memory; and Israel has operated under a declaration of emergency since it became an independent state in 1948. The longer the emergency lasts, the more important it becomes to limit infractions into the rule of law. This lesson has been most clearly drawn by Professor A Rubinstein in his discussion of the Israeli situation:

'Because Israelis believe that this war or semi-war situation is not a short-term affair, they think that the country cannot afford the excesses of other countries in time of war. In other words, because we perceive our semi-war situation as a permanent feature of our national life, we have had to regulate, modify, and moderate the measures that would otherwise have been justified by the grave emergency situation.'[305]

In accordance with this line of thinking, Israel has subjected preventive detention to mandatory court control and made the judges the final

[301] Section 5A of the Public Safety Act 3 of 1953 introduced by s 4 of the Public Safety Amendment Act 67 of 1986.
[302] Clinton L Rossiter *Constitutional Dictatorship: Crisis Government in Modern Democracies* (Princeton Univ Press, 1948).
[303] McDonald Report vol II 922.   [304] McDonald Report vol II 927 & 934.
[305] Amnon Rubinstein 'State Security and Human Rights: The Israeli Experience' in *Human Rights: The Cape Town Conference* eds C. Forsyth and J. E. Schiller (Juta & Co, Cape Town 1979) 138.

arbiters of the right of the state to withhold information on the ground that it is privileged. In Northern Ireland, preventive detention has been allowed to lapse since 1975 and the current policy, expressed in legislation, is to deal with terrorism through the regular processes of the law. While in these two countries there is a clear movement towards the restoration of the rule of law, recent South African measures signify its liquidation.

The combination in South Africa of permanent and temporary emergency measures is therefore fatal to the rule of law in any meaningful sense. It is also politically foolish. One of the reasons for retaining some rule-of-law restraints under emergency government is to limit the social damage of security operations. The indiscriminate use of police power during the 1985 and 1986 emergencies has achieved the opposite by fuelling conflicts, increasing grievances and resentments, and broadening the already dangerous gulf between the security forces and the black people of South Africa. Even if order is restored in the short term, the chances of future peace and accommodation have been gravely harmed by making security authorities in South Africa unaccountable to the law.

The Security System and the Rule of Law—General Conclusions

The South African security system has brought about the root-and-branch elimination of the rule of law; but this rather obvious conclusion is not the only one yielded by the preceding analysis of security legislation according to the yardstick of legality. The analysis has also shown that in two other societies with comparable law and order problems, the violation of the principle of government under law is not nearly so complete. The security threats faced by Northern Ireland and Israel are more daunting in several respects than those experienced recently in South Africa. The terror groups operating in those two countries are superior in training and equipment, and more fanatical and ruthless in intent, than the resistance movement in South Africa. Until quite recently, the loss of life and property destruction caused by terrorists in Northern Ireland has been in excess of the corresponding damage inflicted by ANC terror groups and township rioters in South Africa.[306] Israel is surrounded by formidable enemies and has waged seven major wars against them. In countering these greater security threats, the authorities in Northern Ireland and Israel have shown more concern for the rule of law and have managed to preserve it to a higher degree than in South Africa. This is an important conclusion because it suggests that security imperatives alone have not required the destruction of rule-of-law standards in South Africa. As we shall see later, that destruction is due as much to the preservation of white power as it is to the maintenance of law and order.

The process of the legislative erosion of the rule of law has entailed the fearful corollary of the enthronement of the security authorities as a lawless power in the country. Lawlessness in all its forms is no doubt to be

---

[306] Approximately 2 500 persons have been killed in politically related acts of violence since 1971 in Northern Ireland. Only in 1985, with approximately 900 dead in South Africa, did the death rate assume proportions comparable to Northern Ireland. Of these, about half were killed by the security forces.

deplored; but there is nothing quite so corrupting as official lawlessness. When those who stand officially as the enforcers of the law may dispense with all its traditional constraints, it will not be long before others follow their example even to the extent of losing respect for, and understanding of, the principle of government under law. In this sense the security system has become a potent generator of the disorder it was ostensibly designed to eliminate.

The consequences of undermining legality and converting law into a naked instrument of power are likely to be tragic for all groups in South Africa, including the group responsible for that transformation. The danger of the perversion of legality has been dramatically illustrated in a country to the north of South Africa. The Ian Smith security machine, developed in Rhodesia in a futile attempt to secure white rule by freeing the security forces from legal accountability, has been gratefully accepted by the Mugabe government in 'liberated' Zimbabwe. Among the first victims of the new management of the Smith security machine were some white military officers who were detained without trial and tortured under laws which they had helped to enforce. Such ironic twists of fate are commonplace in history but the lesson which they teach—that freedom is dependent upon the maintenance of the rule of law—has still to be learned. Perhaps the finest dramatisation of that lesson is Robert Bolt's play *A Man For All Seasons* and particularly the following exchange in the play between Roper and More:

> Roper: 'I'd cut down every law in England to do that.'
> More: 'Oh? And when the last law was down, and the Devil turned round on you, where would you hide, Roper, the laws being flat?'

There is no place to hide in modern Zimbabwe for those who incur the displeasure of the Mugabe security forces who have recently enforced the Smith 'laws' without pity against Nkomo supporters. Similar treatment to that being inflicted now on the opponents of the Botha government lies in store for both black and white in any future South Africa with flattened laws. It follows that one of the highest priorities for reformers concerned with freedom and justice is the reconstruction of the rule-of-law state in this country.

CHAPTER 13

The Security System
—A Political Assessment

Democracy and the Rule of Law

The rule of law appears to be related to democracy in several ways. It is related positively as an institution designed to protect certain basic democratic rights of the citizen such as freedom of the person, of expression, of movement and assembly, and of association. The other side of this relationship, the negative aspect, is that the rule of law has always been understood as an institution which limits state power. The rule of law, as a 'weapon against the growth of state authoritarianism' and 'an inhibition on state power',[1] indirectly furthers the democratic style of the management of society. Another way in which the rule of law furthers democracy is 'to bridge the gap between the legal doctrine of parliamentary sovereignty and the political doctrine of the sovereignty of the people'.[2] It achieves this accommodation by requiring statutes to be interpreted wherever possible in accordance with 'general notions of fairness and justice . . . which are taken for granted in the community'.[3] It follows that every violation of the rule of law in South Africa has weakened the democratic elements in conflict resolution and taken the society a step nearer to a system of state absolutism.

Democracy has never achieved anything more than partial recognition in South Africa. The adoption of the Westminster system of government in the Cape Colony and Natal, and the subsequent acceptance of the Westminster style of government at the time of union, provided some justification for the title democracy. However, black participation in the Westminster system was at best nominal and was reduced and finally eliminated after union. The Republic of South Africa Constitution Act of 1983, while providing for the involvement of Indian and coloured persons in central decision-making, set the seal on the constitutional exclusion of blacks, with terrible consequences that are still visible almost daily in the townships of South Africa. Recent reform talk about black involvement at all levels of political decision-making has not been matched by any action, and in any event even the *talk* envisages little more than black membership of the President's Council and the creation of a politically impotent National Council, a body with disturbing similarities to the 'toy telephone' Native Representative Council that failed in the early Fifties. The denial to the black majority of the right to vote for members of, and

[1] Bob Fine *Democracy and the Rule of Law* (Pluto Press, London 1984) 9.
[2] T R S Allan 'Legislative Supremacy and the Rule of Law: Democracy and Constitutionalism' (1985) 44 *Cambridge Law Journal* 111, 129.
[3] At 130.

hold office in, the central institutions of government, is incompatible with all forms of democracy.

When the new constitution replaced the Westminster system with a presidential one, the greater part of government in the Westminster tradition had already been eroded. In Britain and those countries of the commonwealth where the tradition still survives, it operates in a context of civil rights, the rule of law and a parliamentary committee system which, although not comprising committees as vigorous as those of the United States congress, does moderate the executive dominance that is characteristic of two-party democracies. Because the Westminster system in South Africa was steadily drained of its contextual lifeblood, it became even within the limits of white politics one of 'unrestrained majoritarianism' without the compensation of the alternation of parties that is a feature of its operation elsewhere.[4] Repeated assaults on the rule of law and the associated liberties of person, speech, movement, assembly and association, reduced the extra-parliamentary side of democratic freedom to a state of extreme debilitation even for white voters. Extra-parliamentary organisation, association and dissent were seriously limited by detentions and bans of all kinds (bans of individuals, organisations, assemblies and publications) imposed by arbitrary executive decrees. The power of the executive grew ominously while that of Parliament and the people waned. As important aspects of democratic freedom for whites went by the board, the result of the destruction of the rule of law became catastrophic for blacks who, already deprived of formal participation in the political system, now lost the remaining freedoms that we associate with democracy. The outcome has been called a racial oligarchy[5] or alternatively a limited democracy for whites with political tutelage for blacks.[6]

The process by which civil rights have been weakened to the point of extinction has most commonly consisted in the transfer to executive officers of the power, virtually unrestrained by law, to withdraw or suspend their operation either generally or in relation to specific individuals or groups. Every one of the basic civil rights has been affected in this way. Freedom of the person ceased to exist when the minister was given unqualified power to detain. The banning of individuals nullified their freedom of movement, expression and association. The right of assembly has long been a civil liberty casualty by reason of the nationwide ban on almost all outdoor meetings and on many indoor ones as well. Freedom of association has suffered grievously by the banning of over thirty organisations, including the principal black political organisations. The executive withdrawal or suspension of basic rights is regulated neither by clear statutory guidelines nor by effective judicial supervision. This means that an executive officer, usually the Minister of Law and Order, is free to determine who may participate in the political process and thereby to alter the rules of the game to the advantage of his own

[4] L J Boulle *South Africa and the Consociational Option: A Constitutional Analysis* (Juta & Co Ltd, Cape Town 1984) 73–96.
[5] Heribert Adam *Modernizing Racial Domination* (Univ of California Press, 1971).
[6] Theo Hanf et al *South Africa: The Prospects of Peaceful Change* (Rex Collings, London 1981) 41.

party. The minister, or the other officers acting under the direction of the executive, are not independent and dispassionate observers of the political process; they are active participants with a stake in the outcome of the contest. The danger to democratic freedom that is inherent in authorising a participant to draw the line between subversion and legitimate dissent is well captured in Commissioner Gilbert's dissenting opinion on the emergency power recommendations of the McDonald Commission in which he said:

'Because insurrection and dissent are both expressed through confrontation with existing authority, such actions leave themselves open to abuse by that authority. In either case the existing authority tends to react against the aggressor by adopting a posture of self-justification. To sum up, it is not unfair to say that the existing authority is both party and judge in its confrontation with the dissenter, whether he be legitimate or insurrectional. It must be recognised that such a situation easily lends itself to vengeance and to the abuse of power.'[7]

Commissioner Gilbert envisaged this danger even for a society such as Canada where basic rights are well protected by a court-controlled system of legality. This throws into relief the desperate plight of political freedom in rightless South Africa where the government acts both as participant and judge in the determination of the legitimacy of opposition. In such a situation one can no longer speak of a viable democratic right to oppose and dissent.

The removal of rule-of-law controls from security legislation has meant that the circumstances in which civil rights may be withdrawn or suspended are determined by an interested party and, as a direct result of that uncontrolled power, that security-law measures have been used to control opposition as much as subversion. Expressed differently, security laws have placed the ruling party in a position to make its own determination of what is legitimate political opposition and what is subversion, and thereby to control opposition to itself and its policies. This flows directly from the fact that subversion is defined not by law but by the party in power. Of course, the government denies that security law has been misused in this way but the evidence is overwhelmingly against the acceptability or even honesty of such denials. Part of the evidence is to be found in the actual wording of security legislation. The crime of subversion punishes those who seek to achieve any kind of change in South Africa by various means including, for example, means which impede or endanger the free movement of traffic. It is obvious that a programme of political protest marches in a city could impede traffic and therefore lead to a prosecution for subversion. When a law is expressly directed at extra-parliamentary dissent, the government that enacted it can hardly be heard to say that the law is not being used to control opposition. Where the security laws do not in so many words penalise campaigns against the government and its policies, they are vague enough to permit their use for that purpose. Many security crimes in South Africa are so vague and elastic as to make the following remarks apposite to these laws:

[7] McDonald Report vol 2 para 1064.

'In a legal system in which the rules of criminal law are so loosely defined that it is difficult to say in given cases what specific acts, if any, constitute a breach of them, innocence and guilt lose precise meaning, as does proof.'[8]

Where innocence and guilt have lost precise meaning, the use of the law for partisan purposes is a predictable consequence. This is doubly true of vaguely defined powers of detention, banning and the like. Because the grounds upon which the minister or other executive officers may detain or ban are not clearly stated, and because they are subject to no effective external control in the exercise of those powers, these officers may use them for any purpose they choose; and prominent among those purposes has been the control of opposition to the party in power and the policies for which it stands. Under such powers, insurrection and dissent have lost all meaning thereby making possible the removal of democratic rights from the opponents of government. Anyone who has followed the pattern of individual banning in South Africa will know that many of the victims were nothing more than active opponents of apartheid. The same is true of many banned organisations of which the South African Defence and Aid Fund and the Christian Institute are obvious examples. The most telling evidence, however, is to be found in the simple fact that almost every individual or group that is active in opposition to apartheid sooner or later comes into conflict with the provisions of security legislation. Black South Africans in particular have come to learn that actively opposing apartheid even by means that are non-violent inevitably leads to personal experience with the whip, the bullet, a banning order, the criminal court or the detention cell. Opposition and subversion are no longer distinguishable in South Africa.

It follows that a major interest which 'security' laws were intended to further, and do actually further, is the suppression of opposition— particularly black nationalist opposition—to the ruling party and its policies. Even when the laws are invoked against those engaged in violence or insurrection, their legitimacy is weakened by the fact that the subversive conduct is due in part to the denial of other means of opposing the system. The existence of these laws, and the manner of their use, is in fact one of the main grounds for labelling the mode of conflict regulation in South Africa to be coercive. Conflict regulations in divided societies may take one of two basic forms—democratic or unilateral.[9] The unilateral (domination or coercion) model fits the South African institutions, particularly the legal institutions, like the proverbial glove. If it were otherwise, the security system would manifestly have different objectives. The McDonald Commission has plainly and unambiguously set down the purposes of the law-and-order enterprise in a free society:

'Canada must meet both the requirements of security and the requirements of democracy: we must never forget that *the fundamental purpose of the former is to secure the latter.* Those who seek to subvert Canada's democratic institutions would realise an ironic victory if Canadians were to permit their governors to

---

[8] Quoted by Frederick Vaughan in 'The Trial of Socrates: Recent Reflections' (1976) 14 *Osgoode Hall Law Journal* 407, 408.
[9] Sammy Smooha 'Control of Minorities in Israel and Northern Ireland' 22 *Comparative Studies in Society and History* 256 and 'Existing and Alternative Policies Towards the Arabs in Israel' (1982) 5 *Ethnic and Racial Studies* 71.

violate the requisites of democracy in the course of protecting them from their opponents.'[10]

It is significant that the Rabie Commission in South Africa presented no framework of values within which security legislation should be required to operate in South Africa. Apart from an occasional, and usually passing, reference to the need for overall reform,[11] the need to limit restrictions on individual rights[12] to those that are absolutely necessary, and a fairly derisory reference to the rule of law,[13] the Commission's approach was essentially non-normative. It declared, in fact, that its enquiry was to be essentially a legal or juridical one and rejected the suggestion that it should enter upon 'the political terrain'.[14] It is ludicrous to imagine that a desirable security policy can be formulated without a political and, indeed, sociological analysis. One cannot provide satisfactory answers to a meta-legal question through formalistic legal analysis. However, the Commission's reluctance is humanly understandable. Deeper analysis would have shown the South African security system to be precisely one that permits its governors to violate democracy in the course of protecting its requisites from alleged opponents. The fundamental purpose of the violation, moreover, is not to secure democracy but minority control. Normative analysis by the Rabie Commission would also have revealed that security legislation would have to be totally transformed, not just tinkered with as the Commission's report recommended, to make it a vehicle for democratic conflict resolution.

The progressive eradication of democratic rights under the guise of law and order has been accompanied in recent years by a phenomenon that is perhaps even more ominous—the weakening of civil authority over the security forces of the Republic. As we noted earlier, the decline of parliamentary authority and the enhancement of executive power was given further impetus by the creation of a presidential executive under the 1983 constitution. This process of the accumulation of executive authority has been accompanied for some time by a parallel movement—growing security–military influence over fundamental political decisions in South Africa. The security establishment, as Kenneth W Grundy observes, 'has positioned itself at the center of power'.[14a] This second movement is a direct consequence of the militarisation of the society and the semi-war footing on which it has been placed to meet the so-called 'total onslaught'. Within a short time the two movements began to converge as it became evident that the State Security Council, a body in which the security/military establishment is heavily represented,[15] was impressing itself powerfully on the decision-making of the constitutional executive.[16] Signs

[10] McDonald Report vol 1 43 (italics supplied).   [11] Rabie Report para 3.18.
[12] Paragraph 3.33.   [13] Paragraph 3.25.   [14] Paragraph 3.31.
[14a] Kenneth W Grundy *The Militarization of South African Politics* (Taurus & Co Ltd, London, 1986) 1.
[15] See s 4 of the Security Intelligence and State Security Council Act 64 of 1972.
[16] See, for example, Kenneth W Grundy, op cit, 49 et seq. D Geldenhuys and H Kotze, 'Aspects of Political Decision-making in South Africa' (1983) 10 *Politikon* 33; Simon Jenkins 'Destabilisation in Southern Africa' *The Economist* 16 July 1983; and Allister Sparks 'Hawks Back on Top after White Deaths' *The Observer* Sunday 29 December 1985. Defence force raids into Zimbabwe, Botswana and Zambia in May 1986 were apparently carried out without Cabinet approval (*Sunday Tribune*, 25 May 1986) despite the predictable enormous foreign policy damage which they caused.

of the *formal* ascendancy of the security establishment over the civil
authorities have been accompanied by instances of independent and
sometimes rebellious actions by that establishment. Though the full story
behind some of these actions is not known and cannot be revealed by the
actors on account of secrecy laws, there is enough to indicate that the
security establishment is a semi-independent authority in the state and
only partly subject to civil control. Defence department support for the
Renamo resistance movement in Mozambique *after* the Nkomati accord
between the two countries is one example. The aid given to Renamo,
euphemistically described as humanitarian,[17] included the building of a
landing strip and massive amounts of medical supplies.[18] Subsequent
government explanations that the aid was exclusively designed to bring
about peace between Renamo and the Frelimo government in Mozambique will impress only the extremely gullible observer of southern
African politics. Another example is provided by the abortive attempt in
November 1981 of a group of mercenaries under the command of Colonel
Mike Hoare to overthrow the government of the Seychelles. Though in
camera hearings deprived the general public of knowledge of defence force
involvement in the attempted coup, it appears from the judgment given by
the trial judge that there was definite support for the mission by high-up
members of the military.[19] Involvement of members of the National
Intelligence Service, although not capable of definite proof, also seems
clear. It is hardly credible that this foolhardy enterprise, so damaging to
the country's foreign relations, could have had cabinet approval and it
must be seen as a frolic which received clandestine backing from the
military establishment. A third example of the weakening of civil
authority over the security establishment is that of police behaviour
towards the opponents of the government. Despite ministerial declarations condemning torture and the enactment of codes of conduct designed
to protect certain detainees, it is clear that the torture and physical abuse
of political detainees by the police is rife. Direct evidence of physical
assaults on detainees was provided by Dr Wendy Orr, a district surgeon
in Port Elizabeth, in a court application to interdict the authorities from
illegal treatment of certain detainees in that region.[20] Court orders to
restrain the police from assaulting or torturing detainees are becoming
almost commonplace.[21] Police behaviour in controlling unrest in the
townships, both within and outside emergency areas, has been blatantly
lawless. Reports of unprovoked and unnecessary shootings are widespread
and many of these reports appear to be credible. There can be no dispute
about the instant street justice administered by the police when they shot
and killed alleged[22] stone-throwers in the notorious 'Trojan horse' episode

[17] Similar aid given by the World Council of Churches and other bodies to the ANC is
regularly denounced by the South African government on the ground that it furthers the
military struggle against apartheid.
[18] *The Weekly Mail*, 20–26 September 1985.
[19] *S v Hoare* 1982 (4) SA 865 (N) especially at 876.
[20] An interim order restraining the police from assaulting detainees was granted by Mr
Justice Eksteen on 25 September 1985: *Natal Witness* 26 September 1985.
[21] See, for example, *Nordien v Minister of Law and Order* 1986 (2) SA 511 (C). The Natal
court granted three such orders early in July 1986: *The Weekly Mail* 11–17 July 1986.
[22] One of the frightening things about official street justice is that the victims could easily
be innocent bystanders or participants in a demonstration who did not throw stones. Justice
meted out in this way is indiscriminate and excessive; it converts stone-throwing, or
participation in a demonstration where stone-throwing occurs, into a capital offence.

in the Cape township of Athlone in October 1985.[23] These and many other similar incidents present a picture of a police force acting in a lawless and uncontrolled manner; and the heavy censorship imposed in emergency areas was the response of a government unable to discipline its police force and therefore compelled to limit the immeasurable damage to the country and its economy of such brutal repression by throwing a blanket of secrecy over the application of emergency powers. When one takes into account the immense harm that the security forces have inflicted on their own country under emergency rule, it is hard to believe that a government that could have controlled them would not have done so.

We may conclude that the destruction of the rule of law by security legislation has had disastrous consequences for democracy in South Africa. Security legislation has drastically limited the democratic rights of white South Africans and abolished the remnants of democracy that were available to blacks. It has turned conflict resolution decisively, perhaps irretrievably, towards the domination or coercion model. Finally, by freeing the military/security establishment from the restraints of the rule of law, security legislation has gravely weakened control by the civil authorities in the state.

Democracy and Civilised Values

Democracy implies a commitment to standards of civilised behaviour that extend beyond the recognition of formal political rights. It requires governments to observe at least a minimum standard of decency and humanity in the treatment of their subjects. The commitment to civilised values distinguishes democracies in the Western tradition from the so-called totalitarian democracies of the East in which the subjects, to use Arthur Koestler's telling image, may be treated as no more than sacrificial rabbits. When South Africa seeks to place itself on the side of the 'free' West, it undertakes the burden of ensuring that the state, in its dealings with citizens, will recognise their humanity and right to civilised treatment. The same obligation seems to flow, in any event, from the commitment in the preamble to the constitution to 'Christian values and civilised norms'.

There are certain provisions of the South African security system which violate the commitment to decent values and standards of official behaviour. These measures make it impossible to accept the claim of the authors of security legislation that its purpose is to uphold the very standards that are under discussion. One does not uphold standards by denying them. Two features of security law in particular stand out as blatant violations of the state's obligation to maintain acceptable standards of humanity: the provision for indefinite detention of suspects in solitary confinement and the exemption from legal controls granted to the security forces under emergency law. No doubt a case can be made out that other provisions of security law also deny legitimate expectations to civilised treatment. However, these other examples are more contentious

---

[23] Three persons were shot dead and three seriously injured in the 'Trojan horse' shooting. One of those killed was a child of approximately 12 years old: see *The Weekly Mail* 18–24 October 1985.

and the ensuing discussion will focus on breaches of the subject's right to decent treatment that are clear and indisputable.

Even if we grant the state's right to hold suspects for questioning, there is no case in a civilised community for the institution of indefinite detention in isolation and without adequate court control. The medical evidence reviewed earlier[24] has shown that lengthy incommunicado incarceration is in itself a form of cruel and inhuman treatment that frequently results in permanent psychological damage, mental derangement or suicide. It is also a foreseeable and predictable consequence of freeing the interrogators from legal controls that the detainee will be subjected to illegal treatment in the form of assault, torture and the like. The shock waves that reverberated around the world following the horrendous treatment and death of Steve Biko have not put an end to the torture or abuse of detainees. In one of the more recent cases, a detainee was made to kneel on the floor with a pistol against his head and was then shot and killed in circumstances that will never fully be known.[25] The continuation of the practice of torture even after the enormous damage to South Africa's standing in the world community caused by the Biko affair, and the government's subsequent claim that it did not sanction such behaviour, illustrate that maltreatment of detainees is a built-in feature of incommunicado incarceration and that a government which continues to make use of this diabolical institution cannot be too serious about eliminating the abuse of detainees. The treatment of Dr Wendy Orr, who was removed from all contact with prisoners after bringing the court's attention to the systematic ill-treatment of emergency detainees, speaks volumes about the government's attitude to these practices.

Under the emergency regulations promulgated at the time of the declaration of emergencies in July 1985 and June 1986, members of the security forces were exempted from civil and criminal accountability for any action taken in good faith (which is presumed until the contrary has been proved) in the course of exercising emergency powers in dealing with the unrest situation.[26] It is one thing to free members of the military and the police from legal accountability by indemnity Act passed at the end of an emergency but quite another to dispense with legal controls at the outset. The latter is a statutory licence to the security forces to act as they believe fit and it is one, to judge by the reports of police misbehaviour that are pouring in, that has not been neglected. The indemnity clause is a recipe for uncivilised behaviour and one that has no place in a country that is constitutionally committed to 'Christian values and civilised norms'.

The Efficacy of the Security System

Normative analysis of the South African security system has shown that it is irreconcilable with democratic values and civilised behaviour. The

---

[24] See chapter 7 above.

[25] His interrogator received a prison sentence of ten years for culpable homicide; but this cannot recall the life of the victim of this terrible act.

[26] Regulation 11 in Schedule II to Proclamation No R121 of 1985 (*Reg Gaz* 3849 of 21 July 1985) and reg 16 in the Schedule to Proclamation No R109 of 1986 (*Reg Gaz* 3964 of 12 June 1986).

state, to adapt the words of Paul Wilkinson, has pushed itself 'into authoritarianism, and hence into denying its constitutionalism, into dropping all humane restraints and checks on power, and ultimately into becoming a paramilitary or police state, a mirror image of the terrorism it is supposed to be defeating'.[27] The only remaining claim that can conceivably be made for the security system is that it is an effective instrument for securing peace and stability in the country. If in addition to its violation of democracy and civilised standards it fails to pass the test of effectiveness, there is literally nothing to support the retention of the security system in its present form.

The foundation stone of the present security system was laid in 1950 when the Suppression of Communism Act was passed. In that year, according to a report of the South African Institute of Race Relations, the only signs of political 'trouble' were a one-day strike and a mass protest meeting against the policy of apartheid.[28] In the ensuing three decades the ruling National Party secured the passage through Parliament of the battery of Draconian laws that today constitute the security system in consolidated form.[29] The description of the unrest situation by the Institute of Race Relations in 1984, after over thirty years of drastic 'law and order' medicine, makes an illuminating comparison with the troubles of 1950. In 1984, the Institute reported, 175 people were killed in unrest-related incidents and 58 incidents of guerrilla insurgency took place.[30] The death-toll for 1985 stands at almost 900[31] and the killings have not abated in the first half of 1986.[32] These grim statistics are only part of the general picture of 1984, 1985 and 1986 which was one of riots and burnings, boycotts and strikes, and bombs and bullets. The tragic growth of political violence and disorder after three decades of Draconian law enforcement makes it impossible to present security policy as one of South Africa's success stories. In fact, disorder has increased in direct proportion to the application of harsh security measures.

Quite obviously, the security system has failed in the sense that it has neither eliminated unrest nor even contained it; but, more seriously, it is susceptible to the additional criticism that it has contributed to political disorder. The government, though warned even from within its own ranks that drastic measures can be ineffective and counter-productive in the longer term,[33] continues to act as though the iron-fisted application of security legislation has not added to the problem. Police action during the 1976 disturbances provide us with a clear instance, from which the authorities appear to have learnt nothing, of a direct connection between security operations and increased (rather than diminished) violence and terror. When in that year the full force of the security arm of government was turned on the Soweto school demonstrators, an unknown but large number (probably in the region of three thousand) became enforced

---

[27] Paul Wilkinson *Terrorism and the Liberal State* (Macmillan, London 1977) 80.
[28] 1950–1 *Survey of Race Relations in South Africa* 21.
[29] Consisting chiefly of the Internal Security Act 74 of 1982.
[30] 1984 *Survey of Race Relations in South Africa* 65, 92.
[31] *The Weekly Mail* 11–17 July 1986 reports 879 deaths for 1985.
[32] The figure for January to June 1986 is 969 deaths: *The Weekly Mail* 11–17 July 1986.
[33] D P de Villiers 'Change in Respect of Security Legislation' in D J van Vuuren et al (eds) *Change in South Africa* (Butterworths, Pretoria 1983) 393, 415.

refugees from their own country. It was inevitable that these refugees would become conscripts into the guerrilla movement and many have returned to South Africa as trained fighters. The steady growth of incidents of insurgency since 1976[34] is no coincidence and a similar growth may be predicted in the years that follow the heavy-handed and lawless police crack-down in the current unrest. Because the security system puts no effective restraints on police action in unrest situations, the important principle of *minimal force* has been replaced by excessive and indiscriminate repression; and this replacement is creating the guerrilla movements of tomorrow.

The claim by security authorities that they adhere to the principle of minimal force is simply not borne out by the facts. A distinguished foreign correspondent, writing in *The Observer* of 4 May 1986, noted that there had been 1 500 unrest deaths in the preceding 20 months and that *two-thirds* of the deaths were the result of security force actions.[35] Of the 879 dead in 1985, over half (441) were apparently the result of security force operations.[36] The percentage of persons killed by the security forces has been over fifty in the past few years and this must represent a *reduction* since only in the previous two years has the phenomenon of self-directed black violence become a reality. By contrast, of the 2 455 deaths that occurred in Northern Ireland unrest in the period 1969–85 the security forces were responsible for 265—a percentage of 10,8.[37] This means that security forces in South Africa have been responsible for at least five times more killings than their counterparts in Northern Ireland. In 1985 the security forces in South Africa killed over 400 persons as opposed to the 265 killed by Northern Ireland forces in 17 years of civil strife. These comparisons are not meant to play down the horror of opposition violence in South Africa whether it be in the form of necklacing, gunning down officials or bombing soft targets. There can be no objection to strong action *against the perpetrators* of such terrible deeds. What is unacceptable in South Africa is the indiscriminate and excessive nature of anti-unrest operations.

Security laws are contributing to unrest by broadening and intensifying bitterness in the black townships. The bitterness is being broadened by police action against peaceful protestors and demonstrators. Security law in fact compels the police to act against peaceful dissenters because every outdoor meeting is illegal unless prior magisterial permission has been obtained; and as soon as people gather in the open their dispersal is required to prevent violation of a valid but incredibly stupid law. Black anger is also being aroused and intensified by the indiscriminate use of police power in the townships. There are almost daily reports, many apparently true, of unnecessary beating and shooting of children, of the reckless use of tear-gas canisters and of assaults upon innocent detainees. Even if jackboot tactics in the townships succeed in putting down the present unrest, black hatred and anger has been so fuelled that more horrific township strife is probable in the future.

---

[34] See 1984 *Survey of Race Relations in South Africa* 92.
[35] John de St Jorre *The Observer* Sunday 4 May 1986.
[36] Figures supplied by a research officer of the SA Institute of Race Relations.
[37] Information supplied by the Northern Ireland Office, Whitehall, London.

All these considerations amply justify the comment in a recent analysis of the relationship between law, order and state security in South Africa that 'coercion from above . . . tends to give rise to chaos from below' and that 'inopportune behaviour by the authorities that be in the state themselves can also present a threat to state security'.[38] While the basic causes of unrest are undoubtedly social and political, legalised coercion in the form of harsh security laws has become a potent contributory cause. Moreover, the harm caused by the security system is not limited to the direct aggravation of unrest. Because that system empowers the authorities to neutralise or eliminate black leaders in various ways, there is a lowered incentive to engage in a process of negotiation and accommodation. Why talk if you can legally ban, detain, shoot or drive into exile the troublesome opponents of apartheid? The availability of an arsenal of repressive security measures has tempted the authorities into postponing the search for political accommodation, thereby making its achievement infinitely more difficult. As Colin Legum has observed, there is a new generation of blacks emerging who believe that violence is the only language the ruling whites understand.[39] This belief is a direct result of the repression of black political aspirations through the security system and is likely to grow in response to lawless emergency rule; and as it grows, so too will the *political* damage caused by security legislation. That legislation has become a coercive and destabilising substitute for the politics of negotiation and consensus. Far from creating the preconditions for political dialogue it is actually destroying the chances of political reform. In fact, security law has substituted violence for politics as the mode of resolving black/white conflict in South Africa and the drastic amendment of that law is essential for establishing the predominance of talk and compromise over the bullet and the bomb.

The idea that security powers should be reduced is in direct opposition to prevailing conventional 'wisdom' which seeks to fight fire with fire. That conventional wisdom is both shallow and uninformed. Apart from the obvious fact that it is better to fight fire with water, there is evidence that a reduction in security powers in a situation of crisis is not necessarily harmful and that it could be beneficial. The security situation has not worsened in Israel since preventive detention was put under judicial control; nor has it in Northern Ireland since preventive detention was abandoned in 1975. On the contrary, terrorist violence in Northern Ireland has diminished since the authorities ceased to rely on the internment of alleged IRA supporters. Between 1976 (the year after detention was allowed to lapse) and 1984, civilian deaths came down from 245 to 36 and explosions from 766 to 193.[40] Because 'security' laws in South Africa are directed as much against opposition as subversion, the benefits of reduced powers could be greater than in Northern Ireland if by amendment these laws are limited to the real enemies of peace and order

---

[38] Lourens M du Plessis 'Thoughts on Law, Order and State Security' (1985) 3 *Tydskrif vir die Suid-Afrikaanse Reg* 233, 236 and 241. Cf Frederik van Zyl Slabbert *The Last White Parliament* (Jonathan Ball, Johannesburg 1985) 126: 'But there is a direct correlation between the extension of coercive government and the use of violence by those who experience such coercion. . . .'

[39] *Sunday Tribune* of 8 December 1985.

[40] Information supplied by the Northern Ireland Office, Whitehall, London.

and can no longer be used to turn every opponent into an enemy of the
state. Of course, a reduction in security powers without accompanying
reform initiatives is unlikely to accomplish much; but if so accompanied,
security-law amendment offers a real hope of breaking the grim dialectic
of violence and counter-violence in the society.

There is a belief, found mainly on the wilder fringes of South African
politics, that the failure of the security system to contain disorder is
attributable to excessive restraint in putting down political unrest!
Presumably those who hold this belief advocate a Russian-style operation
with tanks in the streets as in Budapest or Prague. Even members of the
government have recently given expression to dark warnings that there
are reserves of military power which will be thrown into the struggle if the
violence continues. There can be no doubt that these reserves exist and
that the government has the *military* capacity to crush its political
opponents by a ruthless deployment of the security forces which, in the
words of Heribert Adam, will make the present methods 'pale into mere
authoritarian dilletantism'.[41] This military capacity is not matched,
however, by a *political* capacity to carry out a Stalin-type oppression of
resistance. The deployment of the reserves of oppressive power, and the
bloodshed that will accompany it, are likely seriously to divide a white
community that, although hitherto tolerant of the injustices of apartheid
and rough police methods against its opponents, will not give general
support to the slaughter of black people. A more formidable political
restraint on full-scale military repression is the vulnerability of South
Africa to international pressure. This country, as Heribert Adam has
shown, is a middle-range power (or 'sovereign protectorate') which, while
generally free to manage its own affairs, is simultaneously dependent on
the great powers of the West; and that dependence means that it is not as
unaccountable for its internal actions as the poorest Third-World
countries whose leaders may maintain systems of brutal repression
without arousing too much international concern or retaliation.[42] South
Africa's dependence on the great powers of the West is due to its strategic
position in the Western orbit, the interlocking of its economy with the
economies of those countries, and its need to achieve international moral
legitimacy.[43] It follows that although the South African government does
have massive reserves of military force which it can deploy internally
against the black people, the Western powers have corresponding reserves
of economic, diplomatic and military power which could be turned
against South Africa if it embarks on a military operation to destroy its
internal opponents. In the present crisis, a moderate use of Western
political and economic leverage has demonstrated the vulnerability of
South Africa to international pressure. Any attempt to improve the
efficacy of the security system by a massive extension of repression will

[41] Heribert Adam 'Engineering Legitimacy and the Politicization of Ethnicity' paper
delivered at the University of Natal Conference on South Africa and the West (Durban, 20–
26 March 1983).
[42] Heribert Adam 'Ethnic Politics, Violence and Crisis Management: A Comparative
Exploration', paper presented at a symposium of the European Consortiums of Political
Research on *Violence and Conflict Management in Divided Societies* (Freiberg, 20–26 March 1983).
[43] Ibid.

add to growing world pressure on the South African government and this in turn is likely to weaken its ability to cope with internal problems.

We may conclude that the South African security system, indefensible by acceptable standards of moral and political judgment, is as great a failure when assessed by its own implicit standard of justification—effectiveness in securing a peaceful and stable society. There is no chance, moreover, of increasing its efficacy by a more rigorous application of security powers. The creation of a peaceful, prosperous and stable society requires just the opposite of that—radical reform of security law in the context of overall political reform.

Security Law Reform—Prospects and Preconditions

The basic function of the security system in South Africa is the protection of the power and privilege of the ruling minority from all forms of attack by the excluded groups. Because it is tied to minority interests, that system is incapable of developing the support and co-operation of the whole people which the McDonald Commission found to be essential to the long-range effectiveness of security laws.[44] The reverse is in fact true —it is bound to alienate the bulk of the population and drive many of those excluded into violent opposition to the government.[45] Official condemnation of violent opposition in South Africa is characterised by strong elements of fantasy and hypocrisy. The security programme is itself a massive, state-directed system of violence designed to render apartheid impregnable from attack; and therein lies the hypocrisy of those who condemn its violent opponents. The fantastical element is the belief that the racially based system of legal discrimination known as apartheid is politically viable although it condemns the larger part of the population to political and social inferiority and outrages the greater part of the world population by proclaiming moral legitimacy for the entire arrangement. Apartheid, the only system in the world that sanctifies a racially based system of injustice, must rank as one of the larger lunacies of world history. As such, it positively requires harsh and inflexible security laws to give it a limited survival chance through coercion of all but those who benefit from the policy. The internal logic or rationality of the security system is to be found in its contribution to the maintenance of South Africa's race oligarchy.

Reform of security legislation is therefore unthinkable while the government remains committed to minority rule and legalised discrimination. The Rabie Commission did not advocate anything more than cosmetic reform of security laws because the real but inarticulate premiss on which the members of that commission acted was that power relations and the fundamentals of the social system in South Africa would remain substantially undisturbed. The government gave the commission no reason to think otherwise and appointed to its membership no person who would challenge the basics of white political thinking on the subject. Since

[44] McDonald Report vol 1 15.
[45] The reason why it is bound to drive opponents of apartheid towards strategies of violence is that security legislation has blocked all non-violent forms of opposition to official policies. A government that deliberately does this has no claim to belief in peaceful politics and no moral right to condemn those who turn to other methods.

the Rabie Commission reported in 1981 the air has become heavy with reform talk, although this talk has been matched by precious little action on the ground. It is vital to the possibility of security-law reform that the rhetoric of change, and the initial hesitant steps that have accompanied it, are part of a process which is intended to abolish legalised discrimination and fundamentally alter power relations, even if the time-scale for change is an extended one. If on the contrary, the reform moves now being inaugurated are no more than a refurbishment of apartheid and the refinement of white political domination, fundamental change to security legislation remains unthinkable and the present security system will (and must) remain entrenched. On the other hand, real political and social change require concomitant reforms to security law since much of that law is inconsistent with, and would be a hindrance to, the creation of an enlightened political order.

The possibility of security-law reform therefore depends upon whether current government moves are directed toward the dismantling or refurbishment of apartheid. The auguries can be interpreted in two ways. On the positive side, there have been changes which cannot be dismissed as cosmetic. The most important are the recognition of black and multi-racial trade unions, the abolition of the pass laws, the grant of long-term tenure, and more recently freehold, to blacks in 'white' South Africa, the integration of many public facilities and the abolition of the concept of inter-racial immorality. There has been political advancement too for Indian and coloured persons who are now incorporated (many would say co-opted) into the central institutions of government. The government has started to reverse the process of denationalising homeland blacks and will reinstitute a common South African citizenship for some of them. Central business areas of some cities have been declared open to members of all race groups. These changes add up to a reform programme that is not insignificant. However, the hopeful signs are contradicted by some darker auguries. The fundamentals of apartheid in the form of the enforced racial categorisation of peoples, and separate areas for the different groups, are still in force and the government retains an inflexible commitment to them. It will not modify residential segregation by permitting 'grey areas' even though this limited reform to enforced segregation appears to follow logically from the recognition of mixed marriages. The grant of trade-union rights has been heavily qualified by security-law restrictions against union officials, particularly during the 1986 emergency which has resulted in the widespread detention of officals of the Congress of South African Trade Unions (COSATU) and, to a lesser extent, of the members of other unions.[46] Much of the freedom of movement restored to blacks may be withdrawn again by rigorous enforcement of squatter, slum clearance and trespass laws.[47] Worst of all, the envisaged *political* reform for blacks appears to be no more than a dangerous kind of tokenism involving 'improvement' to the discredited system of local government, participation in a toothless National Forum and the chance of a few seats in the President's Council. Since meaningful political rights for blacks are

[46] *The Weekly Mail* June 27–July 3 1986.
[47] See, for example, the assessment of the white paper on urbanisation by Pauline Morris in *The South African Foundation News* June 1986.

crucial to the creation of a peaceful and orderly society, the government's inaction, and the poverty of its political thinking in this area, constitute the darkest auguries of all.

Though the darker signs loom larger, it is probably impossible to predict whether the reforming or the conserving tendency will gain strength and ultimately predominate. For purposes of this study, it will be assumed that a process of radical transformation of South African society has begun and that the slowness of reform is in part due to the fact that the 'reformer who attempts to do everything all at once ends up by accomplishing little or nothing'.[48] Piecemeal reform avoids the danger of arousing the simultaneous hostility of all the main vested interest groups. Moreover, it is possible that reform undertaken with a mainly conserving intent could be displaced by genuinely innovative reform as the government loses the power to dictate the direction of change. There are signs that some of the initiative has passed out of government hands into the control of internal opponents and external pressure groups. Therefore, it seems sensible to avoid the futile exercise of prediction and to examine the nature and direction of the social and political change that will be essential to enable the lawmakers to replace the present security system with one that gives substantial recognition to the rule of law.

A precondition of enlightened reform of the security system is a decisive move from the unilateral and coercive mode of conflict regulation towards consensus politics involving all groups at all levels of government. Such a move is also crucial to the containment and reduction of violence and disorder in the society. There are two main reasons why South Africa is prone to violence. The first is that South Africa is a deeply divided or plural society. A plural society is one that is characterised by significant racial, religious, ethnic or linguistic divisions or, as Theo Hanf has put it, one in which people are classified not only by class but by groups, thereby producing a juxtaposition and opposition of social segments.[49] Plural societies are notorious for their political instability and, in the words of Samuel P Huntingdon, 'ethnic heterogeneity is a better predictor of violence than poverty'.[50] There are several reasons why divided societies are prone to violence and therefore have to contend with more intractable security or law and order problems. The most important of these is that threats to the established order come from large and cohesive groups in which a unified culture and identity of interests makes it easier to mobilise opposition to official policies. Furthermore, a group with a specific identity and a common set of grievances, is more likely than discontented individuals to find outside allies and sympathisers who can identify with them culturally, morally or ideologically and strengthen this identification with tangible support. The second characteristic of South African society that makes it more susceptible to instability and violent conflict is the modernisation process to which its peoples have been subject for several decades and which is likely to continue into the next century. Modernisation is a complex phenomenon but its essential features are rapid

---

[48] Samuel P Huntingdon *Political Order in Changing Societies* (Yale Univ Press, New Haven 1968) 347.
[49] Theo Hanf, op cit 3–5.
[50] Samuel P Huntingdon op cit 42.

economic growth and the absorption of the masses into a modern economy accompanied by disruption of the traditional patterns of life, by urbanisation and by large jumps in literacy, education and media exposure.[51] The modernisation process heightens the potential of a plural society for disruption and violence because the masses that are mobilised into the economic system develop a new awareness of improved forms of life and higher standards of enjoyment. Modernisation makes the masses more acutely aware of their disadvantages and deprivations or, in sociological language, of the gap between 'aspiration and expectation, want formation and want satisfaction'.[52] The coincidence of pluralism and modernisation produces a law and order powder keg and great political skill and enterprise is needed to prevent its ignition.

If political reform is to have any chance of neutralising or reducing the conflict potential of a plural society that is in the process of modernisation, it will have to be built around two principles of central importance. The first is the principle of the effective incorporation of the newly mobilised groups into the political process. Since instability in a rapidly modernising society is largely a product of the slow creation of political institutions through which the newly mobilised groups have a chance of realising their heightened aspirations, peace and order are crucially related to the development of strong and adaptable political institutions for the hitherto excluded groups.[53] Failure to do so will inevitably lead such groups in the direction of overt and covert civil strife.[54] The second important principle for political reform is one of constitution-making for the reduction of inter-group conflict and the maximalisation of inter-group co-operation. As Donald Horowitz has shown, well-designed electoral and structural devices can bring about peaceful political accommodation between rival groups in a divided society.[55] In brief, the conflict produced by modernisation requires extended political participation at all levels of government and the instability inherent in social pluralism requires that this participation be constitutionally tailored for the reduction of inter-group hostility.

The main reason why South Africa has a security system that has annihilated the rule of law is that its political responses to the conflict produced by pluralism and modernisation have been the opposite of those just outlined. Instead of political incorporation for black South Africans, the main group affected by the modernisation process, that group has been expelled from the central institutions of government. This exclusion, stamped with constitutional finality by the South Africa Constitution Act of 1983, is directly related to the political violence of today. Though the 1983 constitution incorporates some limited measures for inter-group co-operation between the ruling whites and Indian and coloured persons, it offers nothing in the way of mechanisms for reducing conflict between black and white South Africans. At the same time, enforced legal

[51] At 47.
[52] At 53–4.
[53] At 47.
[54] At 140.
[55] Donald Horowitz *Ethnic Groups in Conflict* (Univ of California Press, 1985) chapters 15 and 16.

discrimination has sharpened hostility by artificially increasing the gap between the heightened aspirations of blacks and the satisfaction of their wants. Seen in this light, the National Party policy of apartheid has been a catalyst for conflict in a plural and modernising society and has necessitated the construction of a security system characterised by unbridled official power and arbitrary and repressive administration.

The direction which political reform should take to reduce ethnic conflict is clear enough—the assimilation of the excluded black group at all levels of decision-making. The specification of the precise nature of the constitutional forms and institutions through which assimilation should be brought about is too complex a task to be undertaken here. However, there are some things that can be said with a reasonable degree of certainty about the assimilation process. The divided nature of South African society demands a constitution with devolved power structures and in-built devices to advance minority protection (not privilege) and inter-group co-operation. Success is unlikely unless the goal of political reform—the replacement of the domination model of conflict regulation by a consensual and co-operative system—is reflected in the means for achieving it. This implies that the continued use of the security system to repress opposition groups is unacceptable and that these groups must be brought into the negotiation process. So long as opposition groups are dealt with by banning, shooting, detentions and prosecutions, so long will reform lack legitimacy on account of its imposed and non-consensual nature. It follows that the government must find a formula to bring presently banned organisations into the negotiation process. It is pointless to denigrate and exclude some of these organisations on the ground that they are committed to violence and to co-operation with the communists. The fact that they are is a reflection of the failure of the system to meet legitimate black aspirations, and the recall of such groups from extremist ideologies and strategies depends upon the immediate implementation of a negotiation process characterised by inclusiveness and accommodation rather than narrowness and inflexibility. Advocating such a programme does not imply support for violence or totalitarian ideology; on the contrary, it seeks to remove the encouragement which the present system affords to all forms of extremism.

Political reform must go hand in hand with staged economic and social reform. The priorities for social and economic change are best determined by identifying the main contributory causes of political violence. In a comprehensive study of political terrorism, Paul Wilkinson has sought to identify the most frequent contributory causes of political violence[56] and of these the following are the most pertinent to the situation in South Africa:

1. Ethnic conflicts, hatreds, discrimination and repression.
2. Socio-economic relative deprivation.
3. Perceived political inequalities, infringements of rights, injustice and oppression.
4. Lack of adequate channels for peaceful communication of protests, grievances and demands.

[56] Paul Wilkinson op cit 37–8.

Just a cursory glance at each of these contributory causes of political violence is sufficient to confirm their relevance to South Africa and to prompt the following priorities for socio-economic reform: (a) The rapid repeal of the remaining ethnically based laws of discrimination such as group areas legislation; (b) Dramatic improvement of black access to the areas of economic opportunity so as to reduce as quickly as possible the disproportion between black and white income and ownership.[57] The disproportion of black to white urban incomes is presently reflected by a ratio of approximately 1 : 5,5.[58] Black access to economic opportunity will never be achieved unless the differentials in educational spending are swiftly eliminated. In the 1983/84 financial year the per capita expenditure (including capital expenditure) on a black child was approximately R234 and on a white child approximately R1 654.[59] It is not surprising that inferior black education is a central cause of grievance and conflict in South Africa. (c) The reduction of official (including police) power over blacks, especially those forms of power which facilitate racial injustice and repression. Officials should not be vested with greater power because the person they are dealing with has a black skin; the decriminalisation of race relations is an urgent necessity; (d) Reopening of channels for communication, protest and demands. This priority involves the restoration of basic civil rights and the removal of official power arbitrarily to suspend their enjoyment.

While there is no doubt that progress has been made towards the realisation of some of these priorities, the changes actually inaugurated have not been decisive enough. Reform, in the words of Albert O Hirschman, is change in which 'the power of hitherto privileged groups is curbed and the economic position and social status of under-privileged groups is correspondingly improved'.[60] The power/privilege balance has barely been touched by the present reform movement. In fact, socio-economic reform in South Africa has almost been vitiated by two strategic flaws: it is unilaterally imposed reform and it bears little resemblance to the rhetoric with which it is accompanied. Imposed reform lacks legitimacy;[61] and indecisive reform, surrounded by the cloudy verbiage of propaganda, is likely to be disbelieved and dismissed. Reform talk, unattended by concrete deeds, produces cynicism, alienation and conflict. An ounce of example is worth a pound of exhortation.

Security law-Reform—General Principles

The foregoing discussion has hopefully made it clear that the assumption upon which reform of the security system is premised is that

---

[57] A recent study made the following significant conclusions about the disproportion: 'Life styles of white South Africans who have free access to the areas of economic opportunity, are the equal of those in countries like Spain, Italy and New Zealand; Rural Black lifestyles, on the other hand, are close to those in Ruanda, Upper Volta and Zaïre': Jill Nattrass *Plenty Amidst Poverty: The Need for Development Studies* inaugural lecture delivered on 21 September 1983 and published by University of Natal Press (Durban 1983) 12.

[58] Estimate given to me by Professor Jill Nattrass.

[59] 1984 *Race Relations Survey* 648.

[60] Quoted by Samuel P Huntingdon op cit 344. See also S C Olivier 'Strategy and Tactics for Change in South Africa' in D J van Vuuren et al (eds) *Change in South Africa* (Butterworths, Pretoria 1983) 379.

[61] S C Olivier op cit 384.

the transformation of South African society will incorporate a movement from unilateral domination towards the sharing of power, and from enforced discrimination towards an equality of income, opportunity and rights. If such a movement does develop out of the present conflict, it is likely to be halting, irregular and troubled by many contradictory ebbs and flows; but given its existence, corresponding changes to security law will become imperative. In fact, the early reform of security law will add impetus to any liberalising tendency while the retention of present security legislation will have a retarding influence. The final concern of this book is the nature of the security-law reform that is dictated[62] by the envisaged social transformation of South African society.

A number of general considerations and principles are crucial to the construction of a security system for a reforming society. The most important of these are the following:

1. The implementation of reforms, especially in an already unstable society, carries the risk of further destabilisation. In the words of De Tocqueville, 'experience has shown that the most dangerous moment for a bad government is usually that when it enters upon the work of reform. . . .'[63] As we have seen, the dangers are greater for a society that is plural and involved in a process of modernisation. The conclusion that follows from these considerations is that the repeal of all security-law powers and controls would be an act of folly equal to the folly of retaining present security legislation during a period of reform. A divided society that is being modernised and reformed will need *some* exceptional measures to arrest a general slide into disorder and even chaos.

2. The choice of security measures to preserve order in a reforming, plural society should be guided by the principle of balance—balance between what Paul Wilkinson has described as the danger of over-reaction (indiscriminate repression accompanied by loss of popular support and legitimacy) and under-reaction (leading to political inertia and the disintegration of the state).[64] Security policy in the past three decades is a classic example of over over-reaction in the sense that the ruling party has enacted and applied measures of extreme breadth and severity against those whom it designates, by an arbitrary process, as enemies of the state. To quote Paul Wilkinson again, this kind of 'slide into general repression generally indicates that the government is exploiting the crisis situation for the enhancement of its own political powers, or to destroy legitimate political opposition'.[65] However, those liberal and radical critics of the government who have advocated the repeal of all security-law measures have insufficiently recognised the opposite danger of a slide into capitulation. The conservative versus radical debate over security in South Africa is very

[62] 'Dictated' is perhaps too strong a word in this context. It is meant to draw attention to the necessary correspondence between the direction of general political and social reform and the direction of security-law reform in particular. Though such a correspondence is essential, it may be characterised by different degrees of proximity and the appropriate fit depends to some considerable extent on conscious design and planning.

[63] Quoted by Paul Wilkinson op cit, 36.

[64] Paul Wilkinson op cit xiv.

[65] Paul Wilkinson op cit 124.

much like the argument between Etienne and Rasseneur which Zola describes in his novel *Germinal*:

> 'The two men had now given up shouting at each other and were coldly bitter and spiteful in their open rivalry. In fact it was what always lies at the bottom of exaggerated dogmas: one man runs to revolutionary violence and the other, by way of reaction, to insincere moderation, and both get carried far beyond their genuine convictions simply because they find themselves cast for parts not of their own choosing.'[66]

To claim, as the conservatives regularly do, that current security legislation constitutes a necessary 'law and order programme', is certainly an example of 'exaggerated dogma'; but so is the view that orderly government will be possible in a reforming, plural society without unusual measures of control. In their justifiable reaction to security force excesses in South Africa, many liberal and radical critics have been 'carried far beyond their genuine convictions' which do not require them to advocate a Weimar-like weakness towards political violence and terror.

3. Gross violation of civilised standards of official behaviour is unacceptable as part of a programme of 'unusual measures' to contain violence and disorder in unstable plural societies. In the course of evaluating reactions to the terrorist threat in Great Britain, Richard Clutterbuck has said:

> 'The middle course of continuing to improve the concept of a tolerant, co-operative and civilised community, which has taken thousands of years to develop, is much more difficult to follow, but more worthwhile.'[67]

The treatment of Steve Biko, and of many other detainees held by the police, and the street justice administered to demonstrators by the security forces, are examples of the grosser violation of civilised human standards. Such official conduct is destroying the possibility of creating a community characterised by tolerance and co-operation. It also directly furthers the strategy of provoking security force excesses so as to increase sympathy for the terrorist cause and promote a de-legitimising hostility to state authority.

4. An internal security system needs to be informed by a set of clear and defensible objectives. Perhaps the most significant weakness of the Rabie Report was the failure to answer the question: 'Whom or what is one seeking to defend?'[68] Inadequate investigation of that question inevitably resulted in almost total endorsement by the Commission of South Africa's repressive security system. By contrast, the McDonald Commission in Canada clearly specified the objectives which Canadian security policy seeks to realise. The security of Canada, the Commission declared, involved the preservation of its territory from attack and 'the need to preserve and maintain the democratic processes of government'.[69] Elaborating on its understanding of democracy the Commission said: '. . . we regard responsible government, the rule of law, and the right to dissent as among the essential

[66] Emile Zola *Germinal* (Penguin, 1958) 232.
[67] Richard Clutterbuck *Living with Terrorism* (Faber & Faber, London 1975) 150.
[68] Paul Wilkinson op cit 118.
[69] McDonald Report vol 1 39–40.

requirements of our system of democracy'.[70] These are the very values that the South African security system has trodden underfoot in the course of securing quite different objectives: the preservation of white minority rule and the policy of apartheid. The sectional bias of South African security law deprives it of a vital prerequisite of effectiveness—the general trust of the entire community. Because security legislation is identified with the preservation of partisan interests and the repression of reasonable majority aspirations, opposition to the authorities that enforce it, including violent opposition, acquires a moral legitimacy that it would not otherwise enjoy. In the words of Paul Wilkinson, 'where a majority is subjected to tyrannical or despotic rule by a minority the minority is imposing its sovereignty by violence and therefore can be legitimately opposed by the force of just rebellion or resistance by the majority'.[71] This passage is cited not to express approval of violence but to condemn the stupidity of investing it with compelling moral force. Only a drastic redefinition of the policy objectives of security law, with a view to directing its sanctions against the enemies of freedom rather than apartheid, can deprive violence and terror of the moral legitimacy which the present system has given them. The central objective of a new security system should be the fostering of the institutions of a free society such as responsible government for all, basic rights and the rule of law, and the preservation of such institutions from violent or subversive assaults.

5. The concession that a reforming and modernising plural society requires special measures for the preservation of peace and order does not imply wholesale derogations from the rule of law. On the contrary, the closest possible adherence to the principle of the rule of law in the formulation of such measures is essential: 'The most evil and dangerous consequence that may follow from repeated overturning of the rule of law is the establishment of the power-hungry security apparatus which acquires a habit of extra-judicial reprisal.'[72] This habit has the further consequence that 'private armies and vigilante groups will spring up like a jungle of weeds almost overnight, adding to the general chaos'.[73] Though these words were not written about South Africa, they describe with chilling accuracy the slide into violence and disorder that has accompanied the erosion of rule-of-law standards in the society; and they underline the urgency of re-establishing the principle of government under law. Bringing the rule of law back into play does not mean that the security authorities will have no special powers but rather that their exercise will be subject to clear statutory standards adjudicated upon by independent courts or similar tribunals. In the context of national security, the rule of law expresses the demand for a clear statutory mandate, which as the McDonald Commission has recommended, should define 'the types of activity constituting threats to security' which are the only concern of

[70] At 44.
[71] Paul Wilkinson op cit 39.
[72] At 42.   [73] At 124.
[74] Frederik van Zyl Slabbert *The Last White Parliament* (Jonathan Ball, Johannesburg 1985) 105.

the security authorities. The rule of law means, in the second place, that any restriction of the liberty of citizens on account of alleged subversive activities must be subject to independent scrutiny and control for the purpose of preventing an abuse of power. Thirdly, the restoration of legality implies that the rules of fair hearing should be available to those against whom the authorities have acted or propose to act. These rules may have to be modified (for example, by in camera hearings) but they should never be abrogated.

6. The imposition of rule-of-law controls over the security authorities, while of central importance, is insufficient and needs to be supplemented by political control. Only those societies that have successfully grappled with the problem of the political accountability of their intelligence and security communities, can have any claim to being fully democratic. As Dr F van Zyl Slabbert has noted, Parliament is nowadays bypassed by the military authorities and the exemption of the security establishment from democratic control is, in his words, 'one of the greatest obstacles to evolutionary and negotiated change'.[74] The basic features of democratic accountability are effective parliamentary control through the regular review of exceptional security measures (which should always be temporary in form) and the creation of a multiparty security committee of Parliament to review the operations of the security forces in an atmosphere that, as far as possible, is 'removed from the realm of partisan politics'.[75] The work of such a committee would be greatly facilitated if it received and debated an annual report from an independent body of senior statesmen[76] set up, along lines recommended by the McDonald Commission and now operating in Canada,[77] to review the actions of the security forces from day to day. As in Canada, such a review body should be given access to all security files.

Security law-Reform—Specific Proposals

According to the six guidelines presented above, the framers of a security system for a reforming South African society should accept the need for special measures but avoid any temptation to over-reaction, eliminate powers that can lead to gross violations of the standards of civilised behaviour, prescribe clear and defensible objectives for the use of the security apparatus, adhere closely to the principle of the rule of law and provide for democratic control of the security establishment. The recommendations that follow seek to give effect to all these broad principles with special emphasis, however, on the re-establishment of a rule-of-law state in South Africa. A return to legality in the context of internal security requires the implementation of at least the following reform initiatives: the enactment of statutory criteria to control the use of security power, the narrowing of security crimes, the institution of rule-of-law controls over detention and banning and the revival of procedural justice in the realm of state security. Each of the suggested initiatives is examined separately below.

[75] McDonald Report vol 1 700.
[76] Drawn from all race groups.
[77] See McDonald Report vol 2 881 et seq.

The Enactment of Statutory Criteria

One of the most fundamental recommendations put forward by the McDonald Commission in Canada was the proposal, since adopted by Parliament in that country,[78] that the mandate of the security authorities in the state should be defined and limited by law. The Canadian example should be followed locally by the enactment of specific statutory criteria to govern the use of state security powers. Taking account of the greater instability of South African society, the following should be declared by law to be the concern of the security authorities:

(a) *Espionage*—defined to mean the passing, or attempted passing of defence (or similarly sensitive) information to a foreign government or organisation (or agent thereof) for a purpose prejudicial to South Africa;[79]

(b) *Violence*—this means the use or threat of violence (other than trivial violence), whether directed against persons or property, for political purposes;

(c) *Subversion*—defined to mean activities aimed at suppressing freedom by setting up a despotic, fascist or totalitarian system of government;

(d) *Encouragement of violence*—the use, in circumstances likely to cause it, of the language or rhetoric of violence.

In addition, the security authorities will obviously be concerned with common-law security crimes such as treason and sedition but both these crimes require statutory narrowing. Their present over-generous contours were established in earlier times of state absolutism and they are unsuitable for modern societies that wish to preserve the democratic right to dissent.

The statutory enactment of the four criteria described above is meant to further several distinct purposes: (1) The first three criteria will be formulated as the principal security crimes; (2) all four criteria will be used to determine whether restrictive measures such as banning and detention should be imposed upon individuals or groups; (3) two of the criteria (criteria *(b)* and *(d)* above) will constitute the basis of a decision to ban a meeting or procession; and (4) the scope for intrusive surveillance by security authorities, whether in the form of electronic interceptions, bugging or spying, will be fixed by all four criteria. Snooping on persons or groups simply because they are political dissidents will therefore fall outside the mandate of the security service. In general, the criteria are intended to set bounds to the legal mandate of the forces of law and order.

The Narrowing of Security Crimes

The first three of the proposed criteria (espionage, violence and subversion) are suggested as the major security crimes for South Africa. They would replace the current crimes of terrorism, sabotage, subversion, intimidation and furthering the aims of communism all of which, to a

---

[78] The Canadian Security Intelligence Service Act of 1984.

[79] This defines espionage more narrowly than under present legislation because that legislation is so broad that the transmission of non-sensitive information, and activities not constituting spying in any meaningful sense, are also covered by the crime: see A S Mathews *The Darker Reaches of Government* 103 et seq and 139 et seq. For the Canadian recommendations, see McDonald Report vol 2 939 et seq.

greater or lesser degree, may be used to punish or harass non-violent opponents of the government. The substitution of three more limited security offences for the broad prescriptions of current political crimes will advance the important objective of detaching internal security law from the protection of a particular government and its policies. The partisanship of South African security law is quite indefensible and, as we have observed, deprives that law of both legitimacy and effectiveness.

Though the proposed crimes of espionage, political violence and subversion are considerably narrower than those they would replace, their enactment would go well beyond what is made criminal in the established democracies. For example, neither political violence nor terrorism is defined as a political crime in Northern Ireland and such activities are criminal there only to the extent that the relevant conduct falls under ordinary offences such as murder, attempted murder, arson and the like, or under statutes dealing with firearms and explosives. The proposed crime of subversion, while narrower than present law, has no counterpart even in countries like Northern Ireland and Israel. The reason for introducing subversion as a crime is to punish non-violent activities that are aimed at replacing the reigning system of government with any kind of despotism whether nourished by the ideologies of the far 'left' or 'right'. Guilt will be conditional on clear proof of an intention to terminate democratic processes within the society. The McDonald Commission in Canada recommended that the security service in that country should be vigilant towards 'revolutionary subversion' which seeks to replace Canadian liberal democracy 'by an authoritarian government of the extreme right or left'.[80] It did *not* propose that revolutionary subversion should be made a crime, only that it would be legal and proper for the security authorities to keep a close watch on people who advocated it. The reason for the proposal that subversion should be enacted as a crime in South Africa is the dangerous instability of the society and the susceptibility of people in such a society to extremist politics.

The suggestion that politically directed violence should be a principal security crime is also controversial but appears to be justified by the deep instability of present-day South Africa.[81] The new crime will cover both terrorism and sabotage in the ordinary sense, but will exclude the use of (or the threat to use) trivial violence. The present crime of terrorism is far too broad because it covers violence of any degree including, for example, an egg thrown at a political speaker or a stone thrown at a building.

The crimes of espionage, political violence and subversion have been suggested as the *major* security crimes in a reformed security system. It goes without saying that there will have to be 'minor' crimes on the statute

---

[80] McDonald Report vol 1 440.

[81] It is arguable that common law provides adequately for the punishment of persons who use violence for political ends in the form of the crimes of murder, attempted murder, assault, arson and the like. This argument is not fully convincing, at least in relation to property since many forms of sabotage are not covered, or are inadequately covered, by common-law offences. The main arguments for introducing a special crime directed at the use of violence for political ends are (1) that it is desirable to give such conduct a special criminal status in a conflict-ridden society; (2) that *threats* of dangerous violence are inadequately punished under the common law and need to be elevated to a higher level of seriousness for purposes of punishment. 'Threats' should be punishable only if they are threats of imminent action. Loose talk about the desirability or necessity of violence should not be made a crime.

book, such as those dealing with the illegal possession or use of firearms and explosives and the destruction or impairment of defence force property. It might be desirable to retain the incitement of racial hostility as a crime provided that it is equally enforced against offenders in all racial groups. Generally, however, the criminal prosecution must be required to rely on common-law crimes and the statutory measures proposed above and not be permitted to make use of dragnet offences of the kind that currently abound on the statute book.

Rule-of-law Controls over Detention and Banning

It is a safe but regrettable assumption that in any transitional period towards a new political and social dispensation, presided over by whatever ruling party, the institutions of detention and banning will be retained as necessary instruments of control. The complete repeal of such measures remains the desirable but not immediately realisable goal. Even during a period of transition, however, they should be temporary measures subject to annual reconsideration and the most grudging renewal. Quite apart from the fact that detention and banning constitute infringements of basic citizen rights, their prolonged use is 'ultimately inimical to community life' and tends to 'form a widespread sense of grievance and injustice'.[82]

Given the prospect of the continued use of detention and banning, both should be subjected, to the greatest possible degree, to rule-of-law controls. With regard to preventive detention and the banning of individuals, the Israeli model of mandatory court review under modified fair-trial procedures is the most appropriate and helpful. This would require that every detention and every banning order should lapse unless brought before the Supreme Court for confirmation within a short period, preferably forty-eight hours in the case of detention and seven days in the case of banning.[83] The court will be required to conduct an in camera hearing at which the detainee (or banned person) and his legal representative may be present unless excluded by the court itself from portions of the hearing in order to protect sensitive information. The court will have access to *all* relevant official information, make its own decision as to what may safely be released to the detainee (or banned person)[84] and have the authority, if it so decides, to depart from the normal rules of evidence. As in Israel, the court must be given power to set aside an order it considers to be unjustified and, where it confirms the order, it should be required to conduct subsequent periodical reviews of the case.

All four of the criteria suggested above as the statutory mandate for the security service should be employed by the authorities and the reviewing court to determine whether a person should be banned or detained. The relevance of the criteria (more strictly, the first three) when expressed in the form of security crimes is to enable the court to determine whether the person before it has *committed* one or more of the prohibited acts (that is, acts of espionage, political violence or subversion) and so is guilty of an

---

[82] These are the words of the Gardiner Committee: see Gardiner Report para 148.

[83] See chapter 12 above for a review of the Israeli detention procedure.

[84] Only so much of the state case as will reveal the identity of an informer or techniques of surveillance and detection should be withheld.

offence. The purpose of the criteria (in this instance, all four of them) in relation to banning and detention is to facilitate a finding on whether a person should be banned or detained because prior conduct suggests that he or she *is likely to commit* espionage, subversion or political violence or to use language calculated to arouse political violence. Where the criteria are formulated as crimes, *actual* commission of the prohibited acts is necessary; but when they are employed in relation to detention and banning, it is *apprehended* commission of espionage, subversion, et cetera which the court must investigate.

The foregoing proposals for preventive detention and the banning of individuals will give greater effect to the principle of the rule of law than the present system because there will be reasonably clear standards controlling the use of security powers, because the applicability of the criteria to the facts will be evaluated in every case by an independent court and because strong elements of procedural fairness will characterise the review procedure. However, adherence to rule-of-law requirements for *pre-trial* detention and the banning of organisations and meetings is best secured along different lines. The evils inherent in pre-trial interrogational detention can be effectively eliminated only by:

(a) Limiting the period of such detention to an absolute maximum of no more than fourteen days;[85]

(b) Declaring that the sole ground for detention is the *reasonable belief* on the part of the detaining authority that the person in question has information about the commission or intended commission of specified major security crimes;[86]

(c) Rigorously controlling the conditions of detention by rules which inter alia require an unconditional right of access to a lawyer after the first seventy-two hours of detention, closed-circuit recording of interrogation sessions, and access to a doctor chosen from a panel of private practitioners. In addition, the rules should place clear limits on the duration of interrogation sessions and prohibit all forms of detainee abuse. There should be no denial of court access to the detainee where ill-treatment is apprehended.

Rule-of-law requirements where organisations are banned could be furthered by a statutory scheme along the following lines: The proscription of an organisation will be justified if it is committed, either by policy or practice, to the achievement of political or social change by violent means or by subversion (the second and third criteria). If, after an informal hearing conducted prior to banning, a proscription order is issued, there should be a right of appeal to a review board and the main features of this procedure should be the following:

(a) *Independent constitution:* The members should have a publicly known independence from government. This will be better secured if appointment is made after consultation with the Chief Justice and judges president of provincial divisions of the Supreme Court.

(b) *Procedural rights:* The organisation should be entitled to (i) a statement setting out the grounds on which the banning order is

---

[85] This is twice as long as the maximum of seven days in Northern Ireland.
[86] The decision to detain would be challengeable on objective grounds before the courts.

based;[87] (ii) to a hearing, with the assistance of counsel, before the review board; and (iii) to confront state witnesses who give evidence to the tribunal unless the tribunal itself decides that representatives of the organisation should not be present when particular evidence is presented on the ground that the identity of informers or other highly sensitive information needs to be protected.[88]

(c) *Security requirements:* Apart from the exclusion of the affected persons from the hearing for reasons just mentioned, the tribunals should generally hold in camera hearings in the interests of state security.

(d) *A right of review:* There should be a right of review to the Supreme Court on the ground (i) of procedural irregularity or (ii) of the absence of a rational nexus between the decision to uphold the banning and the evidence on which it was based.[89] A restricted review of this kind would reserve the decision to ban to the executive and provide the court only with a 'long-stop' function to prevent misuse of the statutory power.

Procedural rights where a publication is banned should be similar except, perhaps, that there should be a right of appeal direct to the courts because of the financial loss implications that may be present in such cases. The criteria for banning a publication should be support for violence or subversion or the regular use of the language of violence (the second, third and fourth criteria).

Controls over meetings and processions in a violence-prone society are obviously necessary and desirable but these controls should not include, as present law does, the power to abolish the right of assembly throughout the land. Bans on meetings or processions should be imposed by magistrates on an area basis when satisfied on reasonable grounds by information provided on oath by a police officer that disorder is apprehended which the police, again on reasonable grounds, believe that they are unable to control. A decision to ban, or to impose restrictions on, a meeting or procession should be appealable to the Supreme Court which should have the power to set aside the order in the absence of reasonable grounds for it.

The Revival of Procedural Justice

The preceding proposals relating to detention and banning included a number of reforms designed to give effect to the procedural justice elements of the rule of law. There are at least three other procedural reforms that are central to the re-establishment of the rule of law in the security field. The first requires that the courts be the final arbiters, as in Israel,[90] of what evidence may be withheld by the executive on the

[87] The statement must provide sufficient detail to enable the organisation to join issue with the state case for banning.

[88] In such a case, the representatives should be provided with a clear statement of the gist of the evidence.

[89] A more restricted right than that of a normal appeal is envisaged here. Appeal usually involves a reassessment of the merits whereas the envisaged review would require the court to satisfy itself that the proceedings were regular and that there was evidence upon which a rational person *could* (not necessarily *would*) consider the banning justified. (The substantial evidence test in administrative law.)

[90] See chapter 12 above.

grounds that it is privileged from disclosure. No tribunal can render proper justice if it is arbitrarily deprived of relevant material. The second reform involves the rejection of evidence procured by undesirable forms of interrogational pressure.[91] The integrity of the criminal justice system cannot be maintained if verdicts are based on evidence that is so tainted. Finally, the use of intrusive techniques of surveillance requires adherence to at least some of the basics of due process. Though it is not possible in this case to give the victim a hearing, there is no reason why warrants should not be a legal prerequisite for surveillance. As in Canada, courts sitting in camera should hear applications on oath for warrants, and should grant them only if a clear need to investigate matters falling within the scope of the four criteria (espionage, political violence, subversion or incitement to violence) is established. Partial adherence to the rule of law is better than none.

Specific Reforms—Concluding Comments

The proposals put forward in this chapter for a reformed security system are no more than a sketchy outline of a viable alternative to the present repressive apparatus. They are not presented as an ideal system since they make provision for restrictions on basic liberties and deviations from the principle of legality. They are offered as the best that can be hoped for in a society riven by conflict. In such a society, as Donald Horowitz has said,[92] the realistic reformer must be prepared to lower his aspirations even though he may wish, as this writer does, for a closer approximation to perfection. As sketchy and inadequate as the suggested reforms are, they do demonstrate that the important task of establishing and maintaining stability in a divided society need not involve the gross violations of freedom and legality to which we have become accustomed in South Africa. More liberty and closer adherence to the rule of law *are* compatible with the creation of a peaceful and stable social system. The search for freedom in any society, but more so in a divided society, is the search for appropriate institutions:

'If we want to be free, we have to work with and through institutions, shaping and re-shaping them in the process, that is building them in the image of the chances of liberty open to us at any one time.'[93]

The rule of law, and the institutions through which it is expressed, are central to the achievement of freedom and South Africans will have to learn again to 'work with and through' the rule of law, and its accompanying institutions, with a view to 'shaping and re-shaping' them for the purpose of securing liberty for our society. Whether they succeed will depend to a considerable degree on the commitment and enterprise of the legal profession and it is to that body, and its wider responsibilities, that the final words in this book are directed.

Lawyers and Security-law Reform

The rule of law was no doubt a predictable victim of the intense struggle of Afrikaner nationalists to secure and maintain power and an inevitable

---

[91] See chapters 7 and 12 above.   [92] In conversation with the writer.
[93] Ralf Dahrendorf *Law and Order* (Stevens, London 1985) 128.

casualty also of the 'no holds barred' campaign to crush African nationalism. To the extent that South African lawyers, who were (and still are) mainly white, identified with the white nationalist cause (or the white protectionism which it embodied), their readiness to abandon, or acquiescence in the dissolution of, the rule of law and similar institutions which barred the straight road to political dominance, is perhaps not surprising. Though not surprising, the jettisoning of rule-of-law values and institutions in the quest for pure power now appears, with the added advantage of hindsight, to have been singularly unwise. If one side in the power struggle is prepared to overturn established restraints on political behaviour, the other side is likely to follow with the inevitable consequence, now before us, of a rampant lawlessness that affects all groups, including the power-holders. While it is possible to understand, if not approve of, the choice made by white nationalist lawyers (and fellow travellers) between the benefits of the quick and easy route to power and the advantages of age-old institutions like the rule of law, the feeble defence of the latter by opposition lawyers is puzzling and in need of some further explanation. Why have non-nationalist teachers, practitioners and judges, who ought to have known and done better, failed to retain the rule of law, if not as a living institution, even as an ideal for official behaviour?

An important part of the answer to the question just posed is to be found in the reigning philosophy of law in South Africa. Legal thinking has always been dominated by positivism and legal positivism, even when not explicitly avowed today, is implicit in the attitudes and orientations of lawyers to their work and discipline. The feature of positivism which has particularly disabled lawyers from being stout defenders of the rule of law, is the rigid separation of law and morality that characterises this approach to legal philosophy. The rule of law, as Roberto Unger has said, tends to flourish in societies that have developed a tradition for judging law by transcendental standards[94] and positivism, by reason of its tendency to relegate moral enquiries about law to the realm of the non-legal, discourages that tradition among lawyers. While enlightened positivists accept the validity of the enterprise of evaluating law by transcendental standards, their insistence that this exercise is outside the concerns of a lawyer *qua* lawyer undoubtedly has the effect of discouraging the profession's interest in the rule of law which is unquestionably a doctrine concerned with the moral quality of the legal order. There are admittedly modern defenders of positivism who recognise that arguments about justice and moral values figure prominently in the judicial process. Professor Neil MacCormick is a representative of this group and in his book *Legal Reasoning and Legal Theory* presents a highly sophisticated and attractive defence of positivist thinking about law. In response to Dworkin's attack on positivism, MacCormick has explained and defended the place of consequentionalist arguments (those about justice or convenience) in legal decision-making.[95] But in defending positivism MacCormick has also transformed it into a phenomenon very unlike the one that has influenced legal thinking for so long. Traditional positivism has always tended to give a pejorative connotation to the moral evaluation

[94] Roberto Mangabeira Unger *Law in Modern Society* 53 et seq, 66, 83 et seq and 104 et seq.
[95] Neil MacCormick *Legal Reasoning and Legal Theory* (Oxford 1978) chapter VI.

of a legal order which it deems to be 'unscientific' and there can be little doubt that the acceptance of this connotation explains the otherwise surprising remark of as perceptive a judge as Oliver Schreiner that:

> 'The charge that the Rule of Law has been infringed is a political charge, not a charge that a law has been contravened. And so the answer must necessarily be a political and not a legal one.'[96]

From this statement it is but a short step to accusing academics who criticise judges for neglecting the rule of law in the state security field of seeking to draw the bench into politics[97] and, by implication, away from their 'true' task of declaring the law 'as it is'. The rejection of judicial concern for the rule of law as an embroilment in politics may not have been an intended result of the positivist approach to law, but it is one that is inevitable given positivism's tendency to 'side-line' moral enquiries.

An anti-positivist tradition in jurisprudence took root and flowered in America with Lon L Fuller being, perhaps, the pre-eminent figure in that tradition. In Fuller's thinking, the moral evaluation of legal rules and systems is not something that begins only when the lawyer has discarded his professional robes and put on the mantle of politician or philosopher. He rejected the traditional fact/value distinction that positivists make and viewed the lawyer's enterprise as one in which the tasks of finding and evaluating the law were inextricably bound together. In the words of Robert L Summers:

> 'In the field of purposive human activity, which includes both steam engines and the law, value and being are not two different things but two aspects of an integral reality. Thus to Fuller the question "Is this assemblage a steam engine" overlaps mightily with the question "Is this a good steam engine".'[98]

It follows that the principles embodied in the rule of law do not cease to be the concern of lawyers because they incorporate an evaluative component. Fuller, in fact, sought to demonstrate that the legality aspect of the rule-of-law doctrine is a notion central to the very concept of the legal order. We cannot speak, Fuller argued, of a legal order without giving due attention to qualities such as certainty, prospectivity, durability and faithful application in practice, to mention the most important of the principles which he designated as the inner morality of the law.[99] It is one of Fuller's most important perceptions that the construction of a system that deserves to be called legal requires adherence to values and institutions embodied in the concepts variously called the rule of law, legality, due process or the rechtsstaats idea. Lawyers, including judges, are not required by their calling or office to distance themselves from these concepts which positivism has relegated to the category of the 'non-science' in law. On the contrary, their office or calling is one which requires that the notion of legality be accorded a central place in the performance of their professional functions.

There is another feature of legal positivism that has had a decidedly

---

[96] O D Schreiner *The Contribution of English Law to South African Law, and The Rule of Law in South Africa* (Stevens, London 1967) 100.
[97] As Chief Justice Steyn did in his address entitled 'Regsbank en Regsfakulteit' published in (1967) 30 *THRHR* 105.
[98] Robert L Summers *Lon L Fuller* (Edward Arnold, London 1984) 25.
[99] See particularly, Lon L Fuller *Morality of the Law* (Yale Univ Press, revised ed 1969).

negative impact on the reforming role of lawyers in the area of security law. Because positivists tend to view law as an autonomous body of rules and to believe that the judge, by a source-based master-test, is able to discover the rule appropriate to the facts of the case before him, the scope for reform through the courts is an exceedingly narrow one according to positivist doctrine. Though positivists acknowledge that there are cases in which the master-test does not yield up a conclusive answer and that the judge therefore has definite but interstitial power to decide the case according to moral or other 'extra-legal' precepts, the areas of uncertainty are of strictly marginal significance in positivist thinking. Disputed cases fall into the 'gaps' of the legal system or in the 'penumbral zone' of legal meaning, both metaphors that strongly suggest a negligible scope for judicial law-making. Transposed into the realm of internal security law, the positivist approach implies that the master- or pedigree test of validity provides the practitioner with almost all the answers to issues that are disputed in the courts and that the scope for enlightened interpretation is virtually non-existent.

The truth is that positivism has been guilty of exaggerating the certainty of legal rules. This exaggeration was perceived long ago by the American realists who, although themselves guilty of an exaggeration in the other direction, were correct in their attack on the then perceived ubiquity of the positivist pedigree test. As Karl Llewellyn declared, in any case 'doubtful enough to make litigation respectable' there are at least two authoritative premises between which the court must choose. Positivists have long managed to preserve the illusion of certainty in the legal order partly by conceiving it as a system of *rules* whereas Dworkin, in his celebrated attack on positivist philosophy, has demonstrated that *principles* (which do not have the 'all or nothing' quality of rules) are at least as prominent as rules in the structure of the legal order. Once we accept that principles play an important role in judicial lawmaking, the scope for a pedigree test of validity in legal disputes is considerably narrowed. It is through principles that arguments about the justice, equity or convenience of legal rules enter into the process of declaring what the law is, thereby undermining the is/ought dichotomy upon which positivists have traditionally insisted. MacCormick, it is true, argues that principles, as much as rules, operate through a pedigree test of validity and that only those principles that comply with the test of consistency and coherence with the rules of the legal system are admissible in terms of the 'rule of recognition'. His extension of positivism is, however, so radical as to make it almost compatible with the thinking of Lon Fuller, that arch-critic of the positivist approach. Fuller would surely have no difficulty in accepting MacCormick's proposition that in every good system of law the judges are 'cribbed, cabined and confined in the exercise of the great powers that they wield'[100] so long as it is conceded, as MacCormick does, that a prominent feature of the exercise of those great powers is the determination of the justice, convenience or moral acceptability of the outcome of judgments. Even if principles have to be filtered through a rule of recognition (pedigree test), they are less determinate than rules and make

[100] Neil MacCormick op cit 251.

the outcome far less predictable and certain than positivists have all along claimed. In short, one of the functions of principles is to reopen large areas of the law to reconsideration and redetermination. Another source of the illusive certainty with which positivism clothed the legal system was a belief in the fixed meaning of language, in the idea that legal texts could have meaning in themselves. The application of the hermeneutical science of language to legal interpretation has exposed the fallacy of fixed meaning and underlined the role of the interpreter in establishing the 'intent' of statutory texts.[101] Positivists who have been influenced by the perceptions of the philosophers of language appear not to have accepted the full implications of their discoveries for the legal order.

Attacks on positivism have generally not disputed, nor is it disputed here, that within every legal system there is what J W Harris has termed 'clear' law as well as 'argued' law.[102] What is disputed is that argued law (Dworkin's category of 'hard cases') is located on an insignificant periphery of the legal system and that the judges are accordingly condemned to tying up the trivial ends of a tidy and well-knit legal order. On the contrary, there is a great deal of untidiness in every legal system and, within such areas, considerable scope for settling disputes that are frequently of great moment. This proposition applies also to statute law, and therefore to the security legislation with which this study is largely concerned:

> 'The law of a statute is not exhausted in its formal wording. Among other things, the content of the law of a statute derives also from interpretations put on it by judges and others. To the extent that these influence the statute's content, the statute owes its status as law not to satisfying an internal criterion of valid law, but to notions that inform particular interpretations and are therefore *accepted* as having rational appeal.'[103]

These important insights have too long been obscured by the positivist approach to law which, particularly in the contentious area of the interpretation of security legislation, has provided the judges with a plausible justification for the failure to assert 'good' law in their reading of the texts. Disputed law, as J W Harris has said, is valid law only 'if its goodness is accepted'.[104]

There is within security law one highly significant example of judicial failure to assert 'good' law over a dubious proposition that owes its resilience to the certainty with which the positivist tradition had clothed it. This example is simultaneously a demonstration that the areas of uncertainty (or argued law) may lie at the centre of a particular branch of law and that decisions seeking to clarify that uncertainty may have ramifications throughout the legal system. The proposition which the courts failed to dispute, and in fact repeatedly applied in their judgments, is that grants of discretion conferred upon officials by verbal formulae such as 'is of the opinion', 'has reason to believe' or 'is satisfied', vest the officials with a subjective power of decision-making. According to a large

---

[101] For a brief survey of the relevance of hermeneutics to interpretation and the judicial function, see L G Baxter, *Administrative Law* 315 et seq.
[102] J W Harris *Legal Philosophies* (Butterworths, London 1980) 173.
[103] Robert L Summers *Lon L Fuller* 25.
[104] J W Harris op cit 173.

number of authoritative judgments given in security matters, when an official is given the power to act—for example to ban or detain a person—upon condition that he 'is satisfied' or 'is of the opinion' that the person in question is a threat to the security of the state, the only question with which the court is (and can be) concerned if the official's action is disputed before it, is whether the official was satisfied or did hold the required opinion. According to this view, the court is not concerned with the question whether adequate grounds existed on which the official's opinion or satisfaction could be based, and judges are precluded by the power-conferring formula from investigating that issue. The judgments in which this proposition was given the status of holy writ appear to have been fortified by the belief that the verbal formulae in question have a fixed meaning and that alternative interpretations have to be rejected as legally wrong. Earlier discussion[105] has shown that several important judgments in Britain, and two recent cases in South Africa, have begun to erode the positivistic certainty with which the subjective interpretation of the verbal formulae was clothed by the judges. It is now clear that it was all along open to the judges to adopt the alternative interpretation that 'if a minister is to be satisfied, he must as minister have reasonable grounds upon which his satisfaction is based . . .',[106] and had they done so, the entire history of judicial involvement in the security field would have to be rewritten. What seems to have precluded the judges from adopting 'good' law is the positivistic infallibility that has become encrusted on to what are merely arguable propositions of law. In the context of public law, judgments may be said to express 'good' law when they tend to further the rule-of-law requirements of clear and consistent standards and fair hearing. Unless forbidden in the clearest possible language, it is the responsibility of the judge to develop rational standards for the channelling of official power and to subject the exercise of that power to rules of procedural fairness. The positivist failure to accept that there is an 'internal morality' to law is the root cause of the neglect of that responsibility. It is misguided to dismiss the view that judges are 'responsible' in this way as an attempt to insinuate politics into the law. The rule of law, as much as parliamentary sovereignty, has juridical status as a constitutional principle; and the legality aspect of the doctrine is implicit in the very notion of a legal order. Inasmuch as the rule of law 'entails a commitment to limited discretions, unambiguous rules of criminal law, the principles of natural justice, and the protection of traditional liberties'[107] it is clear that the judges, faced with the linguistic uncertainty of 'if satisfied'-type clauses, *did* have the option to subject the exercise of power conferred by them to rational standards and acceptable procedures.

We may conclude that the dismal performance of the legal profession in defence of the principle of government under law is attributable to certain deeply ingrained attitudes of mind and modes of thinking that have been nurtured and shaped by the legal philosophy of positivism. It is

[105] See chapter 7 above.
[106] Quoted by C J Hamson *Executive Discretion and Judicial Control* (Stevens, London 1954) 15.
[107] T R S Allan, op cit 138.

inadequate to explain that performance, where it concerns the judges, to a submission to executive power. This is the essence of Christopher Forsyth's explanation after a review of the Appellate Division judgments in the security field. The judges, he says, have shown 'a considerable preference for the executive interest over that of the individual'.[108] This explanation does little more than state the outcome of the bulk of judgments in the security field. Much more illuminating than the obvious outcome of security judgments are the mental processes which enabled judges who favoured the executive by reason of their identification with the white nationalist cause, to present their inclinations in the form of seemingly inevitable legal prescriptions; and which disabled judges who did not share that identification from being more influential in preventing what Lon Fuller felicitously described as 'indecencies in the use of governmental power'.[109] The pressure of professional opinion, as Fuller rightly observes, is crucial to the success of the task of preventing such indecencies, and professional opinion 'can be effective only if it is informed by a sound philosophy'.[110] The unsound aspects of legal positivism, especially its obsessional divorce of law from morality,[111] are at the root of professional, and especially judicial, failure to stem the tide of indecency in the exercise of security power. We have been persuaded far too long by positivistic modes of thinking that large areas of 'settled' law are not open to reconsideration, that lawyers as such have no duty to foster the rechtsstaats idea, and that in legal disputes with political dimensions, the judicial branch should keep its nose clean.[112] It is these attitudes which will have to change if the judiciary in South Africa is to play a decisive part in the rebuilding of the rule-of-law state. It has too long been no more than an elegant frill on the sleeve of state power.

[108] Christopher Forsyth *In Danger for Their Talents* (Juta & Co, Cape Town 1985) 178.
[109] Lon L Fuller 'American Legal Philosophy at Mid-century' (1954) 6 *J Leg Ed* 457, 465.
[110] Ibid.
[111] I accept MacCormick's point that it is equally untenable to draw no distinction between legal and political judgments for, as he says, clear thought requires us to keep distinct 'the description and the evaluative appraisal of legal system . . .': Neil MacCormick op cit 239.
[112] There is a pervasive fallacy that a judge keeps his nose clean by refusing to challenge the use of executive power. The judge who makes a pro-executive decision is as much embroiled as one who prefers to vindicate competing individual rights. It is legal positivism which explains the success of pro-executive judges in passing off their judgments as a form of neutral arbitration.

Postscript

In the final stages of writing an explosion of official activity in all branches of government and especially in the courts, complicated the completion of this book by compelling the hasty revision of several chapters. The continuation of this activity, even while the revised parts were being printed, has necessitated the production of a postscript. It aims to highlight the developments that have occurred between going to press and publication.

The *Tsenoli* saga,[1] felicitously described by a Natal Judge as the dance of *Tsenoli*, came to an end when the Appellate Division delivered its judgment at the end of September. In overall perspective, the pas-de-trois of the full bench in Durban and the similarly constituted ensemble in Pietermaritzburg[2] has dissolved in a rather tame pas-de-cinq in Bloemfontein. In its judgment,[3] the appeal court found the relevant section of the Public Safety Act[4] to be quite unambiguous, despite the conflict between the lower court judgments, and rejected the interpretation of Friedman J in *Tsenoli*[5] as being forced and strained. It will be recalled that Friedman J, on a grammatical and a substantive basis of reasoning, had decided that the State President's power to make regulations for the safety of the public or the maintenance of public order was qualified by the requirement that such regulations should be directed also towards the termination of the state of emergency. Consequently, Friedman J held that the detention regulation which empowered an official to arrest and detain persons who were considered threats to public safety or order simpliciter, and whose detention was not related to the termination of the emergency, was ultra vires and invalid. The grammatical argument is based on the fact that the safety of the public and the maintenance of public order, which are disjunctively linked by 'or' in the Act, are conjunctively linked by 'and' to the termination of the state of emergency, and that it is wrong to treat them all as alternatives as the detention regulation does. The substantive argument is that the legislature could not have envisaged that a common criminal whose violent tendencies make him a threat to public safety could be lawfully detained for conduct that has nothing to do with the termination of the emergency.[6] The rejection of the grammatical line of argument by the appeal court is rather

[1] See pages 263–4 above.
[2] In *Kerchoff v Minister of Law and Order* (see pages 203–4 above).
[3] *The State President v Tsenoli* (as yet unreported judgment of the Appellate Division delivered on 30 September 1986).
[4] Section 3(1)(a).
[5] *Tsenoli v The State President* (see page 203 above).
[6] A better example is the detention of a group of soccer hooligans who undoubtedly threaten public safety but should clearly not be held under emergency law.

perfunctory and offers no persuasive reason for interpreting the word 'and' in the Act as if it were 'or'. The court's rejection of the substantive argument is curious. Rabie J, in a unanimous appeal court judgment, agrees with the lower court that a common criminal cannot lawfully be detained under the detention regulation but this is so because the State President's powers have to be viewed within the overall framework of emergency control. The answer to this finding is surely that the detention regulation does not make this clear and that it would not have been so understood by the officers whom it authorised to effect an arrest and detention. In fact, the Natal full bench in *Kerchoff* expressed the view that it would be perfectly proper for a member of the force to detain a person simply on the ground that he is believed to be a threat to public safety. It dismissed the example of a common criminal being eligible for detention because his activities would threaten specific persons rather than the safety of the public. However, a group of soccer hooligans, in the light of events like the Brussels soccer riots, are detainable in terms of the *Kerchoff* line of interpretation. It follows that what the appeal court regarded as obvious—that the power of detention must be exercised within the context of emergency control—was not understood by three learned judges of the Natal court. Nonetheless, Bloemfontein has the final word and the detention regulation is valid and enforceable in its present form.[7] In upholding the regulation the court also dismissed arguments that it was invalid because the grounds for detention were not specified with sufficient clarity; and it rejected the submission that a person already in custody must be subject to a fresh arrest before he can legally be detained.

There have been a number of positive lower court judgments in the security field. In *Buthelezi v Attorney-General, Natal*[8] the Natal court held that an attorney-general may not deny an accused person the right to bail[9] without affording that person a prior hearing. In upholding the *audi alteram partem* rule, the court expressly dissented from a contrary finding in the Transvaal.[10] Goldstone J in *Mokoena v Minister of Law and Order*[11] refused to hold that a release Mandela calendar which contained excerpts from the Freedom Charter, could be construed as furthering the aims of the African National Congress.[12] In the Zimbabwean case of *Minister of Home Affairs v Austin*[13] the court held a statute empowering detention 'if it appears to the Minister that . . .' did not preclude court investigation into the existence of the facts on which the minister was required to act. In holding that this apparently subjective formulation of the discretion to detain did not debar the judiciary from deciding on the merits, the court drove a further nail into the coffin of those judgments that seek to categorise discretion as objective or subjective by the method of pure

---

[7] The *Tsenoli* saga, even if it had culminated in a declaration of invalidity, would have brought short-lived relief to detainees since a simple amendment to the wording of the regulation would have remedied the problem.

[8] 1986 (4) SA 377 (D).

[9] In terms of section 30 of the Internal Security Act 74 of 1982.

[10] *S v Baleka* 1986 (1) SA 361 (T).

[11] 1986 (4) SA 42 (W).

[12] In terms of section $13(1)(a)(v)$ of Act 74 of 1982.

[13] 1986 (4) SA 281 (Z Sc).

linguistic analysis.[14] The ruling in *Austin* is also useful in spelling out precisely what it means to give a detainee reasons for his detention.[15]

Finally, the constant official rumblings about the United Democratic Front[16] have resulted not in its banning but in a declaration that it is an affected organisation.[17] This cuts off the UDF, but not organisations affiliated to it, from access to foreign funds.[18] The declaration is undoubtedly a body blow to an organisation that does not have access to local wealth (as does the ruling party) and that seeks to redress gross political inequality by recourse to foreign money. The declaration also underlines the limits of internal negotiation in South Africa which still excludes bodies like the UDF as being beyond the pale of possible political consensus.

---

[14] See p 66 above.
[15] In this respect it is much more satisfactory than *Nkondo & Gumede v Minister of Law and Order* 1986 (2) SA 756 (A).
[16] See p 102 above.
[17] Proclamation No 190 of 1986 (*GG* 10486 of 9 October 1986).
[18] See pp 115–16 above where affected organisations are discussed.

Index

307